THE SALOON
Public Drinking in Chicago and Boston
1880–1920

PERRY R. DUIS

THE SALOON

Public Drinking in Chicago and Boston 1880-1920

UNIVERSITY OF ILLINOIS PRESS

Urbana and Chicago

Illini Books edition, 1999
©1983 by the Board of Trustees of the University of Illinois
Manufactured in the United States of America
P 5 4 3 2 1

This book is printed on acid-free paper.

Library of Congress Cataloging-in-Publication Data

Duis, Perry, 1943–
    The saloon.

    Includes index.
    1. Hotels, taverns, etc.—Social aspects—Illinois—
Chicago—Case studies. 2. Hotels, taverns, etc.—Social
aspects—Massachusetts—Boston—Case studies. 3. Pro-
hibition—Social aspects—United States—History.
4. United states—Social conditions—1865–1918.
I. Title.
HV5201.S6D84   1983   647'.9573   83-6971
ISBN 0-252-06781-9

To Cathy
— for all the reasons

Acknowledgments

The creation of a book is a lonely journey, but one that is pleasantly aided by the support and encouragement of others. My teachers at the University of Chicago, especially Arthur Mann, John Hope Franklin, and Neil Harris, were inspirational. The late Bessie Louise Pierce taught me the need for thorough research, while two years assisting Daniel J. Boorstin taught me the joys of thinking on the grand scale; to Ruth and Dan I owe a debt I shall never be able to repay.

The staffs of some two dozen libraries, scattered from Illinois and Kentucky to the East Coast, were all helpful, especially those at the Boston Public Library, the Chicago Historical Society, and the library of the University of Illinois at Chicago.

My colleagues at Illinois gave me unanimous support and encouragement when it really counted, and I raise a toast to this community of scholars. Melvin G. Holli, Gerald Danzer, Leo Schelbert, Peter d'A. Jones, Ronald Legon, Burton Bledstein, Richard Jensen, and the late Shirley Bill deserve special thanks. Others who have been helpful include Frank O. Williams, J. Mills Thornton III, Morris J. Vogel, Harold Skramstad, Frank Jewell, Grant T. Dean, Archie Motley, Zane Miller, Sue Robinson, Louise Wade, and Glen Holt.

My wife, Cathy, gave her unstinting support, as did our cat, Nadia, who kept the pages from blowing away.

Contents

Introduction

WHEN GEORGE ADE published *The Old-Time Saloon* in 1931, he tried to treat the subject dispassionately. The "warts" were all there: broken laws, barroom nudes, and barkeeps that continued pouring for the inebriated customer, along with the usual stories of criminal dives and colorful scoundrels. But Ade's light collection of warm memories had a tinge of bitterness and sadness about it. "Do you recall," he asked, "any prominent and honored citizen of your neighborhood who passed on in 1920 and who is still a topic of daily conversation in the houses up and down your street?" The drys—"white neck-tie preachers"—had killed an American tradition. Drawing on an intimate knowledge of Chicago saloondom of the 1890s and experience in other cities as well, Ade related some of the traditions: straight drinks, free lunches, "regulars," and stolid barkeeps who were always in control of every situation.[1]

While not without insight, Ade's little book strengthened the warm and friendly stereotypes of the place behind the swinging doors. It was humor, folklore, and remembered history. But the story of the urban saloon is much more complex than that, for it touched almost every aspect of city life before 1920. Its absence sold houses in certain subdivisions. Its presence near a school touched off heated debates. Citizens found, much to their dismay, that its license fees constituted a large portion of city government revenues. It was constantly associated with governmental corruption, crime, the assimilation of immigrants, and worries over the moral decay of youth. Hardly an issue of a big city newspaper hit the streets without some mention of a barroom, perhaps as the scene of a crime or a political meeting or as the subject of a human interest feature. The swinging doors seemed to be a ubiquitous symbol of urban life in the half century before 1920.

The story of the saloon might fit into several possible interpretive frameworks. A more traditional approach might examine the epic struggle of prohibitionists and temperance advocates against the liquor interests. Although several interesting works about the anti-liquor crusade have appeared recently, most merely dramatize the fact that temperance in America operated largely according to its own logic. It attracted people who reacted to changes in society and in their personal lives in a particular way that had little to do with the evolution of the liquor industry or with drinking patterns. It is also clear from the journals and books they published that their knowledge of the saloon was often very limited and twisted. Interpreting the saloon through the temperance movement also tends to focus on what a relatively few people *wrote* about the subject rather than on what millions of saloon patrons *did*. Nor did prohibitionists attract more than a small number of followers in major cities. In an urban setting, it is difficult to give their arguments equal weight merely because they represented a particular viewpoint.[2]

The saloon was also the target of other reformers of various types, and this work will duly note the impact of settlement house workers, ministers, and good government groups on the barroom. But reformers were reactors, who responded to situations usually not of their making. In fact, as later evidence will reveal, the forces of urban change and business practices, along with fads and customer preferences, were the prime movers of the situation. While reformers left behind a "paper trail" of manuscripts and publications much larger than those of barkeeps and their allies, there are serious dangers in building an interpretive framework for the saloon out of the ideology of social and political reformers.[3]

A third possible approach might emphasize the saloon's supposed role as a male institution. The great progress in women's history has fostered a reaction in the form of "men's history," which seeks to examine what was uniquely male in society. One such article on the saloon already exists, and its weaknesses mirror those of the entire interpretation. First, the saloon was not a uniquely male preserve. In small "ma and pa" operations the wife was at home behind the bar as well as behind the stove preparing the free lunch. Laws specifically excluding women from the bartending trade always stopped short of banning work by female family members for the obvious reason that their contribution was so essential. Also, German saloons were family-oriented institutions, where the presence of women occasioned no comment.

The crusades against the dance hall and the white slave menace after 1900 also indicate that drinking became less sexually divided as the years passed, while Boston license officials fought a losing cause in trying to enforce temporary segregation-of-sex rules. The fact was that saloons were part of a larger urban society that was male dominated. And for every question about the saloon that might be answered by a "men's history" interpretation, there is another that is much more persuasive.[4]

There is also a temptation to plug the historical saloon into contemporary accounts of drinking behavior. Such excellent studies as Sherri Cavan's *Liquor License* and E. E. LeMaster's revealing *Blue-Collar Aristocrats* yield generalizations and assumptions about today that cannot be readily applied to an earlier era without the obvious danger of historicism. These accounts are based on unique observations of places that might be the exception rather than the rule about drinking behavior today, let alone the social life of the saloon more than sixty years ago.[5]

Instead, the interpretive framework used in this study grew from the sources. It is based on the fact that cities were, and still are, spatial entities that are divided into three basic types of spaces. Some are public: streets, sidewalks, parks, governmental property, and rivers, to name a few. Others, such as dwellings and most business property, were privately owned, with access restricted to invitation or judicial warrant. But midway between these extremes were what might be called semipublic city spaces. The latter were privately owned but allowed public access that was largely uninhibited. The principal motivation for opening up property to others was economic. Stores, theaters, depots, barbershops, blacksmith's shops, and others needed to allow customers access to private property to facilitate the delivery of goods or services.

During the nineteenth century the numbers and types of these semipublic places tended to grow, and their functions became more elaborate. For example, the small wooden depot became the giant rail terminal, the "grand entryway" to the city. The rude inn became the magnificent hotel, and the drygoods shop blossomed into the department store. Theaters became grand affairs, while the popularity of the dime museum and the baseball park demonstrated new profit opportunities in semipublic places of leisure. In part, these developments reflected entrepreneurial initiative and the desire to outdo the competitors. The simple factor of size no doubt contributed to the development of the depot and the hotel, although city boosters realized that civic pride was at stake because those two institutions served many out-of-towners. In part, the department store flourished because the public spaces of the city outside were regarded as dirty, unsightly, and often dangerous. By centralizing shopping and a variety of services ranging from hairdressers, dentists, and theater ticket sales all in one building, the semipublic place became an elaborate city in itself.[6]

These urban institutions generated a sense of excitement, an allurement that almost made people forget that they were private, money-making businesses. Such places as ballparks developed their own etiquette and customs, which one historian has claimed were important in assimilating immigrants. Baseball players and stars of the stage became heroes and heroines of a new sort. Unlike presidents, who were seldom seen by the people, these semipublic celebrities were on view for a price. Novels set in department stores, woodcuts of theaters published in popular illustrated magazines, and gaudy hotel and railroad advertising—all contributed to the growing fascination with the semipublic place.[7]

This development was not, of course, without its controversy. The commercialization of leisure always attracted criticism as a waste of time. Idle hours spent by youth away from home aroused fears of immorality. An image of tawdriness plagued actors, performers in circuses (a temporary semipublic amusement), and operators of dime museum "freak shows." Hotel lobbies attracted "dudes," well-dressed idlers who sat in open defiance of the ethic of hard work. Young women were warned to be wary of strangers in department store lounge areas and on excursion boats, another semipublic enterprise.[8]

There was also a serious question of physical safety. When a stranger entered a semipublic place, who was liable in case of accident? Such calamities as the Iroquois Theater fire of December 1903 kept alive a constant distrust of the claims of fireproofers. But questions of safety also tended to make some private places more semipublic. For instance, city officials were openly concerned about the hazards of tall office buildings. Not only did the upper floors rise far above fire ladders, but elevator accidents became a special hazard. When workers and those visiting the building on business were maimed by incompetent elevator operators, who was liable? The owners claimed that all who entered did so at their own risk, as if uninvited strangers. The courts usually ruled otherwise, and the tall office tower became a semipublic place. Similarly, factory inspection and industrial safety standards transformed the workplace from a purely private building in which employees had no legal claim to safe passage and occupancy into a semipublic place. While the courts were not always consistent on every case, and owners found ways to evade their responsibility, the general trend was toward greater rights for the customer and the visitor.[9]

Finally, the expansion of semipublic places also raised the question of whether or not an owner could exclude particular people or groups. Public accommodations laws and litigation expanded dramatically during the late nineteenth century, not only because minorities were excluded from hotels, restaurants, theaters, and streetcars, but also because the numbers and types of semipublic places were proliferating too rapidly. It was clear that commercial interests were assuming a larger role in American leisure, but the question of minority participation in that trend remained unsolved.[10]

The creation and control of semipublic places were issues that grew out of the processes of urbanization. The agglomeration of population resulted in crowding and increasing dependence on others for the production of food and other vital services. The intensity of land use made it necessary for government to regulate the intrusion of one party's activities into the lives of others. Not only did the debate over such nuisances as smoke and noise intensify, but crowding brought about the need for a new discipline in public places. Traffic control and antispitting laws, for example, were aimed at making streets and sidewalks safe and pleasant. Meanwhile, city dwellers occupied private housing that seemed increasingly unable to satisfy the need to be amused and to find the companionship of others. When separated from the home, work also assumed socializing functions. Thus, an increasing number of daily activities took place outside of the home, some in public places and others in semipublic spots. This blurring of spatial distinctions created enormous problems of social control. Did the semipublic business operate under the law of the street or that of the home? And did the statutes that governed early amusements apply to the new commercialized leisure?[11]

Within this context the barroom evolved as a social, political, and economic institution. The term *saloon* was itself only a generic description, for there were countless variations on the place where liquor was retailed and consumed. Some regional differences were obvious: the frontier bar, the log cabin retreat in Minnesota, and the Bourbon

Street spa in New Orleans.[12] But even the saloons in large industrial cities displayed vast variety, both within the town and from city to city. A tradition of legal localism is partially responsible. Despite the intensity and length of the debate over prohibition, temperance, and liquor, there was remarkably little federal legislation regulating the business outside of such matters as interstate commerce, alcohol on military bases, and taxes. Instead, local traditions, ethnic preferences, and business conditions shaped the regulation of the liquor trade in a patchwork of contrasts.

This study contrasts the saloon as a semipublic institution in two important American cities, Boston and Chicago. Both shared the promise and problems of big cities in an optimistic age. Both were large and growing. Both developed stark contrasts between the splendid homes of the wealthy and the squalor of the immigrant tenements. Both developed a "big city culture," as Gunther Barth has called it, of gaudy vaudeville houses, competitive daily newspapers, crowded baseball parks, fanciful department stores, and tall apartment houses.[13] Both saw the expansion of downtown areas, the development of sweatshop industries, and the outward flight to the suburbs via an urban transportation revolution. Thus, Boston and Chicago, by their similarities, help form the notion that a shared urban experience is a crucial part of the nation's history.

Yet, there is also the nagging problem of differences, the fact that the two cities differed in many respects. In 1913, in *The Personality of American Cities*, Edward Hungerford wrote of "the atmosphere, physical appearance, friendliness, cultural achievement and relative 'hustle' that made one town different from another."[14] In his and other subjective observations the stereotype of Boston as refined, stuffy, strict, and quaint prevails. Perhaps the most succinct form of this image came to this researcher in a comment made by a member of the Cabot family, who was an official of the Bostonian Society in 1971. When asked about turn-of-the-century sources, she replied, "Young man, you must remember that in Boston everything after 1850 is current events."[15] By contrast, of course, Chicago has labored under the shadow of Al Capone, though tempered in later years by the national reputations of Richard J. Daley and Sir Georg Solti. In earlier years it was pictured as vibrant, brash, brutal, and a braggadocio, the personification of the American competitive spirit.[16] An old story told it all. A reporter was ushered into the magnificent library of a meat packer's mansion. Its proud owner pointed to the elaborate leather bindings and said, "See them pretty books? I killed them calves myself."

The contrast, however, went beyond mere images. Chicago actually did grow at a much faster rate—716 percent (from 306,605 to 2,196,238) between 1870 and 1910; during the same period the Hub grew from 250,526 to 670,585, or 268 percent. The Ames Building, Boston's pride, was modestly sized compared to the skyscrapers of Chicago. The old port city, while staging a modest maritime renaissance based on exports during the last years of the nineteenth century, had lost its trading supremacy and was considered to be somewhat isolated because of failure to create direct rail connections to the West;[17] Chicago, of course, was at the center of the iron horse web. And that crucial advantage brought a greater concentration of heavy industry that was able to spread virtually unhampered by geography in three directions from downtown.

Economic differences between the cities also contributed to variations in their ethnic structure during the late nineteenth century. Besides the visible and dominant Irish, Boston also attracted substantial numbers of Canadians and immigrants from the British Isles. Chicago's Irish, on the other hand, were soon joined by a larger German-born population. And while both cities saw the so-called "new immigrants" come from several nationalities, as contrasted with the fewer and larger concentrations of mid-century, the development of steel production and other heavy industries in the Great Lakes region brought a much larger Slavic influx to Chicago.[18]

The reaction of the native-born to the immigrant arrivals also varied significantly. Xenophobia reached its most flamboyant and violent stage in Chicago during the anti-German Lager Beer Riots of 1855. After it died down, the Civil War and the Great Fire and rebuilding occupied the civic attention until the advent of labor disorder. Class hatreds and the rough adjustment to the discipline of the time clock led to local violence during the Railroad Strikes of 1877, the Haymarket Riot of 1886, and the Pullman disorder of 1894. Except for the occasional identification of all Germans as "anarchists," the hatred of immigrants took other forms, such as the struggle for foreign language instruction in the public schools and the Catholic fight to remove the King James Version of Bible recitation from the public classroom.[19]

By contrast, nativism in Boston was both organized and raised to a sophisticated level of intellectual abstraction. Deeply rooted in anti-slavery optimism over the future of the melting pot, the Brahmins found themselves swept aside socially by a new industrial elite and politically by the Irish. Upper-class compassion drifted from mild concern to systematized opposition in the form of the Immigration Restriction League of 1894. Through their chief spokesman, Senator Henry Cabot Lodge, the Massachusetts nativists cited statistics about pauperism, illiteracy, and political payrolls. They used footnotes, where their Chicago counterparts used fists.[20]

But most important of all, the two cities represented radically different approaches to the problem of liquor and society. Boston was the epitome of regulation—not perfect, but strict. All forms of public behavior, including drinking, were prescribed. A complex ordinance book forbade everything from praying aloud on the Charlesbank to whistling in a park. Street musicians had to audition before a licensing board before playing for pennies. That same attitude toward restriction brought the numbers, locations, and ownerships of barrooms under close government control. The object of the regulation was to limit the social, economic, and political role of the saloon in the Hub. Edward Hungerford noted in 1913 that "when you come to the old Bay State town and you suddenly realize that you are being ruled. . . . The effect of many rules and sundry regulations seems to be law and order —to an extent hardly reached in any other city within the United States."[21]

By contrast, Chicago was "wide open." Regulations about the use of public places, from speed limits to peddler's rules, were largely ignored. The streets were filthy, and the same laissez-faire attitude prevailed about crime and liquor licensing. Permits were cheap and unlimited in numbers, at least until 1906, and officials made little effort to restrict locations and enforce ordinances. Because it became almost ubiquitous and its ranks grew to the thousands, the saloon assumed a much more important role in Chicago's everyday life than it did in tightly controlled Boston.

The Hand of the Past

Tradition was a constant companion to the saloonkeeper. The nickel beer, the swinging doors, the sawdust on the floors, and the brass rail represented symbols of the past that were fixed in the public imagination. But the barkeep also had to contend with a residue of legal traditions, some dating back to the colonial inn. Ultimately, these helped make Boston a restrictive saloon town, while Chicago, by contrast, became a wide-open place. One of the most essential differences came from the innkeeping tradition of colonial New England. Virtually all public drinking before the 1830s was done in these unique places. The names of the Lamb, the Liberty Tree, the Eastern Stage House, and the Eagle are a colorful part of colonial history. But it was the special legal status accorded these lodgings that shaped public drinking in Boston hundreds of years later.[22] Because inns were so crucial to the welfare of the traveler when the scheduling of journeys was so uncertain, proprietors legally had to provide lodging, food, and drink at any hour of the day or night, even on Sundays. Only periods of total prohibition abrogated that responsibility. Thus, until the early 1900s the hotels of Boston could sell liquor at any time, when other types of sellers were denied that privilege. Tradition held that customers were legally the friends of the innkeeper, who entertained them in his home, and the imposition of temporal restrictions was an invasion of his privacy.[23]

Colonial legislators in Massachusetts were also aware of the possibilities for abusing the innkeeper's privilege. Their response was a series of laws, enacted between 1637 and 1645, that attempted to depersonalize the relationships between drinkers. Liquor sales were limited to nonresidents, strangers, at first in the hope that locals would remain sober or at least do their drinking at home. This law was as impossible to enforce as it was unpopular, so it was modified to allow townsfolk to enter, but without permission to "drink healths" and tarry at the bar for long periods. Another law, enacted in 1698, limited the location of inns to major roads, again to encourage use by traveling strangers rather than local residents. Although these laws fell into gradual disuse by the late 1700s, they left important legal traditions: a temperate society was one that drank at home, and public imbibing should be stripped of its sociability.[24]

The earliest public drinking places in Chicago were also inns. These were rude structures built and operated by such local pioneers as James Kinzie, Archibald Clybourn, Sam Miller, and Billy Caldwell and bore such names as the Wolf Tavern, the Sauganash, and the Green Tree Tavern. The whiskey and brandy, as well as the food and beds, were important to local travelers, but innkeeping in early Chicago developed with few of the legal restraints found in Massachusetts. By the early 1830s travel had lost much of its awesomeness in the Midwest. In

1848 the first railroad would be chugging west, the same year that a canal route opened to St. Louis. Therefore, because Chicago developed so much later than Boston, the inn was a much less significant part of the lakeside city's early history and legal tradition. There was no innkeeper's privilege.[25]

The tavern of early days gradually gave way to new forms of public drinking. The change was a function of growth and specialization. In Boston, the transition began in the 1700s, as drinkers at first ignored restrictive laws in secret, then openly, before public opinion forced a change in the statutes. The first to go was the role of the innkeeper as the exclusive retail dealer of liquor. The General Court responded to the demand for more drinking places by creating a new category of license in 1832, the "common victualler." This allowed a foodshop to sell liquor without the burden of maintaining rooms. It also reduced the cost of opening a business. Common victuallers opened away from main roads and amidst enclaves of the foreign-born, a trend aided by the elimination of the citizenship requirement for licensees. The fee was negligible, and there was no limit on the number of permits, as had been the case with the pre–1800 inn. Tight restrictions prevented wholesale dealers and grocers from selling retail.[26]

By contrast, liquor dispensing in Chicago evolved from grocery and bulk sales instead of in the early taverns and inns. By the 1850s most retail sales were made in general stores and groceries, while wholesalers opened "sample rooms" for customers to taste what they were about to buy in quantity. The early inns merely faded into the background, displaced by hotels of more spectacular grandeur. By the end of that decade the word *saloon* had begun to appear in city directories, referring to a retail establishment whose primary function was to sell liquor.[27]

The expansion of liquor retailing quickly drew bitter opposition from temperance groups, which adopted two basic tactics. One was the use of persuasion and the pledge, by which the drinker promised publicly to reform himself. The Massachusetts Society for the Suppression of Intemperance, founded in 1813, promoted that approach. Gradually, the state's first temperance society moved toward the idea of total abstinence from all liquor, not just avoidance of the hard spirits. Temperance came to mean more than the rehabilitation of the fallen; it was a positive goal promoted by many who had never touched drink. As the retailing of liquor proliferated during the 1830s and after, the number of pledge-taking societies expanded: the Massachusetts Temperance Union (1838), Washingtonian Society (1841), Sons of Temperance (1844), Independent Order of Good Templars (1844), Massachusetts Total Abstinence Society (1871), and the Catholic Total Abstinence Union (1871), to name a few. All employed the public promise of pure behavior and the maintenance of social activities without benefit of liquor to promote comradeship.[28]

But early temperance movements quickly interested themselves in efforts to end all drinking by legislative fiat. Not only would the soul save itself, but it would save others through prohibition, whether or not they wanted dry salvation. The first taste of success came when the Massachusetts Temperance Union pushed through the General Court the Fifteen Gallon Law of 1838. By limiting the *minimum* sale to that amount and prohibiting consumption on the premises, it effectively shut off the liquor supply to the poor, who could not afford that quantity; the wealthy, who presumably could be trusted with liquor, could drink at home. But the widespread evasion and unpopularity of the law led to its repeal two years later.[29] In 1852, however, Massachusetts passed the so-called Maine Law, which ushered in sixteen years of total statewide prohibition. Widespread violation, along with the shocking disclosures of 1867 license debates, led to a repeal of prohibition in 1868, but antiliquor forces won out again the following year. Except for a brief period when beer sales were legal from 1871 to 1873, the Bay State remained dry until 1875.[30]

The most probing inquiry into the social effects of prohibition came in 1867 during a lengthy General Court hearing. Prohibitionists bragged that liquor consumption had been reduced, that government was no longer in league with the devil by licensing sin, and that liquor could no longer advertise itself through the open barroom.[31]

Other witnesses, however, probed the flaws in prohibition and introduced questions that would influence lawmakers after repeal. The wets claimed that arrests for drunkenness had not really declined as dramatically as citizens had earlier believed. Alcohol was obviously being produced or imported, and a secret distribution system placed it in the hands of thousands of drinkers. One minister described how the crystal decanter had appeared on the home sideboard and how exclusive private clubs had been formed for the singular purpose of secret drinking companionship. Wealthy buyers could afford large liquor purchases from nearby nonprohibition states.

Boston's poor, meanwhile, pooled resources to buy barrels and establish "jugrooms" in tenement basements. Charity workers and city missionaries worried aloud about the social problems that came from this secret consumption. Tenement doors concealed drunkenness, wife beating, and child abuse because drinking had been forced from public view in the saloon, where police, reformers, and the upright citizenry could patrol. Under license, the quality and purity of liquor could be regulated; now, inspection was virtually impossible. Twenty-three dry years left Bostonians very conscious of the legal and social differences between public and private drinking, and when prohibition ended, the lawmakers of the 1880s would try instead to make drinking as public as possible. The licensing process, as well as the daily operation of the bar, would be open to public scrutiny for purity's sake.

The bitterness of the debate and the creation of a vast network of illegal suppliers and outlets left a mark on the Massachusetts liquor industry, but the Maine Law agitation was of minimal importance in Illinois. The first antiliquor group, the Chicago Temperance Society, was founded in 1833, and within a year it had persuaded the Illinois General Assembly to outlaw Sunday drinking. Other temperance groups helped give the raw town an air of respectability, but statewide prohibition was a failure. When the General Assembly enacted one law in 1851, it was overturned in the courts two years later. Another attempt in 1855 failed to gain the approval of voters in a special referendum. Thus, Chicagoans failed to develop the fine art of secret selling.[32]

Part of the reason for the differing traditions in the two states came from the fact that the General Court met in Boston, while the General Assembly convened in Springfield, two hundred miles from Chicago. The Illinois legislators encouraged localism, giving county officials almost complete control over licensing soon after statehood was attained in 1818. In 1839 the legislators transferred those powers to mayors and city councils in incorporated places, but that same act introduced an important principle: counties, townships, and cities also had the right to vote themselves dry. As a consequence, the pressure for statewide prohibition was diffused into hundreds of local battles. Rarely did the General Assembly intrude on the operation of saloons in Illinois.[33]

The locus of authority in Chicago was in the mayor's office. He was a virtual dictator over which applicants would receive or lose licenses, where retailers and wholesalers would be located, and, by practical application, which state laws would be enforced or ignored. The first two prerogatives were upheld many times in the courts; the latter was a part of the political reality. Except for the years between 1861 and 1876, when a board of commissioners controlled the Chicago police, the chief executive had complete command over the enforcement of liquor laws. The desire to be reelected often canceled the intent of a state statute. Some Chicagoans complained, but the Springfield representatives failed to act.[34]

Meanwhile, events in Massachusetts pushed state government toward greater centralization of authority. The General Court blamed ineffective local regulation for an era of debauchery that preceded statewide prohibition; the Common Victualler Act of 1832 had given mayors the power to distribute licenses and enforce laws. Reluctantly, the state legislators decided to entrust the locals once more when prohibition ended in 1875. Each mayor appointed a panel of three commissioners to issue or revoke the annual permits, while authority over the police department remained in the hands of the mayor. This system proved an egregious failure from the start. Appointments to the license boards became embroiled in local politics, while the local commissioners tried to ease the huge underground liquor traffic over to selling legally by ignoring most of the liquor laws. Newspaper exposés revealed that a majority of Boston dealers did not even bother to take out licenses. Amidst the uproar over crime and corrupt police came the election in 1885 of Hugh O'Brien, Boston's first Irish Catholic mayor. Fearing the total moral collapse of the Hub, temperance groups, prohibitionists, nativists, and others began to call for a return to state control.[35]

The change came later that year, when the General Court placed the power to grant licenses and enforce liquor statutes in the hands of a Board of Metropolitan Police Commissioners appointed by the governor. Although Bostonians were unhappy about having their police under state control, the new commissioners immediately replaced the department's top command, began rejecting license applications, and started diverting one-fourth of all liquor fees to the Massachusetts treasury, as the new law allowed. The number of arrests soared as police began to enforce the Screen Law enacted in 1880. The fear of secret debauchery that had appeared so many times in the 1867 testimony had prompted the General Court to forbid the licensee from installing anything that might obstruct the view of the interior from the sidewalk window. While temperance societies objected that the drinking would advertise itself by its visibility, the legislators wanted to make it easier for the police to observe what was going on inside. When the new metropolitan police board decided to bring Boston imbibing into strict compliance with the laws, the Screen Law was an important ally. By contrast, Chicago barrooms could be completely closed to the street while open and had to unshutter their windows only after the legal closing hour.[36]

Thus, the barroom was legally somewhere between the parlor and the curbstone. That constant tension between public and private, between family and larger society, and between personal and common space helped shape the career of the saloon and gives this study its interpretive framework.

CHAPTER 1

From Entrepreneur
to Employee

EVERYONE FORMED an impression of the man behind the bar. To his neighbors he was a sage, an arbiter of small disputes, and an interpreter of the mysteries of politics. His apron, slightly stained by beer or the day's offering at the free lunch table, symbolized his folksiness. The bar rag seldom left his firm grip. But to his prohibitionist enemies, he was a blot upon neighborhood decency. Babies went hungry when their father spent paychecks at his bar. His liquor rendered workingmen inefficient. Criminals, juvenile delinquents, and corrupt politicians poured from his swinging doors. An entrepreneurial imperialist, he drained scarce monetary resources from tenement districts into the coffers of rich brewers and distillers. Flashy clothes, the tendency to "play the ponies," and the diamond stickpin on his ample girth symbolized the arrogance of this "parasite."

Both stereotyped images were rooted in the saloonkeeper's role as a small businessman, and for good reason. Virtually every other aspect of the social and political saga of the barroom ultimately depended on the fact that, before all else, it was an economic institution. Even the most powerful saloonkeeper aldermen worried about the number of nickels left in the till after the bills were paid. And the services the barroom provided, its propensity to run afoul of the law, and its ability to adjust to incoming immigrant groups would all be rooted in the structure of the business.

The economic transformation of the saloon began with changes in the brewing and wholesale liquor industries. An atmosphere of over-competition resulted in an abundance of saloons. As the producers fought to control retailers, proprietors lost their independence, and the barroom came to resemble the prototype of the modern chain store operation.

The Brewery Revolution

The story of the saloon as an economic and social institution was intimately intertwined with the evolution of the brewing industry in the nineteenth century. Like most other manufacturers of the 1820s and 1830s breweries were rather small and unstable. Nearly all of Boston's earliest suppliers had already disappeared by the middle of the century; only the Bunker Hill Brewery survived more than a few years. It had been founded in 1821, and it quickly established a flourishing trade with the hotels, inns, and taverns of Boston. Its success attracted a competitor in 1828, when a group of substantial investors formed the Boston Beer Company in South Boston. But there was still enough trade for both firms to prosper, since the growing concern with temperance converted large numbers of consumers from hard liquor to ale.[1]

The brewing industry appeared in Chicago at the inception of the village. In 1833 a pair of transplanted New Yorkers, William Haas and Andrew Sulzer, opened a small plant on the outskirts of the town and began selling ale to the few thousand residents. During the next decade the founders sold out to William Lill, an Englishman, and to William B. Ogden, the city's first mayor and premier promoter, who eventually sold his interest to raise money for railroad investment. In 1841 Ogden was succeeded by Michael Diversey, a milkman, and the company became known as Lill and Diversey.[2]

The following decades saw a proliferation of new brewers in both cities. In Boston a total of twenty-two opened before 1860. The entrepreneurs of this generation were significant in two respects. First, they all located in the Roxbury section and helped establish it as the primary German neighborhood of Boston. Most of the employees lived near the breweries, which were among the most substantial factories in a city noted for its lack of heavy industry. Since the firms had extensive storage cellars and warehouses that could not be moved, the result was a population far more stable than those in the transitory North, West, and South Ends. As one guidebook noted decades later, "A large area of country in the Roxbury District is covered with their [German] solid brick buildings, yards, and vaults."[3]

Even more important, the new brewers of the antebellum decades introduced lager beer to millions of urbanites. This new brew first entered the country in 1840 when John Wagner began a small experiment in the rear of his Philadelphia home. He had brought lager yeast with

him from Germany, where it had already gained widespread popularity. And within a few months Wagner's fledgling company had orders
that exceeded its capacity. Wagner soon found himself overshadowed
by imitators all over the East. Within half a decade, a lager brewery
owned by Michael Ludwig began operation in Roxbury. The Germans
of the area were so anxious to purchase his product that they came directly to his door to buy the barrels; Ludwig bragged that he never had
to introduce a delivery service. Eventually, Ludwig sold out to John
Roessle, who used aggressive marketing and delivery to make the company one of the largest in the country. Others who crowded into Roxbury concentrated exclusively on lager products, leaving ale and porter
for a few Irish and British plants in South Boston and Charlestown.[4]

The migration of lager beer production closely resembled the movement of population, especially the German-born, from east to west.
After its introduction on the eastern seaboard, it next appeared in upstate New York, then in Pittsburgh, Cincinnati, and St. Louis. In 1854,
Valentin Busch and Michael Brand brought it to Chicago. The pair
had started an ale plant a few years earlier, but the competition from
Lill and Diversey and the half-dozen other ale companies had forced
them either to innovate or to close. So they moved to the limestone hills
of suburban Blue Island, cut storage cellars in the ground, and began
brewing lager beer. Within a few years they had become one of the
largest companies in the Midwest.[5]

By 1860 what would be the future pattern of Chicago's brewing industry had become evident. First, Busch and Brand proved to be correct; the future lay in producing lager rather than ale. From the 1860s
on, nearly all the successful midwestern companies either started with
that product or later switched over to it. Lill and Diversey continued to
produce ale and could still claim leadership in production, but their
economic position became increasingly fragile, and they had to seek
new, out-of-town markets to compensate for a home consumption that
was rapidly disappearing. The company never rebuilt after the fire of
1871.[6]

Something else had also become clear: the field was becoming increasingly competitive. In Chicago there were fourteen brewers in
1860 and twenty-three a decade later. Moreover, the industry was also
assuming a "David and Goliath" appearance, with the field divided between the giants and the upstarts. There were many small newcomers
crowding the field. Typically, their founders were penniless immi-

grants who had spent their first years in America working in someone else's brewery. Once they had accumulated enough capital, they had struck out on their own and added another name to the list of brewers. The pattern was repeated in Boston. The twenty-two brewers of 1860 had grown to thirty in 1870 and forty-five by 1880.

In the Hub and in Chicago, the newcomers employed imaginative gimmicks to capture a share of the business. James W. Kenney, whose Armory Brewery Company opened in 1877, oriented his ale and porter business toward the Irish sections of Boston. The Fortune brothers, natives of County Wexford, did the same in Chicago. The latter city's ethnic heterogeneity accounted for at least a half-dozen companies aimed at fellow countrymen from Bohemia and Poland alone. Others attempted to create a taste for Weiss beer, an especially light variety with a negligible alcoholic content.[7]

During the next decade the larger Chicago companies continued to build their capacity, while the smaller ones increased in number. Although the city was growing at a spectacular rate, critics began to express fears about the future. The market was growing, but production capacity was expanding even faster. Yearly sales figures lagged far behind, because industry leaders overexpanded far beyond their ability to sell. Huge investments sat idle and failed to produce a profit.[8] The situation was not as critical in Boston; its capitalists had been more conservative in their market forecasts. But the potential problem was there; twenty new firms appeared between 1881 and 1890.

In both cities new entrepreneurs were discovering an essential fact: brewing was, and still is, technologically one of the simplest among the large industries. It consisted primarily of a system of heated and cooled containers; the production itself was carried on by nature. At least until mechanical refrigeration appeared, the investment was mainly in buildings. With this fact obvious to hundreds of brewery employees, the temptation to start yet another brewery remained strongly fixed in their imaginations.[9]

The local situation in both cities was complicated by still another problem: outside competitors. Cross-country shipment of brewery products had been going on for years; the flat and inert qualities of ale and porter had made that possible. Lager presented more difficult problems because of its effervescence and the possibility of spoilage. Some early Milwaukee brewers had been able to ship their product the eighty-five miles to Chicago, and several of them opened Chicago offices at a rather early time in the Windy City's history. Philip Best (now Pabst) opened an office in 1857, while Valentin Blatz and Joseph Schlitz entered the city in 1865 and 1868 respectively. But it was the great Chicago Fire of 1871 that allowed the beer barons of Milwaukee to expand their sales. That catastrophe destroyed much of Chicago's productive capacity long enough for the Wisconsin brewers to establish a market. When one of them later advertised that it was "the beer that made Milwaukee famous," it was referring to the barrels that it sold in postfire Chicago. Other producers, from such places as Watertown, Wisconsin, Waukegan, and Blue Island, tried to capitalize on Chicago's misfortune.[10]

Even after the city rebuilt, Chicago continued to attract outside competition. When pasteurization and refrigeration techniques were perfected in the 1870s and 1880s, there was almost no limit to the market. By 1885 between 15 and 20 percent of Pabst's output alone found its way into Chicagoans' steins — almost twice as much as Milwaukians consumed; the rest went to scattered parts of the country, including Boston. Anheuser-Busch of St. Louis developed perhaps the most aggressive national marketing program of all: by the summer of 1877 its rubber-lined cars were carrying beer as far as Galveston, and before the beginning of the next decade, Budweiser and its other brands were being sold on both coasts.[11] The Best Brewing Company alone kept forty-five teams and drivers in Chicago busy delivering its 115,000 barrels, while Schlitz and Blatz sold 50,000 and 45,000 respectively — 32.3 percent of all beer sold in Chicago. That "invasion" from Wisconsin led Chicago brewers to petition the City Council for relief in the form of a substantial license fee levied against the "foreigners." The pleas were unsuccessful.

Every technological improvement seemed to make the future more disquieting for the older hometown producers, especially in Chicago. Artificial refrigeration of storage cellars meant that Chicago and Milwaukee lost their most important advantage — a plentiful and cheap supply of ice. Inland companies could now avoid the cost and trouble of importing the natural coolant. Refrigerated railroad cars, the completion of the basic rail network, and pasteurization meant that beer could be shipped almost anywhere. And finally, newness itself was an advantage in an industry that eagerly adopted the latest techniques in production, handling, and packaging. New companies with sufficient capital could avoid the encumbrance of outdated facilities. Moreover, during the 1880s, when labor unions were attempting to organize the industries, the higher the level of automation, the greater the economic advantage to the brewer.[12]

In Boston during the mid-1880s, out-of-town brewers were also scrambling to capture as many customers as possible. Philadelphia and New York beer invaded the Hub first, but by 1883 Cincinnati's Moerlein Brewing Company and Schlitz from Milwaukee were advertising in the *Transcript* alongside companies from Rochester and Lowell. Eventually these brands were joined by Stroh's from Detroit and Anheuser-Busch.[13] But the comparative isolation of the Hub and its smaller population made it far less attractive than Chicago to out-of-town brewers.

The Problem of Prices

The new forms of competition ultimately affected the industry's price structure. The impact was less severe in New England, where competition was only moderate and the producers managed to form a viable trade organization. The Brewers' Association of New England, formed in 1872, included nearly everybody who either produced beer in the region or shipped it there. For most of the rest of the century that group maintained a stable price of twelve to fourteen dollars per barrel.

But in Chicago no such organization existed, and the wholesale rate of ten dollars in 1873 had become eight dollars at the end of the decade.[14] Any discussion of a price increase aroused the saloonkeepers' anger. On April 30, 1880, they held a meeting, the results of which were extensively reported in the press. The foreman of the Binz brewery made a formal affidavit that the production costs never exceeded four dollars a barrel, and as a result the assembled saloonkeepers went on record opposing any more than a 100 percent profit or eight dollars a barrel. The brewers replied that materials and federal tax alone cost $3.88 per barrel, but that figure did not include capital cost and finance and depreciation. The producers noted that beer in New York and other eastern cities sold for ten dollars and that the cost of hops had escalated from twelve to forty-five cents a pound. They also went on to note that saloonkeepers grossed twenty-eight dollars per barrel at retail, leaving twenty dollars clear profit. Barmen had no reason to complain.[15]

The antagonism between brewer and saloonman that had been building for so long finally broke into the open. From that point on, at least in Chicago, the producers and the dispensers would unite only when necessary to battle the common antiliquor enemy. And for the next forty years they would make an obvious falsehood out of the temperance attack on a unified liquor interest.[16]

The brewers then formed the Chicago and Milwaukee Brewers' Association. This was a strange organization that amounted to little more than formalization of good will. It established a minimum price of eight dollars per barrel for standard beer and required its members to agree to end the practice of granting discounts.[17] The organization appeared to be effective for a few years. The wholesale price remained stable, but the real reason lay in the rising cost of production which counterbalanced the effect of competition. Raw materials became more expensive each year, while the relative success of the Brewery Workmen union boosted the labor costs for most of the companies. These forces curbed the temptation to underprice the market.[18]

By the mid-1880s the brewing industry was in chaos. A tenuous truce halted the price war. Beer from a thousand miles away competed with hometown brands. Small companies, which refused to join the brewers' associations, threatened to undersell the larger ones. And all of this contributed to the unpredictability inherent in the brewing industry to begin with. The condition of the market was always at the mercy of the weather and economic conditions. A cold season or an increase in unemployment might leave a brewer with a surplus, while failure to plan for increased demand meant the loss of potential business. The aging time of beer, which was usually at least six months, left the brewer guessing about the future. Even the cost of raw materials, which were also directly affected by the weather, could fluctuate widely from year to year.[19]

The Beginning of Brewery Control

This instability could not help but affect the relationship between the brewers and the saloons. For decades the two segments of the industry had operated independently. The man behind the bar had traditionally supplied his own capital or borrowed it from a bank or his friends. He paid his rent and utilities and went downtown himself each year to purchase his license. His barroom reflected his personality and tastes — honest or crooked, fancy or plain — because he owned his fixtures. If he conducted his business properly, he prospered, and it was his decision to close and sell out when the nightly receipts in the till failed to meet his expectations or pay the bills at the end of the month.

This independence had given the saloonkeeper a distinct advantage in his relationship with suppliers. The price and quality of the products and perhaps the personality of the salesman motivated him to choose one brand over another from representatives of various jobbers and wholesalers of hard liquor and breweries that made the rounds occasionally. The whiskey trade especially left a great deal of room for experimentation. There were hundreds of brands on the market, and the decision to purchase a case or a small barrel of one of them had little long-term consequence for the saloonman's business.[20]

A similar degree of freedom characterized the saloonman's connection with the brewer. Their relations were frequently cordial and extended over many years. Fritz Sontag, for instance, spent twenty-eight seasons as a salesman for Anheuser-Busch in Chicago and was well-known in saloons throughout the city. But it was always the saloonkeeper's prerogative to weigh each brewery's offer, test the product, and bargain for discounts. The only real limitation on his choice was the awkward size and complexity of the tapping apparatus and the fifty-five-gallon barrels.[21]

By the 1880s the chaotic situation in the Chicago brewing industry had begun to change all that. Overcompetition among brewers meant that beer salesmen tried to outdo each other with promises of rebates and discounts. The price proclaimed by the brewers' association remained at eight dollars in Chicago, but in reality the salesmen brought it down to nearly half that amount. Companies also tried such public relations gimmicks as purchasing blocks of tickets to balls and parties, many of them held in saloons.[22] This activity alone cost breweries up to $10,000 each year.

Every year the variety and number of gratuities increased. Salesmen from Anheuser-Busch distributed thousands of free "samples" to saloonkeepers and bought rounds for customers. Brewers began offering free trays, interior advertising displays, and complimentary glassware to sweeten the sales pitch. Lithograph novelties, calendars, bottle openers, pocketknives, and postcards that carried the name of the saloon as well as that of the brewer began to appear in salesmen's kits. Anheuser-Busch started supplying large wall prints, including scenes of "Washington Crossing the Delaware" and "Custer's Last Fight." Other companies supplies such standard barroom nudes as "Andromache at the Bath."[23]

The evidence of the brewers' competition appeared in the exterior of the saloon as well. For many years proprietors had used signboards which, like the interior fixtures, reflected individual personalities and tastes. Some were elegant and fancy, with large gold letters that promised expensive whiskey. Others were unique, such as the large schooner ship over Michael "Hinky Dink" Kenna's door; the "schooners" he served inside were of another variety. Other places employed a simple red light, which in Chicago could indicate a respectable saloon instead of a brothel, or the most common inscription, "Wines, Liquors and Cigars" with the proprietor's name.[24]

By the early 1880s the brewers began furnishing signs as gratuities. As the years passed, some of these extravaganzas were made of glass and eventually electrified; they cost $250 to $300 apiece.[25] Some observers saw this competition as an evil forced on the brewers by their inability to cooperate. In 1879 the Boston correspondent for the *Western Brewer* wrote that the brewers should "proceed to cut off the sign nuisance, so prevalent in most cities, which compels them to furnish kindling wood to their saloons in the shape of costly signs that sooner or later make their way into the fire-box, to make room for other signs more elaborately painted by a competitor. We could name a single brewery whose sign bills average from $300 to $500 a week."[26]

The character of the salesmen who called on saloons also changed. The old-time brewers' representatives had once spent most of their time merely servicing the needs of long-standing customers, thus earning the nickname of "collectors." But increased competition transformed both the type of men who went into sales and the methods they used. They were now boisterous, free-spending "drummers," who were expected to distribute gifts and appear to take an interest, however contrived, in the personal lives of the men behind the bar.[27]

Often, the brewers found potential salesmen among the most successful and upwardly mobile saloonkeepers. The career of a Chicagoan named Phil J. Sommer was typical. Born of humble circumstances, Sommer had been a manual laborer before opening his first barroom on Halsted Street adjacent to Jane Addams's Hull House. He prospered at this location, but envisioned even greater profits near the outskirts of the growing city. He chose West Pullman, a semiindustrial section near the sleeping car manufacturer's model town, and in October of 1892 he purchased a plot of land and began making plans for his new venture.[28]

The bitter winter ended any hopes of beginning the construction until spring, but before then Sommer's career abruptly changed course. One day Gustave Trapp, an agent for the Gottfried Brewing Company, stopped by the Halsted Street place with an attractive job offer. Gottfried, from whom Sommer bought his beer, had been impressed with the young saloonkeeper's personality and wanted him to head a new branch warehouse and sales operation in the very neighborhood where he had intended to build his new saloon. The salary of eighty dollars per month, plus forty cents for each barrel returned, was irresistible. Sommer sold his Halsted Street bar and abandoned his plans to build in Ninety-Fifth Street.

His new duties were complicated and taxing. First, he helped the company select a site for its new warehouse and arrange for the construction of a new rail siding. Then he began soliciting trade among the army of competing collectors. He visited fifteen to twenty saloons a week, spending nearly $300 each month on good will — far more money than he earned in salary. The brewery, in fact, spent nearly forty cents in salesmen's expenses on each three-dollar barrel of beer it sold. When Sommer signed up new customers, it was his duty to see that deliveries were made on time, that empty barrels were returned, and that customer complaints were answered. It was difficult work, but Sommer was a success, and before he left the employment of the company, he started another Gottfried branch in suburban Crete.

The Takeover

The process of winning customers was costly and often led to open discord between the brewer and the retailer. Disreputable saloonmen accepted offers of special discounts, gifts, and even small, interest-free loans from one company, only to switch suppliers a few weeks later and pocket the gratuities of both. Some breweries allowed customers to accumulate a monthly tab instead of paying the driver on delivery, only to discover later that many dishonest barmen refused to pay. Bill collection and court litigation were too expensive to pursue in most instances, but the accumulated chicanery of hundreds of saloonkeepers could cost the brewer a substantial amount of money.[29]

The growing popularity of bottled beer further complicated the matter. A saloonkeeper might accept gifts or even mortgage money from one company, but quietly sell other brands in bottles because they did not require the cumbersome barrels or tapping apparatus. The saloon owner could adjust his stock more easily to suit his customers' tastes, but the brewers saw it as one more way in which unscrupulous saloon-keepers took advantage of the competition in the industry.[30]

Finally, an accumulation of such intangibles as ethnicity taxed the patience of the brewers. One salesman, John S. Pierce of Chicago, wrote to Pabst, "We are getting along first rate with the Bohemians. Have not lost Gep or any of them as yet. Of course they want a Bohemi-an agent, but my experience in life is we don't always get what we want. It is trouble enough to have to look after the Bohemian custom-ers to say nothing about an agent of that nationality."[31] With stories of this nature becoming increasingly common, the *Western Brewer* took the occasion to suggest an answer: direct brewery control of their own retail outlets.

The idea of producer-controlled retail outlets originated in England, where the "tied-house" system had been in operation for nearly a cen-tury. Since the 1790s such companies as Guinness had used it almost ex-clusively, and by 1830 the brewers had almost completely monopolized the pub licenses.[32] The adoption of the plan in the United States was gradual and uneven. A few brewers had introduced it on a limited scale before the Civil War. In 1859, for instance, Philip Best owned the Milwaukee Lager Beer Saloon and Restaurant on Chicago's Randolph Street, while the Valentin Blatz Company operated a similar facility next door.[33]

But it was not until after 1880 that the brewers began the takeover in earnest. First came rental of bars, mirrors, sideboards, and other fix-tures to saloonkeepers. By January 1884 the *Daily News* counted over 200 such arrangements, but its survey was incomplete. Less than a decade later the brewers were renting $210,565 worth of fixtures to several thousand saloons. Finally, by 1916 the companies owned the equipment of 4,679 of the 7,000 bars in Chicago.[34] The quality and cost of the fixtures varied considerably. Those who had previously been in business needed only a few accessories, while newcomers needed a full complement of equipment.[35] For instance, when Fred Rahlf signed up with Anheuser-Busch in 1904, his fixtures cost $1,400. But his loca-tion — only a few doors from the southwest corner of Lincoln Park — showed great promise. In return for eighteen monthly payments of $75 and an agreement to dispense only the St. Louis brewer's beer, he received everything he needed to start in business:

> One back bar with mirror, one front bar and workboard, one cigar case, one bottle case, one front partition and doors, one ice box in saloon, one lunch counter, one wire partition, nine tables, thirty-six chairs, one steam table, two swinging doors, one cash register No. 274473, two card machines, one bath tub and washstands, one furnace, one gas stove, one kitchen range, all gas and eleric light fixtures, four electric fans, all glassware and bar fixtures and implements, all kitchen furniture, fixtures and cooking utensils, all dishes, and cutlery and all other articles belonging to the saloon and lunch business at premises below described.[36]

The practice of furnishing fixtures was not an act of benevolence. The mortgage guaranteed that the brewery would eventually be repaid. It was an investment that gave the beermaker a secure and exclusive retail outlet. A common clause in chattel mortgage agreements prohibited the saloonkeeper from selling anyone else's beer. Furthermore, the saloonkeeper was obligated to pay "the current market price" or, in other words, what the brewer demanded. These provisions were naturally unpopular, but in all major cases the courts of Illinois and Massachusetts, as well as English common law, upheld their validity. The saloonkeeper had to make his own arrangements to purchase hard liquor.[37]

Another important factor in the evolution of the saloon business was the high license movement of the 1880s. Advocates argued that if the annual fee were sharply raised, saloonkeepers would finally begin to pay their share of the increased police and welfare costs that resulted from liquor consumption. The plan would also provide additional revenue to finance expensive public works projects so badly needed in the expanding city. Proponents also argued that because dealers would have a larger financial stake in their business, few would risk losing their expensive license through illegal sales. Drunkenness and sales to juveniles would disappear. Marginal saloons, so often labeled the most serious troublemakers, would be forced to close, and ownership would be concentrated in more responsible hands. Furthermore, increases would also provide a good opportunity for differential licensing, with dispensers of hard liquor paying much higher rates because those drinks reputedly caused more social disorganization than did beer or wine.[38]

High license became a national movement during the early 1880s, but the idea was adopted with much more enthusiasm in Boston than in Chicago. In the Hub the first serious consideration of the idea began in 1883. The following year, the license authorities raised the rate from $125 for all sellers to $150 for beer only and $250 for beer and whiskey licenses. It was the Board of Police, installed after passage of the metropolitan police act of 1885, that took the high license arguments seriously. Within two years the rate had been raised to $500 for everyone. By 1890 the board had developed an elaborate scale that differentiated between the various kinds of sales. Large hotels paid $1,500 and their smaller counterparts were assessed $300 less. The most shocking change, however, saw the common victualler, or saloon, rate jump from $500 to $1,000 for the right to sell all kinds of intoxicants. This made Boston's license rate the highest in the nation.[39]

By contrast, the increases were much more modest in Chicago and were the result of a different kind of lobbying effort. The mayor enjoyed the power to distribute and rescind licenses, but he had no control over the license rate. That had to be done by a mandate from either the General Assembly or the City Council. The latter body was hostile to the idea, however, perhaps remembering the bloody Lager Beer Riot that had followed an attempt to raise license fees in 1855. Efforts focused on Springfield, where downstate legislators finally passed the Harper High License Act of 1883. Named for William H. Harper, a silk-stocking attorney-legislator from Chicago, the bill established a statewide minimum of $500. In an attempt to make the proposal look unnecessary, the Chicago City Council had already raised fees from $52 to $103, but the Harper Law passed anyway. All the Chicagoans could do was change the dates of the license year in an attempt to save the saloonkeepers a few dollars.[40]

The liquor dealers could marshal little resistance to the high license panacea. They warned that marginal dealers would turn to crime to supplement their proceeds, rather than go out of business quietly. Massachusetts saloonists predicted that those who could not afford to stay open legitimately would sell in secret; time would prove the prophecy correct. Meanwhile, legislators ignored the advice that the high fee would cause bars to attempt to draw customers from the competition with fancier fixtures, music, and other trade-building gimmicks. The saloon would not be reduced in importance, only entrenched more securely than ever.[41]

Temperance reformers also unwittingly contributed to the growth of the tied-house system through the high license by creating a serious need for additional capital from outside the retail trade. Independent saloons faced bankruptcy, while outlets supplied with brewery-owned fixtures once again turned to the brewers for aid. The producers accepted the burden without hesitation. The passage of the Harper Law in Illinois closed 780 of Chicago's 3,500 saloons in 1884, but 516 new ones opened the following year, largely with the help of the brewers. During the next decade the vast majority of the retail trade would make the transition, until a handful of brewery representatives replaced the long lines at the license windows at City Hall.[42]

In part, the brewers were merely trying to regain some of their lost profits. Generally, the retail value of a barrel of beer remained stable, varying from saloon to saloon according to the size of glasses used and the portion of the house's trade devoted to the "growlers," or large tin pails. The most important variable was the wholesale price to the saloonkeeper; the lower it fell, the more profit was transferred from the producer to the retailer. And on a total production of thousands of barrels, the difference between a three-and a fifteen-dollar wholesale price could be very important. The brewers did the obvious thing in attempting to regain some of their lost profit by selling the fixtures and the license to the dealer.[43]

The result was a continued surplus of saloons. The ratio of people per barroom in Chicago stabilized at 203 to one in 1885 and slowly inched downward. There were more bars in that city than in all fifteen southern states combined, a fact that dismayed temperance and liquor spokesmen alike. Organizations representing both sides of the alcohol issue demanded that the City Council enact some type of limitation law, but these efforts were in vain. In the long run it was not the climate, nor the number of foreign-born, nor even the corrupt Chicago Police Department that had created the situation. Rather, the cause lay in the artificial props erected by the city's brewers in their desire for a more secure portion of the market.[44]

The condition of the trade did not necessarily mean that independents could not turn a profit. Some even created successful nonbrewery chains. The two largest were both started by wholesalers. Chapin and Gore began as a grocery at State and Jackson in 1865. A few years later the owners added a line of liquors, which they found so profitable that when they rebuilt after the Great Fire they specialized in whiskies.

During the 1880s their sample room evolved into a chain of retail outlets, numbering five in 1891. Their principal competitor, Hannah and Hogg, began in 1873 when they bought an interest in an extant saloon named the Thistle. From one bar the partnership grew to include eight places by 1888. Besides the retail trade, Hannah and Hogg and Chapin and Gore both carried on a large wholesale business with hotels, saloons, and private homes.[45]

Transforming Boston's Saloon Business

While the high license law and competition among breweries were responsible for the revolution in Chicago's retail liquor trade, other factors prompted changes in Boston. One was the strong reaction to the private evasion of the midcentury prohibition law. When it ended in 1875, officials were determined not only to use the law to make drinking as public as possible but also to reshape drinkers' buying habits. The return to legal liquor in Massachusetts had little immediate impact on Boston's "wet trade." The number of sellers was supposedly reduced. In 1870 there had been 2,584 illegal places known to be in operation, or one for every ninety-seven people, including women and children. Five years later a special License Board, established to administer the law, approved only 1,897 applicants, or a ratio of one license to 180 people. The real extent of the reduction will never be known, however, for large numbers of concealed places continued to serve their private customers.

But whatever its other failings, the pre-1885 License Board had managed to concentrate the off-premises sales in grocery and wholesale liquor shops, eliminating most of the other sellers. It found greater difficulty, however, in reorienting the private drinking customs of the prohibition era. In 1875 little more than half (50.9 percent) of the licensees were innkeepers or victuallers. The remaining places (49.1 percent) sold to people to carry home. A decade later, the on-premises salesrooms still constituted only 56.3 percent of the total. Only a combination of changing personal habits, which made public drinking more acceptable, and a careful redistribution of licenses by the authorities finally changed the pattern. By 1896, 79.3 percent of all dealers were hotels or restaurants which provided facilities for public imbibing, and for the next decade and a half these two types of sellers would together constitute about 80 percent of the total.

If more Bostonians were drinking in front of each other than ever before, they were doing it in restaurants rather than in hotels. The number of innkeeper's licenses remained steady, never exceeding 4 percent of the total licensees before 1889. Instead, an increasing proportion of the applicants asked for common victualler's licenses. The requirement remained that food of some sort had to be available, but this was easily evaded by providing simple sandwiches or cheese. Since the proprietor did not have to provide lodging for guests, the victualler's license was the least expensive and easiest form of the liquor trade to enter. Its attractiveness, along with the gentle encouragement of the licensing officials, made the restaurant the most common place where liquor was sold. In 1875 it constituted 42.6 percent of the licenses, while two decades later nearly three-fourths (74.4 percent) of all sellers held the victualler's permits. As a result, the restaurant became Boston's version of what was the traditional saloon in other cities.

The greatest loser in this transition was the grocery store. During prohibition the food shops had been a major source of liquor, especially in poorer neighborhoods. In 1867, for instance, they constituted 42 percent of all sellers, but with the return of legal liquor, that portion rapidly disappeared. In 1875 it was 29.4 percent, and in the next two years half of that trade disappeared. By 1900 only 9.2 percent of the licensees ran grocery shops. It is difficult to trace the precise reasons for the change. Undoubtedly, the growing popularity of cheap barroom-restaurants in tenement neighborhoods was a contributory factor. No matter how ramshackle, they still were more comfortable and commodious than grocery stores. But a most important cause was undoubtedly the conscious policy of those who granted the licenses. Perhaps the long, agonized debates of 1867, over the demand for open and public sales, prompted officials to close off the major source of alcohol for tenement home consumption. Whatever the reasons, the transition from private to public drinking, from grocery store to common victualler, however subtle, indicated an important change in Massachusetts society. Ultimately, that transition would affect the law, politics, and the social relationships of its citizens.[46]

Another temperance statute that dramatically affected Boston's saloons was the limitation law of 1888. Public drinking would never again be the same. The roots of this legislation went back to colonial statutes that were based on the assumption that fewer licenses meant

fewer opportunities to drink and a more sober community. The idea reappeared in 1878, amidst the poorly regulated flood of postprohibition
barrooms, and was the subject of a decade of debate. Antiliquor interests denounced it as a compromise with the devil, while saloonkeepers
were nervous about the unanswered question of how many fewer licenses there might be. Finally, in 1888, the General Court arrived at
the ratio of one license for each 500 citizens.[47]

The impact was devastating. On May 1, 1889, only 780 of what had
been 2,286 dealers survived. There were numerous charges of political
favoritism. The press was also puzzled by the obvious attempt to reori-
ent Boston's public drinking habits. Wholesale licenses were often
paired with victuallers and hotels; the purchase of a bottle to take
home would thus be more likely to be done in front of a crowd — a sobering thought for secret drinkers. Wholesalers also gained control of a
greater share of the retail permits. Finally, more of the licenses were
concentrated on major thoroughfares, even in poorer neighborhoods,
and downtown, leaving few drinking spots in comfortable residential
districts. This momentous event was followed a decade later by another: in 1899 the total number of Boston licenses was frozen at 1,000,
no matter how much more the city grew. Thus, compared with Chicago, which would not enact a limitation law until 1906, the saloon business in Boston was restricted to the few rather than the many.[48]

Proponents had argued that the limitation law would make the remaining barrooms much easier to patrol. Reduced in ranks and clustered in accessible locations, survivors did find visits from patrolmen
and officials more frequent than before. But the artificial scarcity of
permits, combined with the continued desire of hundreds of people to
go into the business, produced an unforeseen consequence. It gave the
right to hold the license, as well as the license itself, a certain monetary
value. This "license premium," as it was called, lacked official sanction. It was purely a matter for the marketplace to determine.[49]

This development disturbed many observers on both sides of the temperance issue. Antiliquor spokesmen complained that it was unfair to
allow a privilege granted by the government to be sold at personal
profit. Proponents replied that the situation was not unlike the granting of franchises for the exclusive use of streets or the rental fees paid by
peddlers for the space on the public streets. The license premium assumed a certain degree of stability, an assurance that officials would

renew the permit from year to year. But after numerous attempts to abolish the premium failed, it became a standard extra expense in purchasing a Boston saloon license.[50]

The artificial value quickly exceeded the cost of the permit itself. Initially, dealers had feared that the police commissioners might not automatically issue renewals. And, indeed, for the first few years after 1889 there were a few surprises when the official dispensations were announced. But by 1893 the demand had pushed the premium up to $3,000 to $5,000. That remained the standard price for some years, although during 1910 there was a surge in demand, pushing values to $8,500. By May 1 of the following year the unofficial price for the privilege ranged from $11,000 to $15,000.[51]

There were several reasons why the value soared so high. First, the license officials approved the recognition of the premium as an asset in bankruptcy or probate proceedings and allowed it to be sold or inherited. It was also clear that in Boston the enormous majorities in favor of legal liquor would prevent any attempt to vote the city dry. At the same time, the license law of 1899 guaranteed that there would not be any more than one thousand licenses granted, regardless of how rapidly the population grew. With each licensee all but assured of increased revenue, potential entrepreneurs were willing to pay fantastic prices to enter the business. And this, of course, led to quiet monopolies by those who could afford the premium.[52]

While the brewing companies used the license laws quickly to seize control of Chicago's retail liquor trade, they were far less active in Boston. They did set up a number of individuals in business, following the standard procedure of selling fixtures to the new entrepreneur on a long-term mortgage. Brewers from outside the Boston area engaged in this practice as often as those from the immediate area. But as late as 1891 the beer makers owned few licenses in the city. There was far less competition among brewers, because Boston was a smaller market than Chicago and was not as well endowed with rail connections.[53]

Instead, the high cost and limited number of licenses drove many Boston proprietors into partnerships. Where multiple owners were relatively rare in Chicago, they were common in Boston, even outnumbering the independent entrepreneurs in 1891. That plan allowed the owners to share the burden of soaring license rates and provide for a smooth transition when one partner died or decided to sell out.[54]

The most significant share of Boston's saloons, however, fell under the control of wholesalers. The reasons for that transition were rooted in the quest for profit, but they also included an important transition that took place in the whiskey trade between 1860 and 1890. During the early years the wholesaler had actually been a less important part of the trade chain. Federal law required distillers to keep their product in bonded storage for only three years; at the end of that period, they were anxious to move it out. At the same time, because there were relatively few distillers, the wholesalers found themselves competing to purchase the annual whiskey crop. It was not uncommon for wholesalers to buy an entire half of an annual production at once and tie up as much as $150,000 in stock, on which they also had to pay the federal tax. The investment and the cost of maintaining a huge warehouse were enormous and allowed only a few, well-financed wholesalers to be successful.[55]

Most of the men who entered the field at mid-century had made large amounts of money elsewhere, mostly in the grocery trade, and had sold liquor as a sideline. S. S. Pierce, for instance, had opened his grocery business in 1831, using a wheelbarrow to make deliveries. By the time he issued his first price list in 1849, most of the 265 items were alcoholic. Similarly, Jeremiah Ford, an Irish immigrant, had invested his profits from grocery retailing in a wholesale liquor business, and Adams, Taylor and Company and John Lyons grew from similar roots. Some had sample rooms for the benefit of customers, while most depended on jobbers to distribute the goods to retailers.

During the postbellum years, however, the hard liquor business underwent two fundamental changes. One was the advent of new distillers. Although the rate at which new places appeared did not match the brewing industry, the new companies created more of a buyer's market. No longer did a wholesaler have to snatch up as much of the distiller's product as he could. The second change was the extension of the bonded storage time from three to eight years. This meant that the distiller, not the wholesaler, had to pay the costs of extended storage. The result of these changes was an increased profit on a smaller investment for wholesalers, and that, in turn, attracted many more competitors.

The new competition in the wholesale trade had two principal results. First, it all but eliminated the middleman role of the jobber. Wholesalers hired their own salesmen and sought customers, rather than waiting for them to come to the business. More importantly, it also encouraged wholesalers to go into the retail trade on a grand scale to insure markets. The sample room, once hidden away in a dark corner, became the most prominent feature of the storefront. Some Boston wholesalers opened chains of saloons, much as brewers did in Chicago. Furthermore, the advent of cheap, throw-away quart and fifth bottles brought many wholesalers into a vigorous bottle trade. An advantageous location near a railway station insured many customers who were on their way to dry states in New England. Many a revelry in Maine originated in a sale made near a Boston depot.

Many Boston saloons also fell under the control of wholesale liquor dealers because the Boston Police Commissioners actually encouraged it after the enactment of the limitation law. The consolidation of the two branches of the trade obviously facilitated the job of policing because it reduced the total number of places where liquor was sold. But the policy also helped attain the long-standing goal of making liquor sales as public as possible. A person afraid to be seen purchasing intoxicants could steal into a wholesale store and make his transaction with relative anonymity, but with the bottle trade conducted in a saloon, there might be hundreds of witnesses. Likewise, bartenders might be less inclined to sell a bottle to someone who was intoxicated if they thought that plainclothes police or temperance spies might be watching.

Finally, these contrasting patterns of ownership were largely the result of the drinking habits of the residents of the two towns. Chicago had a much larger German population, who made lager beer their standard drink. On the other hand, fragmented evidence indicates that Boston retained its Irish character much longer. Germans never constituted a large portion of the Hub's population. As a result, there was a higher per capita consumption of whiskey in Boston than in Chicago and, therefore, an added incentive for hard liquor interests rather than brewers to become involved in the saloon business.[56]

The Loss of Independence

By supplying the license, the brewer — or, in the case of Boston, the wholesaler — had replaced the independent outlet with someone whose loyalty he could command. Now the saloonkeeper not only paid a monthly installment on his mortgage, but gave the beer delivery man an extra ten dollars each week to cover the payment for the license. The formality of a written legal agreement seldom covered the new arrangement, and for good reason. Initially brewers and wholesalers were unsure whether the law of chattel mortgages covered licenses. So, to protect themselves, they seldom entered the saloonkeeper's name on the permit itself, using the name of a brewery employee instead. This not only concealed the true ownership of the license from the prying eyes of the temperance press, but also allowed the brewer or wholesaler to end the career of an unprofitable saloonkeeper without formal notice. Thus, through a curious set of unexpected results, the high license movement took control of the saloons of Chicago and Boston away from the saloonkeepers. The new investors eventually recovered the cost of fixtures which often had been constructed with brewery labor that might have been idle in slack seasons. The brewers and wholesalers also regained the investment in the licenses, and, most important of all, they were assured of outlets for the sale of their product.[57]

The same interests also provided the saloonkeepers with surety bonds. In Chicago, private companies and politicians provided a quarter of the bonds, the rest coming from breweries. One firm, the Czech-owned Atlas Brewing Company, even organized a subsidiary, the Chicago Bonding and Surety Company, to service the needs of the brewer's saloons.[58]

In Boston, the role of the breweries and wholesalers in the bonding process was much more limited after the mid-1890s. An exposé in 1884 revealed that brewers had signed hundreds of certificates, perhaps overextending themselves beyond the property-holding requirements. A. J. Houghton of the Vienna Brewery alone appeared on 116 of them, while Robert Engle of the Smith and Engle Brewing Company was listed on thirty others. Distillers and wholesalers provided the bulk of the remainder. The demand for reform soon faded away, but five years later L. Edwin Dudley of the Law and Order League charged that a "liquor oligarchy" of wholesale suppliers still furnished the bulk of the bonds. Finally, in 1895 the Massachusetts General Court imposed a limit of ten bonds for each surety. This act did not disconnect the supplier from the seller, but it did promote a wider distribution of bond holding. Wholesale dealers and brewers continued the practice, but such outside corporations as American Surety of New York assumed a greater portion of the burden.[59]

Restructure: Promise and Failure

Despite the competition, the brewing industry in New England and the Midwest gave the appearance of steady growth in the late 1880s. The wholesale price of beer remained at about twelve and eight dollars, respectively. New companies entered the field, but the number of beer consumers grew as well. German immigration reached its peak in 1890, and a gradual shift of American drinkers from hard liquor to beer was well under way. On the whole, the gentlemen's agreements limiting competitive pricing seemed to be working. Finally, the gradual adoption of the tied-house system had given the brewers both additional revenue and an assured market. Everything looked favorable, but this state of stability and growth contained the seeds of its own destruction, for it attracted the very factor that once again plunged the industry into ruinous competition. This was the entrance of British capital.

American industry looked especially promising to overseas investors. Economic opportunities at home were limited by comparison with the untapped potential of the United States, and after 1886 they bought up controlling interests in a number of companies: a flour mill in St. Louis, New England tanneries, the Elgin Watch Company, and paper mills in upstate New York, to name a few. English capitalists were seldom interested in forming new corporations or constructing plants. Rather, they preferred to purchase firms already in operation, especially ones that had already proved their profitability and could be managed from the other side of the Atlantic. It was not surprising, therefore, when they began buying breweries. That industry already had a substantial physical capacity and capital maturity, and it was highly competitive. The English investors were confident that they could buy several companies and operate them at a greater profit by reducing competition.

This program of acquisition began on the East Coast in 1888, first in New York City and then in Philadelphia. Before the year was over, they were negotiating in Chicago. In March 1889 Charles McAvoy announced that his place had been sold and within the next year eighteen Chicago malthouses and breweries became part of five giant companies.[60]

These acquisitions evoked a wide variety of hostility. The press termed it an invasion, while independent brewers denounced the "wildcatters" and foreign money as an affront to American nationalism. The brewing journals claimed that the sellers had been tricked into accepting too little payment.[61] The saloonkeepers also viewed the British invasion as a deceptive means to raise the wholesale price. One of them, Michael Koch, refused to pay his bills to the F. J. Dewes Company, claiming that Illinois antitrust law negated any debts owed to an illegal "trust." He lost his case in court, but his fellow members of the liquor dealers' association vowed to use "every legitimate means . . . to defeat the insidious designs of the English beer trust."[62]

At first the trusts bypassed Boston. In March 1889 they acquired the Frank Jones Company of Portsmouth and the smaller Bay State Brewery in the Hub. But Samuel Untermeyer, the purchasing agent for the Englishmen, rejected a bid to sell four of the largest Roxbury concerns — Houghton's, Roessle, Burkhardt's, and Pfaff's — claiming that the investors were more interested in flour and rolling mills at the moment. A year later, however, Untermeyer negotiated the purchase of the Boylston and Roessle companies of Roxbury, Suffolk in South Boston, and the Stanley Brewery in Lawrence. These became the New England Breweries, Ltd., and ended the British investment in the Boston area. A total of £1,910,000 was pooled for the purchase, an insignificant amount next to the £6,088,000 spent in Chicago.[63]

The English trusts initially displayed unbounded optimism. They closed some of the unprofitable plants and consolidated certain operations in others. The savings resulted in enormous profits during the first year and rosy predictions that foreign capital had drained the local industry of destructive competition. But before another year had passed, the true conditions became obvious; the basic problems of the industry remained unsolved. First of all, only twenty of the fifty-three breweries in Chicago and six of twenty-seven in the Boston area fell under the control of the syndicates. Such large producers as Anheuser-Busch, Joseph Schlitz, and Pabst remained independent and were willing to support the brewers' associations and abide by standard prices. But a third group refused to cooperate. These were the small companies, many of which had been formed for the primary purpose of being sold to syndicated investors. Others had been established in suburban areas to sell to upwardly mobile German-Americans and others who had moved outside of the city. But in all cases, these smaller competitors began producing and selling beer at a price low enough to pose a threat to the larger producers.[64]

From 1890 to 1893 the number of brewers and their capacity grew rapidly in both cities, but in Chicago the industry underwent the greatest expansion. The World's Columbian Exposition provided most of the incentive. Retailers and producers both invested heavily in anticipation of the millions of visitors. Seven hundred new saloons opened. New brewing companies appeared every month. In 1892 whiskey interests formed the Monarch Brewing Company, which promptly announced that it would sell its beer for four dollars a barrel, or one-half the price established by the brewers' association. The latter group countered by lowering its members' price to six dollars and then announced that it would use its influence with city officials to block the construction of any more breweries. The ineffectiveness of that announcement was made obvious later that year; in the first two weeks of December 1892 four new companies opened their doors.[65]

The resulting competition was disastrous. Despite almost weekly reports in the press that the "beer war" had been ended, the wholesale price continued to fall. The competition came from outside the brewers' association. Mavericks secretly offered discounts and rebates worth almost a dollar on each barrel. In addition, some 100,000 barrels of low-priced beer came from outside the city. Companies as far away as Peoria, Freeport, Fort Wayne, and Racine discovered that their production and delivery costs were cheap enough that they could ship and sell beer in Chicago for three dollars and still turn a profit. The ineffective brewers' association quietly dissolved in December 1894.[66] In desperation the Chicago brewing interests, both in and outside the syndicates, turned to the idea of taxing the delivery of out-of-town beer. But the Illinois Supreme Court proclaimed that a city's streets were open to anyone who did not physically harm the pavement or morally injure the community; that included out-of-town beer wagons.[67]

The depression of the mid-1890s created further difficulties. The artificial stimulus of the World's Fair only postponed its impact on Chicago. Even at a wholesale price of $4.00, a barrel of beer in 1893 had produced $1.22 in net profit to the English syndicate investors; large-scale production had resulted in more efficient utilization of facilities and economies of scale. But two years later, the burden of unused capacity and sharply reduced sales, paired with a stable selling price of three dollars and dividends to pay, brought the net profit per barrel down to fifteen cents. Overcapitalization in the industry amplified these difficulties. In the decade after 1890, the total investment in American breweries increased 54 percent, far faster than sales warranted. Part of the capital went to increase total brewing capacity, most of which went unused. The rest consisted of the inflated value placed on the properties purchased by the English syndicates. Most financial observers agreed: the British had sold an excess amount of stock in order to buy breweries priced higher than their actual worth. As a result, too much of the syndicates' revenues were being applied to depreciation and dividends.[68]

These conditions took their inevitable toll as the trusts failed to make dividend payments and tumbled into bankruptcy. Boston breweries were facing similar problems. The wholesale prices in the Hub had never before fallen so low; six dollars was the bottom, while eight dollars was average. The Frank Jones Brewing Company, Ltd., fell behind in its dividend payments, and after 1897 it too failed to turn a profit.[69]

The brewing industry remained in chaotic condition even after general prosperity returned in 1898. Brewers faced new problems. First, the United States Congress enacted a special war tax of one dollar on each barrel of beer produced in America. Most producers passed this new cost on to the saloonkeepers, but a few absorbed part of it themselves in an attempt to enhance their competitive position, perpetuating the industry's price war. Then, in 1899, the British courts dealt a serious blow to the English combines by ruling that they were liable to pay a substantial income tax to the British government on profits earned overseas. This ended any plans for further capitalization or expansion in America and ruined the value of the syndicate stocks on the British exchanges.[70]

The desperate condition of the industry drove it toward further consolidation. It began in August 1898 when Chicago distilling and wholesaling interests began acquiring the assets of thirteen nonsyndicate Chicago-area plants through a holding company chartered in New Jersey. The new management hoped to rationalize and streamline the operation by closing down inefficient plants and using compatible facilities in others. By limiting competition and cooperating with a revived Chicago Brewers' Association, it hoped to raise the average price to saloonkeepers above the present level of only four dollars.[71] But even this plan failed its promoters' expectations. Managers of plants designated for closing successfully delayed that action for a number of years. In the meantime, however, the parent company began losing money, and in

1903 it was back in federal court again, this time for bankruptcy and reorganization proceedings. A similar American-owned combine, the Massachusetts Brewing Company, was formed by ten Boston-area companies, but the comparative quietude of brewery competition in New England made it a financial success. [72]

Real Estate: The Ultimate Control

With profits sharply reduced and all attempts to fix prices in Chicago obviously unsuccessful, the brewing companies broadened their search for revenue. Their rationale was simple: if they could not make more profit on each barrel sold, they could at least sell more beer. This prospect was especially attractive in Chicago, where the burgeoning population produced a substantial increase in beer consumption each year. The brewers' objective, then, was to insure a market for their product, and the means of achieving it was through the control of real estate. The plan ultimately cost the brewers millions in capital investment and resulted in the beer makers becoming some of the larger and more influential landlords in Chicago.

When the brewers began paying the rent on the storefronts, they also assumed more direct control over the fate of each saloon. Decisions about where to locate were made more often in the corporate headquarters rather than over the saloonkeeper's kitchen table. Substantial financial backing allowed more outlets to be opened near major intersections or along heavily-traveled streets — locations that independent saloonmen could seldom afford. And because the brewery's name appeared on the lease, a proprietor who failed to turn an acceptable profit might find his business career summarily terminated. Even if the fixtures remained in his possession, he might not have a building in which he could install them. The brewers simply moved in another tenant. [73]

These instantaneous removals brought the real estate interests and the brewers into direct conflict. While the beer makers searched for new tenants, they often let property remain unoccupied for long periods of time. And if they decided that the location was hopeless, they frequently broke the lease. Landlords protested that this practice left their property poorly maintained. Idle buildings appeared abandoned, giving the impression that they were not useful for any purpose and making it more difficult to rent to someone else. In 1898 the Chicago

Real Estate Board publicly rebuked the brewers and warned its members of the dangers involved in renting to tied saloons. By that time, however, the breweries had already embarked on an alternative arrangement: purchasing the properties themselves.[74]

Breweries expressed only a limited interest in Boston real estate. The Hub was experiencing far more limited population growth, 24 percent between 1880 and 1890, compared with Chicago's 118 percent. The complex of liquor regulations in that decade had made the acquisition of saloon property in Massachusetts more difficult. The Police Board continued its policy of carefully regulating the location of the limited number of licenses, so that a brewery that purchased and equipped a place outside the downtown had no permanent guarantee that it would always be able to operate a saloon at that location. An abutter's law, which allowed adjoining property owners to veto applications, added to the difficulty. Scattered evidence indicates that only two breweries each owned a small parcel of downtown real estate.[75]

In Chicago it had long been a different story. The brewers had dabbled in midwestern real estate as early as the 1860s, but mainly for speculative purposes unrelated to beer sales. A few companies such as Pabst had begun purchasing saloons in the early 1880s, first in Milwaukee and then elsewhere, but it was not until the beginning of the next decade that the producers began a systematic acquisition of land and buildings. In September 1892 the two major English companies announced the incorporation of subsidiary real estate departments. Not to be outmaneuvered, the Joseph Schlitz Brewing Company, which remained independent of foreign control, established the Edward Uihlein Real Estate Company to handle its purchases in Chicago.[76]

The English combines issued special bonds to finance their purchases and, during the next few years, spent some six million dollars on Chicago real estate, primarily in outlying neighborhoods and business centers. The more spectacular purchases were made by the independent nonsyndicate brewers, who bought heavily in the downtown district. Anheuser-Busch bought the defunct Grand Pacific Hotel and spent a million dollars in refurbishing and advertising the place. The St. Louis brewer also bought the Wyoming, another hotel bankrupted by the post-Exhibition depression, and converted it into an elaborate restaurant, the Kaiser-Hof. Pabst bought the Union Hotel and the Great Northern Theater, one of the largest in the city.[77]

The Milwaukee independents were also the first to construct their own saloons in outlying neighborhoods. In 1897 Edward G. Uihlein, the Chicago agent and younger brother of the family that controlled Schlitz, quietly arranged for the erection of a $40,000 building near the busy six-corner intersection of Milwaukee, North, and Robey (now Damen) avenues. Competitors quickly copied the idea. Several of them, especially the English-owned Schoenhofen and Gottfried companies, invested several thousand dollars each month in such properties. But neither became as involved as Schlitz, which constructed fifty-seven saloons worth some $328,800 during the next eight years.[78]

The Schlitz barrooms were of mixed design. Some were plain, with the saloon and rear quarters for the proprietor and his family on the first floor and an upstairs divided into small flats. In others the second floor was devoted to halls and meeting rooms. The structure at Ninety-fourth and Ewing avenues, in the South Chicago mill district, was topped with two floors of small sleeping rooms for workers. On the fronts of its buildings Schlitz installed enormous stained glass windows and roofline ornaments, both depicting the company's globe trademark.[79]

The custom-built saloons were most frequently located in relatively new residential areas several miles from the center of downtown, but seldom in neighborhoods with a substantial temperance following. In all cases, they were established either directly on or adjacent to main streets that carried heavy pedestrian traffic. There was no apparent ethnic specialization, except that a large number did appear in German districts of the North Side.[80]

A keen eye for potential business also brought Uihlein and Schlitz to the bargaining table with a curious seller, the Pullman Land Association. The founder of the sleeping car company had himself banned saloons from his model town; the only bar was in the Florence Hotel, and it was reserved for company executives and honored guests. Workers had to trudge several blocks away to purchase liquor from the bars that lined the shopping streets of the Kensington and Roseland communities. But in October 1904 the Land Association, in need of money, sold Schlitz a choice, ten-acre plot just across the Illinois Central tracks at 115th Street. The association had earlier sold an adjacent plot to the South Park Board for $1,500 an acre, but the Milwaukee brewer was so eager to move near the throngs of thirsty workers that it paid nearly three times the price. Almost immediately Uihlein went to work constructing "Schlitz Row," a two-block string of saloons, stables, and apartments decorated with the distinctive globe trademark at the roofline. Nearby the company built houses and more apartments for the use of branch managers and for rent to the general public.[81]

Although the connection may not seem obvious at first, the evolution of the saloon closely paralleled the growth of the chain store in American retailing. Begun in 1859 with Huntington Hartford's Great Atlantic and Pacific Tea Company, it underwent tremendous growth during the last years of the nineteenth century. At the heart of the system was the notion that a large number of identical retail units could be more profitable than competition among dissimilar retailers. Standardization was the key. A&P stores were essentially all alike, just as brewery-made fixtures and beer and brewery-dictated sales policies and expectations of profit standardized brewery-owned saloons. The tradition of the five-cent beer also proved helpful, as did occasional threats by city authorities — never carried out — to establish a uniform minimum amount allowed in a shot and a drink glass.

Other aspects of saloon operation made the chain store operation a success. There were economies of scale in the large-scale purchase of food for the free lunch and the distribution of money to cash paychecks. Careful scientific research brought outlets to locations where the maximum walk-in trade could be found. Finally, even the signboards out front were symbolic of change. In days past, the owner's name or that of his house were the most prominent words hanging over his door. But after the brewer took over, its brand and its symbol were the largest things on the sign. This had its parallel when an A&P, a Woolworth's, or a Walgreen Drugstore moved in: the name of the manager was less important than his efficiency and the profit he turned for the company. The entrepreneur had become an employee.[82]

Conclusion: Transforming an Industry

Brewing was, by nature, a relatively simple process that was swept up by the expansive optimism of the 1880s. The burgeoning of immigrant communities, especially the Germans, had evoked expectations of an unlimited expansion of thirst and a tendency to overcapitalize. Supply exceeded demand, especially in Chicago. A second disquieting factor which also appeared during the 1880s was the disruption of localized brewing trade patterns by new bottling technologies, refrigeration, and high-speed rail shipment. The insularity of urban markets — especially in Chicago, the nation's rail hub — was lost in the strenuous efforts to enlarge production and reduce unused brewing capacity. The proximity of Milwaukee and St. Louis, both of whose breweries made far more beer than local populations could consume, made Chicago's beer wars even more lively. Boston's location in the northeast corner of the nation reduced its role as a rail center and allowed it to miss much of this overcompetition.

Thus, by the mid-1880s the brewers were making more beer, but its abundance and frequent market invasions by outsiders drove down the price. In a desperate search for a way to build stability and predictability into their industry, the beer makers turned to trade associations. While these enjoyed some success in Boston, they were an abject failure in Chicago. Brewers finally settled on the tied-house system, a British tradition, as one way to insure outlets for their product. Gradually, brewers began to assume direction of the saloon trade. That move found an unintentional ally in antisaloon forces that promoted the plan of increasing liquor license fees to cover the social cost of the drinking problem in society. Instead, the higher annual fee helped drive the individual dealers into economic dependency on their suppliers. In Chicago, brewers began by supplying outside signs and eventually sold the fixtures, necessary surety bonds, and even the license to prospective retailers. In Boston, a much higher license rate, coupled with a severe limit in the number of licenses — a feature not found in Chicago — brought about a different pattern of control. Although brewers did take over some outlets, the large Irish population and their preference for hard liquor allowed wholesale spirits dealers to assume domination of most others. The Hub's licensing authorities also encouraged the consolidation of barrooms and package-goods stores under multiple-outlet management in order to simplify law enforcement and the investigation of applicants' backgrounds.

By the end of the 1880s it was clear that not even the tied-house plan could stabilize Chicago's saloon trade. The $500 license gradually became less of an obstacle to ambitious independents, while expectations of a bonanza because of the World's Columbia Exposition brought an influx of out-of-town brewers. The entrance of British investors, who purchased the ailing breweries and consolidated the strongest into trusts, failed to stabilize the competition, as did an attempt to create an American-based trust at the century's close. The abundance of producers who remained outside of these arrangements kept the wholesale price of beer in Chicago extremely low, making it possible for thousands of marginal retailers to eke out a small profit and survive. All that the major brewers could do was move into the real estate market so that they could insure perpetual domination of the best locations.

By contrast, Boston's saloon trade was tranquil. Where the Windy City had witnessed an attempt to consolidate the business vertically, from the hops bin to the stein, the Boston liquor trade underwent horizontal integration into chains and partnerships. The limited number of licenses soon commanded substantial premiums: the right to buy the license assumed a value itself. Ownership became increasingly elitist. The lighter competition guaranteed greater profits, as did the deliberate policy of the license authorities to steer licensees toward the most heavily traveled thoroughfares.

The most important legacy of this dramatic business transformation could be measured in the numbers of swinging doors in the two cities. In Boston, where the saloon ranks were limited by legislation to a ratio of one for each 500 residents, competition was predictable and fairly limited. By contrast, the lack of regulation in Chicago resulted in a free market for saloon retailing. The brewers and the dwindling ranks of independent retailers determined the number of outlets and their locations. Only rarely did mayors exercise their right to turn down applicants or veto proposed locations. As a result, Chicago drinking spots were both numerous and ubiquitous. And the proprietor's search for the furtive nickel in order to survive would bring a vast expansion of services.

CHAPTER 2

The Saloon
as a Small Business:
The Function of Failure

To its enemies the saloon seemed ubiquitous and omnipotent. The words *the liquor interests* evoked images of manipulative, faceless, evil people conspiring to ruin youth, drive the family to poverty, and bring crime to the community. But few temperance and antisaloon critics understood the reasons for the enormous number of barrooms. The literature of moralistic reformers is remarkably unsophisticated in its treatment of the economics of the brewing and distilling industries. Nor could even the friends of the saloonkeeper really comprehend why so many in the business moved so frequently, suddenly changed brands of beer, or shuttered their doors for good with so little notice.

The story of the saloonkeeper provides a rare portrait of a seldom-studied phenomenon: small-scale entrepreneurship in the large city. Often illiterate and lacking business experience, these small merchants kept very few records. An unheralded first appearance in a city directory and, perhaps, a listing in the "closings and judgments" columns of *Mida's Criterion*, a wholesalers' journal, were the only recorded rites of passage for most saloons. For some, success brought status in the community and entrance into a "profession," complete with organizations, journals, and standards of conduct. As part of a vital middle class, successful liquor dealers could become neighborhood civic leaders taking home comfortable incomes. But for every diamond stickpin there were several failures. Opening-day optimism turned to disappointment, a frantic search for gimmicks to draw the crowds, promises to creditors, and, ultimately, a sad closing. And with the disappointment came bitter divisions in the supposedly solid phalanx of the liquor interests.

The Function of Failure

Thanks to the brewing companies, a saloon was, in the words of one proprietor, "the easiest business in the world for a man to break into with small capital."[1] The lucky beginners who could provide their own rent went to brewers only for the bar and other large fixtures. As one Chicago barkeeper remembered: "All you need, you might say, is the key to the place, and you can get that by paying the first month's rent. You go to the brewery agent (any of them) with the lease for the place and the rent receipt and they'll have the fixtures out at the dump before you can get back on the streetcar."[2]

Occasionally, a lucky beginner might be able to purchase the other necessities — glasses and the like — from someone who was selling out. In this case he was responsible only for repaying the license at $1.50 a day, plus a premium on the price of each barrel to cover the payment on the chattel mortgage for his fixtures. It was even easier to start the business completely from scratch. All that was required was a month's rent money in advance and perhaps a small deposit. As another Chicagoan described it:

> Oh boys, it was a fierce jolly those brewery people threw into me when I handed over the forty bucks. They predicted that, being a popular young fellow, I would make all kinds of money if I ran the place on business principles. I was all swelled up over it, and maybe I didn't hand them a little stiff talk myself. All the money I had in the world was $85, but I gave the brewery people the impression that I had a trunk full of it. I had one $50 note and the rest was in ones, making a roll big enough to throw a street car off the tracks.[3]

Many new saloonkeepers turned directly to the brewers for everything. Company craftsmen were kept busy delivering and erecting fixtures. When a tipsy customer or an irate wife smashed a stained glass window or a mirror, it was the brewery that fixed it. The brewery handled complaints to the landlords, when it was not the landlord itself, and often paid taxes and water assessments.[4]

The increasing cost of setting up a new place drove many neophyte saloonkeepers into total dependency. Inflation was partly to blame, but many newcomers disliked the austerity of "standard grade" fixtures supplied by the brewery, because they were often shopworn by numerous removals and reinstallations for previous owners. Mass production resulted in a sameness, a standardized appearance that distressed many prospective proprietors and prompted one newspaper to comment that all Schlitz saloons looked alike.[5] The alternatives were very expensive. Even the everyday items of utilitarian necessity cost more than one might anticipate. Cuspidors were $1.50 each, lunch counters averaged $1.50 per running foot, and rattan swinging doors ordered from Albert Pick and Company cost $1.80 a square foot. Fancier cut glass or stained glass panels for screens, backboards, and doors featured in the catalogs of Pick, Charles Passow, and the Brunswick Company cost many times that amount.[6]

Glassware was another troublesome expense which also involved a crucial business decision: what size should the saloonkeeper choose? There was always the temptation to stock several sizes, but the cost was prohibitive. The cause of his dilemma was the tradition of the "nickel beer." The price was standard in nearly every saloon; only the quantity or the quality of the beer varied from place to place. This meant that the selection of his standard size glass virtually froze the retail value of a barrel. As long as the wholesale cost remained low, he made a profit, but every time the brewers threatened to raise it, the saloon owner was faced with earning less on each barrel he sold or reequipping the place with smaller glasses for his nickel beers.[7]

Beer pumps also became increasingly complicated and expensive, as did the seemingly simple matter of counting and protecting the receipts.[8] Proprietors, especially those in debt to a brewery, became increasingly concerned about their exact income and less trusting of their bartenders. Saloonkeepers eagerly experimented with various money-counting devices, including the earliest cash registers. Customers knew the amount of the sale and an adding device inside gave the proprietor an exact total of the sales. The National Cash Register Company played upon the theme of insecurity in the frequent advertisements it placed in the *Champion of Fair Play*, the Chicago liquor dealers' newspaper. "NO NEED TO WORRY," proclaimed its messages:

> A proprietor need not have all these worries . . . today all these can be taken care of by automatic machinery . . .
> Automatic machinery . . . will require no attention. It will pay for itself with the money it saves, and you can pay for it as it saves. It gives you leisure. It relieves you of worry . . .
> [And] by appearing free from worry . . . [the owner] will inspire confidence and will induce people to come oftener to his place — to

hesitate to leave him for the newer places that start from time to time . . .[9]

The Help Unionizes

If the rising cost of entering business drove the saloonkeeper further into debt to the brewery, the enormous expenses of operating the business made it more difficult to repay it. Besides the cost of beer, whiskey, and the liquor license, the proprietor faced an unending series of bills. One of these was labor. The cheapest places to run were the small, family-operated affairs. There were no wages to pay, but the business was little more than an extension of the household which resided in the back rooms or upstairs apartment. The children performed clean-up chores and worked the basement beer pump, while the wife carried out her own important tasks.[10] As one study of the near northwest side of Chicago remembered:

> The wife of a saloonkeeper, however, often led a strenuous life. Keeping up the noon lunch was no small task, and she had to do all her family work in addition, and was often called on to help with handling drunken men. The effect on the family depended on whether the family life could be maintained independent of the saloon. In one case that we know the children were brought up with ideals and the son never touched a drop of liquor. In other cases demoralization was inevitable, as saloons were often hangouts of disorderly characters in the neighborhood.[11]

The use of female and child labor in saloon work greatly disturbed antiliquor interests. In Massachusetts they unsuccessfully attempted to make it illegal for the saloonkeepers to reside in the same building as the business. Child labor laws in both the Bay State and Illinois generally excluded the hiring of nonfamily minors. In 1897 the Chicago City Council passed a law banning female employees not related to the licensee. While essentially an antivice measure, this ordinance reduced the ranks but did not eliminate female bartenders. Wives and widows of saloonkeepers in both Chicago and Boston continued to serve drinks and hold liquor licenses.[12]

The most controversial labor issue, however, concerned the unionization of bartenders. Organization began in the 1860s and 1870s as "clubs," usually short lived and ineffective. The nature of the occupation helped make organization difficult since potential members were scat-

tered throughout the city, where pretelephone communication was difficult. The dispersal of bartenders also made individuals more vulnerable.
Unlike railroad or heavy manufacturing labor, there was seldom a concentration of more than a few bartenders under any one proprietor; a
walkout in a single place could hardly cripple the whole industry.[13]

The first successful bartenders' and waiters' union in the United
States formed in Chicago in 1866. The only labor organization in the
West to have its own hall, the Bartenders' and Waiters' Union of Chicago proved to be one of the most stable in the country. It survived a
brief entanglement with the Knights of Labor and managed to evade
the antilabor climate of the Haymarket era, despite its own strike for
shorter working hours.[14] The brief walkout in early May of 1886 did,
however, evoke a caustic comment from the *Tribune:*

SHORTER HOURS FOR BAR TENDERS

The community could stand it even if the strike of bar-keepers
were of long continuance. The community could endure a lock-
out. It is the one eight-hour movement which ought to come above
all others, and a six-hour movement would be better still. Where
are the men who should be in the battle's front on this the fateful
1st of May? Will they, behind the reeking bars, still bow the head
to the oppressor, or will they resolve to work for fewer hours, or
die, and so do well for the community?[15]

During most of the 1880s, the unionization movement grew slowly.
Benefit balls and relief work among its own members occupied most of
its attention. But the increased labor agitation of the 1890s brought a
renewed interest in substantive issues of wages and especially working
conditions. The saloon was frequently open from 6:00 A.M. until midnight, with the bartender putting in a lengthy workday. In fact, they
often worked longer hours for less pay than any other service industry.
By 1900, for instance, the Illinois Department of Labor reported that
bartenders averaged only twenty-five dollars a month compared with
fifty to eighty dollars for chefs, twenty to seventy-five dollars for jani-
tors, and forty to sixty dollars for bookkeepers.[16]

The movement in Chicago, however, divided into several ethnic and
neighborhood factions, just as the saloonkeepers' associations had
done. The original union of 1866 split into a half-dozen competing
branches, each of which grew rapidly during the World's Columbian
Exposition season but declined near the end of the decade. Meanwhile,

in Boston the Waiters' Alliance claimed 1,600 members in 1892, but it is impossible to determine how many worked as restaurant waiters and how many were genuine bartenders.[17]

After 1900, however, unions became an unavoidable reality to Boston bar proprietors and a troublesome possibility to their Chicago counterparts. The demands became specific: a "closed shop," overtime pay, and at least one day off each week; the latter issue was especially controversial in Chicago, where bars remained open on Sundays. Bartenders also demanded protection against unexpected dismissal or irregular employment dependent on seasonal fluctuations of the trade.[18]

The bartenders now realized that the proprietors were highly vulnerable. Control by the brewers meant that rent and mortgage payments on fixtures were inflexible; if a bar was closed any length of time or had to operate with a reduced staff, the future of the place was doubtful. Moreover, bartenders discovered the value of alliances with other labor unions. In 1902 Bostonians saw the start of a "blue button campaign" in which members of other trade organizations were asked to patronize only bartenders who belonged to a union.[19] The Hub correspondent to the *Mixer and Server*, the national trade periodical, warned: "There are several places which are patronized almost exclusively by union men and still they do not employ union waiters. But let the union waiter buy a hat, pair of shoes, or cigars and tobacco or patronize a bar where they do not employ union bartenders, then see how quick he will get a call-down. 'O consistency, thou art a jewel.' "[20] The union employed the blue button plan as well as the threat of a strike with some success in several areas of Boston.

In Chicago the bartenders also appealed to fellow workingmen as a bargaining weapon, but the Chicago Federation of Labor officially refused to recognize the bartenders' union because of bitter factional disputes. Membership numbered no more than 500 in 1905, indicating some progress in organizing the Loop district but little success in the neighborhood barrooms. That year Boston, with only a fraction of Chicago's saloon licenses and population, had three times as many unionized bartenders.[21] The president of the Chicago bartenders' union blamed the relative lack of success on one factor — the ease with which people of marginal means could get themselves into business. Advocating a license fee of $1,500, he noted:

The great trouble with the business for the owners and for the bartenders is that the Chicago saloons are too cheap. It does not cost enough to get a license. And the places are fitted and run on the same cheap basis.

If the license fee was tripled we would not have half the number of drinking establishments, but they would be a credit to the city. It would be worthwhile to own one and worthwhile to work in one. They would be furnished right and would attract the better trade and repress the poorer.[22]

Free Lunch and Public Bar

Shortly after the Great Fire of 1871 a Chicago barkeep named Joseph Chesterfield Mackin unveiled a new attraction in his saloon. After that event, no American saloonkeeper's life would be the same. "Chesterfield Joe" had tried almost everything to attract customers away from his rivals. A minor politician himself, he had attempted to make it a hangout for local "solons," but not many became regulars. He built a library in the backroom, equipping it with files of sporting magazines and papers, but gamblers and horse-betters would not give him their undivided business. Finally, he began serving a hot oyster free with every drink. Although the claim is impossible to verify and his competitors quickly copied the scheme, Joe Mackin had immortalized himself in saloon history. He had invented the free lunch.

Proprietors in other cities adopted the giveaway to drum up trade, but in Massachusetts there was little choice. The inn shaped the saloon. In Boston liquor dealers faced an additional operating expense mandated by the General Court. The central question was whether the public drinking place was really a saloon or a restaurant. One of the most important requirements of the 1875 licensing act had evolved from the widely held belief that liquor served with food was less dangerous to the drinker and to society than liquor served at a public bar. The clause also helped mollify the antiliquor sentiment which hoped that food might curb the imbiber's appetite for drink. In other words, in postprohibition Boston the hotel and the restaurant replaced the saloon in its familiar form.[23]

The provisions of the new law were quickly ignored. A few liquor dealers bought stoves and tables to show the license officials, but disposed of them in secondhand shops. By 1878 the *Transcript* could report that hundreds of saloonkeepers merely placed signs in their windows advertising "rooms and meals by day or week" or "meals served at all hours." Inside they were no more than common grog shops. As a result of these disclosures, the legislature enacted a new law requiring strict inspection and compliance, but this new command from the General Court had little impact.[24] Boston police authorities were preoccupied with the growth of the unlicensed trade, and the more stringent the requirements, the greater the likelihood that the dealer would try his luck without any permit at all. Officials gave a broad hint that applicants need not have facilities to cook food or lodge guests.[25]

The liquor dealers hated the law. The *New England Trader*, a weekly saloon trade journal, labeled it "one of the relics of the puritanical period." Many proprietors who were merely ignorant of the law, it added, would probably be punished.[26] The Police Board joined in the complaint. Noting that it was nearly impossible for the officer on the beat to distinguish the intent of each and every liquor sale, it recommended the repeal of the public bar law and gave its tacit approval to efforts in the legislature to legitimize liquor sales without food.[27]

The metropolitan police law of 1885 meant administrative reform at the top of the police department, but it did not alter the actions of the officer on the beat. All around the city, barrooms opened in defiance of the law. There was no pretense of serving food, and the familiar bar, complete with backboard mirrors and brass rail, became a common feature of Boston. All of this was in open defiance of the law, the legislature, and the state supreme court.[28]

During the winter of 1890 the General Court forced a crackdown. Amidst increased criticism of the Police Commissioners for numerous other shortcomings, the House passed a resolution condemning public bars and calling on law enforcement officials to remove them. On April 26, 1890, the police finally acted.[29] Many liquor dealers were faced with the prospect of actually having to sell food for the first time. Those who occupied long, narrow buildings in the downtown district had to find ways to squeeze tables into rooms only five or six feet wide. Tearing out the existing fixtures and purchasing tables and chairs proved costly; the *Globe* estimated that the 700 liquor dealers in the city might collectively spend $12,000 on the conversion. And finally, there was the issue of labor. The bar was actually the model of efficiency as a means of serving drinks. One bartender could serve dozens of patrons. But tables and chairs required great amounts of labor to wait on cus-

tomers. Even the suggestion that Conkling's, a newspaper hangout in
the *Traveler* Building, import English barmaids could not humor the
angry saloonists.[30]

The fatal day came on the nineteenth of May. "The Corpse is
Ready," proclaimed the *Globe*, " 'Twill be Cracker and Cheese with
Lager . . . 05 Cents."[31] Some barmen were confused about whether or
not they had to supply food, but most warned their customers to become "diners" and order food first, then liquor; that way there would
be no question about compliance with the common victualler law. A
majority of the places also purchased the proper fixtures, estimated by
the press to be no fewer than 50,000 chairs and 15,000 tables. Only a
few of the holdouts decided to place a few tables in view of the door
and conduct their primary business behind a newly installed screen
that shielded their bar.[32] Some clever proprietors decorated their windows with signs reading "Family Wine Store" or "Lunch Room." A
common barroom now labeled itself as a "Cafe."[33]

The fall elections of 1890 supplied the liquor dealers with bouyant
optimism. They had raised a sizeable war chest to defeat public bar
supporters in the legislature and had succeeded in removing the most
vocal of them. The debate over a constitutional prohibition proposal in
1889 had left an unfavorable impression with many voters who had
tired of temperance arguments. Much of the grumbling over the ab-
surdity of food before drink and other provisions of the public bar law
focused on Governor John Q. A. Brackett, who stood for reelection. He
had prodded the Police Commissioners to enforce the unwanted law in
the first place, and his actions in 1890 cost him the next election. The
new chief executive, William Eustes Russell, proved more amenable to
the liquor sellers; one of his first administrative statements called for
the final repudiation of the public bar law.[34]

Within a few months the General Court began discussing the repeal
measure. By far the most important statement came in February when
the saloonkeepers' attorney, Louis D. Brandeis, made a most impas-
sioned plea before the Joint Committee on the Liquor Law. He pleaded
that the best way to improve the conditions of drunkenness and crime
in Boston was not to abolish the saloon; that had already proved to be
an unworkable alternative.[35]

Brandeis went on to condemn the renewed enforcement of the public
bar law. It had reduced neither drunkenness nor the desire for "alcoholic refreshment" which brought people to drinking places. After fif-

teen years of neglect, "the law, if it still exists, is a dead letter . . . ."[36] Finally, he ended his remarks by asking the legislature to amend the law. The local licensing board, he said, should be empowered to decide the types of furniture and food it wanted in the saloons under its jurisdiction.[37]

A majority of the Massachusetts legislature agreed. After a few more months of bitter debate and a determined attempt by the prohibitionist speaker of the House to rule any repeal bill out of order, the public bar law ended its controversial sixteen-year career. On June 4, 1891, Governor Russell affixed his signature and perpendicular drinking was once more legal. Saloons no longer had to furnish food and the "long mahogany" reappeared. Bartenders were overjoyed; temperance advocates vowed revenge. And the used furniture stores were flooded with thousands of tables and chairs.[38]

After that, most Boston saloons seldom bothered to supply much beyond a few heavily salted crackers, intended primarily to make the customer want to drink more. The limitation law of 1889 controlled the competitive tendencies of licenseholders, and with no great necessity to lure customers with elaborate "spreads," the Hub's saloonkeepers escaped that burdensome expense.[39]

In Chicago, however, the lunch supplies occupied an important place in the saloonkeeper's budget. A few purchased cheap, low-grade meats; others contracted with caterers like the William Davidson Company, which specialized in daily service to saloons. But most often the lunch was the major contribution to the business venture made by the proprietor's wife.[40] The more elaborate meals cost great amounts of money. One large saloon near the Chicago Commons settlement on the near northwest side reputedly spent thirty to forty dollars each day on: "150–200 pounds of meat, 1½–2 bu. potatoes, 50 loaves of bread, 35 pounds of beans, 45 dozens of eggs on some days (eggs not usually being used), 10 dozen ears of sweet corn, $1.50–$2 worth of vegetables."[41] Five lunchmen were employed to serve the feast. Exorbitant costs often drove barrooms into bankruptcy. Two competitors on South Clark Street between Van Buren and Harrison gave away "free bracers" and up to 100 pounds of beef liver each day. Both went broke during the same week of 1913, prompting the *Champion of Fair Play* to repeat the same warning that it had been making for over a dozen years: "Most of the modern free lunch 'layouts' would kill a horse. They consist of a dozen different kinds of food, and nothing that would really appeal to the palate. One good joint of roast or corned beef is better than a dozen dishes of pickled this, and pickled that, and pickled almost anything that was never eaten in Germany."[42]

Costs of Doing Business

Besides the major costs of labor, rent, fixtures, and lunch, the saloon-keeper also faced a series of small but troublesome expenses that drained funds from his cash drawer. One of these was the cost of ice. In the winter most cooling problems were easily solved, but the rest of the year saw a constant stream of complaints against the "ice trust." Large firms like the Knickerbocker and Jefferson companies in Chicago and the Bay State Company in Boston had long ago cornered the market. A warm winter followed by a hot summer usually meant a small harvest, intense demand, and a sharp increase in price. At times the expense drove the saloonkeepers to join municipal reformers in the unsuccessful demands for regulation of the ice business as a municipal utility or for the construction of a city-owned ice plant. But each season the saloon-men had to face the iceman's bills — at least two dollars a ton in winter and four dollars in summer — and the possibility that the weather might drive it even higher.[43]

Saloonkeepers also found it increasingly difficult to obtain fire insurance coverage, and premiums were much higher than for other businesses of similar size. Saloon fires seemed disproportionately frequent, in part because there were so many barrooms. Most incidents, in fact, resulted from the usual causes: children playing with inflammables, mice chewing on matches, and defective heating appliances or wiring.[44] But insurance companies claimed that a number of fire hazards were unique to saloons. The rapid turnover and geographic mobility of the business meant that many premises were ill equipped for the preparation of free lunches and that makeshift kitchen facilities in the rear room greatly increased the likelihood of some kinds of conflagration, as did drunken brawls and tipsy proprietors who overturned oil or gas lamps. And, finally, a high rate of business failure and the danger of prohibition or some type of localized dry law were invitations for arson. One Italian woman, whose autobiography presents an excellent view of immigrant life in turn-of-the-century Chicago, told of the misfortunes of the saloonkeeper in whose building she lived. When his seasonal supply of homemade wine spoiled, he tried to set fire to the building in order to collect the insurance. Even this desperate act failed, but his story was repeated hundreds of times, each incident contributing to the other saloonmen's higher insurance rates.[45]

The same kind of problem faced the liquor man who tried to purchase life insurance; if he could obtain it at all, he had to pay more for it. Some companies refused altogether to write a policy for a saloonkeeper, claiming that he was likely to become an alcoholic. If he was not a drunkard, perhaps he was overweight; indeed, the stereotyped image of the man behind the bar always presented a portly figure whose girth was draped with a tent-sized apron. Some companies claimed that he was perpetually tired or "nervous," even if he owned a National cash register, because of his long workday and rush hours at noon and in the evening. And, finally, insurance spokesmen claimed that the saloonkeeper was always in danger of physical assault. A customer's angry wife might attack the owner as well as the backboard mirror, or unruly patrons might turn on the bartender at some late hour of the evening.[46]

The Unpredictable

The saloon was also subject to many unforseen expenses and financial emergencies that were serious enough to put the place out of business. The late night hours and what were sometimes substantial amounts of cash in the till made the bar especially vulnerable to robberies of various kinds. This problem became so common that the Chicago Liquor Dealers' Association offered a standing reward of 100 dollars for information leading to the arrest of those who victimized its members. Unsophisticated bartenders fell for schemes that varied widely in ingenuity. Two perpetrators might stage a fight in front of the saloon, wait for the owner to investigate, and thus provide an excellent opportunity for a third member to enter from the back and remove the money. Another trick employed a barefoot boy, who ran into the barroom and promised to watch the place while the bartender took a bottle of beer to the youth's father, who was parked nearby in a carriage or wagon. While the barman was gone, the youngster made off with the day's proceeds.[47]

Holdups were a common problem. When darkness thinned out the street life of the city, the intimate relationship of the barroom and its environment made it the ideal and often the only target available in the early morning hours. And the reputed wealth of the saloonkeeper only made him even more attractive as a victim.[48] Some bandits rode horses, and a few bold ones even rode streetcars, but it was the automobile that provided enough speed, flexibility, and anonymity to create a serious security problem. In 1912 the *Champion of Fair Play* warned its readers that "the 'auto holdups' are out in full force . . ." and went on to comment: "Another thing to those living on outskirts. Don't be left alone in your saloon until the closing hour. If your regular customers depart early, better to close up and lose a few straggling nickels than have your friends say next day, 'How natural he looks,' 'Wonder who did it?' . . . Many good fellows have been shot down in cold blood for keeping open too long chasing the nimble nickel."[49]

Danger appeared to be everywhere. One trade journal suggested that larger places should keep stoves and lanterns inside their walk-in refrigerators since holdup men frequently locked their victims in the cooler. Saloons on corners were cautioned that bandits who sought them out often worked in pairs, with the additional man used to cover the side entrance. Another sign of concern was the great frequency with which alarm systems were advertised in the liquor periodicals. One of these, endorsed by the *Champion of Fair Play*, was similar to that employed in banks. The bartender tripped a floor switch which set off an outside gong, "thus scaring the hold-up man away and at the same time summoning police."[50]

Former or present employees created another potential source of economic ruin. Bartenders or managers occasionally ran off with large amounts of money. One spectacular case involved a cashier at one of the branches of Chapin and Gore in Chicago. Distinguished in appearance, so much so that he was nicknamed "Grove" after Grover Cleveland, L. A. Hopkins fled to Canada with a young lady and $3,500 of the firm's funds. The incident was described in great detail in the sensation-seeking press, but earned a more permanent fame in a fictionalized form. The woman in question was the sister of Theodore Dreiser, a regular customer of the saloon, and Hopkins became the tragic George Hurstwood in the novel *Sister Carrie*.[51]

Saloonkeepers who frequently lacked prior business experience were also easy marks. For confidence schemes, Chicago swindlers operating in the early 1890s posed as agents who would assist aspiring entrepreneurs in setting up businesses independent of the brewing companies. One Bohemian tailor traded his house for a "fully stocked" saloon, only to find the bottles filled with vinegar and water. Another victim purchased a place that supposedly grossed $165 each day, only to discover that its actual trade amounted to a fraction of that. Still others unknowingly bought places that were heavily encumbered with debts.[52]

The public nature of the saloon, with the steady stream of strangers drifting in from the street, encouraged a number of swindling schemes that victimized unwary proprietors. All varieties of bad check artists plied their trade in the barroom. One popular swindle involved a stranger who cashed a few genuine checks for small amounts of money to establish his credibility. Then he wrote a worthless one for some large amount of money. In another scheme, a pair of crooks posed as plumbers who were working on a building nearby. They came in complaining that they had been paid by checks, which they asked the bartender to cash. Thirty-five proprietors on Chicago's North Side discovered that the checks were worthless.[53]

Finally, the saloonkeeper encountered numerous people who tried to lure him into various protection schemes. They offered some kind of "pull" or inside information that might allow him to delay payments on his license or avoid prosecution for selling to minors and drunkards. A "Chicago and Suburban Saloonkeepers' Protective Bureau" promised to investigate salesmen and provide legal advice for just twelve dollars a year, less than the dues of the Liquor Dealers' Association. The *Champion of Fair Play* exposed it as a fraud.[54]

While many of the saloonkeeper's economic problems were caused by his own lack of business skill, others were beyond his control. Fluctuations in the local economy could encourage hundreds of new places to open in good times and put as many others out of business when times became lean.[55] As one whiskey industry spokesman put it: "The brewers felt it first. The foreign laborer, who largely drinks beer, was the first to have his wages cut down. He stopped drinking his glass of beer, and the demand diminished. The Americans drink the whiskey. They were the last to have their salaries cut. When they stop drinking, the distillers appreciate the fact."[56]

Depressions such as that of the 1890s were especially wrenching. Only moderate turnover occurred in Boston, largely in the small neighborhood places. Larger ones downtown were best able to withstand the economic shocks. And the total number of liquor licenses did not decline because even in the worst part of the depression, there were more people who wanted into the business than the limitation law allowed.[57]

By contrast, Chicago's saloons felt the full impact of the depression. The World's Fair had delayed the onset of high unemployment, but afterwards the sheriff's sale became a common sight. Mayor John P. Hopkins, who was normally allied with the retail liquor interests, sent city police to help brewery and wholesale whiskey salesmen collect payments on overdue bills. Notices of bankruptcies swelled the columns of *Mida's Criterion*, a wholesale trade periodical. Those listings kept salesmen abreast of their customers, but in retrospect, they also provided a sad record of failures, judgment suits, and voluntary closures. What had been a small list in previous years swelled to dozens in each fortnightly accounting.[58]

The city newspapers and the "Business Record" columns of the *Criterion* revealed another fact about the impact of hard times on the Chicago saloons. Although the total number of barrooms declined only slightly between 1894 and 1896, an average of 17 percent of them changed hands in each quarterly license period. Individual owners were forced out of business by the brewing companies that controlled them, only to be replaced by newcomers who took out chattel mortgages on the fixtures left behind by predecessors. The brewers were compelled by their enormous investment in real estate and by the continuing competition in their industry to keep their tied outlets open, while the depression itself eliminated the weakest among the retail dealers. Those saloonkeepers who survived had to face not only the threat of foreclosure, but also a nearly stable number of competitors for a dwindling number of paying customers.[59]

The seasons and the weather added another element of unpredictability. Much of the trade was irregularly distributed throughout the year. In the winter beer sales declined far below the summertime peak. Lent and Advent seasons made temporary abstainers out of the more religious citizens, especially when such influential priests as Father Dorney of Chicago's Back-of-the-Yards area persuaded social clubs to suspend their weekend saloon dances. The saloonkeeper had to rely on his warm-weather profits to make up for the lean months, and cool summers created obvious problems because of such inflexible expenses as rent, license, and mortgage payments.[60] Other summers were unpredictably hot. In June 1901, for instance, Chicago and Boston witnessed one of the most severe heatwaves in American history. Dozens died of heat prostration, and Chicagoans alone consumed an estimated 35,000 barrels of beer during each day of the warmest period. A similar three-day hot spell a dozen years later saw the city's population reportedly consume a million gallons a day, an average of six glasses for every man, woman, and child in the city![61] But soaring thermometers introduced the prospect of disgruntled "regulars" crowded out or ignored. Proprietors also found it very difficult to keep their storage cellars cool enough to prevent the barrels from exploding; nor could they secure ice. To guard against the possibility of running out of beer, saloonkeepers tried to anticipate demand by purchasing reserve supplies. But if the weather suddenly cooled, as it often did, they ended up with more beer and whiskey than they could sell in months, along with large bills that drained their cash reserve.[62]

Blind Pigs and Kitchen Barrooms

Another uncontrollable factor in the saloon business was the presence of unlicensed competitors. These places had to display a judicious mixture of enough anonymity to avoid prosecution and sufficient publicity to attract business. In Boston they were called "kitchen barrooms" in apparent reference to their frequent appearance in tenements. That phrase, which was eventually applied to all illegal liquor sales in the Hub, was also related to the excuse frequently given to police during raids: that the customer was really a friend or relative who had stopped by the owner's kitchen.[63] Chicago, perhaps reflecting its more rustic tendencies and its stockyard interests, called its unlicensed barrooms "blinds pigs." The origin of that phrase is lost in saloon folklore. The term "blind tiger" was common in other parts of the country, and the word *blind* almost certainly refers to its semisecret nature. One legend held that early in Chicago's history the police raided an illegal barroom marked by a sign with only the letters A P G. When a newspaper reporter inquired about its ownership, an officer answered, "A pig with its I knocked out" — hence the term "blind pig."[64]

Regardless of the origins of its popular names, the unlicensed barroom had become a noticeable problem long before the Civil War. Chicago officials estimated that in 1849, only twelve years after the city was incorporated, there were already twenty-six unlicensed dealers and only 146 legitimate ones. Throughout the 1850s temperance advocates complained loudly that secret places were probably three times as numerous as legitimate ones. Boston, meanwhile, had encountered a similar situation, made even more acute by the periodic imposition of prohibition in the state.[65]

Everyone guessed about the extent of unlicensed sales, but it was not until 1862 that local authorities in both cities had an accurate account. That year the federal government began requiring an annual retailer's tax. Its small cost—twenty-five dollars—and the belief that federal agents were difficult to bribe prompted almost everyone, even bordellos, to comply, regardless of whether or not they purchased a local license. Gradually, lists of those holding these stamps came to be viewed as an excellent means of tracking down blind pigs and kitchen barrooms. Federal authorities were reluctant at first to reveal this information and thus involve themselves in local law enforcement matters, but gradually the legislatures, the courts, and the Congress forced a change in this policy.[66]

The disclosures proved disturbing to the saloonkeepers as well as to temperance advocates. The Liquor Dealers' Association called attention to the fact that its members paid their fair share and more to support local government, while the blind pig caused the city to lose revenue and gave the legitimate traffic a bad name. The association then pledged to help the police find violators. Members watched their neighborhoods, asked questions of customers, and reported their findings to their branch meetings. The information was then turned over to the police, much in the same manner as quasi-legal groups like the Law and Order League searched for dramshop violations.[67]

Despite these efforts the extent of the violation remained enormous. In 1884, the year before the Metropolitan Police Act, there were 1,300 unlicensed places in Boston and only 2,808 legitimate ones; Chicago recorded 5,000 federal licenses in 1882—one for each twelve legal drinkers—but only 3,500 legitimate saloons. Mayor Carter Harrison, armed with a list of federal stampholders, promised to "make it lively" for blind pigs, but he failed. By 1894 there were over 2,000 unlicensed places, many of which had been legitimate during the World's Columbian Exposition but which were now unable to afford the local license fee. In following decades the situation worsened: in 1900, there were over 10,000 federal stamps, but only 6,400 were saloon licenses, while three years later the total of nonlicensed sellers had risen to 4,600.[68]

There were obvious reasons for the existence of so many blind pigs and kitchen barrooms. One was lax police enforcement. The number of arrests in either city seldom amounted to more than a fraction of the total.[69] In Boston, for instance, there were only sixty-one arrests in 1884. And *Chicago Tribune* reporters were able to turn up 192 places without any city license, thirty-three with mutilated ones, and another twenty-one that had expired — all in the matter of a few hours. Every one of them, however, had a federal stamp. This situation remained unchanged except during periodic crackdowns.

The success of the high license movement was another contributory factor. Many of those who could not afford $500 or $1,000 each year and were refused aid by the breweries took their chances at operating without any license at all. And each increase in the fee also seemed to evoke more creative responses. During the 1870s, when Massachusetts had low licenses and limited liquor sales to beer, saloons used the malt product as a cover for illegal whiskey. Later, when "Berlin beer" (less than 3 percent alcohol) could be served in any unlicensed place, the bartender carried bottles of beer or spirits in his pocket or placed them near a drain in case of a raid. Other sellers piped beer from barrels in adjoining houses or hid whiskey behind pictures in the wall. One man in Chelsea even devised a trap door which emptied the liquor and the vessels holding it into large vats of lime.[70]

The most ingenious of all the blind pigs, however, were the bumboats. Boston had a few of these floating saloons, so named because they sailed beyond the territorial limits and outside the license jurisdiction of any state, but it was in Chicago that "Black Jack" Yattaw developed the practice into a fine art. He was a colorful gambler whose Yacht Club House was a floating barroom-restaurant with a dance platform on the roof. Each day Black Jack would maneuver his craft up to the government pier and attract the waiting customers on board with what the *Tribune* in 1880 described as "a painted and bedizened harreds." Then, with a full load on board, his boat slid out into the lake, safely beyond the power of local authorities.[71]

Yattaw was arrested several times after he began his cruises in the late 1870s, but his capers never went beyond municipal court. Powerful political friends, like Democratic chieftain and fellow-gambler Michael Cassius McDonald, would prevail upon the mayor and extricate Black Jack from jail. By the 1890s he had in fact become enough of a lovable popular hero and tourist attraction to make it into the World's Columbian Exposition guidebooks, and that notoriety probably prevented his incarceration. What his bumboat and its several deriv-

ative competitors did accomplish was to keep alive the controversy over
how far the city's police powers actually extended into the lake and
what kinds of private economic enterprises could be pursued on its
waters.[72]

Old Competitors: Legal or Not?

Besides the blind pig or kitchen barroom, the saloon also had to contend with a large and varied group of competitors — some legal, some
not — who sold liquor as a sideline. These sellers were the product of the
same historical forces as those which shaped the saloon. This point is illustrated by the problem of wholesale dealers who sold liquor in quantities less than the legal limit. They were always tempted to sell directly
to the consumer. In fact, for many decades it had been the accepted
business practice to do precisely that. A buyer, especially a rural or out-
of-town buyer, expected to be able to taste what he was about to purchase in quantity. Dealers then began to set aside space as a "sample
room." Over the decades, when retail selling became a specialty, some
saloons called themselves sample rooms, even if selling by the barrel or
bottle was only a sideline.[73]

When the high license movement gained major victories in the
1880s, lawmakers in both Illinois and Massachusetts imposed lower
fees on the wholesaler. Those who sold in quantities of five gallons or
more and primarily to retailers or to consumers for home use supposedly created less of a policing problem than did the saloon. In Massachusetts a license of the Fourth or Fifth Class (Wholesale) cost only about
one-half the First Class (Retail) rate. Chicago had no wholesale license
at all until 1885, when the City Council fixed it at only $250. In 1896
the aldermen responded to political pressure and lowered it to only
$100 a year. This situation in both cities produced an enormous temp-
tation to cheat.[74]

Unlike the secretive blind pig or the kitchen barroom, this form of
competitor was much more widely known to the public and included
department stores, whose entire business was based on a city-wide or
regional reputation. When they began retailing liquors, everybody
knew about it. This saloon competitor also had a mid-nineteenth-
century precedent. The general merchandise store had always carried a
stock of whiskey and beer, which it was equipped to sell retail on the
premises as well as in packages to be carried away. And so, when the

department store came into wide popularity in the later decades of the century, the function of liquor dispensing appeared prominently among the various lines of merchandise.[75]

Another of the saloonkeeper's competitors was the grocery, which carried a wide variety of merchandise. Both urbanites and rural people who came to town bought perishables in the market place, but went to the grocer for such other foods as molasses and flour.[76] Liquor was often sold in large quantities, and grocers equipped themselves with a cellar and frequently with a room to sample the goods. As one Boston grocer remembered about the 1830s, "A man would hardly have dared to go into business without it."[77]

As saloons developed into specialized businesses, they increasingly viewed grocers as burdensome rivals. In 1881 one saloon spokesman estimated that 800 of Chicago's 4,000 retail licenses were held by grocers and that a huge number beyond that operated illegally. The barkeeps turned to the city police for help and gained an unexpected ally in the temperance movement. The Women's Christian Temperance Union, the Christian Prohibition Union, and the Catholic Total Abstinence Society all began boycotts of grocers who sold liquor openly or secretly in closed crocks and disguised bottles.

The liquor men agreed with the ultimate goal of dry groceries, and in 1896 they got the Chicago City Council to pass an ordinance requiring every grocer to pay a $500 license fee even if all liquor sales were made in packages and bottles to be carried off the premises. The matter caused little comment for several years, but when evasion became widespread, the saloonkeepers pressured the police to initiate a crackdown. Although the law withstood several court challenges, unlicensed sales from the grocer's back door and under his counter continued to drain away scarce profits from the barkeeper's till. And the temperance organizations continued to worry about the impact of this secret drinking on the family.

Bottled Goods: The Portable Pig

Saloonkeepers also had to contend with another development in the liquor trade—the proliferation of cheap, mass-produced bottles and what it did to the portability of beer. The saloonists viewed the bottle trade with mixed emotions. For many years it really posed no threat to the regular business. Bottles were in such short supply that an industry

group, the Cook County Bottling Protective Association, actually sued
to prevent junk dealers from carting the containers out of town. Scav-
engers resold the bottles to the brewers for six cents a dozen for the
small size and up to four cents each for larger sizes. The association
finally stopped the elusive practice by prodding the Illinois legislature
into passing a new law: no bottle could be resold without permission of
the trademark holder. And finally, bottled beer was sometimes difficult
to sell over the bar because of a long-standing rumor that its contents
were in reality lifeless dregs that no self-respecting saloonkeeper would
ever put in a schooner or schnits.[78]

By the late 1880s, however, bottled beer was no longer a novelty but
a threat to the saloon. The problem was portability, not out of the saloon but from the back of a wagon. The first to discover this new
method of retailing were an assorted group of independent bottlers
who bought beer from brewers by the barrel and resold by the bottle.
They peddled door to door or sold to anyone on the street — an annoy-
ance to the regular keeper.[79]

But before long the Chicago brewers themselves hit the streets. They
made substantial sales by selling directly from the wagon to congrega-
tions of thirsty people. The beermakers rationalized and enlarged upon
the business acumen of a few of the pioneer independents, such as
Thomas Ludington. Back in the 1890s, he had received a regular license for a "saloon on wheels," complete with sandwiches as well as
beer. His favorite customers had been the gangs of workers installing
new sewers in new neighborhoods. But when the brewers took over,
street vending became a big business. Between twenty and thirty wagons rolled through South Chicago alone, following city construction
crews. In an age of labor-intensive construction, when manpower
rather than machines performed public capital construction and maintenance tasks, beer peddling could be a very profitable business.[80]

Boston had no specific license for beer peddlers, and by the late 1880s
the trade was so extensive that horsecar drivers accused beer wagons of
being one of the greatest single obstacles to traffic. These four-wheeled
saloons followed a regular route that covered all types of neighborhoods, from the slums of Village Street to the new residences of the
Highlands and the fashionable homes of Back Bay and Beacon Hill.
The brewery normally sold the beer to the deliveryman, usually at the
cost of one dollar for a case of twenty-four bottles. The latter, in turn,
resold it for whatever he could get. The standard price was $1.25, but

single bottles brought a dime each, and so a fortuitous stop to serve curbside customers could produce an extra $1.15 in windfall profit. And each year the number of bottles in circulation increased and, with it, the beer trade outside the saloon.[81]

The saloonkeeper gradually realized that bottled goods were undermining his trade. Not only did the brewers indirectly compete with the retail outlets they themselves owned, but peddlers sold the bottled beer at prices not much higher than the wholesale barrel rate to the bar proprietor. One saloonkeeper, who was also an alderman from the South Chicago steel mill district, expressed his frustration: "The beer wagons in South Chicago are making more money than the saloonkeepers. The wagons go around and fill people up with beer right on the street. Some of them sell whiskey and cigars and are practically saloons on wheels. They pay no license and still compete with the saloonkeeper who has to pay $1,000 a year."[82]

The saloonkeepers could find little encouragement in the legislative process. The Chicago Corporation Counsel advised against enacting a special license on beer wagons, declaring that the council could not tax the brewer who made the beer and tax him again when he sold it; a tax on a tax was illegal.[83] During the following year, the Chicago liquor dealers lobbied for a bill that would have banned all house-to-house and street sales, but the City Council instead recommended that the police department be encouraged to halt all deliveries except those made in response to a specific order. Officers were ordered to stop all delivery wagons and examine the dispatch books, but police reputedly used the occasion to collect bribes and shakedown payments. But even if the authorities had strictly enforced the law, the rapid adoption of the telephone made the delivery business more efficient and popular.[84]

Newspaper advertisements tempted the reader to "phone before eleven" and the beer would be "delivered before seven."[85] Large display ads, now directed at the consumers rather than the saloonkeepers, always included the brewery's phone number and an enticing statement on the ease of ordering beer through the comfort and privacy of one's telephone.

"Trying to Make a Buck"

The most serious problem that proprietors in Chicago and, to a more limited degree in Boston, faced was competition among saloonkeepers themselves. The enormous number of licenses issued each year, especially in Chicago, where they were unlimited until 1906, reduced the chances of surviving long enough to apply for a renewal. At the same time, the brewing companies, whose entrance into the retail trade was largely responsible for the overcompetition, demanded at least a minimal profit from their investment. Caught in between, the saloonkeeper grasped for anything that would give him an advantage over his rivals. Sometimes it led to crime, but more often it resulted in a determined effort to be different, to offer something more — some service or attraction that the place down the street was lacking. The competitive urge itself was nothing new, but the form and intensity that this struggle later took was indicative of the condition of the trade.[86]

Some saloons tried consciously to avoid the standardized look of brewery domination. Most could afford little more than a fancier stained glass window or some other minor amenity, but the ideal which so many sought could be found in the downtown area. In Chicago the drinker might encounter a branch of the Hannah and Hogg chain. Each one had large stone caricatures of people in the sidewalk out front. Chapin and Gore, another chain which, like Hannah and Hogg, eventually decided to specialize in the whiskey distilling business, was best known for its large, cartoon-like paintings of famous personages that adorned the walls of its seven downtown locations. To show off its artwork, "C and G" installed the first electric lighting in any barroom in the city.[87]

Soon almost every one of the big bars boasted of some unique attraction. Hester's Fish Camp had a large pond filled with live fish. The bar in the Planter's Hotel was hewn from the Queen Jane's Oak, reputedly 480 years old, while the one at John Harding's, at 100 feet, was advertised as the longest in the city. Colonel Squire T. Harvey's Ye Wayside Inn had over $2,000 worth of twenty- and five-dollar gold pieces, Queen Victoria Jubilee coins, and silver dollars inlaid in the floor and bar. And the bartenders at Lansing and McGarigle's, a favorite political gathering spot, worked behind a perfectly round mahogany bar.[88]

None, however, could compare with Heinegabubeler's on State Street. Part of a national chain, it was a museum, peep show, and amusement park as well. "Motographoscopes" showed treats like "Night at Vassar" and "Midnight in Paris" in "natural motion." It had gymnasiums, reception rooms, reading rooms, and a roof garden. But most important was its reputation for making greenhorn newcomers the butt of gags and pranks. Holes in their mugs leaked beer on their shirts. The vending machines dispensed rubber gum and the washroom bowl collapsed. Customers who complained were ushered to the sidewalk, while those who laughed at themselves were treated to free food and drink, as well as being able to witness the adventures of the next unsuspecting victim.[89]

The novelty bars were not entirely confined to the downtown district, although most were located there. For instance, Rudolph Voss's place at 8956 Superior, South Chicago, had a "model coal mine" and a "village blacksmith shop" in full operation indoors. Grenier's Garden at Madison and Throop Streets on the West Side attracted customers with six-day bicycle races on its grounds. The most unique of these places was the Relic House near Lincoln Park. It capitalized on the Great Fire of 1871. Built entirely from the fused remains of what had been the largest wholesale hardware concern in the city, it became one of the city's best-known sight-seeing attractions and contained a small museum of paintings and other fire memorabilia.[90]

A few bar owners tried to use their famous names to draw customers. Malachy Hogan, a former prizefighter referee, opened a bar after his retirement. But the most famous of these bars belonged to the boxers themselves. Paddy Ryan, a Chicago favorite, opened a place on State Street in 1882, while "Joe" Goss, Jim Keenan, and others did likewise in Boston. The Hub's most spectacular saloon opening involved its favorite pugilist, John L. Sullivan. The *Temperance Cause* commented that "Boston got a taste of Westernism in municipal experience" when a "howling crowd" of curiosity seekers filled Washington Street in search of a drink or at least the owner. Police considered it a riot and summoned reserves and additional aid from the suburbs. This venture failed a few years later, but in 1895 Sullivan opened again, this time in partnership with a former actor named Mike Clarke. The boxer's drinking problem ruined this business also, and by 1902 he was broke. Ironically, the last notable job this would-be saloonkeeper held was as a lecturer for the enemy. The Anti-Saloon League sent him across the country on speaking tours, where he warned youth about the dangers of alcohol and how the saloon bankrupted the nation's morality and its economy. In this job he proved effective, to a large extent because of his deep familiarity with his subject.[91]

Chicago also had a saloon operated by a boxer whose career outside the ring was as famous as his pugilistic triumphs. In July 1912 Jack

Johnson opened his Cabaret de Champion, which was perhaps more of
a nightclub than a saloon.[92] As he later remembered, the black champion "spared no effort" in gathering a spectacular collection of decorative items:

> Having traveled extensively, I had gained a comprehensive idea of
> decorative effect; I had viewed some of the most notable amuse-
> ment centers of the world, both as to their exterior and interior ar-
> rangements. I also had collected many fine works of art, curios
> and novelties. These I used in providing the attractive features for
> which my cabaret gained considerable distinction . . . In the art
> collection were paintings of myself and wife by a portrait artist
> who was rated as one of America's best. Other paintings were of
> my father and mother. I displayed a few real Rembrandts which I
> had obtained in Europe. Adorning the walls were original paint-
> ings representing Biblical and sacred history scenes. Another
> painting was of Cleopatra. These were only a few of the art sub-
> jects which adorned the walls of the Cabaret de Champion.[93]

Johnson's place also attracted a huge crowd the night it opened and,
like Sullivan's, soon fell into trouble. Mayor Carter Harrison revoked
Johnson's license the following October on the charge that he ignored
the closing-hour ordinance. Accusations that he was involved in the
recruitment of prostitutes led quickly to the demise of Johnson's career
as a cabaret owner. By the end of the year, the Cabaret de Champion
had closed.[94]

While most saloons out in the neighborhoods could not afford such
extravaganzas, they were able to devise their own methods of attracting business. Some involved an attempt to cast the proprietor in the image of good will and generosity. The custom of giving Christmas gifts
to regulars took on new meaning in an atmosphere of intense competition, as each proprietor tried to outdo his neighbor. The various liquor
dealers' associations condemned the practice as foolish; saloons which
did not wish to participate or could not afford to were now forced into
this frivolous draining away of profits. In 1895 the Chicago police ordered its officers to "request" that saloonkeepers end the practice. The
problem of public drunkenness always seemed to increase during the
holiday season, and the fact that the liquor was given rather than sold
created difficult legal problems concerning the saloonkeeper's responsibility under the dramshop act. But in Chicago, at least, these statements
had little effect. From the mid-1880s until well past 1910, the liquor
dealers' association issued its annual order, even threatening to fine and

expel its members who failed to comply. And every year the Christmas giveaway continued unabated.[95]

Only in Boston, where the number of saloons was small, concentrated in a relatively limited area, and could be closely watched, was there any effective control. On November 14, 1911, the license authorities issued an order forbidding gifts of liquor during the holiday period. That ended the tradition in the Hub.[96] That year the license authorities in Boston also outlawed the long-standing practice of giving "trading stamps, coupons, bonuses," and other gratuities. As early as 1902, the M. H. Cobe Company, "Boston's Biggest Wholesalers and Retailers," began giving away a free clothes brush with every purchase, as well as "Green Trading Stamps." Other souvenirs followed, many of them supplied by the brewers: memorandum books, card cases, pocketbooks, and matchbooks, among other items.[97] What they did to increase business is debatable, but in the case of one South Chicago proprietor, they proved disastrous. Theodore Kurowski decided to give away White Eagle trading stamps, along with prizes of whiskey and cigars. The customers readily accepted the latter two items, but the white eagle was the national bird of Poland, and patriotic groups were incensed. His trade nearly ruined by boycotts, Kurowski quietly destroyed his stamps.[98]

The cash drawer also benefitted from a number of other sideline items dispensed across the bar. Cigars were a staple item. Although few bars bothered to purchase the proper licenses, most of them sold some form of tobacco. A supply of two hundred "nickel movements" and the same number of ten-cent "good ones" cost about eight dollars wholesale; they retailed for thirty dollars. Saloonkeepers also diversified these supplemental profits with such items as buttermilk, which some bars sold as a chaser. By the turn of the century, they had added headache powders, bonbons — nicknamed "wife pacifiers" — and a laxative called Veronica Water. A cold snap in the autumn brought out the beef tea, which the meat packers supplied complete with urns, pots, and mugs. And finally, the desire to promote the profitable mixed drinks led some saloons to sell Coca-Cola, which had been introduced in the South as a temperance drink.[99]

The search for customers and extra revenue also brought a series of mechanical novelties to the saloon. Some required no skill. If a bell sounded when the bartender rang up a sale on the Automatic Trade Clock, the customer won a prize. There were coin-operated whiskey dispensers; two nickels produced a one-ounce bottle. An Automatic Lunch Counter was designed to extract a few pennies from free-food patrons; its design resembled that of the Automat restaurant machines. The Albert Pick Company even sold a countertop device that gathered in coins from those who needed matches. "A penny burns a hole in a man's pocket," the seller's catalog advised. "He wants to spend it." Thus, by capitalizing on the drinker's fascination with gadgets, the mechanically inclined proprietor hoped to realize extra profits from the customer he had attracted.[100]

This search for additional revenue turned the saloon into a game room and quasi-gymnasium. Some bars had full-sized handball courts constructed in the back room, but others settled for a Chicago Pigeon-hole Table for forty-two dollars and a Self-registering Tivoli Table for twenty-five dollars. Box-ball, which Albert Pick guaranteed would produce "1200% profit," was a derivative of the bowling alley. Players paid a nickel for a five-minute game, and it showed the potential, at least, of large amounts of revenue if kept in constant use. It also had the advantage of portability, and the manufacturer would custom-fit it to any saloon.[101]

The most common table game was billiards. Uncounted hundreds of saloons used it to hold customers in slack hours and, in some cases, to gain a few additional nickels from table fees. The city of Chicago was supposed to license these games, but each time the mayor or the council considered enforcing the law, the saloonkeepers issued boisterous threats about what might happen at the next election. So the use of billiard tables grew until by the end of the century saloons deliberately sought out alliances with billiard halls, which had maintained a separate existence in Chicago since the Civil War era and had once offered a popular spectator sport. But by the 1890s the pleasures of drinking and playing billiards began to appear in tandem. One study in 1900 estimated that there were 140 such arrangements in Chicago, while a similar survey nine years later set that number at nearly half of the 7,600 saloons in the city.[102]

By contrast, most saloons in Boston remained relatively free of such artificial attractions. Barrooms distinguished themselves by the general opulence of their quarters, rather than by any gimmicks. Fine hotels had a posh bar replete with fine inlays and marble fittings. A poor man's bar had only the simplest of fixtures and little else. The lunch fulfilled the minimum requirements of the law, with no attempt to supply an opulent feast in the slums. There might be a deck of cards, but never a conscious attempt to turn the barroom into an amusement park.

The utilitarian quality of the Hub's drinking spots was due to a pair of factors. First, there were ordinances and Police Board rules against the mixing of liquor sales and amusements. In part, the traditional dislike for the temptation to tarry over a drink had prompted officials to ban the presence of certain gaming devices or music where liquor was sold. They felt that games might also attract youngsters, who should be kept away from saloons. But the primary reason for the barroom's austerity was the monopolistic situation created by the limitation laws. Boston's saloons simply did not have to engage in the same kind of desperate competition that prevailed in Chicago. Thus, in the evolution of the retail dealerships, the strictures of the liquor law had helped shape the saloon as a small business, and that process had, in turn, helped determine the extent to which the dealer would try to make his place a social amusement center.[103]

Grim Realities of Failure

It is nearly impossible to calculate the amount of business and profit generated by the individual saloon. Federal statistics measured only the amount of liquor manufactured, not the quantity sold. As a consequence, the large volume of beer transported from St. Louis and Milwaukee and the hard liquor made in Peoria went to unknown destinations. The statistics that temperance people claimed to be Chicago's "drink bill" were merely wild guesses. Thus, *Chicago's Dark Places*, a temperance tract promoted by the WCTU, could claim that in 1891 every man, woman, and child in the city spent $33.25 to purchase, on the average, fifty-three gallons of beer each year. This tab of $40 million did not even include hard liquor. Germans, reputedly more temperate, consumed only twenty-five gallons per capita. Those figures appear inaccurate, especially in light of the brewers' estimates of beer sales. The *Champion of Fair Play*, for instance, estimated that the total of all liquor business in Chicago amounted to no more than $21 million for the year 1899.[104]

It is certain, however, that unpredictability, competition, and questionable profit margins produced a high rate of geographical mobility. This was one of the most important characteristics of the saloon. If the original turned any kind of profit, it was a move up, a change to a more desirable site with better facilities. More prosperous men frequently moved several times in the neighborhood, perhaps from an out-of-the-way location to a major street. Then, if they were especially successful, they made the big plunge and opened up downtown. Charles Keller, for instance, began on Carroll Avenue on the West Side and moved to 832 West Lake. William Rust, vice-president of the *Alter Wirths Verein*, started on Halsted Street in 1880 at age thirty-five, moved to Waller and Twelfth Street in 1885, back to Halsted Street in 1887, and finally ended operating the Hofbrau Exchange and Restaurant on Washington Street downtown in 1890. Geographic mobility was so common that nearly every one of the saloonkeepers appearing in the biographical section of the World's Columbian Exposition souvenir published by the Chicago Liquor Dealers' Protective Association had moved at least once in his career.[105]

For a saloonkeeper in trouble, departure from the old location represented either a last-ditch attempt to save oneself or the final admission of failure. When those who owned their own places finally closed, they inevitably tried to cover up the real reasons in their newspaper advertisements: "Reason for going: owner has to go to California for his health," or "For Sale — two first-class saloons — each taking in daily $140 for whiskey alone" — optimistic appeals for the next generation of hopefuls.[106]

Some of these excuses were undoubtedly honest, but there was the tremendous rate of failure among saloons, giving mute testimony to the long-term effects of competition and uncertainty in the business. In 1880 Chicago's Mayor Carter Harrison reported that he was transferring nearly twenty licenses each week, 1,000 per year out of 3,090 issued. A work slowdown in the stockyards during 1895 claimed twenty casualties in a few days. In the license renewal period in the fall of 1901, no fewer than 960 saloons had folded and turned in their licenses, and another 468 had sold the license with the business. Two years later, 950 closed in four months.[107]

Brewery control of licenses complicated the matter. In Chicago their economic backing inflated the total number of barrooms and neutralized the intended effect of the high license. Blame for the high rate of turnover fell largely on the brewers. It took so little capital to enter the retail liquor business that the saloonkeeper had very little stake in the enterprise. If he prospered, he gained favor with the company, but if he did not, he could be evicted immediately. As early as 1881, when brewers were just beginning to become interested in the saloon business, the German Tavern Keepers Association (*Alter Wirths Verein*) lodged a formal protest against the fact that "decent German saloonkeepers" were being "forced out of business by brewery concerns." It even went so far as to suggest a boycott of Joseph Schlitz products because it was "one of the offenders."[108]

Often the failing saloonkeeper had no time to plan for his closing. The brewery simply locked him out. For example, Richard Berlizheimer once ran the Blue Ribbon Cafe in Chicago. But one day in 1901 he came to work only to find his stock of hard liquor, which he himself owned, out on the street. The locks on the door had been changed. Not content with his embarrassing loss, Berlizheimer got a lawyer and initiated what became three years of litigation. He finally lost out because the court decided that the Pabst Brewing Company owned the place and he was merely an employee. At least this disappointed barkeeper might have taken comfort from the fact that in the year of his final defeat, fully 60 percent of the brewery-owned saloons in Chicago changed hands.[109]

The brewing companies greeted the high rates of failure with apparent indifference. In fact, it was easy to argue that the beer makers actually benefitted from the situation. This did not include any immediate profit that might be derived from forfeited deposits or rents. The trouble of removing the fixtures and changing the company books was probably worth more than the forty or fifty dollars involved. Furthermore, the brewer also had one of his valuable licenses tied up for at least a few months in a location that made no money. In both cases, the company suffered a direct out-of-pocket loss.

But the constant fluidity of the retail trade provided a trio of benefits that would prove more valuable in the long run, something worth the trouble. First, it provided the brewing companies with an efficient way of removing the people who lacked business talent. The brewery agents could never accurately predict success or failure on the basis of brief introductions. Too often, the promising newcomer who appeared so bright and eager knew nothing about balancing books, ordering supplies, or attracting customers. This way, the agent's mistakes would not be around for very long, and since the brewer owned the license and probably the fixtures and the lease, the failure had no legal right to remain in what had been his saloon.

The American version of the tied-house system also allowed the brewers to adjust to the changing social and economic structure of the city. The saloon depended largely on people's immediate choices and desires. The demand for drink was seldom deferred to another day. The desire to purchase a cap might remain for several days, but thirst or the need for the companionship that a saloon might supply were things that were much more transitory, strong one minute, gone the next. This fact made the brewers especially conscious of every fad, every new thing that might appeal to the whims and fancies of their potential customers. A newly opened saloon might become a testing ground of sorts. The brewery's real estate agents were constantly looking for profitable saloon sites, and the eager applicant who had his own lease gave the company an opportunity to test new markets with even less risk. Similarly, such auxiliary features of each barroom as the lunch or entertainment required considerable planning. The success or failure of each change could be determined only by experience, and the bright new face behind the bar provided that important commodity.

The city, of course, provided a constantly changing landscape of economic functions and uses. The brewery had to be able to respond to every transition in the neighborhoods where it wanted to do business. When a new factory opened, the beer men crowded in nearby. Often they would seek out popular tradesmen or labor leaders as potential entrepreneurs. By 1881 the Chicago Labor Union had become greatly troubled by this avenue of social mobility. "The union," they proclaimed, "is not in favor of an unlimited number of saloons, repudiating the notion that as soon as a man becomes disqualified or incapacitated for manual work, he should drift into the saloon business."[110] But the practice continued. Even Richard Powers, a Chicago seaman who was the first head of the Federation of Organized Trades and Labor Unions, opened a barroom in the Loop.[111]

"A Headless Segregated Army"[112]

In the strange democracy of failure that prevailed in the retail liquor business, one man's dreams were often built on the ruins of someone else's misfortune. The proprietor and the brewer were in almost constant conflict over a variety of nagging disagreements. In 1898, for instance, the federal government imposed a war tax of one dollar on each barrel of beer sold in the United States. Most brewers passed it on to the retailers, who could not pass it on to their customers because of the nickel beer tradition.[113] Each attempt by the brewers to increase the wholesale value brought a volley of complaints which were routinely dismissed. Saloonkeepers charged that they were being shortchanged through barrels that were only partly filled. One Boston saloon owner, Lawrence Killian, even sued the Harvard Brewing Company, claiming that he and other saloonists were cheated regularly by standard barrels that were not completely full. The brewers replied with complaints that saloonkeepers failed to return the barrels, either piling them in the basement or breaking them up for firewood.[114]

Controversies over the wholesale price of beer prompted some Chicago saloonkeepers to go into the brewing business themselves. When hostility over the price of ale prompted a short-lived boycott in November 1867, a group of dealers resolved to found a cooperative brewery. It took nearly a year to gather sufficient capital, but the Chicago Union Brewing Company finally opened its doors in 1869. The cooperative idea gained wide popularity during the 1880s, as several of the neighborhood liquor dealers' associations attempted to set up their own plants. Their efforts accounted for much of the unprecedented growth in brewing capacity of Chicago during that decade. The announcement of still another new co-op greeted the established brewers when they attempted to increase prices, but the amateur nature of most efforts produced a high rate of failure. An accumulation of minor successes, however, left seven surviving cooperatives by 1913.[115]

As the years passed, the gap of misunderstanding between brewers and retailers widened. There was an understandable coolness between the brewers and the liquor dealers' association. By the late 1870s the beer barons had already withdrawn from active participation in retail groups. By the early 1890s the brewers' policies were being mentioned as a raison d'être for the saloon associations in the first place. Brewers became the butt of jokes, the subject of caustic editorials, and the center of inflated controversies. In one such instance in 1907, Adolphus Busch, the St. Louis brewer, reportedly came out in favor of the principle of local option; people should have the choice, he said, whether or not they wanted saloons nearby. The *Champion of Fair Play* splashed hostile stories and editorials across its front page and dealers' groups threatened to withhold their trade, until Busch withdrew his statement.[116]

For the most part, however, the brewers ignored such criticism. In fact, the conventions of the United States Brewers' Association seldom mentioned saloons at all, except to condemn them for causing crime. In 1878 the *Western Brewer* condemned saloons for a lack of "a sense of public decency" and "a sense of personal responsibility."[117] Coming at a time when most states were enacting dramshop laws, such remarks were not appreciated by the bartenders. When the brewing industry began giving financial support to saloons, it also began to chastize saloonmen who took the money and then used their places as centers of various criminal activities. By the turn of the century, such statements appeared with increasing frequency: it was the seller, not the beer, that caused the crime; it was the wicked saloon that would bring prohibition. In 1907 a Chicago brewers' group started a cleanup movement. It pledged full support to local law enforcement officials and promised to withhold aid from anyone convicted of a crime. And, of course, it disclaimed any guilt on its own part.[118]

The retailers answered such statements with equal vehemence. Tim McDonough, who headed a national saloon organization, described a "dive" as "typically a brewery saloon." The *Champion* also tried to link brewery support to the presence of crime. By demanding every possible penny, the brewery created an atmosphere in which the proprietor had to employ every means possible to survive, even crime. It was the brewery, then, aided by the high-license fanatics, who drove a few saloonmen to criminal activities.[119]

As later evidence will reveal, both sides were partially correct. But instead of resolving their differences, they enlarged the conflict to include the hard liquor interests as well. Most of the latter had remained uninvolved in the retail trade. Very few distillers had any direct financial investment in saloons, although many of the Boston wholesalers had added bars to their premises. But in no way had the whiskey producers become as enmeshed in the daily operations of the men who ultimately sold their products. It was, therefore, with an element of surprise that the hard liquor interests encountered the blasts of their partners in the drink trade.

The three sides fought over a number of issues. Wholesalers claimed that the brewery ownership of saloons had made the beermakers "partners in crime." Wholesale journals warned that an aroused public might demand prohibition as a result. The brewers answered by posting the well-worn argument that beer was a "temperance drink" which did not create drunkards, drain pocketbooks, or drive men to crime.

The *Western Brewer* proclaimed: "Whiskey makes a man ugly and corrodes his stomach. Wine dazes him. Water thins him, lowers his physical tone and makes him frigid, besides filling him full of all manner of strange animals. Beer, on the other hand, mellows him, links him with the universal brotherhood, superintends a physical and moral serenity, and makes him a friend to his kind. . . ."[120]

The brewers and distillers also argued over the purity of their products. Long before the Pure Food and Drug Act of 1906, they accused each other of peddling "poison." Brewers claimed that whiskey was no more than alcohol with bogus coloring and flavor-enhancing chemicals added; by contrast, beer was "nature's drink," a healthful blend of natural ingredients that nourished the body. The distillers spread rumors about the impurities in beer and reprinted a *Scientific American* article that claimed that beer was dangerous to humans because it promoted obesity. Beer also produced what was termed "the very lowest kind of inebriety," and the "most dangerous class of ruffians in our large cities." Articles in *Mida's Criterion*, a wholesale journal, claimed that artificial coloring produced dark beer and that barrels of brew that had gone flat were frequently rejuvenated with bicarbonate of soda.[121]

The major cause of the conflict was economic. Although they both shared retail outlets, the brewers and distillers were competing for customers. Except when a beer drinker demanded a chaser, the consumption of one product usually excluded the other. Throughout the preprohibition years, each side tried to gain the advantage. Distillers accused brewers of lobbying in Congress for higher taxes on distilled goods that would make whiskey relatively more expensive and relieve the pressure to increase the beer excise. Brewers also gave open support to the idea of differential local licenses that favored beer-only saloons.[122]

The conflict between beermakers and liquor wholesalers was especially bitter when it involved the problem of collecting payments from saloons. After the takeover of the 1880s, the advantages clearly fell to the brewers, who could demand instant payments to the delivery man by threatening to lift mortgage or license. Wholesalers, a dozen of whom might visit a saloon each week, were too numerous and had no control over their customers unless they owned the retail business, as they frequently did in Boston. Furthermore, the system of delivering hard liquor invited collection problems. Shipment followed the order by several days or weeks and billing was common. Wholesalers frequently extended interest-free terms but found too often that the saloonkeeper failed to pay at all, leaving the matter up to collection agencies and the courts. There was little that distillers' representatives could do but publish lists of bad debts, bankruptcies, and mortgages in *Mida's Criterion* and complain. Business sense warned against attacking saloonkeepers in public. Instead, the *Criterion* publicly blamed the brewers for the mess: " 'Collections are slow' is the usual complaint of the wholesale dealers, and why? Because the brewers forestall them by gobbling up receipts of the saloon men."[123]

The retail trade attacked the hard liquor business as well as the brewers. Saloon publications printed complaints against collection procedures, calling them unnecessarily harsh and "ruinous," and attacked the whole notion of a wholesale trade. If brewers sold directly to the sellers, the distillers could also. Standard Oil had eliminated the middleman. Michigan furniture manufacturers sold directly to customers through magazine advertising. A saloon magazine quoted a distilling company president that some $40 million was "lost" every year to wholesalers and that a salesman's travel expenses alone consumed 20 percent of the value of his sales.[124]

The highly tenuous nature of the retail trade led too easily to conflict between retailer and supplier. The saloonkeeper was nervous about his future. Profits were unsure. Hundreds of his fellow keepers closed each year. Would he be next? In Chicago the brewer was the landlord; the distiller was the scheming bill collector; and both wanted to squeeze the last dime from him. In Boston the roles were often reversed. The brewers, on the other hand, saw the maximization of sales as their final goal. For them the end really did justify the means. The saloon was merely an intermediate step, a sales mechanism that had to be operated to turn a larger profit. If it didn't contribute toward that goal, they changed the barroom by moving it elsewhere or replacing its proprietor until it did. In a brewery-owned saloon hard liquor was a necessary accommodation to a competitor. In a wholesale-owned saloon in Boston it was the beer that was the sideline.[125]

Association and Disunity

Internal divisions also hampered the development of strong dealers' organizations. As the decades passed, unity became increasingly difficult. During the early 1870s Chicago saloonists had banded together to form the Liberty League to counter the high license and Sunday closing movements and to encourage members to keep free of crime. In the turmoil following the Great Fire of 1871, Mayor Joseph Medill had blamed the liquor interests for corrupting city government and, therefore, for the inept response to the conflagration on the part of the fire department. The dealers helped defeat the Medill forces and elect a proliquor candidate, Harvey Colvin, in 1873. Soon afterwards, the Liberty League disbanded.[126]

A permanent successor did not appear until three years after Illinois passed the Dramshop Act of 1872 and the number of cases began to grow. That law made dealers responsible for damages their intoxicated customers caused; dependents of a drunkard could also sue the saloonkeeper for financial support. A group of liquor sellers met at Charles Koester's barroom on Clark Street and formed the *Alter Wirths Verein*. It excluded owners of criminal resorts and hired an attorney to defend members from dramshop suits.[127]

By 1881 the Chicago dealers had erected an elaborate hierarchy of protective associations. In September of the previous year the Illinois Liquor Dealers' Protective Association was formed to lobby against temperance legislation in Springfield. But the creation of other levels of trade groups revealed weaknesses rather than strengths. One problem was physical distance. This had not been an important issue when Chicago had been a compact town. But urban sprawl and the settlement of Cook County made it more convenient for dealers in such places as Hyde Park, Lemont, Harlem, and the Town of Lake to form their own organizations, rather than make the lengthy trip downtown. Many of the smaller, outlying dealers also began to resent what they thought was domination of the *Alter Wirths Verein* by downtown saloons. The creation of the Cook District Liquor Dealers' Protective Association was supposed to unify its constituent groups. But instead, lagging membership, "locals" that faded in and out of existence, and newspaper stories of internal discord meant that the Cook District was a loose confederation at best.[128]

Ethnicity was another troublesome problem. The *Alter Wirths Verein* had obviously been dominated by Germans, and the Irish dealers had tolerated their minority status until 1882, when the Germans decided to hold the meeting in their native tongue. That insult led to an Irish secession and the founding of the Chicago Liquor Dealers' Protective Association. Soon Swedes, Bohemians, and several other nationalities established their own groups, often subdividing again into regional associations. By 1891 there were thirteen member groups in the Cook District confederation.[129]

Unity also eluded Boston's dealers. In May 1882 a small group of English-speaking sellers formed an association "to make their business . . . rightfully recognized and respectable . . ." and to defend members against a wave of dramshop suits. The group quickly disbanded, but after a few years German saloonists and brewers revived the Personal Liberty League in Roxbury. Their Irish counterparts did the same in Chelsea, South Boston, and Charlestown. They all joined together to form the Massachusetts Liquor Dealers' Association, which lobbied on their behalf on Beacon Hill, hired lawyers to defend them, and published a newspaper, the *New England Trader*.[130]

The apparent harmony soon disappeared amidst the economic changes in liquor selling. In 1884 wholesalers formed the Massachusetts Wine and Spirits Association to protect their interests, which often conflicted with those of the retailers and brewers. The old arguments over lower license rates for selling beer and the supposed wholesomeness of beer-drinking as opposed to imbibing spirits brought the conflict between the associations into the open. Each claimed that it was leading the fight against prohibition, with the MLDA accusing the MWSA of having a "large surplus [of money] always on hand, while the retail dealers are constantly being compelled to pay large fines."[131]

A further division occurred in the ranks after enactment of the metropolitan police act in 1885. A group of retail dealers blamed both existing organizations for failing to kill the law, which placed the Boston police under the control of the governor. The dealers' groups had refused to become involved in politics, and the result was the formation of yet another association, the Massachusetts Liquor League, in 1886. Its founder, John J. Walsh, was a former Boston alderman who also owned six saloons. He was convinced that political organization was the key to survival. The MLL endorsed only those candidates who agreed to sign an "iron-clad oath" against antiliquor legislation; those who refused were labeled temperance fanatics in league propaganda. A war chest of $300,000 provided funds to purchase influence when necessary. Walsh also hired a professional staff to organize locals across the state and instruct members in the art of lobbying against prohibitionists. Finally, whenever a committee of the General Court heard testimony on proposed legislation, a representative from the MLL was always there to present the dealers' side of the issue.[132]

The liquor dealers' associations were many things to many people. They were fraternal organizations, providing insurance, picnics, and other social occasions. When local chapters of some national brotherhoods began banning members of the liquor trades — some Masonic orders during the 1880s and the Knights of Pythias and Fraternal Order of Eagles after 1900, for instance — the liquor men countered with the Knights of the Royal Arch.[133] The new organization was complete with secret rituals and insurance benefits. While constitutionally separate, these fraternal orders maintained close relations with local dealers' groups.[134]

Liquor trade associations also reflected the saloonkeepers' concern with the law. Each group hired an attorney, who assumed a leading role in its hierarchy. Trade journals that were closely affiliated with organizations — the *Champion of Fair Play* in Chicago and *New England Trader* in Boston, for instance — carried regular columns explaining court decisions. *Mida's Criterion*, the *Western Brewer*, and *Brewers' Journal* provided the same functions for their readers. These publications not only reported local news in exhaustive detail, but carried columns from other cities and reported on lobbying efforts in the U.S. Congress. In 1893 various state dealers' groups had joined to create the National Retail Liquor Dealers' Association to counter efforts to pass restrictive legislation on the national level, and the locals were anxious about its success.[135]

Conclusion

For many immigrants, ownership of a saloon was part of the American Dream, an avenue to financial comfort and status in the community. But frustration and failure greeted many newcomers. The problem was one of economics, especially the inflexible financial demands of license fees, mortgage payments, and liquor bills in a rapidly changing and highly unpredictable urban world. Every saloonkeeper had to worry about the high cost of a license, rent or property taxes, bills from the brewer and wholesaler, grocery expenses, and insurance premiums. Those who had borrowed to purchase fixtures, license, lease, and stock found themselves facing still other required payments. But the uncertainties of the weather, economic conditions, crime, and even the cost of ice made it impossible for many dealers to have the payments ready for collection on time. Competitors, ranging from department

stores and peddlers to a variety of illegal blind pigs and kitchen barrooms, added to the unpredictability.

Boston saloons were somewhat less vulnerable than their Chicago
counterparts. In the Hub, the limited numbers of licenses virtually insured success by virtue of less competition. The higher $1,000 fee and
the prohibitively high premium that arose from the limitation law
screened out most of the marginal and inexperienced hopefuls before
they could go into business. Since Boston saloons tended to operate as
partnerships or small chains, investors took a direct hand in the day-to-
day operations; they were not gambling with someone else's money.
Often large in size, Boston saloons were secure enough to be regarded
almost as a utility: in exchange for a high license fee and the agreement
to abide by certain rules, the saloonkeeper received a perpetual right to
operate in a location that was virtually assigned by the licensing
authorities. This did not mean that Hub saloonists were free from
financial worries, for they faced higher beer costs and what amounted
to a mandatory free lunch. But most were secure enough to survive the
unpredicted.

By contrast, the Chicago saloon was like a cork in an ocean. Unlimited and relatively cheap licenses, along with the extensive help provided by the brewers, made it easy — too easy — to enter the business.
The intense competition among brewers allowed thousands of marginal
outlets to open, only to fail during the next economic downturn or cool
summer. The turnover became so rapid that failure became almost the
norm rather than the exception. Brewers began to use the unsuccessful
dealers as marketing tools to weed out the best locations and discover
entrepreneurial talent. Failure had a function. In turn, saloonkeepers
whose mortgages were foreclosed felt that they were being cheated out
of their downpayments and their hard work.

The result was an atmosphere of tension and discord among the supposedly unified liquor interests. Saloonkeepers attacked both brewers
and wholesalers over credit collection and prices. Wholesalers and distillers blamed brewery domination of saloons for criminal activities
within, while the beermakers complained the cause was the whiskey
that passed over the bar. Brewing companies also fought the hard liquor interests over the idea of differential license rates that assessed
beer-only saloons at a lower rate. Brewers also openly labeled their
product a nutritious "food," while blaming whiskey for physical as well
as social dissipation.

Most important of all, knowing the history of the saloon as a small business is essential to understanding the expansive social and political role that it played in the American city. As later evidence will reveal, economic considerations would be central in the saloon's attempts to attract trade by opening its doors to the neighborhood and functioning as a semipublic place.

CHAPTER 3

The Saloon and the Public Neighborhood

SOCIAL CLASS MEANT many things in Victorian America. It signified the difference between the educated and the untrained, the comfortable and the miserable, the secure and the fearful, and the well-fed and the hungry. It fed emotional images that social groups created for each other: the "economic oppressors" on one hand and the "dangerous incendiaries" and "rabble-rousers" on the other. The striking social contrasts that existed within a few blocks of each other remain one of the most significant facts in the social history of the metropolis. But there was another dimension to the issue that sheds light on the meaning of social class in the city dweller's everyday experience. This was the way that one's station in life determined the relationship between social levels, the significance of mobility, the programs of reformers, and the functions of institutions like the saloon.[1]

In the Victorian city, an increase in the amount of living space and privacy in one's life was an essential part of social mobility. The class scale had a distinct spatial dimension. On the bottom were the drifters and transients who had no privacy at all; on top were the wealthy who lived in a world of closed carriages, private schools, exclusive clubs, reserved church pews, and opera boxes. Scattered in between were respectable bachelors and single women who occupied private rooms, families crowded into tenements, artisan classes which saved their wages for bungalows, and the middle class which purchased spacious townhouses or frame homes in subdivisions. This spatial scale of class demonstrated how the move upward in income frequently meant not only a move outward toward the city limits but also a greater degree of isolation. Whether by a raised stoop, a wooden picket fence, or decorative ironwork surrounding estate grounds, the comfortable family insulated itself from the city outside.

The spatial scale of class is important in interpreting the differences between saloons that relied upon a mobile street trade of strangers and those that catered to neighborhood drinkers. The dimension of social space provides a framework for interpreting the many functions of the saloon and helps explain why the barrooms seemed as essential as churches to the life of many neighborhoods. Ethnic groups used the public spaces of the city in different ways, just as the saloons of each nationality had unique features. Finally, the concern with privacy and the uses of public areas explains many of the attitudes of social reformers and how they confronted the problem of semipublic drinking.

Tramps: The Most Public People

At the very bottom of the social scale were the tramps, hobos, and other transient types whose "floating" lifestyle prevented accurate enumeration. The so-called tramp problem was not small; both Boston and Chicago numbered their drifters in the tens of thousands. The Hub was wintering port for thousands of idle seamen each winter, but the largest unemployed group could usually be found in Chicago. The confluence of railway lines brought more than 30,000 homeless men to its streets each year at the turn of the century, the number swelled by seasonal unemployment in agriculture and maritime work. A national economic crisis drove the number even higher, with such moderate depressions as that of 1907 leaving over 75,000 drifters filling every type of free sleeping space and overwhelming local charities.[2]

Some men — and women — consciously chose the transient lifestyle, while others tumbled into it through misfortune. In either case, they were the city's most public people. Their poverty was constantly on display. Their livelihood came from temporary day labor agencies that were located near transient districts. The jobs open to the drifter were simply scrawled on a blackboard. There was no choice, no individual bargaining, nothing personal, private, or permanent about it.[3]

Home for this floating population was very public and temporary. In the summer it was outdoors, the public places of the metropolis. Warm weather permitted a night out in the park or under an elevated sidewalk or in an alley. Hobo jungles grew up along transportation routes, such as the Mystic River in Boston or the mouth of the Chicago River or almost any railway; although the latter was privately owned, the lack of security allowed free access. Most other citizens knew little of this lifestyle and were shocked to discover "bums" in Lakefront (now Grant) Park in Chicago or panhandlers in Boston's Public Garden. Angry comments about the "Bum Row" along a sidewalk in the Boston Common could be found in 1890 and repeated two and three decades later.[4]

The small plots of greenery provided almost as much permanent privacy as the flophouses the transients patronized in the winter. The best ones were managed by widows and "old sailors" who attempted to keep individual rooms clean and quiet.[5] But the more typical "bunking shops" were filthy rookeries created in old warehouses, apartments, and hotels. Large rooms gave way to tiny cubicles with cardboard or chickenwire partitions, while in other places the beds were lined up in long rows in a common room. Hallways, floors, and straw mattresses were urine-soaked. Everything crawled with vermin, forcing the more ingenious tenants to fashion heavy, sacklike coverings to protect themselves in bed. Almost every spare inch of space in the building was given over to housing, even dark basements befouled with broken sewer pipes. Sanitary facilities were crude and filthy, since all of the men washed in a common bowl and used the same towel.[6]

Transient districts also perpetuated an alcoholic subculture. Drink provided an escape from misery, while at the same time being a central reason for the downfall of those who were formerly respectable. Ben Reitman, the maverick Chicago physician and paramour of Emma Goldman, maintained that the tramp drank primarily because it was the easiest thing to do. It required less effort than shaving, bathing, or even eating, and it was an excuse for unemployment and the lack of personal cleanliness.[7]

Reitman's explanation was credible because it pointed out the ubiquitous availability of liquor in the transient district. Whiskey was popular because of its portability and the ease with which it could be concealed, useful attributes for those who lacked a permanent and private space to store and consume it. It also produced instant warmth in winter weather. Transients consumed wine in great quantities because of its cheap cost. Beer was also inexpensive, but it lacked easy portability, because it required a growler or a bottle deposit to be carried from the premises. Both of the latter were frequently beyond the means of the transient.[8]

A large number of saloons supplemented street drinking. "Barrelhouse" bars were common. Washington Street in Boston and West

Madison and South Clark streets in Chicago were lined with broken-down dives. These saloons supplied a multitude of services to the homeless, including shelter. During the winter proprietors allowed some customers — trusted regulars — to sleep on benches or on the floors in exchange for help with the after-hours cleanup. Other saloonkeepers ran upstairs lodging houses. Some were clean, while others were undistinguishable from the rest of the flops in the area.[9]

The daily cycle of life on the skids minimized the hours spent off the street. The transients were evicted as early as 5:00 A.M., while some patrons left voluntarily in search of the day labor jobs that were assigned at that hour. If they had any money, they stopped at a nearby saloon for an "eye opener," although hunger and a lack of coins might drive them to accept a free or one-cent breakfast at such places as the North End Mission in Boston or Chicago's Salvation Army. Mission meals, however, were too often accompanied by a mandatory church service. The vast majority of drifters chose hunger or the saloon.[10]

Competition among bars in these districts was intense. In order to drum up daybreak trade, one enterprizing proprietor in Chicago's West Madison Street gave away one free drink to each customer between 6:00 and 9:00 A.M. He reasoned that his grizzled customers would feel obliged to buy another drink or perhaps a third. The resulting goodwill trade more than made up for the cost of the first shot, and the saloonist acquired enough capital to open two other places in the neighborhood.[11]

The early hours of the morning were only the beginning of the transient's relationship with the saloon. At noontime he was back again, this time to sample the free lunch. Most flophouse dwellers were lucky to get cheap cold cuts, a few boiled eggs, and cheese with crackers. The proximity of both cities to large bodies of water made fish an important sideboard staple. In better neighborhoods the free lunch was designed to supplement the customer's appetite for drink, but the tramp needed the food for survival.[12] One denizen of the street told a *Boston Globe* reporter:

"Have you no home? Where do you sleep?" [asked the newsman]
"Last night I took a good snooze in a stable, the best I've had for a week. Night afore I got a nap up in Franklin Park among the bushes. I was afraid the police would find me all the time, and slept with one eye open. No sir; I have no home. I ain't had one for a year. They put me out because I couldn't pay my rent, and I ain't

been able to pay any since; so here I am, no better than a tramp."

"Where do you get your meals?"

"Where you just seed me. I bum my way at the free lunch dishes of the barrooms. It is poor fodder sometimes, but cheap, and a man can't kick who is trying to hold soul and body together. How long ago was it you put me out of here?" [he asked of Fitz, the saloonkeeper]

"About two weeks, I guess."

"Right you are. Just about two weeks. Since then, I have done the whole city, and now I am going my rounds again. I'll see you again soon. Say, was you going to give me another drink, mister?"

"How did you get the five cents you had when you came in?"

"Beat it out of a sucker. Told him I was hungry and wanted a plate of beans. He gave me ten cents. I got it changed and came in here. This is the twin to it. That will get me a supper. See? It is cheaper to live at the barroom than at the poor beaneries."[13]

That small drama was replayed countless times each day — tramps trying to squeeze the maximum lunch from the minimum liquor purchase. The generosity of the bartender in this matter touched off a minor debate among students of the transient problem. Ben Reitman and an associate dressed as tramps and canvassed saloons near downtown Chicago in search of handouts of meals and money. They received only seven dimes, one quarter, and two nickels in visits to twenty-two bars. On the other hand, begging at 100 churches across the city produced thirty-nine meals and money from thirty-two others; only twenty-nine churches turned them down completely. As a result, Reitman complained that saloonkeepers were only interested in profit and exploited the poor in the same manner as day labor agencies. Boston settlement house worker Robert Woods echoed that opinion when he noted that "in the case of the poor man, the street is the hospitable club rather than the saloon. Here [the curb], he will meet his companions, resorting to the saloon for drinking only." Woods also noted bars in his city's transient district had few stools and seats and that bartenders discouraged loitering.[14]

The views of Reitman and Woods ran counter to one of the most widely held beliefs about the drifters' bars — that they were quasi-charity agencies. The popular press focused on the Workingmen's Exchange, operated by Chicago Alderman Michael Kenna. Tramps from around the country reputedly traveled to Chicago just to see it. A dime purchased "the special," which consisted of a pair of huge porkchops, a heap of fried potatoes, four slices of toast, and one of Hinky Dink's famous twenty-five-ounce schooners of beer.[15] Similar generosity prevailed at Alderman John Brennan's place, over on the West Side. The boss of the Eighteenth Ward, Brennan drew favorable comment from some reformers, despite the illegal votes he exchanged for his generosity. Raymond Robins, director of the Municipal Lodging House and a friend of social settlement leaders, proclaimed that "John Brennan comes nearer to living up to the teachings of the scripture than a great many who make greater pretentions to morality. He controls the people of his ward, not because he is base and corrupt, but because he is simple and democratic. He has . . . given more food to hungry men . . . than perhaps any other man in Chicago."[16]

Whether a saint or scoundrel, the saloonkeeper hosted a mixed army of transients. Observers frequently mentioned the heterogeneous ethnic and racial mixture of customers. There were young boys and old men, criminals and noncriminals, professional hobos and heads of families who were temporarily dislocated. The saloon was their shelter from the weather and the place where they learned the means of survival. And, on occasion, it was the place where their friends gathered to bid farewell; during the early 1870s urban missionaries in Boston's North End noted the use of saloons as funeral chapels for transients.[17]

Reformers in both cities hoped to close the flophouses and "stale-beer dives" by providing cheap, but wholesome, alternatives. Instead, they found themselves merely supplementing the existing system. At first, city officials only allowed the homeless to sleep in the hallways of police stations and other municipal buildings.[18] But when the problem began to appear permanent, the response became institutionalized. In 1879 Boston established one of the earliest municipal lodging houses in the country, while Chicago finally did so in 1901. Here a man could obtain a meal, a hot bath, and a bed. But both facilities required a few hours work in return. Although the rule was frequently broken in Chicago, it was strictly enforced in the Hub; everyone had to toil in the Hawkins Street Woodyard.[19]

In supplementing these municipal efforts, private philanthropies displayed a wide variety of approaches to the problem of the drifter and his saloon. Dr. John Harvey Kellogg, a nutritionist and physician from Battle Creek, Michigan, established a free dispensary in 1893. Later renamed the Workingmen's Home and Medical Mission, it emphasized

medical care and a wholesome penny lunch as an alternative to the
nearby dives on Chicago's Custom House Place.[20] The Salvation Army
in both Boston and Chicago employed inexpensive food, along with
prayers, as a means of uplift,[21] as did St. Stephen's Rescue Mission in
the Hub. The Boston Industrial Home and similar institutions in both
cities tried to provide employment as well as food and moral instruction.
Finally, there were the Mills Hotels and Dawes Hotels. The former,
designed to appeal to poor men seeking steady employment, was a
chain that opened its first Chicago facility in 1899; the Boston Mills
Hotel opened three years later. In 1914 Charles G. Dawes, the Evanston
banker who would later become vice president under Calvin Coolidge,
opened the Rufus Dawes Hotel in memory of his son. A Boston branch
went into operation in 1916. Both provided beds for seven cents and
private rooms for a dime. There were showers, inexpensive meals, and
reading rooms. Dawes established the rates and insisted that his hotels
turn a small profit, thus removing them from the category of purely
philanthropic ventures.[22]

The record of the private substitutes for commercial flops and bars
was mixed. They did provide clean facilities, good meals, and fumi-
gated beds. But they certainly failed to drive their competitors out of
business. In 1889, when John Bogue and the Improved Housing Association investigated the transient situation in Chicago, the four charity
operations had seventy-one competitors and held only 1,142 of a total
skid row sleeping capacity of over 9,000 beds. Another study a decade
later found 142 flop houses ringing the Loop.[23]

While the numbers and ubiquity of the flops and dives within the
transient district overwhelmed the philanthropic substitutes, many
drifters resented the rules and the kindness of do-gooders. Compulsory
bathing, during which their clothes were disinfected and searched for
liquor, interfered with what some thought was their right to be filthy.
Meals at the Salvation Army and similar city missions were accompanied by mandatory sermons. Some places asked too many questions
of the applicants, leading the Dawes hotels to advertize that "we wish
to assure our patrons that so long as they are orderly and deport themselves in our hotels, their independence will not be interfered with, nor
will they be affronted by unasked advice or interference in their private
affairs." The fact that the Dawes management had to post such a sign
in its lobby indicates at least a reputation for meddling. In the saloon,
the transient knew that he was a paying customer. The use of the sa-

loonkeeper's semipublic space required no moralizing and no answers about personal matters. Many of the men who lived on the street at least could keep their life stories private.

Finally, charity reformers failed to realize the internal contradiction in their philosophy. Most firmly believed in environmentalism or, as one report put it, that "the character of the lodgers is greatly elevated by familiarizing them with sanitary and cleanly operations. . . . Becoming accustomed to better accommodations they will gradually pay more attention to their personal appearances and finally become self-respecting citizens." Yet, at the same time, virtually every charity flop shunned repeaters who returned for more than three or four nights. The process of uplift did not work that quickly, and the city's most public people continued to crowd the curbstones, toss down the nickel for a night's shelter, and push their way to the bar for a drink of cheap liquor.[24]

Tenements and Urban Space

The tenement dwellers of the city were also intimately familiar with the street. Their poverty and insecurity resembled that of the homeless transients. But most people in the slums tried to maintain some degree of privacy, some tenuous difference between their living space and the world outside. Their struggle to retain that distinction and the role which the saloon played in sorting out what was private and what was public provide meaningful insight into their lives.

For many slum dwellers the streets and sidewalks were an arena of economic survival. There were countless peddlers who sold from carts and wagons, while other portable entrepreneurs made their living recycling other people's castoff items. This business provided an important economic link between neighborhoods of differing social classes and ethnic groups. The junkman diligently picked through the piles of debris swept nightly to the curbstone in front of stores. If lucky, he might find some scrap of metal or other object that possessed a resale value.[25]

The housing situation was common in almost every major American city. Ramshackle structures, remnants from an earlier and less-congested age, held dozens of families where few had once lived. Back-lot slums were common. In Chicago they were often older homes carried to the rear of the property to make way for larger buildings that would front on the streets. Boston's hilly topography and irregular street pattern created a form of hidden misery all its own. Its rear yards, although irregularly shaped, had proved tempting to speculators and landlords and were quickly filled with jerry-built housing that covered nearly every square foot of land. In either case there was little or no open space for air and light. Some residents of Chicago's near West Side, in fact, had fewer cubic feet of breathing space than the state law required of flop houses.

Inside the tenements the presence of nonfamily lodgers aggrevated the crowding problem. Nineteenth-century immigration had brought vast numbers of single men to America. Some had left their families behind and were trying to accumulate enough money to pay additional boat fares; shared housing facilities helped to reduce living expenses. Others made so little money that they could not afford private quarters. In either case the members of the most recently arrived nationalities — Bulgarians, Serbs, Croations, Greeks, Italians, and Poles — set up cooperative housekeeping efforts in tenements and cheap rooms over saloons. One in their group served as boss and handled the cooking, rent collecting, and other business of the surrogate family.[26]

Tenement life almost completely lacked privacy. Overcrowding left living spaces with undifferentiated functions. The family cooked, ate, slept, laundered, and passed idle hours in a common room. According to Northwestern University Settlement House worker George Nesmith, they bathed with "frequent infringement upon the sense of modesty." Internal privacy was further compromised by the frequent presence of boarders, taken in to defray the burden of rent.[27] The instrusion of home manufactures brought the sweatshop into the living space, where the temporal rhythm of quitting time was lacking.[28]

The lack of facilities within the tenement also brought its residents in constant contact with the street. The lack of running water meant frequent trips to a common tap or well. Coal or firewood in amounts larger than a basket was too great an investment, and the family lacked a place to store it.[29] The only toilet facility was a common vault in the basement. In some Chicago neighborhoods the elevation of the street grade left the first floor of the house lower than the pavement surface. Planks over the subterranean front yard linked the street with the new front door on the second floor. Residents frequently carved a privy into the side of the embankment, where, symbolically, they found relief in the middle of the street.[30] Finally, the lack of refrigeration and storage space meant that the poor had to purchase their food almost daily or survive on nonperishabiles; this meant another trip to the market, peddler's cart, or grocer.[31]

The public life of the poor disturbed social reformers. The filth of the streets invaded the home, where residents' personal traits of hygiene, dress, and behavior reflected the garbage-strewn streets of the slums. Such groups as Chicago's Municipal Order League believed that the environment made the people; cleaner streets meant less social disorganization. Boston's Robert Treat Paine saw criminal behavior among youth spread by the "constant contact and dangerous intimacy" with the street. The cure was "the privacy of a separate home." Similarly, model tenement schemes called for conveniences obviating dependence on the street.[32]

Milk, Water, and Beer

Liquor, in one form or another, played an important part in the domestic life of the slums. Many residents saw it as the only pure and wholesome drink available. The water they carried away from the common tap was often barely potable. Bostonians were more fortunate, since the general scarcity of fresh water had prompted the city government to construct the Cochituate Reservoir and enforce the maintenance of ample pipes to service the needs of its citizens. Even then the water often emitted a strange smell and was seldom crystal clear. But the problems encountered in the Hub were never as serious as those of Chicagoans. The ample supplies in Lake Michigan — preserved by reversing the flow of the Chicago River — along with the ease of drilling into the high water table underground had made Chicago's government unjustifiably self-confident. Frozen pipes halted service in winter, and small fish flowed from faucets in summer. Backyard wells, placed too close to privy vaults, were easily contaminated.[33] By the 1890s, Chicago's problems had even gained national fame. As *Puck*, a New York humor magazine, quipped: "Mr. Murray Hill [a New Yorker]: Do you have mixed drinks here? Chicago Bartender (pouring a glass of water): Yes. How does that strike you?"[34]

Nor could many mothers trust the milk supply. In most large cities it was either unsafe or widely thought to be suspicious even when it was pure. It frequently spoiled enroute from farm to table, and negligence at each step along the way increased the hazards. Unscrupulous dairies skimmed the cream, watered the remainder, and added a blue coloring to hide the milk's deterioration. Wagons that delivered the product used unclean containers and were not refrigerated. The sanitary conditions of the neighborhood stores were frequently quite poor; the same problems of broken sewer pipes, vermin, and dirt that characterized housing could also be found in the shops where the tenement residents purchased their food. Finally, few homes had facilities to keep the milk cold; it had to be consumed immediately or thrown away.[35]

The poor quality of public water and milk supplies encouraged many families to turn to substitutes. Few could afford to purchase purified water in bottles, and many turned to beer. There was a widespread belief that it had great nutritive value. Despite the contrary advice of temperance propaganda, most people believed the legendary Martin J. Dooley, when he advised that "liquor is food. It is though. Food — and drink."[36] Beer had been pasteurized, so customers felt that it was pure. The saloons where they purchased it were often the cleanest places in the neighborhood. More demanding patrons could even carry it away in bottles that provided even more insurance of purity. Beer was cold when purchased, but it could also be consumed at room temperature; unlike milk, it would not spoil. Since parents frequented the saloon anyway, it required little extra effort to bring home a pail for the children or to send the youngsters after one. The daytime hours, when most working men were preoccupied by their labors, saw a healthy growler trade that was destined for consumption by women and children. According to one account, tenement wives in Chicago's Italian neighborhoods carried on extensive socializing that was initiated when someone produced a growler of beer.[37]

The brewers, seeing the potential for profit, consciously played on people's fears. As one advertisement in the *Boston Globe* announced in 1901:

Sterilized?

Sure! We are very particular on that point — as it is the satisfying touch that makes "Roessle Premium" (Export Brand) complete, and not only safeguards it as regards stray germs, but renders it "immune" from chemical change.

If you regard your health, pay strict attention to the particular brand of lager beer you drink. *You can* trust "Premium."[38]

Ads like that sold a lot of beer in middle-class neighborhoods where the water was bad, as well as in the slums.

Beer was frequently cheaper than milk, and that fact brought settlement houses into the dairy business. Not only did the reformers aim a constant stream of criticism at the laxity of health officials, but they also began to supply milk directly to tenement families. Chicago settlements established some eighteen milk stations in congested districts. Handbills, printed in foreign languages as well as English, told mothers that *"Latte Puro Pei Bambini,"* or "Pure Milk for your Babies," was available at eight ounces for two cents. The dispersal of the milk stations was designed to challenge the ubiquity of the saloon and the cheap grocery store. While the settlements undoubtedly fell short of the latter goal, the tens of thousands of bottles of milk they distributed had an enormous benefit in slum neighborhoods. The publicity surrounding the project stimulated health officials into action against the adulterated product.[39]

Public Eyes: The Law and Order Movement

Drinking by children and habitually inebriated adults, especially in the tenement districts, revived a long tradition of sumptuary legislation to protect the unfortunate from the effects of their own actions. The role of government as the policeman of personal excesses dated back as far as colonial Massachusetts. A statute enacted in 1630 banned liquor sales to children, Indians, and drunkards. Since innkeepers might have some difficulty recognizing the latter, authorities were to circulate a "drunkards list" of forbidden customers. To facilitate enforcement, a 1798 law encouraged leading citizens to visit the town's drinking places and watch for violations. Thus, for many of the poor, imbibing was becoming an increasingly public act.[40]

With the return of legal liquor after the demise of the mid-nineteenth-century Maine Law agitation, the legislatures of Illinois and Massachusetts reinacted sumptuary legislation in the form of dramshop acts. Passed in Illinois in 1872 and in Massachusetts three years later, these statutes not only reiterated the old prohibition of sales to minors and drunkards, but also made both licensed and illegal sellers financially responsible for the actions and fate of those forbidden customers and their dependents. During ensuing decades of litigation, the courts of both states tended to broaden the dealers' liability to include such things as the physical damage an inebriate might inflict on the property of others and financial responsibility for the effects of lost income on his family. The devastating impact of liquor on a child's health could also be measured in monetary terms by a court.[41]

The dramshop acts, however, had one practical flaw; they depended on the aggrieved to initiate a law suit. Since many of the poor had neither the sense of efficacy nor the funds to hire an attorney, the laws were ineffective through most of the 1870s. It took a dramatic event in Chicago, the Railroad Riots of 1877, to inspire a concerted effort to make the dramshop acts a powerful tool against saloonkeepers. That cataclysmic strike led to street violence in several major cities, including Chicago, where thirteen men were killed. In the aftermath a group of prominent business and civic leaders met secretly to discuss the causes. It was their consensus that intoxicated minors had been responsible for much of the bloodshed and that saloonkeepers and inefficient police shared the blame for supplying the youths with liquor. That November the new Citizens' League of Chicago for the Suppression of the Sale of Liquor to Minors and Drunkards went into business. Drawing upon the old principle from colonial liquor law that the substantial citizens had a special duty to provide sumptuary guidance to the poor, the league also took advantage of the fact that the saloon was a place of public access. Platoons of volunteer and paid agents went to work with the announced purpose of helping the police watch for violations. The Chicago effort gained national publicity and spread to several cities, including Boston, where the Citizens' Law and Order League was formed in May 1882. Eventually, it became a national movement.[42]

"The law and order crusade," as it was popularly known, employed several methods of gaining evidence. Often the league agent simply entered the barroom, watched whom the bartender served, and obtained the names and addresses of minors or inebriates by following them home. Then the agent would file an affidavit and complaint with the police and try to persuade relatives to sue. On occasion the league men would be accompanied in their rounds by a youth nearing adulthood; despite the obvious entrapment of the saloonist, the league usually made the charges stick. Other personnel kept a constant vigil in the courts, watching for cases that might lead to dramshop suits. Agents would approch a potential plaintiff and promise free legal service. As a result of these efforts, the number of dramshop cases rose dramatically. In its first full year, 1878, the Chicago group won 164 of 241 cases; in

1884 the success rate was 1694 of 2042 suits, this, when there were only 2928 saloons in the city. The Boston league claimed a similar rate of prosecutions.[43]

The saloonkeepers' response was predictable. They claimed that they were being singled out unfairly and that not even gun dealers were liable for murders carried out by their customers. League "spotters," as they were called in Boston, lived dangerously. The *New England Trader*, a liquor journal, published "Wanted" posters bearing likenesses of league agents. During the 1880s investigators in both cities were severely beaten by saloonkeepers and customers. Andrew Paxton, owner of a temperance restaurant and head of the Chicago league, was set upon in the street by one dealer, emboldened by several glasses of what the *Tribune* called "Dutch Courage." Paxton nearly died.[44]

Despite the terror they caused the liquor trade, the law and order movement faded into obscurity during the 1890s. It became nearly impossible to find men willing to risk life and limb as an agent. The leagues also gradually lost their uniqueness, in part because other temperance groups imitated their use of the dramshop law and also because the leagues themselves widened their activities to include lobbying for other antisaloon legislation. In doing so, they began to compete more directly against other groups for funds. Finally, and most important, the press and the judges tired of the growing excesses of the leagues. By the 1890s the Illinois courts were routinely dismissing cases involving minors hired to entrap sellers, and the newspapers no longer spoke of the leagues as if they had any semiofficial status. Only once, in 1878 in Chicago, could league agents actually arrest violators, but there were numerous instances in both cities where they burst into saloons claiming to be "special police" and smashed the fixtures and stock. Near the end of the 1890s both leagues were having trouble raising funds, and in 1901 the Boston Citizens' Law and Order League quietly folded. Its Chicago counterpart, meanwhile, was absorbed by what was about to become the state's leading antiliquor group, the Anti-Saloon League.[45]

Street Children and the Saloon

The goal of the citizens' leagues in separating youth from liquor was also hopeless because poverty thrust minors into the same dependence on public and semipublic spaces as their parents, and liquor was such a pervasive element in that lifestyle.[46] Tenement children grew up in the

street, which served as their playground. Lax enforcement of weak truancy laws also made the sidewalk their school. For thousands of mes-
sengers, peddlers, newsboys, and bootblacks, many of them homeless,
the street was residence and workplace as well.[47] George Needham's
1884 study of *Street Arabs and Gutter Snipes* had aroused considerable
sympathy for the homeless youth, and some of the earliest charities in
both cities tried to provide shelter.[48] As social worker Philip Davis of
Boston noted: "Street Children, like the streets, are in a peculiar sense
public property of which the community is trustee. As the street department represents the community's sense of obligation towards public property of one kind, so the education and recreation must reflect
concretely its sense of responsibility toward the children of the street.
The streets, heretofore no body's special business, ought in this sense to
become our common concern."[49]

Many observers regarded the abundance of urchins as more than a
series of individual tragedies. Not only were they the products of in-
human flaws in the American economic order, but they also symbolized
the collapse of the family. Children's labor had long been considered
an important supplement to the family economy in rural areas, but
charity and social workers of the late nineteenth century began to see
youthful employment in cities as a different matter. The child on the
street dissolved the bond of protective private intimacy that was the
very essence of family life. And it was in the slum district that the social
malady became so common.[50]

Educators also had to compete with the alluring attractions of the
street. The crowd provided the anonymity necessary for pranks or petty crimes. It offered countless ways to earn a penny and even more
places to spend it. The school could not win back the child's interest.
One observer of the high rate of truancy was Chester Carney, a University of Michigan sociology student. While on a fellowship to study slum
life near the Chicago Commons settlement on the near northwest side,
Carney observed:

> Every jangling street-car leads to the fairyland of the unknown.
> Shop windows are full of a thousand wonders for a boy of ten, if he
> can never own the toys in the flesh he can possess them in spirit as
> he flattens his nose against the plate-glass; magic mills run by real
> water from a yard-long river; clowns tell the wonders of a cure-all;
> street fakirs will sell a whole tool kit for ten cents, if one can get to
> him through the crowd of admiring little arabs; there is the ever-

present street-piano, with its strangely dressed man or woman; for his diversion the animals in the park are next best to a circus; is he hungry, a corner fruit-stand gives him a chance to test the adage of "stolen fruit."[51]

In the opinion of many observers the street became a direct threat to the well-being of the child. Not only were there physical hazards in playing in front of wagons and streetcars, but there were moral dangers as well. Seduction by "white slavers" awaited careless girls. In 1902 one Boston minister proclaimed that "picture windows daily feed the eyes of many of these children with mercilessly vicious illustrated materials," and "gross and lurid billboards" were all too visible "in the streets where men and women are housing their children." But to that same observer, the saloon was the most familiar and had the easiest access of any public room for many boys and girls. Liquor became one of the greatest threats to the wholesome lives of city children.[52]

There were several ways in which a child might come into contact with alcohol. Reformers periodically complained that the innocents were able to purchase candy that was filled with liquor. The Citizens' Law and Order Leagues and, later, Chicago's Juvenile Protective Association instigated inquiries into the sale of the potent bonbons, but were able to do little to stop the problem. Dealers were scattered across the city and remained mobile. The secrecy of the trade, which few children bothered to report, made it difficult to trace and control.[53]

By contrast, liquor sales by unscrupulous bartenders were more common.[54] Occasionally, it was a neighborhood kid who wanted a drink, and the dealer willingly granted the request. A newsboy who sold papers in saloons could often obtain a "nip" to help him face the cold wind outside. The bartender could also be drawn into the deed by a "young mustache," who appeared to be twenty-one but really was a minor. Not until world war brought the selective service card could a dealer be sure. But most saloonmen who slid the glass across the counter to a boy were really after a few more nickels in the till. That was just as true when a Chicago grand jury investigated the problem in 1883 as it was two decades later, when Chicago teachers discovered that their students had "beer cards." The proprietor of a nearby drinking house punched the card each time the youthful bearer sneaked in for a drink. At the end of each month, the boy with the most punches received a prize.[55]

The involvement of children in street gangs was another serious problem. The friendships and social contacts children made in the street assumed a structured hierarchy of power and authority. Acting as an "army" against "invaders" from other neighborhoods, they adopted certain places as their headquarters.[56] Often, they chose a local saloon. There they played pool, drank beer or whiskey, and planned their activities. If they committed petty thievery or picked pockets, the proprietor might serve as a fence. But in any case, the barroom was a convenient and private refuge from the street.[57] Reformers could do little to stop the youth-gang saloon. The police refused to prosecute the offenders, and the secretive nature of the activity made it difficult to trace.

Instead, the juvenile advocates concentrated their efforts on attempting to end a more obvious and public contact between youth and liquor, the growler trade. The homely tin pail was almost universally found in the immigrant neighborhoods, where it served many purposes. It was cheap and nearly indestructable, especially when equipped with a homemade lining of tar, and served many purposes for adults. It could protect a lunch from the jostling bumps of a streetcar crowd or from the weather. It carried coffee and a small bottle of whiskey for consumption during the working hours of the morning. But at noon and again at home in the evening it held about a half-gallon of beer, and that proved to be the most controversial aspect of its existence.

Although there was a large growler trade among the tenement housewives, "rushing the can" was primarily a noontime ritual. Each day dozens of boys would flock around the factory gates to pick up the workers' pails. By placing a six- or eight-foot pole on their shoulders, the heartier youths could carry a dozen or more in one trip. Each got a penny for his efforts, and the workers who carried their lunches were able to avoid wasting their precious break fighting the saloon crowds. Out in the stockyards district of Chicago, dozens of boys who were out of school found this a profitable form of self-employment. An eager "rusher" might also receive an offer to help the proprietor clean the place. And for a fortunate few, it even became the first step toward setting up their own saloons.[58]

Customers and bartenders also engaged in a subtle "battle of the foam." The man at the tap attempted to produce a larger head. He added a furtive pinch of salt or rinsed the glasses in salty dishwater. A few shook the glass while filling it. Crafty drinkers attempted to obtain more beer and less suds by rubbing the walls of their growlers with soap or tar. This reduced the friction and allegedly produced a heavier can of beer. No one, however, mentioned what it did to the taste.[59]

By the 1880s, the can trade had become a regular feature of the factory district. Even then, few people other than the drinkers and the rushers were happy about it. Temperance advocates complained that the cheap nickel or dime price caused workers to consume too much. Health specialists warned of the physiological dangers of gulping down large quantities of cold beer after heavy labor. Juvenile reformers claimed that tender youth was introduced to the barroom habit at an early age.

Some of the most severe criticism came from the liquor interests themselves. As early as 1889 the West Side Saloonkeepers' Association complained that filling growlers amounted to selling beer wholesale to the public. That practice sliced their profits, but all of the dealers would have to join in the effort to end it; a few holdouts could ruin everyone. This failed because little more than half of all proprietors belonged to the association.

After that initial attack, the organized liquor trade continued its efforts to persuade Chicago dealers to curb the growler sales. Every few years the members of the various local divisions listened to angry speeches and passed strong resolutions condemning the homely can. But none of these efforts had much of an impact. In 1906 the Liquor Dealers' Association attempted to induce its members to raise the growler price to a dime. The headquarters sent out large announcement cards for the members to display on their backbar mirrors. The *Champion of Fair Play* even printed stories disclosing that the Health Department was about to investigate the quality of the beer used in the growler trade; rumors circulated that some saloonmen collected dregs and leftovers from customers' glasses and secretly dispensed them to the unknowing can rusher. None of these scare tactics worked. Despite another attempt to revive the issue in 1912, the price of a growler remained the same down to the last day of legal beer.[60]

Voluntary actions were apparently of no use, so the antigrowler retailers turned to the legal system. One way to reduce the can trade was to eliminate the practice of allowing youngsters to purchase beer. The adult himself or herself — women went to the back door — would have to go to the saloon, and here he might be tempted to join his friends and purchase a standard-size glass. This would not only increase the dealers' profits, but it would also make them appear to be gravely concerned about the future of American youth. The first legislative action came in 1893, when state representative Michael McInerney introduced a new temperance bill in the General Assembly. The former Packingtown saloonkeeper wanted to have a parent thrown into jail for sending a child after beer. This bill was defeated in a house floor vote, seventy to thirty-six. Eleven years later John Powers, boss of the Nineteenth Ward (Near West Side), sponsored a similar bill during his short term in the state senate. The press ridiculed the measure. "Powers as a Reformer," read the headlines, and local politicians like Judge Adolph Sabath disagreed with it publicly. The jurist argued that the working man deserved a break after his hard day's work. Besides, solitary drinking in the privacy of the home had its advantages. It was a painless solution to the problems of treating friends to rounds, and, at the very least, the growler kept the family together during the evening. "Johnnie da Pow" saw his bill die in committee.[61]

In 1904 the Chicago City Council accomplished what the state legislature failed to do the previous year. By an overwhelming vote of fifty-four to ten it adopted an ordinance that ordered the saloonkeepers not to deliver any liquor to minors, even if they had a note from their parents. The issue divided the six liquor dealers sitting in the council, and its passage immediately threw the growler trade into confusion. Some of the Polish saloonmen on the Southwest Side called for its immediate repeal, claiming that the "laboring people loudly demand it." But the real source of concern was whether or not it would ever be enforced; law books were filled with ordinances that most people ignored. The liquor men tried to use their downtown contacts to learn the answer, but after a few symbolic arrests the fate of the new law was clear. In a few months children once again were carting growlers home to papa and rushing cans at the factory gate.[62]

The 1904 law was a failure. No one doubted that. The Citizens' League of Chicago, now merged into a larger organization known as the Anti-Saloon League, wanted to revive the idea that all respectable citizens should help the police ferret out offenders. A child carrying a growler, after all, constituted an obvious violation of the law. But the age of citizen-policemen had all but passed. For three years, the police made no attempt to enforce the law, but their inaction helped forge one of the strangest alliances in the history of the saloon. It began in

1907, when the leadership of the dealers' association held its regular monthly meeting. There were seven visitors that afternoon — a priest, a minister, two businessmen, and three matronly women — and they looked peculiarly out of place at a saloonkeepers' gathering. They were reformers, representatives of the Juvenile Protective Association. The latter group had been formed only a few months earlier in order to publicize the adverse living conditions of wayward youth and to lobby for remedial legislation. After a few nervous moments the barkeepers extended a warm welcome. The JPA stressed its belief that "90 percent" of the city's barmen were honest and refused to sell liquor to children. The saloonkeepers' association, which was anxious to eliminate the growler, reiterated its desire to abide by the law. And so that afternoon the two groups initiated an alliance. They exchanged cordial correspondence, and when the Cook County dealers held their annual banquet, the representatives of the JPA were honored as special guests.[63]

The détente lasted for a few years before it gradually dissolved. The liquor men helped to prosecute a few dealers and continued to warn their members about the evils of selling to minors. And when the JPA's chief publicist, Louise DeKoven Bowen, attacked the saloon dance halls, she was always careful to point out that these were run only by the most disreputable dealers. The reformers even made vaguely favorable comments about the Liquor Dealers' Association, which basked in the positive publicity. Of the two groups, the liquor men clearly had the most to gain. Not only did the relationship enhance their image in the community, but it helped the honest saloonkeepers police their own trade, something they had never been able to do previously. But the initial purpose of the alliance was never fulfilled. The cheap growler, delivered over the bar to a youngster, remained a feature of the working-class saloon up to the beginning of prohibition.[64]

The Saloon as an Extension of the Home

One of the most important aspects of the saloon's flexibility was its unusual ability to adapt its services to the temporal rhythm of the neighborhood. During the early morning hours — most places opened at either 5:00 or 6:00 A.M. — it served the working men, who sought a morning bracer with the coffee they often carried in their lunch pails. At noon there was the lunchtime crowd. There were dozens of men grasping for the free food, while the can rushers pushed their way through the throng. The afternoon hours saw a busy trade at the back or side door, when women would come to the barroom entrance or send their children after a can of beer or a little whiskey or wine for "cooking" purposes. Finally, for the late afternoon and evening hours, the barroom became the man's domain once again.[65]

The attraction of the workingman to the saloon was mysterious and magnetic, involving both "push" and "pull" factors. Charity and settlement workers alike accepted the notion that the dreary monotony of slum life drove people to drink. In its various forms, alcohol was the most ubiquitous opiate, the cheapest escape. But the problem affected men and women in different ways. According to one account, "A woman's drinking brings both the liquor and its effects more directly into the house than does his." And since "a woman's acquaintances are apt to be her immediate neighbors, . . . her drinking habits are often directly due to the influence of these neighbors."[66] In other words, those reformers who saw the ravaging effects of alcohol on the family were quick to believe that, even among the lower class, drinking among women was more private than among men. They perceived the significance of the fact that women, or their children, toted the growler from the saloon to the home during the day, while the men left the home as much in search of a place to drink as of something to drink.[67]

Tenement women were also deeply involved in the illegal liquor traffic, especially in Boston. The scarce licenses and high fees had produced a demand for drink that far exceeded its lawful availability. Municipal authorities had tried to concentrate legal bars along heavily traveled thoroughfares, supposedly sparing the neighborhoods from the saloon evil. The result was a lively kitchen barroom trade, so named because many back-door sales were actually made over the kitchen table. Much in the manner of the sweatshop and other domestic industries, economic activity had penetrated the division between the family's private space and the public areas and people outside. And because women were so often home, in the kitchen, they played a significant role in this trade.

The kitchen barroom arrangement in Boston was convenient. The location of the place was common knowledge among neighborhood drinkers, but sellers also had to remain secret enough to evade honest police officers. On occasion, when knowledgeable police felt compelled to make a raid, they temporarily traded precincts where, in the words of one observer, they could "keep out of embarrassment." When "pulled," sellers could claim that the authorities had barged in on a private home. The liquor stock was commonly distributed throughout the place, so that family members or lodgers could claim ownership of the bottles. The proprietor then introduced the customer as a friend being treated to a neighborly drink. Those dealers too timid or handling too much business to use these excuses had to resort to standard ways of concealing their stock. Bottles disappeared into secret panels in walls and into oversize waste pipes under sinks. One genius even installed a tank in his wall and dispensed liquor through a gas jet.[68]

The volume of these sales upset neighborhood settlement workers, whose fears closely resembled those expressed during the 1867 hearings on the failures of statewide prohibition. When Vida Scudder, Helen Cheever, Emily Green Balch, and Laura Cate founded Boston's Denison House in 1893, they began keeping a detailed diary which made frequent mention of the problem. On January 15, 1892, Helen Cheever noted what happened when she visited one tenement building: "Went to Mrs. Julia Sullivan's—While there a dazed sort of man came in and asked for ten cents worth. Mrs. S. protested she had no money. He said he did not mean that, but ten cents worth. Mrs. S. whispered that he could get what he wanted upstairs. . . . Soon afterwards we heard a man put downstairs and out of doors, and Mrs. S. remarked that the man upstairs was rolling in money for selling liquor, and then when one of the poor fellows who paid him got drunk he was put out that cruelly."[69] Thus, not only did the kitchen barroom bring strangers into the tenement building, but in cases where the dramshop acts might apply, it was harder to prove the identity of the seller. Finally, many kitchen barrooms sold the worst quality liquor. Often it consisted of "barrel washings," adulterated but cheap.[70]

The saloon, legal or secret, also became involved in the problem of domestic tranquility. Here it played a curiously ambivalent role. There was an element of truth to the standard prohibitionist argument that it was a housebreaker. Hours spent at "Dinny's" were hours away from the family. The debilitating effect of the alcohol could make a workingman less productive and more liable to lose his job. The temptation was always present to squander the paycheck on the way home. There is no accurate way to measure the extent of the problem, but its emotional appeal made it one of the most frequently mentioned and poignant antiliquor arguments; little Nell, searching for her "pop" amidst the drunken revelry in a barroom, was frequently the object of pity in

morality plays. Not even the saloon's strongest defenders could deny
that to some extent they were true.

But the saloon was not the only villain of the piece. Conditions in
many families had deteriorated on their own, a fact that many social
workers were only too quick to admit. Drink was the symptom rather
than the disease. Workers at the Northwestern University Settlement,
on the Near Northwest Side of Chicago, blamed poor home life and a
significant lack of warmth and privacy for the saloon's popularity.
Loving parents would deter the growth of street gangs, and a tightly
knit family would insure that the homeward-bound father would by-
pass the swinging doors. To add to the argument, Judge Greenbaum of
the Chicago Municipal Court warned that it was their wives' atrocious
cooking that drove men to the free lunch table. Court statistics ranked
drinking low on the list of causes of divorce. And a few settlement
workers even went so far as to say that the corner saloon was responsible for saving as many marriages as it broke up.[71]

The saloon, then, could function as a family safety valve, a convenient way for men to escape from the crowded tenements. But this was
not the only economic institution that offered this kind of semipublic
service. Robert Woods, the settlement house leader, noted that there
was also a marked increase in the number of restaurants in Boston's
slums near the turn of the century. Families sought out eateries operated by their fellow countrymen and spent their last pennies on cheap
food, mainly as a way to escape their domestic surroundings. This development worried the charity and settlement workers, for it indicated
the decline of the dinner table, one of the last important family functions left at home. When that was gone, the family as an institution
was itself in danger.[72]

The reformers responded by establishing various kinds of domestic
science training programs. Settlements like the Chicago Commons and
Hull House started cooking schools to improve the skills of immigrant
housewives. Other programs taught the basics of household sanitation,
and the University of Chicago even compiled a booklet of public health
ordinances for housekeepers. The Chicago Woman's Club established a
voluntary School of Domestic Arts and Science, which trained servants
as well as others, and then successfully lobbied for the establishment of
such courses in the public school system.

Meanwhile, philanthropic Bostonians set up the New England Kitchen in 1891. This charitable enterprise was designed to train servants

and to provide low-cost meals that tenement wives could take home to their families. These activities, as well as others mentioned above, were designed to make the home a more attractive and efficient place. And, indirectly, they had as their goal the redemption of husbands from the saloon.[73]

The domestic science movement was only one of several ways in which social reformers attempted to alter the relationship between the tenement family and its public environment. It was difficult to change the habits of the poor and equally hard to remake their living places. But it was relatively easy to establish substitutes or supplements for what was lacking at home.

For example, Boston began discussing public bath houses as early as 1860. A special committee, appointed that year by the Board of Aldermen, recommended that some means be found "for making them [the 'poor classes'] clean and enhance their health."[74] Privately owned commercial baths were too expensive for the "middling class" single people of the respectable boarding houses, let alone the slum dweller. The committee suggested that the waterfront be used first, but it took another seven years before Boston opened the first of its "floating baths." These were the earliest publicly managed swimming facilities in the United States, and their immediate success prompted the city to open fourteen indoor baths and several other outdoor ones in the following decades. The addition of swimming pools provided year-round recreation in the tenement neighborhoods where it was needed the most.[75]

Most of Boston's baths had already been erected before Chicago finally opened its first public facility. The latter city's government had always held a laissez-faire attitude toward its public places. Street trades operated freely, and thousands slept in the parks. Chicago, for want of interest or funds, was unwilling to invest money or space in enterprises to help its poor. It took considerable pressure from the private reform groups, especially the Municipal Order League, to shake officials from their lethargy. But finally, in 1894, the Carter Harrison Bath opened on the Near West Side, the first of twenty-one such facilities that would be scattered through the slums by the end of World War I. Even then, Chicago's baths were strictly utilitarian and contained no swimming pools or recreation facilities of any other kind. Anything that would promote loitering or provide anything beyond basic services met stern disapproval from the tight-fisted Health Department.[76]

The idea of providing semipublic institutions to bolster the family met its most severe test during the warmer months. The summer heat greatly intensified the public orientation of tenement life. The buildings became unbearable, and the residents virtually abandoned them to join the more transient classes outdoors. At night, adults could commonly be found where children played during the day. "The people sleep on the streets, sidewalks and the yards, where there are yards," observed the social critic Robert Hunter in his study of Chicago slums.[77] Social life and most family activities moved to the porches and steps. As a Boston newspaper reporter noted, "It is on the roof of the tenement that many of the poor spend the best part of the summer evening," and during heat waves those tarred boards were covered with sleepers.[78]

In Chicago the poor were effectively closed off from the major parks and beaches by the physical size of the city and the isolation of the tenement neighborhoods. Nickel fares, often without transfer privileges, made it too expensive for the workingman to take his family on the streetcar, and the distance was too great to walk. Some of the most congested neighborhoods were as much as five miles from the nearest parklands, while the web of railway tracks crossing at grade level made it difficult to travel out of some neighborhoods. As one commentator put it: "While Chicago has provided liberally for her people in the matter of large and beautiful parks, it has been discovered now that it is too late, that their parks are enjoyed only by the rich. Their homes surround them, their carriages cover their drives, and the fresh air and the blooms exist only for them alone. . . . Accordingly, the class that does not need the park, or at least is able to pay for its fresh air, monopolizes it, while the class that needs it above all and for whom it was especially designed, is debarred from its enjoyment."[79]

Conclusion: The Saloon and the Poor

Americans have always had great difficulty deciding the question of how public or private the lives of the poor should be. During the first half of the nineteenth century institutionalization was widely accepted as the proper policy toward those on the public dole. Isolated, supposedly to keep them in a protective and uplifting environment, almshouse inmates were denied both the privacy of the family domicile and access to the public streets, where they might beg and loiter. Society could thus avoid the unpleasantness of encountering its failures. But scandal, cruelty to those confined, and the inability of facilities to keep up with the expansion of the ranks of the poor brought "indoor relief" into disfavor. "Outdoor" aid allowed recipients of the dole to live in their own quarters, supposedly with much greater privacy and dignity than life in the poorhouse could provide.

In reality, however, the postpoorhouse period saw the thin line between public and private dissolve. The lower the depths of poverty, the greater the dependence on the public space of the streets and sidewalks for survival. Transients spent their summers squatting outdoors and their winters in saloons and flophouses, both of which were semipublic places. Life allowed few long-term plans beyond daily survival and even fewer economic choices: panhandling, jack-rolling, and day labor were their means of making a living. Tattered clothing was a visible sign of low status that led to exclusion from the rest of society. And the presence of this floating population contributed to the American notion that the streets of the large industrial city were dangerous, unsightly, and filthy.

Charity workers could do little to alleviate the problems of single transient men, aside from providing wholesome semipublic alternatives to the flop and the bar. But families in tenement districts presented greater possibilities for reform, clouded by sadder consequences of failure. The poor of the North, South, and West Ends of Boston and Chicago's Maxwell Street and Back-of-the-Yards lived at more permanent addresses and enjoyed more privacy that did flophouse dwellers. At least the tenement had a front door. But even then, the lack of food and fuel storage space, toilets, and water within the tenement unit brought residents constantly to the street. Cramped, stuffy quarters drove them to seek leisure on rooftops, fire escapes, and sidewalks. And such semipublic spaces as the saloon for men, the grocery shop for women, and the cheap theater for families became, in effect, extensions or enlargements of inadequate living spaces. The poorhouse had represented one type of public living space; life outside merely saw the substitution of other nonprivate living areas.

It was the saloon, however, that attracted the attention of charity and settlement house workers and moved them into the antiliquor camp. The barroom provided intoxicants that left the breadwinner an inefficient worker, more likely to be unemployed. Too many paychecks never made it home. Family ties weakened because husbands spent idle hours away from home, while the lack of a stable and private home life allowed youth to stray into the saloonkeeper's grasp. Rushing the growler led to drinking from it, while youth gangs made saloons their headquarters and graduated to more serious offenses. The saloon even took advantage of the lack of toilets, the poor milk, and the shortage of clean water in the neighborhood to lure customers who, in turn, were expected to purchase the obligatory beer.

While there was, of course, a strong element of truth in the reform indictment, the involvement of the barroom in the social lives of the poor was as much a matter of effect as it was cause. The tenement dwellers turned to the saloon because there were few alternatives, while the proprietor gladly catered to them because the marginal economics of his business forced him to chase every nickel.

Social reformers of various types approached the problem from several directions. The earliest religious missionaries established tenement outposts and attempted to appeal to a sense of self-preservation and self-control among the poor. Those who publicly signed pledges swore on Bibles never to drink again.[80] The notion of appealing to self-preservation also prompted the Scientific Temperance Instruction that began in Boston in the 1870s. By the end of the century most states required that children receive a minimum number of hours of course work on the adverse effect of alcohol on the human body.[81] The great educational efforts of the Woman's Christian Temperance Union, through tracts and rallies, were likewise designed to reach the drinker's sense of reason. But the drink problem grew.[82]

The vast expansion of the saloons' ranks by the 1870s, fueled in the following decades by investments by brewing companies, brought a response in the form of the dramshop acts and the Law and Order Leagues formed to enforce them. They emphasized the role of the drink dispenser, rather than the drinker, as the cause of the problem. That crusade continued until the early part of the new century, when its supporters lost interest.

A third approach attempted to use the law to drive barrooms out of the slums. Boston licensing authorities, for instance, rejected many applications because the proposed bars were located too far from major commercial streets in poor neighborhoods, while the Abutters' Law allowed adjacent property owners to raise objections to applicants located too near schools, charity offices, and similar uplifting institutions. In 1888 temperance organizations pushed through the General Court a controversial law prohibiting liquor sales in dwellings of all types. The drys were consciously trying to separate the private life of the family from the public life of the saloons, both legitimate and kitchen barrooms. Although the tenement bill was enacted into law, the Massachusetts Supreme Court nullified its effect by approving residences above saloons, provided that there were separate entrances for each.[83]

The fourth attack on the saloon came mainly from settlement house workers, who promoted competitive substitutes on the neighborhood level. The reform of the tenement home played an important part in this approach. Domestic science classes were designed to make wives better homemakers, while followers of the Arts and Crafts movement promoted the unadorned, angular, Mission-style furniture as having great potential use in uplifting the home lives of the poor. Not only was the latter cheaper to build, but its plain design was considered masculine. Men would be less likely to drift off to saloons if they had comfortable places to spend their evenings at home and food, prepared by a domestic science graduate, that was superior to that found at the free lunch counter. In addition, of course, settlement houses also tried to compete with saloons by opening their doors to men's organizations and athletics.[84]

All of these antisaloon efforts essentially failed despite some minor successes. The poor were simply too dependent on the public and semi-public spaces of the city to consider privatizing their life-styles. Despite a valiant try, settlement and charity workers were outnumbered and outfinanced by the inviting phalanx of swinging doors.

CHAPTER 4

Public Politics
and the Saloon

Few aspects of the liquor business attracted as much comment as its relationship with electoral politics and the legislative process. To temperance speakers, the saloonkeeper-politician symbolized all that was wrong with the political system. He stood in the way of civil service reform. He paid off his cronies. He corrupted the scruples of the malleable immigrants. He wielded his influence to break the law. Settlement house worker Albert Kennedy recalled that in Boston "the affiliation between the saloon and politics was so close that for all practical purposes the two might have been under one and the same control."[1] And Massachusetts temperance writer Henry H. Faxon told civil service reformers that their goal must be to separate "the halls of legislation" from "the dramshops of the street."[2]

Everyone had his own explanation for the relationship of liquor and politics. Some attributed it to the Irish, and for years some of the most flamboyant politicians were also Irish saloonkeepers. Chicago's "Bathhouse John" Coughlin, whose loud dress and equivalent demeanor made him famous, graduated to saloonkeeping from the less-admired massage trade. His partner, Michael "Hinky Dink" Kenna, ran a pair of cheap lodging-house saloons just south of the downtown. There was Barney Grogan, who was important on the West Side, and Edward F. Cullerton, who reputedly made no speeches. In the Hub Patrick Kennedy and Jerry McNamara, both of South Boston, and Phil O'Brien of Charlestown were powerful Democrats.[3]

Another theory which borrowed heavily from temperance rhetoric maintained that the saloon sought protection and political privilege *only* because it provided an opportunity to break the law. There may have been some truth to the charge, but many divekeepers became involved in criminal activity *after* they had established their political base.

The large amount of saloon license revenue collected each year also endowed the liquor trade with a vested interest in government. Every increase in the annual fee made the municipalities more dependent on the white-apron brigade. This was less so in Boston, where license revenue in 1880 provided only 2 percent of the total city income; in 1895 it amounted to 6.2 percent. The severe limitation of licenses meant that the Hub City had to find other monies. By contrast, in Chicago there was no limit to the number of permits before 1906. In 1880 license revenue accounted for only 1.6 percent of the total, rising in 1886 to 12.4 percent. But the passage of a $1,000 license in 1906 meant that no less than 22.1 percent of all city income came from saloon license fees.[4] The situation led one observer to remark that "while much has been said about the evils of saloons in large cities, the fact is that we are dependent on the saloons to enable us to eke out a municipal existence. The taxpayers of Chicago ought to take off their hats to them."[5] Little wonder that some barmen thought they owned city hall.

This dependency also provided saloonkeepers with a means of protecting themselves against prohibitionists. It was especially true in Massachusetts, where local voters chose between legal liquor and prohibition at each December's elections. The Massachusetts Liquor League issued an annual warning that a dry vote meant fiscal suicide for municipalities. When Chelsea, an industrial suburb of Boston, experimented with prohibition in 1884, it had to increase its tax rate, impose new licenses on dozens of businesses, and even turn to requests for donations in order to keep its city government in operation. The same thing, the League warned, could happen in Boston. In 1889, when the high license and limitation bills were being considered by the General Court, the liquor dealers even threatened to join ranks with the No License League unless the measures were defeated.[6]

In Chicago the loss of license revenue was a more serious threat. As early as 1886, the *Western Brewer* noted that Illinois local governments received over $3 million in liquor license fees. Even the City Club of Chicago, a business-oriented governmental reform group, had to admit that the saloon licenses were a vital part of the city's income. Although good government interests felt that the license should be increased even more, they would not admit what would happen to city government if the high fees drove most bars out of business or turned them into blind pigs. Finally, in order to emphasize the dependency, in 1910 Alderman Anton Cermak led the City Council in directing the mayor and corporation counsel to report on ways to replace the $8 million received from saloon licenses. The answer was obvious before the inquiry began: there was no alternative. The General Assembly had frozen Chicago's ability to raise tax rates or float bond issues. Saloon license fees were the only means of averting municipal bankruptcy.[7]

Finally, saloonkeepers were naturally interested in politics because they believed that their trade was in constant danger at all times. No business remained as encumbered by as many regulations for as many years as did the saloon. In Boston the need to control the city government was less important, because the General Court traditionally enacted the liquor law and a police board, appointed after 1885 by the governor, handled its administration. But the composition of Chicago's City Council commanded constant vigilance. *Mixed Drinks*, the liquor newspaper, remarked: "It is time to stop being kicked and cuffed around, and for the saloon men and all lovers of personal liberty to take off their coats. . . . [The] silk-stocking Christians are quietly at work, and by all kinds of blandishments are endeavoring to elect a majority of their tools to the City Council, with the sole view of squeezing another $100 out of the saloon men in the way of a license fee and to deprive them of the profits of a day's work."[8]

The vigilance of the individual saloonkeeper and his trade organizations was especially important in Boston and Chicago because neither had a Tammany Hall-type centralized political structure. This situation, with power dispersed into many hands, built an element of unpredictability into the legislative process. There was always the nagging fear that a temporary alliance might decide to punish the liquor interests or, in a moment of fiscal embarrassment, press for a hike in the license fee. On the other hand, a dispersal of power into the hands of ward chieftains did allow talent to work its way upward from the precincts, rather than being imposed downward from a central organization.

Politicians in both cities found themselves working on two levels — the neighborhood and the larger world of the party. The latter was a diverse collection of competitive interests with no one faction gaining complete control. The trend in the last two decades of the nineteenth century was, in fact, in the opposite direction. Boston's most prominent ethnic political strategist of the 1880s had been P. J. Maguire, who served as chairman of the Democratic City Committee. Under his guidance Irish voters finally united as a bloc in 1885 to elect Hugh O'Brien, the Hub's first Catholic mayor. Panic-stricken Brahmins, who saw their power slipping away in favor of the Irish, quickly pushed through the General Court a law giving a board appointed by the governor complete control over the Boston police and all liquor licenses. But the fears of moral anarchy and governmental chaos were unfounded. O'Brien and his successor, another Maguire follower named Nathan Matthews, both proved to be fiscal conservatives. And neither allowed city hall to be sacked by the patronage-hungry ward politicians.

Boston's political system became more fragmented during the 1890s, when a new generation of ward bosses overthrew the aging Maguire in 1894. None of the newcomers — "Smiling Jim" Donovan, Joseph Corbett, John F. Fitzgerald, Patrick J. Kennedy, John A. Keliher, or Martin Lomasney — was powerful enough to seize even the limited authority that Maguire enjoyed. After warring for a few years they came to an uneasy truce in the form of a regular meeting group known as the Board of Strategy; only Lomasney, too much a maverick to be trusted, was excluded. The board promoted such mayors as Josiah Quincy, whose Brahmin name and deep desire to improve public facilities for the poor provided a perfect cover for the overloaded ward payrolls, nefarious city contracts, and campaigning at city expense. By the end of the 1890s corruption had come to Boston on a grand scale.[9]

Meanwhile, city hall politics in Chicago was even less centralized during the 1880s and decidedly more corrupt than in Boston. The chairman for much of the decade was Michael Cassius McDonald, a colorful gambler who used his earnings and "inflooence" to construct the Lake Street elevated line during the early 1890s. The mayoralty was dominated by Carter Harrison I (1879–87, 1893). Kentucky-born, wealthy, a commanding horseback figure with his familiar slouch hat, Harrison was personally honest, but he presided over a city government marked by nonstop scandals in the form of franchise bribes, padded payrolls, and every other form of malfeasance. Harrison's assassination in 1893 and McDonald's financial and political collapse as his elevated line sank into bankruptcy in the depression of the decade removed the party's two most influential figures. Party politics then fragmented completely into shifting coalitions and alliances of convenience motivated by the search for spoils. And a procession of one-term mayors, limited by their narrow charter powers, watched the corruption continue.[10]

Politics on the second level, the neighborhood, was more closely related to *how* an ambitious person got involved than *why* he did it.

Fame and fortune on the city hall level might have provided the lure, but almost everyone's career was rooted in the parochial concerns of the ward. Here, power operated according to a different set of values. Personality, rather than the ability to inflict damage on others, was the key, and everything depended upon the primary relationships of family or the secondary ties of friendship and much less on the tertiary contacts between strangers drawn together by some abstract ideology. At this level the saloon became a critical institution, a stepping-stone to the rank of statesman.

Information was the cornerstone of neighborhood political power. Detailed knowledge of the "small change" of everyday life — the labors, expectations, and problems of the citizenry — helped garner the votes. A variety of occupations, all related in some way to meeting people on the street or in some semipublic business, provided an education in communications for aspiring young politicos. Michael "Hinky Dink" Kenna had been a newsboy, while "Bathhouse John" Coughlin, coboss of Chicago's First Ward, had been a masseur. In Boston, Martin "The Mahatma" Lomasney started as a lamplighter, while "Smiling Jim" Donovan was a butcherboy. Two giants of a slightly later generation in Chicago, Republican Fred Lundin and Democratic Mayor Anton Cermak (1931–33) both started as peddlers, the former dispensing a temperance refreshment and the latter selling firewood. In all of these cases — by no means an exhaustive list — contact with future constituents taught what people expected from government as well as the complexities of how people communicated.

Keeping in Touch: Information Networks

The pattern of inner-city residence consisted of not just one community, but many of them, piled up as if in overlapping layers upon a single area of geographical space. Some parts of both cities had relatively homogeneous sections, such as the Italian and Jewish districts of Boston's North End or the vast German-speaking patches of Chicago's North Side. But in other areas a neighborhood might consist of a few buildings in one block, four or five in another, and still more a few blocks away. Thus, in West End Boston, the block bounded by Phillips, Cedar, Grove, and Revere streets contained blacks, Irish, "Americans," British Provincials (probably French Canadians), plus an unidentified mixed population. Only one clear pattern emerges — the tendancy toward what might be called "corner dominance." In virtually all of the intersections in West End Boston, a single group occupied at least three corners of virtually all intersections. The same was true in Chicago's Sixteenth Ward, while the generalization was slightly less accurate in the Hull House district. This pattern left interior alleys and midblock lots as ethnic boundaries and probably produced a distinct tendancy toward streetcorner neighboring. There is no precise way to determine how often it occurred, but if true, then a corner location would be all the more advantageous for a saloonkeeper.[11]

Community in the usual sense of the word was hard to identify. There was a constant turnover of population, with people moving as often as every few months. The housing became filthy, or the neighborhood became too crowded, or the breadwinner changed jobs; all of these causes could produce a hastily-planned move to another tenement. That fact, along with the mixture of people, often produced a condition of geographical proximity combined with social distance.[12] One description of Chicago's Near South Side Italian neighborhood, which was part of the city's vice district, noted that: "Italians, dirty but honest, men and women of decent character, so far as the moral code goes, are housed with the outcasts, the lowest and vilest in the city. They live side by side in the same building, and usually on terms of neighborliness with each other. Italians, Syrians and Arabians go there because they fancy rents are cheap. They speak their own language, herd together, make merry among their own people at weddings and christenings, and what goes on in the next flat or the next door or half a block away is nothing to them. Nobody in that district is exclusive."[13]

Yet there were also certain forces within each group that helped hold the neighborhood together. Alvan F. Sanborn, a resident of South End House settlement, wrote of "Bulfinch Street," a fictitious name he applied to one of the nearby tenement alleyways. Despite the poverty and the geographical mobility — "The Whitings have moved sixteen times in eight years" — there was still a sense of community. People shared each other's griefs and participated in a lively street life. They could spot strangers instantly. A common temporal rhythm governed their conduct. Neighboring was most intense during summer evenings, but the mingling went indoors during winter. Saturday night brought more drunkenness to Bulfinch Street, while the residents made "very noticible efforts" to "distinguish Sunday" by dressing up in their newest clothes "to attract the attention of neighbors." Monday was always wash day, unless it was a holiday.[14]

The tenement was a permanent part of urban life, and with it came a community life that thrived on the streets and in saloons. Some type of communications network, some kind of place for people to exchange information, was necessary in order to maintain neighborhood cohesiveness. For whole families, it was the porch; for children, it was the street; for women, it was the clothesline or the back stairs. But for men and, occasionally, their families, it was the saloon.

The most basic communications function was simply providing a place for face-to-face contact. This was especially important in areas with very low rates of literacy. An 1893 survey of several square blocks of tenements near Hull House revealed that only 34 percent of the population could read English; another 32 percent could read another language. This meant that somewhere between one- and two-thirds of the people there depended completely upon oral communications. Nearly 70 percent of one specific group, the Italians, were totally illiterate.[15] In Packingtown, another neighborhood of low literacy, a Bohemian real estate man commented on the verbal interchange around the barroom: "The saloon is a very wholesome discussion center. Here men bring their ideas and compare them. It helps to get at the truth in a situation and fight manipulation by unscrupulous men."[16]

In circumstances like these, it is easy to see why the saloon became the major repository of neighborhood information. This was the place where the newly-arrived Bostonian or Chicagoan learned how to get downtown on a streetcar or where to contact a lawyer. The bartender knew who ran the ethnic benefit societies. He could be trusted to spread the news if someone's child was missing. And, despite the high rate of business mortality, the saloon was still one of the most stable institutions in the neighborhood. Immigrants who frequently moved used the bar as a permanent mailing address. When many of their relatives arrived in Chicago from the old country, the address they clutched nervously in their hands was often that of a saloon. This practice was so widespread that numerous proprietors complained that their basements were always filled with trunks and packages as yet unclaimed by their customers.[17]

The saloonkeeper not only helped outsiders find their way around the immigrant community, but he also interpreted the outside world for his customers. He read letters for illiterate friends, and in the period prior to postal substations and letter boxes, his bar was an unofficial post office.[18] Finally, literate drinkers could always find the saloon well stocked with newspapers. One investigation of saloons on Chicago's Near Northwest Side reported that 139 out of 163 bars had at least one paper. Besides a daily "rag," the proprietor could subscribe to appropriate choices among a large number of foreign-language newspapers. On the eve of national prohibition, Boston had twenty-three of them, including four Armenian, three Lithuanian, and two Albanian, besides the regular complement of German and Italian publications. Chicago, because of its size and diversity, had many more — 106 to be exact — including fifteen German and fourteen Bohemian titles.[19]

The adaptability of the saloon extended to its role as a center of communications. When new forms of information media appeared, the larger barrooms were among the first to adopt them. "Special wires," really no more than leased telegraph lines, linked certain bars with major sporting events. Fans, equipped with scorecards which were also furnished "on the house," could keep up with baseball games without taking a foot off the brass rail. Many of the youthful saloon employees were kept busy marking the latest results on large chalkboards suspended near the ceiling at one end of the room.[20]

Finally, saloons were among the first semipublic places in the city to make telephones available to customers. These devices were most commonly used as the neighborhood's link to the outside world: a call to a hospital, to city hall, or to a relative in another city. Since few people in tenement areas could afford them, they lined up at the barroom phone. The number of callers made little difference, since early phone subscribers paid a flat rate, regardless of how many calls were made. Later, when message units came into use and pay phones appeared, the man behind the bar sold or gave away the token necessary to make public calls. At every step of the way, the saloon adapted itself well to new means of communications.[21]

The Saloon in Joy and Grief

The lack of alternative space brought many neighborhood people into the saloon. Most of this traffic was casual and unplanned. But at certain times of great joy or grief the activity in the barroom had a special significance, for the lack of privacy in the neighborhood meant that those antipathetic events were shared by the whole community. For instance, the traditions of many ethnic groups prescribed that large wedding celebrations supplemented the religious ceremonies. Instead of a church parish hall, many families rented the public halls that were above or next door to many saloons. These were sometimes free, provided that the guests visited the adjacent bar.[22] Such practices dismayed many reformers like Jane Addams, who wanted to remove "such innocent and legitimate" events to settlement houses.[23]

Tragedy in Victorian America was also a public event. On a national scale, disasters and assassinations of political leaders kept salesmen busy distributing maudlin books, banners, and other paraphernalia of mourning. The leaders of government traditionally received large public funerals. But misfortune among the urban poor was even more a matter of public knowledge and record. Before the mid-nineteenth century those who lacked self-sufficiency could spend their lives in the poorhouse. Here, they would have no more privacy than the common vagrant, for a family's individuality was lost along with its pride.[24]

During the latter decades of the century, the poorhouse gradually gave way to outdoor relief. The impoverished no longer went to the institution, but help, in the form of the charity worker, came to the home of the poor. This was a significant step toward the privatization of misery, but many aspects of misfortune in the tenement districts remained public. The home and the family life it contained continued to be open to the inspection and questioning of strangers. And whatever privacy this system afforded could easily be lost by the unforeseen event. Depressions put even the relatively comfortable artisans out on the street; the severity of the economic slump could be measured by the numbers of otherwise respectable men who slept in the parks and by the size of the soup lines. And various groups of defectives, foundlings, and delinquents continued to remain in hospitals, asylums, and other institutions.[25]

The idea that the poor had all but lost their identity was slow to die. As late as 1878 the Boston City Council seriously debated whether or not paupers had the right to determine the disposal of their own dead bodies. So much personal dignity had been lost through institutionalization that their corpses had become, in effect, municipal property. Council members were shocked to learn that these bodies were routinely donated to medical schools for instructional dissection. That practice saved the city the cost of burial in potter's field.[26]

The pawnshop was a familiar landmark on the road to poverty. Here, too, the poor were constantly reminded of the public nature of their misfortune. Items of the greatest personal value — usually watches and rings with family inscriptions — were their most marketable assets, and these ended up on display before the gazing crowd of strangers. Ultimately, it was the social class of the patrons that determined the degree of privacy that surrounded the transaction. The wealthy who were financially embarrassed could visit a "diamond broker" in the center of the downtown district. Although the pawnbroker knew the names of his patrons, his place of business was a respectable office building.[27]

Pawnshops provided considerable opportunity for corruption. Not only did these places easily become criminal fences, but their extortionate interest rates robbed the poor. Reformers created competing institutions — the Workingmen's Loan Association of Boston (1888) and the Illinois State Pawner's Society (1899) — which helped to curb such abuses by providing honest competition. But many poor people objected to the prying questions about their background, their place of employment, and their ownership of real estate. The Boston association even insisted upon visiting the home of the "applicant." Nor would the reform groups accept items other than valuables, like jewelry, that might be sold at auction.[28] In desperation, many turned to mortgage sharks, who accepted furniture as collateral, and to loan sharks, who lent small amounts of money at usurious rates.[29]

When the impoverished needed a quick, unsecured loan, there were few honest places to turn. There was an occasional "street angel" like Boston's Marcus Masse. He loaned money to thousands, charged them little or no interest, and never had an office. But more often people could turn to the saloonkeeper. When they had valuables, they could store them in his safe. Ironically, one of the most open and public places in the neighborhood was also the most secure. And when they needed money, regular customers could often obtain a quick advance on their word alone.[30]

Death was a frequent visitor in the slums. The unsanitary environment produced mortality rates several times those of the better neighborhoods. In 1890, a child in the Packingtown district of Chicago had a poor chance of surviving to age five. Emissions from gas factories and tanneries, filth, and garbage helped give the Sixteenth Ward (Near Northwest Side) the distinction of having the city's highest death rate in

1899.[31] Frequent industrial accidents left behind many widows and orphans, and spectacular fires that swept the tenement districts often wiped out whole families.[32] The funeral was a common social gathering in the slums. Shared grief helped unite neighbors, but according to Mrs. Annie Carlo, who owned a saloon and served as a visiting nurse in a Chicago Italian neighborhood, it meant more than that. "A death in the family is sad," she noted, "but it gives occasion for a fine funeral, and a funeral is a sure indication of social status."[33] It was the fear of a pauper's burial that drove many to join mutual benefit insurance societies; security was often defined as having enough money to avoid potter's field. And it was the desire to give a loved one a proper funeral that led many of the poor to spend beyond their means.[34]

During emergencies like this the saloon performed one of its most important functions. The proprietor, along with doctor and undertaker, played a prominent role in managing the ethnic insurance societies. The dealer's social status in the community, his long business hours, and his safe all made his business one of the places sought out by those in need. If there was little or no insurance money, then the persuasiveness of the bartender could coax donations from his customers. He could pass the hat or leave a dish or cigar box on the bar. Larger efforts were able to use the saloon hall as a meeting place. For instance, when Chicago police officer John Heubner was killed early in 1882, his friends and neighbors met in Adam Och's bar at the corner of Milwaukee and Division streets. Here they organized a neighborhood canvass which ultimately paid off the mortgage on the officer's house. Such meetings were common before prohibition.[35]

Saloon men were also prominent donors to various charitable enterprises. Medical institutions, like Boston's Irish-operated Carney Hospital, welcomed donations of wet goods. Whiskey, wine, and brandy performed an important medicinal function, and the saloonkeepers could obtain it at wholesale prices.[36] Finally, various ethnic relief organizations like Chicago's German [Aid] Society counted saloonkeepers and brewers among their most generous benefactors. Such gifts, when recognized on a list of donors, also served as modest advertising for the dealers.[37]

Organized charities also paid an occasional visit to the saloon. The Salvation Army and the Volunteers of America, although against liquor, invaded their enemy in search of donations. They were successful, but their brazen acts infuriated the saloonkeepers' organizations. A major controversy arose in 1908, when the Chicago press reported that the city had become the target of bogus charities whose solicitors wore uniforms similar to those of the Salvation Army. At that point, the dealers' newspaper, the *Champion of Fair Play*, advised its readers not to allow anyone "suspicious" through the door. It went on to say that the Army's "money did not always reach the poor anyway."[38] Some months later, when the Army marched in a temperance parade, the *Champion* sent out a special circular that advised, "Kindly, but firmly, TELL THEM TO KEEP OUT."[39] More than one "lassie" landed outside.

The saloon lunch also fed the hungry. W. T. Stead, the English journalist, claimed that Chicago's saloons daily kept 60,000 people alive during the Depression of the 1890s. Even settlement workers who were unfriendly to liquor conceded the enormous size of this informal philanthrophy. The dealers' groups, which had little sympathy for a genuine loafer, made puffed-up claims about the good they did society.[40] In 1913, for instance, the *Champion* argued: "Some people say that a dollar spent in a saloon is lost. Now let us consider one item, that of the Free Lunch. The cost of the free lunch given away in a saloon will easily average $10 per day. There are 7,152 saloons in Chicago, and at $10 each, that amounts to $71,520 per day given away in food to hungry persons by the saloonkeepers of Chicago, or $26,104,800 per year. . . . How much do the churches give away to the hungry?"[41]

Nickels and Votes

Dependence on public spaces for survival, the inability to plan for the future, and a sense of helplessness were among the most salient characteristics of life in the slums. Moreover, there were few accepted ways in which those with funds felt they could help. Charities of various types were one way to funnel money and services to the poor. Governmental aid was another, although the dole, like the almshouse, was never popular among taxpayers. But for many immigrant poor the key to survival lay in government's role as an employer and purchaser of goods. Taxing and spending represented a redistribution of resources. It was a source of income for the unskilled and an emergency fund to aid the victims of tragedy. Furthermore, perpetuation through political machines not only instilled a sense of efficacy through the process of getting out the vote, but it provided an element of predictability in the lives of thousands of impoverished constituents. And at the center of it all could frequently be found the saloon. As a political headquarters, it was an ideal "store," from which an ambitious proprietor could "sell" services along with beer and whiskey in exchange for nickels and votes. The same openness of the saloon that brought about so many restrictive laws and regulations contributed directly to its role in the political process. It was perhaps the most open social institution in the neighborhood. By operating all hours of the day and night, the proprietor was accessible to thousands. In this position, he was known to everyone in the procession of hundreds who daily passed through his doorway, and in return he knew much of his clientele by their first names.

The accessibility and openness of the saloonkeeper-politician was a characteristic that attracted a great deal of attention. In 1898 someone in Chicago humorously suggested that the library rooms in City Hall be turned into a saloon; the New York-based *Liquor Trades Review* applauded the notion. Because the aldermen were always drunk, it would turn a profit, and constituents would only have to look in one saloon instead of several. "Once again," the journal commented, "does Chicago thus prove her leadership in the world."[42] In a more serious vein, William Howard Taft told an audience of Yale students to get acquainted with the prominent men of the ward:

> Get acquainted not only with the well-to-do in your ward but with the artisans, with the saloonkeepers, and whoever are the controlling factors, although they may not be elevating to be associated with. There are many honest and hardworking saloonkeepers. They are up early in the morning, and they stay up late at night.
> (Here the audience broke up with laughter). I see you are familiar with the habits of the saloonkeeper. In the city he is the proprietor of the social club of his neighborhood.[43]

The services that the saloonkeeper provided the neighborhood also enhanced his popularity. The social role of his place as the center of communication made it a natural listening post for gossip and political news. Since people were likely to express their opinions to each other orally, without the privacy of the telephone, he was in an excellent position to know about the sidewalk that needed fixing, the dead animals in the alley a few blocks away, or the community's desire for a park to keep the children off the street.

The saloonkeeper was no stranger to the private tragedies of the citizens as well as their public needs. If a house burned, he knew of it almost as quickly as the fire department. The same held true for the other privations that beset the urban poor.

The saloon almost personified the politics of dependency. People needed something and the politician supplied it, and if he happened to tend bar, he knew about it all the more quickly. It frequently played upon the misfortune and the grief of the poor. It reemphasized the thin line between public and private that characterized the lives of the indigent. Personal suffering became public knowledge in the crowded neighborhood. And the politics of the slum was also peculiarly domestic in its outlook: jobs, family security in the face of injury, and coal. Just as the saloon functioned as an extension of the family kitchen, the issues of daily survival spilled from tenement apartments to the streets and the barrooms. And standing there with aid at his disposal was the saloonkeeper.

There were also many saloons near police stations to help people in trouble. That location guaranteed a steady clientele drawn from off-duty officers, who cashed their checks and ate their lunches there. But many of these bars were also the headquarters of bailbondsmen. The lights burned late, and that made it convenient for offenders who were charged at night; widespread violation of closing ordinances kept some bars open every hour of the week. The saloonman also had a safe, often a rarity in outlying neighborhoods, and he could store hundreds of dollars to put up each night in bond money.[44]

The saloon also became involved in sidewalk-level politics because the proprietor usually spoke the language of his customers. He often became the primary source of information about the new world. In the words of one settlement report, he was "with the ward politician the only interpreter of American institutions."[45] The fact, then, that the particular neighborhood place attracted a clientele of a certain ethnicity made the owner that much more persuasive as a political advisor to his newly-arrived brethren. In the oral society, characterized by low literacy rates and patchworks of languages, newspapers and handbills were often ineffective in getting out the vote. Personal contact was the key to success. The political organization canvassed the neighborhood door-to-door, or the saloonkeeper used his position behind the bar to contact the neighborhood as it passed through his swinging doors. The effect was the same. As one saloon newspaper reminded its trade readers: "See to it that every man you know and who frequents your place is registered on March 15th; ask everyone you know, *Have you moved since the last election?* If he has moved, write down his name and address so that you will be prepared to get him out on registration day and have him registered."[46]

Politics was also part of the saloon — along with the barbershop and poolhall — because there were few alternative locations for partisan discussion. Schools, libraries, baths, or other types of municipal property were off limits. The city of Boston did provide wardrooms for meeting purposes, but these were meant for nonpartisan uses and were never adequate in size or number. In Chicago, it was well into the twentieth century before the community center movement popularized the idea that local government should maintain places for nonpartisan discussion of governmental issues. As one observer noted, there was "no public place where men may meet on a common footing to discuss the political questions before them and select from their number those who are to be in authority."[47]

Excluded from other meeting places, political groups flocked to the only facilities large enough to handle their gatherings, the saloon halls. The newspapers carried dozens of meeting notices: "The Thirteenth Ward Republican Club will meet at Benz's Hall," or "The Sixteenth Ward Republican Club will assemble at Mayer's Hall." Such semipolitical groups as the Land Leagues, which were organized to give financial aid to that Irish movement, also rented saloon halls. A few barrooms even changed the names of their establishments to recognize the meeting hall trade. Frank Lehr's place at 117 Clark Street became the Town of Lake Headquarters, while a bar on the Northwest Side called itself the Democratic Headquarters of the Eighteenth Ward.[48]

The saloon provided a base of operation for many notable politicians. One of the first "statesmen's bars" in Chicago belonged to the flamboyantly-attired "Chesterfield Joe" Mackin. Influential in Democratic circles, he had also been responsible for the introduction of the free lunch to the city. That fete gave him the additional nickname of "Oyster Joe." For many years before his conviction — he got five years in 1885 for stuffing the ballot boxes in favor of brewer Rudolph Brand's state senate bid — Mackin's place had been the unofficial headquarters of the Cook County Democratic committee. And from behind his bar he also directed the operations of the First Ward "Levee" vice district, drawing a percentage of the take from gambling and prostitution to help finance his political career.[49]

Many other political bars flourished in Chicago. Fred Busse, who served as mayor from 1907 to 1911, once told reporters, "They don't need anyone sleuthing around after me. They can always get me any evening at J. C. Murphy's saloon, Clark Street and North Avenue."[50] Carter Harrison II met his friends at Vogelsang's, while the Monarch Buffet, in the shadow of City Hall, was a favorite hangout of aldermen and municipal clerks. Joseph Cerveny, who purchased the latter place in 1904, became a close adviser to his politically ambitious friend, a future mayor named Anton Cermak.[51]

All of these places were well known, but the most famous proved to be the small bar owned by Jim McGarry on Dearborn just north of Madison Street. The owners of the property would not rent to a saloon unless some other, more substantial interest shared the lease; Chapin and Gore, a large saloon chain and whiskey wholesaler, agreed to back McGarry. His warm wit and sagacious wisdom about politics endeared him to dozens of those prominent in politics. Police Inspector John Shea dropped by frequently, as did John J. McKenna, a Brighton neighborhood notable and member of the School Board. There was nothing fancy to attract them. Casey, the bartender, either refused or didn't know how to mix drinks. Nor would the place even sell cigarettes, only cigars. All through the day the chatter continued.

As the reputation of McGarry's place spread, it attracted the notice of young newspaper writers who sought stories about the everyday life of the metropolis.[52] Among that group was Finley Peter Dunne. He had been so amused by McGarry's comments that he began recording them on paper. And then, during the World's Columbian Exposition, he published the first of what would become perhaps the most famous continuing observation of the American political scene, the Mr. Dooley series. McGarry's bar was moved to "Archey Road" (Archer Avenue) in Bridgeport, and McKenna became "Hinnissey," but the brogue and wit were the genuine article. Nothing was above Mr. Dooley's gentle ridicule: politicians, reformers, mayors, and even "Tiddy" Roosevelt were all the subject of Dunne's friendly exaggeration. The column began as a once-a-week feature on the *Chicago Post* editorial page, but in a matter of a few years it attained national syndication. Some of the columns were republished in book form.[53] Despite the publicity, McGarry still refused to serve mixed drinks or even provide a free lunch. After all, his place was "a drinking place for gentlemen — not a restaurant."[54]

Visible Politics

The electoral process in the Victorian city was a highly visual experience. While information and ideas were transmitted by word-of-mouth, a larger sign, more colorful bunting, or a greater torchlight crowd could create a favorable impression. The street assumed a quilt-like appearance from the billboards, while in the saloon posters, matchbook covers, buttons, and almost every other visual gimmick of political technology could be found. When a saloon carried a particular candidate's paraphernalia, it was meant not only to be an endorsement by the proprietor, but also a warning to the customer not to argue in favor of an opponent.[55] On occasion, however, independence was the best policy, especially in a close contest where support for the loser could bring sad consequences. "Don't commit yourself to anybody," the *Champion of Fair Play* cautioned. "Wait and let your organization deal with the political powers. Don't get scattered, but stand together like a company of regulars on the line of battle."[56] Few barkeeps heeded that warning.

Election time also meant extra revenue for the saloon. In many neighborhoods it was customary for candidates to court potential supporters over a glass of "strong stuff." Office seekers migrated from bar to bar buying drinks, making speeches, and passing out cards. One Chicago aldermanic candidate, who also enjoyed the support of the mayor, was accompanied by a pair of police officers; whether they were along to protect him from his enemies or merely to add credibility to his claims of influence is not known.

If a saloonkeeper remained neutral, he might enjoy the gratuities of both opponents. In Boston candidates not only purchased rounds but did not ask for the change from the large bills offered in payment.[57]

Proprietors, however, were wise not to be overly optimistic about the amount of "wet-goods electioneering," as many found out in Chicago's Seventeenth and Eighteenth wards in 1894. Initially, barkeeps expected a tough race for the state senate seat to be filled that year. But when one candidate withdrew, his opponent, tightfisted John Gaynor, refused to spend any money over the bar. The dealers were stuck with huge reserves of "election (i.e., expensive) brands of whiskey and cigars." As the *Daily News* reported, "The natural desire to unload on a falling market has resulted in the liveliest saloon competition which had been seen on the West Side for years."[58]

During elections those with a vested interest in government wanted the voting under their personal supervision. And to insure the results they frequently had the polling place located right in their own saloon or in one owned by a trusted friend or lieutenant. This was much less common in Boston, where the tradition of using such public places as schoolhouses and wardrooms as polling places dated back to the early nineteenth century. But in Chicago, the Committee on Public Services of the Cook County Board bent to the wishes of the Democratic party leaders. Prior to 1886 voting booths appeared in the back rooms of saloons and sometimes directly in the front of the bar. This put the appropriate bribe of a free drink only an arm's length away. No one was quite sure how often this practice took place, especially since polling places were frequently moved at the last minute away from announced locations. But the newspaper estimates of at least half of them being located in saloons may be accurate. The press usually blamed Mike McDonald, the saloonkeeper-gambler who reputedly controlled the Democratic party during the 1880s. For years one of his favorite projects had been the control of the election committee of the County Board, and the distribution of polling places was his personal decision.[59]

The affinity of liquor and balloting attracted the attention of the saloon's opponents. In Boston, where the liquor interests had less representation on legislative bodies, the Board of Aldermen demanded in the early 1880s that the list of polling places be publicized well in advance of elections. Temperance and other reformers then had a chance to raise objections to locations too near liquor licenses. To complement this reform, Massachusetts also joined the first states to order all liquor dispensaries in the state closed on election day. Enacted at the height of the police reorganization controversy of 1885, it was one of the first and most comprehensive statutes of its kind in the nation. All license holders, including inns and victuallers, had to lock up their liquor for the entire twenty-four-hour period. Moreover, the new Police Board enforced the law strictly. Newspaper reporters seldom found saloons operating during elections. At least while the polls were open, the saloon and politics were momentarily divorced.

By comparison, election reforms were an abysmal failure in Chicago. Midwestern reformers went through the motions, but the results were minimal. In 1886 and 1887 the Illinois legislature passed a series of measures designed to disarm the saloonkeeper-politician. A comprehensive election code required that the selection of election judges be made public; "responsible citizens" might then be able to publicize and challenge the appointment of barkeeps and other "disreputable" people. The maximum number of voters in any precinct was also reduced, supposedly to eliminate the long lines of voters at the polls. Its real purpose, however, was to enlarge the number of polling places in order to make it more difficult for bosses to exert central control. Other laws required that voting booths be at least 200 feet from saloons and, finally, that all liquor licensees be closed down during the balloting. In February 1886 even the Chicago council temporarily became reformers by passing a law declaring that no voting or registration could take place where liquor was sold.

On paper the Illinois enactments were impressive; in reality they never worked. One newspaper jokingly commented that the 200-foot law was inoperative in the Seventh Ward; there was a saloon on every block! Most barrooms also remained wide open, especially those located adjacent to polling places. The daily press gave lengthy descriptions and lists of the lawbreakers, and the police made a few symbolic arrests. But most were set free with minimal punishment. Instead of conforming to the law, barroom operators seemed bent on making their activities as wide open as ever.

Brawls, bribes, and ballot stuffing were so visible to the public view that the trade papers began to call for saloons to shut their doors on election day so that the proprietors could be free to campaign for pro-liquor candidates. The liquor press also warned that citizens were gradually becoming less tolerant of the defiant saloonkeeper, who was also doing irreparable damage to the image of the trade! Few in Chicago, however, were listening.[60]

Most political activities in saloons were relatively open and public, but the Grey Wolves, as the crooked elements in Chicago politics were called, planned their strategy in the back room. In 1881, for instance, there was an altercation in the rear room of exalderman Julius Jonas's place on Washington Street; four "city fathers" engaged in a brawl when someone defamed the character of a fifth one who failed to show up with bribe money. Fifteen years later, during the height of the streetcar franchise scandals, the *Chicago Evening Post* confidently blamed the back rooms of several saloons as if they were accomplices to the graft and bribes. And even the chicanery in the outlying wards was apparently coordinated and planned behind the same closed doors. In the scandals surrounding the Republican primary of October 1883, the strategy employed by those who "stole" the election was planned in the rear room of a downtown LaSalle Street bar.[61]

Organizing the Floaters

The astute politicians in both cities also made careful use of the large numbers of homeless floaters. For years Boston boss Martin Lomasney based his Ward Eight (West End) organization on their votes. Because there were few legal saloons in the immediate area and the "Boston Mahatma" was a very temperate man, his Hendricks Club, a meeting hall, instead became the headquarters of his machine. Hundreds of casual laborers and drifters, nicknamed the Sons of Rest by the newspapers, normally crowded the cheap hotels and roominghouses along Causeway, Pitts, and Lowell streets. Lomasney's army was not huge, but at election time he mobilized it effectively by transporting his troops around to the various precinct voting places and letting them vote several times. During one investigation of the ward, one denizen of the district bragged that he had voted seven times in ten minutes. Lomasney apparently used cash and jobs as well as liquor to pay his "constituents."[62]

"Colonization" was much more open and common in Chicago. Not only were there more saloons, but the city's position in the national rail network kept its transient lodging houses filled. At election time newspapers regularly revealed how thousands of vagrants became voters.[63]

There were two areas where lodging house voting was practiced to perfection. Out in the small vice district just west of the Loop, Alderman John J. Brennan perpetuated his power by rounding up denizens of the street and herding them into polling places. This Irish saloonkeeper, whom the *Tribune* in 1883 had described as "a Democrat of 'inflooence,' " had once been a detective at the Grand Pacific Hotel. During the early 1880s he opened a saloon in the rear lot of a district police station, where he made a good business out of providing bonds for petty criminals. The place also turned a nice profit for the owner of the building, whom Brennan paid $120 a month; the landlord was Carter Harrison I, mayor of Chicago.[64]

Brennan had little trouble getting elected for most of his twenty-two years in the City Council. But in 1895 he faced what appeared to be his strongest competition from another West Side lodging house keeper, John A. Rodgers. Both men used the same attractions to reward the faithful. As one bemused observer, a student at Northwestern University, noted: "All day, while the polls are open, the bar tenders of the two candidates were busy treating friends of the respective office-seekers. Wagon-loads of half-drunk Irishmen, whose native wit never seemed brighter, were driven around to the different saloons to drum up straggling votes for their candidates. Intoxication was everywhere. Madison Street, just west of the river, was a listless, drifting throng of toughs and bums out for a gala day of free drinks, boozes and fights. Brennan was re-elected, and that night his saloon was the scene of jollification, hilarity, and drunken jubilee, which lasted into the early hours."[65]

To the south of the Loop Michael "Hinky Dink" Kenna presided over one of the most sophisticated colonization plans in the city. Before each election, national as well as local, the population of the saloon-lodging houses under his influence would swell with floaters imported for the occasion. Housed and fed for a few days before the vote, they were organized into regiments and properly instructed. Then they were transported around the ward where needed. When combined with the votes from various brothels in the Levee district, this itinerant constituency was an unbeatable force. And because Kenna and his fellow-alderman "Bathhouse John" Coughlin could wield unquestioned influence over the police and over the renewal of the licenses held by other saloons, nearly everyone was happy to cooperate.[66]

One of the best-documented vote-fraud cases involved another Levee saloonkeeper, Solomon van Praag. Born in Chicago in 1859, "Solly" entered the liquor business at age twenty-three. The Owl, his resort on South State Street, was well known for its petty gambling, whoring, and narcotics sales to Levee inmates. The bar also assumed distinctly political orientation as its owner rose quickly in the ranks of the Democratic party. Solly's reward for hard work came in 1890, when his party's convention slated him for the General Assembly, an honor for a man barely in his thirties. His first victory was easy; vote stealing was uncontrolled and the Republican opposition was weak and disorganized. But his attempt to retain his post two years later proved to be quite another experience.[67]

The fall election of 1892 was one of the more unusual in the state's history, because the Australian ballot was being tested for the first time. Reformers' interest in privatizing urban life extended to ballot boxes as well. Corrupt political managers were uneasy, because they could no longer watch the "residents" take a ballot from either the Democratic or the Republican worker and deposit it in the box. Instead, voters received identical printed sheets which they marked themselves. The bosses had reacted to the reform by inventing a technique called chain balloting, which they were testing for the first time. Party leaders illegally received extra copies of the official ballot. They gave their first voter a premarked ballot, which he deposited in the box. Then he took his blank ballot, which the clerk had given him, and returned it to the boss outside the polling place. The boss marked this ballot and gave it to the next voter. The process repeated itself all day. Wagons shuttled fresh battalions around to the precincts on regular schedules, and these "patriotic citizens" enjoyed a liquid reward at each stop. Chain balloting allowed the bosses to neutralize the reformers' attempt to inject privacy and choice into the voting process in the transient districts.

Political Mobility and the Saloon

If one believed the temperance literature, a majority of the urban legislatures at the turn of the century were populated exclusively by barkeeps, each festooned with cigar, fedora, outlandish vest, and diamond stickpin. The image seemed to personify corruption. But in reality the saloonkeepers were far less significant in numbers than the historical image suggests. The facts do not discount the importance of the saloon in campaigning, but they do reduce the size of the army of "barwipers" who answered to the title of alderman or councilman.

The saloonkeeper-alderman was, above all else, a public politician. His political style was not unique. Others, whose economic backgrounds and careers also had a distinct neighborhood orientation, shared his secret: accessibility, personal contact, and a parochial interest in the ward. Other retail establishments, such as groceries or even the shops of blacksmiths and other self-employed artisans, also became casual meeting places where the proprietor could use friendships and a detailed knowledge of the neighborhood to launch a political career.

In Boston the pattern of political participation among liquor dealers depended largely on whether the individual was a retailer or wholesaler. The Hub City had a bicameral legislature. The Board of Aldermen, with one member elected from each ward, held all of the power to make law, while the Common Council acted as ombudsmen, voicing the opinions of their constituents, recommending laws to the aldermen and passing resolutions of approval or disagreement with the upper house.

Traditionally, the aldermen tended to be men of substance, while the council members came from more plebeian backgrounds. In 1870 Boston's Board of Aldermen consisted primarily of large downtown merchants, rather than the neighborhood shopkeepers, but the Common Council contained a number of public politicians. Of the sixty-four members of the latter body — four from each ward — five (7.8 percent) were retail grocers, three (4.7 percent) operated lodging houses, and two (3 percent) were saloonkeepers. One councilman was a wholesale liquor dealer and another operated a cigar store. These men represented the "low-number wards" of the tenement neighborhoods and wharves of the North and South Ends. Only one, John Quinn, had a distinctly Irish name. The other wards sent fourteen (21.9 percent) small merchants and an equal number of skilled artisans. There was also a sprinkling of teamsters, clerks, and even a farmer. Significantly, there was only one doctor, one manufacturer, and a pair of lawyers.[68]

By 1880 the Common Council had expanded to seventy-five members, three from each ward, but the most significant change was in the character of the men who sat there. The public politicians had nearly disappeared. There were still three liquor dealers, who now made up 4 percent of the total, but there was only one other neighborhood merchant, a confectioner who had his store in the same ward he represented. There were only four (5.3 percent) other owners of small businesses and seven (9.3 percent) artisans. The replacements included nine (12 percent) lawyers and ten (13.3 percent) "manufacturers." While some of the transition might be due to individuals or the directory company redefining occupations, there was clearly a shift in power away from the small neighborhood retailer whose business contacts with customers gave him votes. Meanwhile, the character of the Board of Aldermen remained unchanged.[69]

A decade later there were still three (4 percent) saloonkeepers and nine (12 percent) lawyers in the Common Council. The number of skilled artisans and small merchants remained stable as well. The most notable change came in the growing number of people who held white-collar jobs working for someone else. They were either salesmen or clerks (6 or 8 percent each) or insurance agents or managers (2 or 2.7 percent each) and a bookkeeper and a stenographer. This group now constituted a fifth of the Common Council. Once again there were three saloonkeepers. While the lower house was in transition from economically independent to dependent occupational groups, the Board of Aldermen was suffering a similar decline in status. Now, among the dozen men, a stevedore, a butcher-shop clerk-turned-fireman, a grocery clerk, and a belting company worker who also worked in the city's sewer department shared decision making with merchants and lawyers.

At the turn of the century the transition was nearly complete. In 1902 there were virtually no neighborhood merchants and only one saloonkeeper on the Boston Common Council. Clerks and salesmen made up over a quarter of the membership, lawyers another 10 percent, and the rest were scattered through a number of nonself-employed occupational groups. By this time, the scarcity of liquor licenses meant that their owners were usually men of reasonable wealth. And benefitting from that position, two retailers and one wholesaler sat on the Board of Aldermen in 1900.[70]

Even in Chicago the numbers of saloonkeeper-aldermen were actually quite small. In 1870, for instance, the Chicago Council had forty members, but only two (5 percent) of them—P. B. Sheil and James Walsh—operated saloons. Five (12.5 percent) operated groceries, which might also have dispensed liquor, but there is no indication that this was the case. Two other members, John McAvoy and K. G. Schmidt, were prominent brewers, while one wholesale whiskey man also held office. The majority of the council was made up of small merchants, a few skilled craftsmen, three realtors, and three lawyers. In 1874 the numerical count of liquor representatives remained about the same: two saloonkeepers, two brewers, and a wholesale dealer. The addition of a distillery foreman, Thomas Bailey, from the Ninth Ward (Near West Side) brought the number to six, or 15 percent.

During the next two decades the visible political power of the Chicago saloon reached its peak. The redistricting of 1876 reduced the number of wards from twenty to eighteen, each still entitled to two representatives. But intense pressure from temperance groups, especially the law and order league, and the first attempts to create permanent liquor associations brought more retailers into politics. By 1880 the brewers and wholesalers had disappeared temporarily from the council. In their place appeared six saloonkeepers and a hops merchant. Six years later, the addition of one more saloon man brought the total liquor representation to eight out of a total of thirty-six members, or 22 percent.

The saloonkeeper-aldermen of the 1880s were a mixed lot. A. J. Kowalski, for instance, was notable because he was the first Polish alderman, a considerable feat considering the small size of the city's Slavic community in 1887. He also founded the Polish Saloonkeepers' Association.[71] The most notable of the lot was Edward P. Burke. An Indiana-born stonecutter, he entered politics and the liquor trade at about the same time. Burke Hall at Halsted and Thirty-fifth Street was a favorite gathering spot for neighborhood politicos, and from it he launched a lengthy career. In 1880 he became Fifth Ward alderman and was reelected once; in 1886 he returned to the council for three more terms.[72]

Chicago saloonkeepers held their greatest share of City Council seats during the early 1880s. At the beginning of the decade there were six liquor dealers and one hops merchant (19.4 percent) among the thirty-six members, and in 1886 seven retailers and one wholesaler could be counted among the aldermen (22.2 percent). While their numbers did not slip precipitously during the next few years, their share of the total did. The annexations of 1889 were largely responsible. The ward boundaries in the old part of the city were left untouched, but new areas expanded the number of wards from eighteen to thirty-four. Thus, of sixty-eight seats in the inner-city wards, eight elected saloon-keeper-aldermen in 1890 and twelve in 1894, but now the barkeeps made up only thirteen percent and 17.6 percent of the council, respectively. When the city was redistricted again in 1900, creating thirty-five wards and seventy seats, there were only seven retailers (10 percent) among them. And in 1906 only five remained among a total of seventy (7.1 percent). Thus, by the time that the Municipal Voters' League and other reformers had begun to notice the saloonkeeper-alderman, the liquor dealer was disappearing from politics. Mayor Carter Harrison II sensed the transition in his City Council. Speaking before the Yale Law School Political Club in 1905, he noted:

> I recall when in 1897, a photographer for an Eastern magazine was engaged in taking a flashlight photograph of the city council, several of its members seemed ill at ease; to calm their restlessness I announced the photograph was not intended for the Bertillion system of [criminal] identification. Today these seats are filled by lawyers and progressive business men, who esteem it an honor to

be members of what was once a justly abused body. I do not mean to say the reform had been complete. It is a fact, however, that a majority of the present council is made up of men whose sole concern is the welfare of the interests they have been elected to conserve. In doing away with the old-time aldermen, we have made a riddence of his hangers-on and satellites. [73]

Harrison's estimate of the quality of Chicago politicians may have been exceedingly optimistic, but he did correctly note their changing backgrounds. With each passing decade, the ranks of small businessmen and self-employed craftsmen in the City Council gave way to lawyers and other professionals. More of them owned or ran companies that could sell something to the city, and after the great annexation of 1889, realtors and builders emerged as a major block of aldermen. What better way to insure city services in new subdivisions than to sit in the City Council? As a result of these shifts, the pattern of council membership after 1900 began to show lawyers and realtors from a ring of wards that surrounded a dwindling number of saloonmen and other small businessmen who represented inner-city wards, especially those near the branches of the river. And in the midst of this transition, the uncouth saloon alderman began to look more like a rough-and-tumble remnant from a frontier past. [74]

The small number of liquor dealers who survived this political transition were also significant for their long tenure in office. What had been temporary public service during the 1870s became careers by the turn of the century. John Coughlin and Michael Kenna served forty-five and twenty-six years respectively, while John Brennan represented the Eighteenth Ward (West Side) for twenty-two years. Just south of him, John Powers ruled the Nineteenth for some thirty-eight years. The saloon alderman who served a short time became the exception rather than the rule, a fact made more meaningful by one statistic. The eight saloonmen who held office in 1890 had aldermanic careers that ultimately totaled 179 years. [75]

This longevity is best illustrated by the story of Edward F. Cullerton, whose council service spanned five decades. He was born in 1842 in Chicago, and after the usual public school education he opened what became a thriving livery service, boardinghouse, and bar. In 1871, a few months before the Great Fire, he was elected an alderman of the Seventh Ward. A term in Springfield briefly interrupted his local

career, but state politics proved too boring for him, and once again he
was back in the council, this time supporting Harvey Colvin's People's
party movement in 1873. From that point on, he served in the council
continuously — with the exception of six years in the 1890s — until the
beginning of national prohibition.[76]

Cullerton's longevity did not result from his speechmaking ability.
Rather, his nicknames of "Crafty Ed" or "Smooth Eddy" best explain
his talent for survival. He was a master at producing more supporters
at the polls than were legally registered to vote, while at the same time
using imaginative excuses to explain their presence. In 1886, for instance, he announced plans for a new brewery in the ward. Construction was set to begin on election day, and at the appointed hour he
assembled an army of 600 laborers from all over the city to begin dig-
ging. Before a single spade was turned, he gave them time off to vote,
and before they could return to their bogus labor, he announced a
change in his business plans. There was, of course, to be no brewery,
but each worker received a day's pay for his trouble.[77]

Many other liquor dealers used their neighborhood status to obtain
political jobs rather than office. They could join the municipal payroll
while continuing to operate their private businesses. If he could afford
a bartender, a saloon owner was capable of being away from his place
during the daylight hours when business outside the downtown areas
was often slow anyway. Many of the city jobs also required only a few
hours' work each day; the rest of the time could be devoted to managing the bar.[78]

Saloonmen in such positions were frequently the target of exposés. In
1894 Chicago's mayor, John P. Hopkins, learned through the *Tribune*
that barkeep Charles Mulbrauson, who was a member of the Seventh
Ward Democratic committee, was a street foreman on the side. A year
or so later the *Herald* disclosed that another liquor dealer also super-
vised a bogus street repair crew. He merely distributed the payroll
money to lodginghouse loafers who promptly spent it over his bar. Ten
years later, Richard Fox, the Chicago street superintendent, filed
charges against John H. Cronin, a minor Fifth Ward politico. Fox revealed that Cronin not only did no work, but collected extra city revenue as rent for the headquarters for the ward's street crew. The "office"
was actually his back room, and the "ward yard" was his back alley.[79]

Conclusion: Interpersonal Politics

After the muckraking journalist Lincoln Steffens repeated the story in *The Shame of the Cities*, it became a famous joke: the fastest way to empty the City Council chambers was to stand at the rear and shout, "Your saloon's on fire!"[80] In reality barkeeps were not that numerous in municipal legislative chambers, but the men behind the bar came to symbolize an era of American city politics. Their power was nothing grafted on the city by design, but instead political power grew naturally out of the barroom's social functions in the working-class neighborhoods that became their constituencies. The key was information, first-hand knowledge of the triumphs and tragedies of people living on the edge of dependency. In an oral society that deemphasized written communication, the saloon's crucial role as a center of gossip armed the ambitious politician with a shopping list of jobs, city services, and welfare help that he needed to bring to the ward in order to exchange for votes. The proper political connections in city hall meant municipal and state jobs for loyal workers, while the honored position of alderman might mean employment "voluntarily" offered by streetcar companies or major businesses enjoying city contracts. Larger firms within the ward also found it advantageous to allow politicians to have a hand in hiring practices, lest a swarm of fire or building inspectors declare the premises unsafe. With a pipeline of money from downtown and the saloon as a listening post that informed him of the community's needs, the saloonkeeper had certain distinct advantages over rivals for political careers. Only a few of the semipublic businesses which also functioned as neighborhood social centers — grocers and blacksmiths, for instance — shared the barkeep's access to information.

The saloonkeeper was also a highly visible person in an age of visual politics. The torchlight parade, the half-tone or line drawing of the candidate's likeness, bunting and flags all helped establish the image of popular support and legitimacy, especially for those who could not or would not take time to understand the issues. Thus, visible saloon politics fit well an urban age in which signboards became a common nuisance and electricity found one of its earliest applications in illuminating advertising "transparencies" on storefronts. Advertising increasingly turned to illustrations — word pictures that spoke every language — to sell everything from houses in working-class subdivisions to soap, while newspapers sought illustrators to portray news events in woodcuts. While all of this image building was crude compared to that of the 1960s and after, the saloonkeeper-politician, nonetheless, was a public celebrity who could be consulted for the price of a nickel beer.

Personality was also critical to the barkeep-politician's rise, for the warm word of condolence, the hat passed down the bar, and the free food were often the only standards by which constituents knew how to judge the performance of an officeholder. This situation, of course, appalled political and social reformers. Their goal was a well-informed electorate that carefully weighed the issues, investigated the qualifications of candidates, and then cast ballots untethered by extraneous considerations. That goal remained elusive. The Australian ballot, introduced in Massachusetts in 1888 and in Illinois four years later, was designed to purify the voting process by privatizing it and removing it from the view of bosses, but in the end it made little difference. Efforts to remove the ballot box from the barroom and close the latter on election day also found only limited success.

To reformers, then, the saloon symbolized everything wrong with the political process. It was, in effect, a political hiring hall that fostered overstaffed inefficiency which wealthier voters had to finance. Its appeal to the visual and emotional campaigning ran counter to attempts to educate voters. Its ability to communicate in foreign languages, as the next chapter will reveal, frustrated Americanization and assimilation programs. And most important of all, the saloonkeeper-politician represented a stubborn parochialism that seemed to contravene the efforts of reformers to look to larger metropolitan goals. The barkeep and his entourage seemed most interested in neighborhood issues and the day-to-day survival of customer-constituents, while reformers constantly looked toward the future. Such grandiose ideas as Daniel Burnham's Plan of Chicago or "Boston-1915" generated little enthusiasm from those whose concerns were limited in both extent and time.

One of the most popular Boston bars during the late 1870s and the 1880s was Jacob Wirth's, for years a fixture on Eliot Street. (Courtesy Boston Public Library)

The Bay State Brewery stood on Sumner Street in Boston and was in its prime during the 1870s and 1880s. (Courtesy Boston Public Library)

The Pabst and Fred Miller breweries, both of Chicago, operated adjacent beer depots in South Chicago. The year is 1900. (From the author's private collection)

By Authority of the City of Chicago.

Permission is hereby given to Nicholas Kuttn — to keep a Brewery on N. Water St bet Dearborn & Clark St —

and to sell, vend and retail vinous, spirituous and fermented liquors by the small quantity for and during the space of one year from the date hereof. A bond having been filed pursuant to the laws of the State of Illinois and the ordinance of the said City of Chicago in such case made and provided.

Given under the hand of the Mayor of said City, and the seal thereof, this first — day of May — A. D. 1847.

L. D. Boone

Acting **Mayor and Presiding Officer of the Common Council.**

ATTEST, *Henry B. Clarke* ——— **Clerk.**

Levi Boone, the acting Chicago mayor who signed this 1847 saloon license, precipitated the Lager Beer Riot in 1855. As mayor, he targeted German saloons for his nativist wrath. (Reprinted from *History of Chicago and Souvenir of the Liquor Interests* [Chicago: Belgravia Publishing Co., 1892], p. 125)

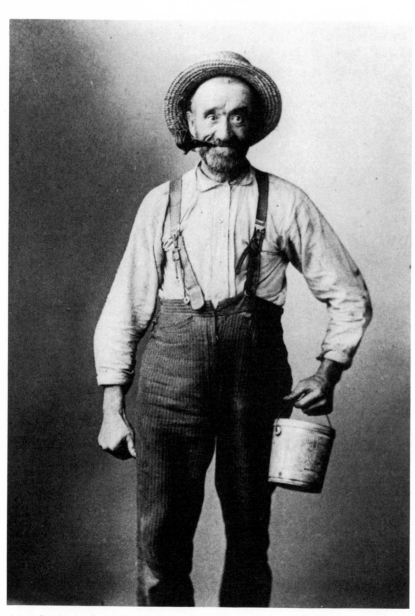

According to author John Ritchie, "the growler is a cosmopolitan vessel, and it is rushed in every language that finds a roosting place in Chicago. . . ." (Photograph from Sigmund Krausz, *Street-Types of Chicago* [Chicago: the author, 1892], p. 6)

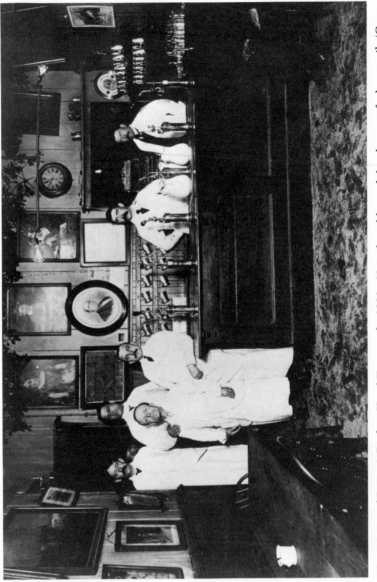

The interior of Boston's Bird-in-Hand Tavern, the 1890s. Note the tables and the absence of a brass rail. (Courtesy Society for the Preservation of New England Antiquities)

Phone
before eleven

delivered
before seven

Phone
Canal 9
The
"Edelweiss
Line"

THE PETER SCHOENHOFEN BREWING CO.

Beer delivery to the private residence cut deeply into saloon revenues. (From an Illinois Theater program, Oct. 15, 1916)

Besides his more famous Workingmen's Exchange, Michael Kenna also owned this fancier bar a block north on Clark Street, Chicago. (From the author's private collection)

Chicago's Masonic Temple Buffet, c. 1900, was a good example of a high-toned, but public, barroom. (From the author's private collection)

The exterior of the saloon of Michael T. McGreevy.

Soon after McGreevy went into business in 1894, his bar became the leading spa for baseball fans for the next twenty years. (Courtesy Boston Public Library)

This South Chicago saloon was located near the city's iron and steel center, c. 1910. (Courtesy the McLaughlin Family Collection)

CHAPTER 5

The Public Melting Pot

If the saloon was a particularly public institution, it was also one which seemed ubiquitous, especially to its critics. It was not only public space, but it also seemed to be universal space. But when many anti-liquor publicists railed against the barroom menace, they incorrectly tended to assume that all drinking places were either "low dives" or "gilded dens." What they failed to recognize was that the saloon, being both a small business and essentially an extension of the sidewalk, reflected the diversity of Chicago and Boston perhaps more than any other social institution. With a license to population ratio that reached as low as one for each one-hundred-fifty men, women, and children, almost any narrow community of tastes could be sufficient to support a license. It might be a particular ethnic group or those seeking a special atmosphere or physical location. Just as the variety of licensing systems created variations in barrooms from city to city, so too did different tastes create an enormous diversity of drinking places within a city.

Accessibility meant that the neighborhood, its residents, and the users of the public space outside the swinging doors were the major factors in creating the variety of barrooms. Proprietors who could not cope with that fact failed. Those who could adjust turned a profit.

Ethnic Space

The saloon in the tenement districts had to adjust to many changes in the neighborhood. It had to weather the shocks of unemployment and strikes. It had to adjust to the changing land-use patterns in some areas as commercial and industrial districts expanded into residential areas. The character of the housing stock changed, usually undergoing a decline in quality. But most important of all, the ethnic character of neighborhoods was constantly changing. The saloonkeeper, whose business was practically an extension of the sidewalk, soon realized an important fact: the city's tenement residents did not all use public and semipublic places in the same way. Rather, their ethnic backgrounds and traditions, although modified in the urban matrix, produced certain distinct differences in the street life of each group. This variety, in turn, had its parallel in the several ethnic forms of saloons.

Ethnic specializations had developed in many of the street trades and survived when those activities moved indoors. Italians and Greeks operated pushcarts or green groceries and were most numerous among those who eventually opened fruit and produce stands. Jews were predominant among the rag pickers and owned the more permanent versions of those same activities, the junk and pawn shops. Most of the portable craftsmen, such as scissors grinders and itinerant handymen, were Germans; when they accumulated enough capital, they opened construction firms or engaged in other artisan activities. Even the army of newsboys on Chicago's street corners was unevenly distributed among different nationalities. One study, conducted by the Chicago Federation of Settlements, revealed that over a fifth of the news vendors were Italian children, a number far larger than their proportion of the population in 1903.[1]

National origins shaped other forms of public behavior as well. Robert Woods compared the Jewish and Italian districts of North End Boston and found the former to be far more sober and serious than the latter. His viewpoint may have reflected the commonly held stereotypes of his day, but he was correct in contrasting the character of their religious ceremonies. The Jewish Sabbath was often celebrated in the privacy of the home, while the most important Italian religious days involved the whole community. In Chicago's South Side (Wentworth Avenue) Sicilian colony the *Festa della Maria Virgina* included a large procession and sidewalk booths containing religious shrines. One description of the annual mid-August event pointed out that "in such public celebrations and in the persistence of tradition and customs we find the village of the old world often transplanted and flourishing with little change in the heart of our great cities."[2] Native costumes, dances, street games, and music added further to the distinctions between the various ethnic enclaves.

National origins contributed to ethnocentrism and interethnic hostility. Contemporaries made frequent reference to it. Robert Woods observed that Boston's Irish disliked Italians and Jews and mixed with them only for political purposes; Canadians and English-born immigrants disdained all other groups.[3] In Chicago ill feelings imported from the homeland set Poles against Prussians and Irishmen against Englishmen. According to one source, when Italians moved into a building, everyone else moved out.[4] Juvenile gangs in both cities often organized along ethnic lines and contributed to the most violent and noticeable conflict.[5] Chicago settlement worker George Nesmith believed that such discord was itself a reason to develop small parks in tenement districts. These breathing spaces would improve the standard of local health, but the more that open spaces were decentralized, the easier it would be to adapt each of them to the uses of the specific nationality surrounding it.[6]

There were many complex reasons for these ethnic differences in public behavior. Some traditions had been part of the cultural heritage brought from the old country. Others were acquired after the settlement in the city. But what is significant is the role that ethnic traditions played in the development of the saloon as a public place, for their ubiquity and adaptability made them important institutions in almost every neighborhood. This could happen because each group modified the saloon to meet its own unique demands. As a result, there was really no such thing as "the saloon," but rather, there were as many different kinds of saloons as there were neighborhoods.

The variety of ethnic saloons seems confusing. Every group had its favorite beverage, spoke its own language freely, told its own jokes over the bar, and enjoyed its own delicacies at the free lunch sideboard. Most groups, however, fit easily into four basic categories. The first may be called "universals." Consisting primarily of the Irish and the Germans, they were widely dispersed across the city and entertained a clientele of mixed ethnic background. They were predominant in Chicago's Loop and in downtown Boston, and they enjoyed the patronage of busy thoroughfares. Their opposite counterpart might be labeled "ethnocentric." These were bars which catered to a single ethnic group and were located within that group's neighborhoods. While outsiders were not necessarily unwelcome, the proprietors made no special effort to attract the trade of other language groups. A third group consisted of nonsaloon ethnics who utilized other social institutions in place of the saloon. Finally, there were the black residents of

both cities. While their activities roughly resembled those of the ethnocentric groups, the growing level of discrimination and segregation
they faced created a unique situation.

Our Own Saloons: The Ethnocentric Bar

The ethnocentric saloon was a sign that a neighborhood had turned
inward. The ties of language or customs were much stronger than the
centripetal forces of ethnic intermixing and dispersal. This characteristic was not confined to immigrants from any particular region of the
world. Members of the so-called "old immigration," as well as the new,
found the saloon to be a comfortable complement to their ethnicity.
Scandinavian saloons, especially those run by Swedes, were located almost entirely within their tightly concentrated neighborhoods. During
the mid-nineteenth century the Swedes had settled in the poverty-
stricken Near North region of Chicago, and as late as the 1890s they
were still welcoming drinkers along Chicago Avenue on the North Side
to accommodate a small settlement. During the 1870s many lodging
house keepers also operated bars in their basements; these places were
usually filled with the newest arrivals.[7]

A few Danes and Norwegians owned places on the fringe of the neighborhood, but they, like the Swedes, designed their places to appeal to a
narrow ethnic audience. In biographical sketches, such as those in the
History and Souvenir of the Liquor Interests, the most prominently
mentioned feature was their interest in serving neighborhood families.
Nearly all featured Swedish punch, a few even posting it on their signboards. Axel Nilsson operated a "Texas" buffet adjoining his bar, while
Scandia Hall hosted ethnic labor meetings, and Swedish singing societies met at Andrew Johnson's. Even within the liquor business itself,
the Scandinavians were among the first to create their own ethnic liquor dealers' association.[8]

Among the more notable of the ethnocentric saloons were those operated by Italians. These displayed several unique characteristics. They
were probably the only barrooms where the drink sold was of relatively
minor importance in attracting customers. Most Italian households
made and stored an ample supply of the community's staple beverage,
a native red wine. Any surplus was easily sold to neighbors by the jug
or by the drink. This meant that in Italian communities the favorite
drink was as easily obtainable outside the barroom as it was within.

Bartenders sold wine but never consciously tried to cut into this trade. Instead, they catered to the interests of the brewing companies which had set them up in business and tried to convert the customers to "American" drinks like beer and whiskey.[9]

The Italian saloon attracted a narrow clientele that did not depend on the street traffic that passed its door. The casual non-Italian drinker who stopped in because it was convenient was a rare customer. Contemporary observers frequently commented that in the North End of Boston and the Hull House neighborhood of Chicago, only Italians patronized Italian saloons.[10] The negative publicity of the press, especially in Chicago, undoubtedly drove away many non-Italians. The appellation "dago bar" was a common synonym for criminal saloons in exposé stories about the city's low life, and this usage probably attached a certain stigma to the Italian drinking places in at least one segment of the public mind.[11]

The Italian saloon survived primarily because it provided certain services to the neighborhood. Customers seemed to flock to the places simply to pass the time and visit. Many men held unskilled jobs and were idle during seasons of the year. During summer they sat on benches in public places like Boston's North Square, but in the colder months and at night year round, they filled the barrooms of Ann Street. Many customers came in just to read the newspapers. In Chicago's polyglot West Side the bars all carried copies of *L'Italia*.[12]

Many other customers sought information about jobs. They could not have found a better place in Italian neighborhoods; the proprietor was also a labor boss. A number of barrooms served as employment agencies for railroads, hiring labor for track maintenance gangs. And when these seasonal workers departed, the saloons of the neighborhood seemed almost deserted. As *L'Italia* commented: "The saloons of South Clark Street, of Fourth Avenue, of Ewing, Taylor, Desplaines, and the small decent cottages are empty. No longer are there deafening shouts, the pounding of fists on the tables, the playing of cards or the drinking of beer. Goodbye to the days passed idly, seated near the hearth, around the benches of the saloon, along the streets. All are at work!"[13]

Other saloons became involved in the *padrone* business. They operated in the midst of large numbers of poor and uneducated bachelors who were the victims of the labor exploitation business. The saloonkeeper became the intermediary between the individual workers and the larger society. The helpless immigrants already admired him as an authority in politics, law, and even the rules of card games. He could also get them jobs, and in return the barroom proprietor could enlarge the meager profits of the liquor business in an impoverished neighborhood. As a result, an unknown number of lower-class Italian saloons — probably twenty or thirty in Chicago alone — were also headquarters for *padrone* operations.[14]

The social structure of its neighborhood largely determined the character of the Italian saloon. In both cities, unmarried males made up a substantial portion of the populace, 60 percent in Boston in 1900. Most had migrated by themselves and saved or spent their money at their own discretion. Many moved in with families or rented small rooms.[15] Even in places like East Boston, which was comparatively uncrowded and not a slum, the physical environment encouraged alternatives to home leisure activities. As one commentator put it, "The decreased size of the tenements and rooms everywhere makes it evident that the life not only of the laborers, but of the middle class as well, must find an increasing part of its expression outside of the home."[16] The saloon filled that need.

Another group that tended to frequent their own barrooms was the Bohemian population. Few of them settled in Boston, but Chicago's colony became one of the largest in the United States. Beginning with a few emigré intellectuals in the 1850s, it had grown to several thousand by 1900. But the majority of the people, unlike the earliest arrivals, were poor. Those with tailoring skills opened sweatshops, while many others became involved with the monotonous job of cigar making. Their poverty placed them in some of Chicago's most dilapidated neighborhoods, first in Prague, a slum located just southwest of the downtown, and by the 1870s in Pilsen. The latter was a settlement of run-down frame buildings that escaped the conflagration of 1871. Poor sanitation and rear alley tenements, in which over a quarter of the population still lived in 1914, made the district one of the shabbiest in the city.[17]

Many families supplemented their incomes by renting to lodgers, and the overcrowding that resulted helped orient the social life of the community away from the home. But a lively street life was difficult amidst the unpaved byways strewn with garbage, and the intensive use of land precluded the establishment of beer gardens as they had existed in the old country. Sunday strolls, another tradition, were difficult because Chicago's large parks were so far away. Instead, much of the socializing remained indoors. In the 1860s they opened the *Slovanska Lipa*, a community building, and by the end of the next decade they had also established a pair of *sokols*, or gymnastic societies. These institutions, along with church parishes, became the principal centers of Bohemian leisure and benevolent activities.[18]

The saloons provided a valuable supplement to this active community organization. They provided the usual attractions of tables for playing cards and subscribed to *Svornost* and *Denni Hlasatel*, the local newspapers. But the meeting hall upstairs or next door was in many ways the most important part of the Czech or Slovak saloon. Substantial evidence indicates that no other ethnic group in the city made as frequent use of that type of saloon facility. Certain barrooms became the centers of the local Free Thought movement, which actively protested the dominant role of the Catholic church in the community and sought to establish their own informal educational system. They became social outcasts and in some parts of the community encountered difficulty in gaining access to many meeting facilities. And so certain saloons became their unofficial headquarters.[19]

Dozens of other community groups rented the saloon halls. They held large weekend dances to raise funds for various benevolent purposes and made them the focus of neighborhood social life. Institutions such as the *Utulna A. Sirotcinec*, or Old People's Home, depended almost entirely on these gatherings for funds. An inexpensive bar permit license from the city and a twenty-five-dollar federal tax stamp allowed the revelry to continue until 4:00 A.M., long past the normal saloon closing hour. The most serious problem was in finding a hall to rent, as some were booked up months, even years, in advance. One group solved that problem by purchasing an entire saloon, just so they would have their own hall to use each weekend.[20]

A fourth group which frequented the barrooms of their fellow countrymen were the Poles. Few of them had landed in the Boston area, and those who did had chosen to live in the peripheral sections of Cambridgeport, South Boston, Dorchester, and Roxbury, rather than in the central part of the city. But Chicago and the other industrial cities of the Great Lakes region became the home of thousands.[21] In 1890 there were only 24,086 Poles in Chicago; two decades later there were 126,059. Not only did they grow rapidly in numbers, but they also distinguished themselves by remaining in compact communities longer than other groups. That fact, along with their poverty, directly shaped their community life.[22]

There were four major Polish communities in Chicago. The oldest was on the Near Northwest Side, near Milwaukee Avenue and Division Street. Later settlements developed just west of Bohemian Pilsen, out near the stockyards of Packingtown, and, finally, near the steel mills of South Chicago. These communities suffered from the common problems of tenement neighborhoods: garbage in the streets, filthy food, unwholesome milk, and overcrowded housing. But in the case of the Poles, the misery was compounded because the neighborhoods they inherited were third- or fourth-hand. What had been decayed tenements when the Germans left had deteriorated even more with the arrival and departure of the Irish, Scandinavians, and even the North Side Italians. But the Poles held tenaciously to housing that was within walking distance of work.[23] And when they erected magnificent churches like St. Stanislaus Kostka, built in 1892, they also created community anchors that resisted later decades of residential mobility.[24]

The Polish saloon was devoid of distinguishing characteristics. It had a few tables and a bar; it sold both whiskey and beer, but little wine. It was strictly an indoors institution, and it sold enough beer to keep the Polish-dominated White Eagle Brewing Company busy. But what was most curious about the Polish saloonkeeper was the way he came under attack within his own community. Other ethnic groups had their temperance societies, but probably no other nationality of dealers was subjected to such a constant stream of verbal abuse as were the Poles.[25]

Several factors contributed to such overt antisaloon feelings. First, there was the problem of image. Poles, as among the later of the immigrant groups, seemed especially sensitive about the way they appeared to outsiders. Saloonkeepers, by filling their countrymen with whiskey, degraded the respectability of Polonia. *Dziennik Zwiazkowy*, a local newspaper, editorialized, "We implore you to behave yourself respectably, as cultured people. How can we ever hope to gain any respect among other nationalities when disorderly drunken conduct is permitted among Poles."[26] Leaders implied what sociologists like William I. Thomas and Florian Znaniecki later concluded—that the unsettling conditions of immigration had created an extraordinary amount of social disorientation among the Poles.[27]

According to the newspapers, drink did its most serious damage to the traditional family structure. Parents no longer provided a positive example for their offspring to follow. "Men are drunkards, women are drunkards, and the innocent looking at this get used to bad habits," complained the *Narod Polski*.[28] But it was the dance hall issue that aroused the greatest amount of anxiety in the community. This problem, like that of housing, became more difficult to solve because of the relatively late arrival of the Poles. Near the turn of the century a dancing craze swept the imagination of Chicago's young people. Saloons in many parts of the city, including Polish neighborhoods, opened halls. And when the children of the most recent immigrants began to attend, the saloon was drawn into the common intergenerational conflict. "The fondness of dancing," complained one observer, "makes young girls subject to excessive spending. Their clothes wear out quickly and soil easily, so more often the thoughtless girl buys dresses, ribbons, and other adornments, instead of saving her hard earned cash."[29] Moreover, young girls gambled and drank in front of everyone, "so openly and publicly that it looks as if all gentlemen saloonkeepers belong to the same protection as our glorious police."[30]

Some of these antisaloon attacks may have been rooted in a traditional ethnic bias imported from the homeland. As *Abstynet*, a community temperance tract, complained:

> In Poland, most of [the] saloons are operated by Jews, because a real Pole and Catholic thinks himself too respected and too honorable to operate such a vile business. And this is the reason that saloonkeepers and saloons in Poland are insulted and become mean to the Polish people. And for that reason Poles are filled with antipathy and anti-Semitic aversions. In America it is the opposite. Polish Catholics are operating saloons because it is simpler and more profitable than any other business.
>
> To be a saloonkeeper every ordinary man with the ambition of a good drunkard or plenty of "gab" will do. Even the brewery helps them financially when it comes to the rent, fixtures, merchandise and furniture; they give them these for credit.
>
> Poles willingly give their support to their countrymen, go to the saloon and support them in the name of patriotism, and saloonkeepers good-heartedly serve them drinks of any kind, domestic or imported.
>
> Business is going good. Support your fellow countrymen with the aim of solidarity.[31]

But despite the complaints of temperance interests, the number of Polish saloons continued to grow.

Ethnic Universals

The other type of ethnic saloonkeepers, the "universals," included
the Germans and Irish, as well as the "Americans," who were either of
native stock or the descendants of earlier foreign-born arrivals. Their
bars were widely dispersed around the city; few wards in either city
lacked an Irish saloon. And in Chicago where the Germans were much
more numerous, a "Kraut" saloonkeeper could be found even in such
unlikely places as the South Chicago steel mill district or the teeming
Near West Side neighborhood of Hull House. In 1893 the latter area
was predominantly Italian, Austro-Hungarian, Russian (Jewish), and
Polish; Germans and Irish were a very small percentage of the population. But, nonetheless, of the 118 saloons, no fewer than fifteen had
German proprietors and eight were operated by Irish. Even the densely
populated North End of Boston, which moved through a succession of
Irish, Jewish, and Italian dominance, had one or two German places
that survived until prohibition.[32]

The Irish were among the earliest participants in the saloon business
in both cities. In Boston the operation of a small hotel, restaurant,
boarding house, or saloon became a favorite first step in economic mobility. The crowded streets of the North and South Ends where the
Irish resided at mid-century carried names such as O'Malley and Kennedy over the saloon doors. Along with the church, the barroom became a vital center of neighborhood social life. When the bulk of the
population moved elsewhere and the Irish that remained in the South
End could be described as a "people with ancestry," or fairly well assimilated, the saloon remained in the community, hosting dances and
relief benefits and serving as the meeting place after wakes.

Chicago's Irish community dispersed as rapidly as Boston's, if not
more so. Where that group remained the predominant foreign group in
Boston until nearly the turn of the century, Chicago experienced a
large German migration that submerged the Irish culturally if not politically. People talked of Chicago as a German city, rather than an
Irish one. The ranks of the latter declined proportionately as well as
absolutely as the decades passed. In 1870 they constituted 13.4 percent
of the total population; in 1880, 8.8 percent. By 1890 there were
70,028 in the city, or 6.4 percent of the total population; this also represented only about 15 percent of the foreign-born. During the next
two decades the number of immigrant arrivals and births failed to off-

set the deaths and dispersals to suburban and other out-of-city locations, and the absolute number fell by nearly 4,000. The influx of other groups, in the meantime, reduced the Irish percentage figures to about half of their previous level.[33]

Despite this statistical decline, Chicago's Irish continued to enter the saloon business in large numbers. In part this reflected a national trend. Census figures indicate that from the turn of the century until 1920, the Irish actually demonstrated a rather stable or slightly increasing tendancy to remain in the retail liquor business across the generations. Where nearly every other ethnic group saw the first arrivals enter the saloon trade in larger numbers than their proportion of the population, the next generation did so in decreasing numbers. In Chicago, the Irish actually became increasingly entrenched in the business. In 1880, 410, or 14.7 percent of the city's 2,782 saloonkeepers recorded in the Federal census were Irish; in 1900, the 1,286 Irish bar proprietors made up 21 percent of the 6,130 saloonkeepers.[34]

Most Irish barrooms were more distinguished for the facilities they lacked than for those they contained. The interiors often were unspectacular; marble wainscoting seldom adorned the walls, and the spittoons bore evidence of thousands of kicks. The lunch was plain, more of a standard fare than something designed to attract crowds. The favorite drink was whiskey. Only gradually did the Irish accept the German's brew. In both cities that was probably due in part to the fact that Irishmen who purchased breweries in the 1870s and 1880s could appeal to the ethnic pride of their fellow countrymen. Perhaps the most unique characteristic of Irish bars was their aversion to tables; they were stand-up places. There was an old myth that an Irishman could down a greater volume of whiskey if he remained in an upright position. But, then, the Germans, who enjoyed drinking at tables, had their own mythical abilities to consume heroic quantities of alcohol. "If a Slav ever tried to imitate a German in his drinking habits, he will drink himself to death," complained a Polish newspaper.[35]

The typical German saloon is also hard to describe. The downtown places were fancy and primarily serviced the noon-hour trade. These places were not designed to appeal to family or neighborhood social life. The German bars in the outlying neighborhoods, however, tended to be quite different. Where the Irish bar tended to be dimly illuminated, the lighting in the German place was as bright as daylight. This might have reflected a more substantial investment or a superior building, but it probably reflected the family orientation of the place. The German saloon was as much a family institution as the Irish bar was a man's world. Unescorted women were not welcome because they might be prostitutes, but the entire family was, including the children. Thus, the common complaint that the saloon destroyed the family had far less relevance in German communities.

There were also few comments about crime in German saloons, leading some observers to believe that the barroom was a stabilizing rather than a disruptive influence in the adjustment of immigrants to Chicago life.[36] The peaceful barroom of Otto, Fritz, or August was usually depicted in the press as an honest operation. Disreputable women seldom entered, and drunkenness was uncommon.[37] As one German saloonkeeper who operated in the North Center area of Chicago commented: "The story goes that when a German comes to America, he looks for just three things — a saloon, a church, and a singing society. . . . When Germans drink they do not get mad, but just happy and want to sing and be friendly."[38]

Some German theaters and Turner halls, gymnasium-headquarters of athletic societies, served beer, but the most unique form of German drinking place was the beer garden. This institution traced its origins back to the continental custom of enjoying an outdoor Sunday afternoon with the family. Transplanted to urban America, the Turners frequently enjoyed outings at picnic grounds like Colehour's in South Chicago. Entrepreneurs like Peter Rinderer also realized the potential profits in locating near a crowded city like Chicago. In 1865 he opened Ogden Grove, named for the land company from whom he purchased the ground. Others followed and combined their beer gardens with the inns that were designed to accommodate traveling farmers. Thus, a person who sold the family livestock or grain in the city could enjoy an overnight stopover at Chicago's Bismarck Gardens as well as a beer in an outdoor setting.[39]

The beer gardens were as varied as other public drinking spots. No two of them were exactly alike, but most were as ornate and attractive as the competition demanded. All had tables and chairs rather than a bar, and the food they served was often as important as beer in attracting trade. Music was essential, but what started as small brass bands eventually evolved into orchestras, famous soloists, and vaudeville-type performances. The Summer Bazaar Garden, which occupied Boston's Mechanics' Hall Building in the late 1880s, had a military band as well as a full orchestra and included billiards, bowling, rifle practice, dancing, and skating among its attractions. Fischers, on the shores of Lake Michigan on the northern edge of Chicago, advertised its cool breezes and bathing beach. As the years passed, mechanical contrivances rivaled natural features. In 1901 when the Keeley Brewing Company built the commodious Heidelberg Gardens, seating 444 at 121 tables, it installed a rock fountain on which a gardener had induced moss to grow. Thirteen years later Frank Lloyd Wright's Edelweiss Garden (more commonly known as Midway Gardens) featured an electric fountain that played colored lights on the water sprays.[40]

Most of these places were more impersonal than the corner saloon. Nearly all collected admission fees as a cover charge; this was usually a quarter — a fairly large amount for the late 1880s — which made up for the freeloaders who wanted to do a lot of listening but only a little drinking. Public transit also became an increasingly important factor in the trade. Resorts in both cities clustered near streetcar lines, with a location at an intersection considered especially choice. Two Boston places, Maolis Gardens in Nahant and Melville Garden at Downer Landing, reminded guidebook readers that only a pleasant boat ride separated them from Boston's India Wharf. Many Bostonians also rode to bucolic relaxation on trains. By 1879 there were dozens of picnic groves scattered near rail lines, five of them operated by the railroads themselves. That year picnic passengers going to and from Boston numbered 125,000 on trains, and in 1878 harbor boats transported nearly 300,000 in each direction. Three of the Boston parks reported their aggregate attendance for 1879 at over 450,000.[41]

The beer gardens were especially attractive to families who found them pleasant places to spend a summer afternoon. Some reform-oriented commentators thought the mixed company was a favorable influence on drinking practices, but Mrs. E. Trask Hill of the Massachusetts Women's Christian Prohibition League fumed, "This may be tolerated in atheistic Germany, beer-loving Chicago and Milwaukee, licentious Paris or cosmopolitan New York, but we cannot tolerate it in Puritan Boston."[42] Temperance advocates argued that children and young men and women were exposed to the evils of the drink trade at a tender age. The presence of attractive young girls and drink at the same location aroused irresistible temptations among men.[43] Finally, the influx of large numbers of strangers on Sundays worried many residents. In 1880 Henry F. Coe, a Boston City Council member from Roxbury, complained that "in the last year or two a number of places of public resort have been opened and great multitudes of people have gone out to these gardens. The consequence has been that these people have spread out over the country round about, and there has been an insufficient force of police to protect the property of those living in the vicinity."[44]

On the surface, the Germans and Irish seemed to have a community of interests in the liquor business. Members of both groups had invested a great amount of money in the business; both had been in it a long period of time and claimed a common enemy in the "temperance cranks." But actually there was a large amount of hostility between the two ethnic groups. The problem of language divided the Chicago liquor dealers' associations before they had a chance to become influential. The Irish became irritated when the Germans insisted on using their native tongue during meetings; the latter group complained that many of their members knew no English. The resulting split never completely healed. The Irish always held little more than a secondary role in the hierarchy of the liquor dealers' protective associations, despite their numbers. In fact, only one Irishman, Thomas Nolan, ever headed the county-wide federation known as the Cook County District.[45] The opposite was true in Boston, where the Germans were the minority among saloonkeepers.

The dissension went far beyond matters of language. Germans and Irish operated barrooms all over the city, not merely in their own neighborhoods, and were competitors in a very real sense of the word. Had their clientele been drawn wholly from the small ethnic islands and enclaves, as it was with most other foreign-born groups, perhaps the conflict might not have been so sharp. But even this factor was overshadowed by others. Differences in drinking habits added further political overtones. The Irish claimed that the idea of a differential license rate, with beer assessed at a lower rate than whiskey, was a plot hatched by German saloonkeepers and legislators. The "Krauts" could have their beer at a lower annual fee, and the whiskey-drinking Irish had their whiskey. When the matter of Sunday closing came up, the Germans claimed that the Irish, who lacked the traditions of the Continental Sunday, cared little whether the saloons were officially open or closed. The Irish, they argued, had no particular attachment to Sunday opening, and if an Irish barkeeper chose to keep in operation that day, he could always pay off the Irish cop. The German, on the other hand, suffered while the Irish laughed.[46]

The Saloon and the Blacks

Black residents faced institutional as well as residential segregation. Social customs had excluded them from certain places for many years but had grown in scope and rigidity with the increasing numbers of new arrivals from the South. Although there had been a civil rights law, which gave them full access to public and semipublic places, on the books since 1885, there was no guarantee of enforcement. The legal machinery of the state, county, and city usually took the side of the minority group, but the punishment given offenders was minimal.[47] In 1893, for instance, Chapin and Gore refused to serve a black customer in one of their downtown locations; the fine was twenty-five dollars.[48]

The defendants in early public accommodations suits claimed that the state law did not specifically mention saloons. In 1896 the Illinois Supreme Court remedied that shortcoming by identifying a long list of businesses, including saloons, that were to be covered by the act. And in 1903 the General Assembly finally amended the statute to recognize its broader coverage.[49] Even then, there was no guarantee of service for blacks. Because it was not classified as a criminal law, the police made no arrests for its violation; someone had to go to court and institute civil action. In one notable case J. S. Thurman, a black attorney, was refused service at Riley and Early's saloon on Randolph Street downtown. He collected $200 in damages when the defendents refused to show up in court. The black press gave the case considerable publicity, prompting *Mida's Criterion* to warn its liquor-dealer readers that "the civil rights business is a two-edged sword, and it does not pay to monkey with it, especially in Chicago."[50]

The liquor dealers themselves frequently ignored the official city position on the matter. Confrontation led to occasional physical violence. For instance, during the long 1905 teamsters' strike, blacks attacked Ludwig Lewi's saloon at Twenty-Ninth and Armour. The neighborhood was undergoing a racial transition, and Lewi had been known to exclude blacks. The use of 600 blacks as "scab" labor by the team-owning interests added to the tensions. Then one day in late May, Lewi's bartender shot and killed a black who was involved in a fight just outside the door; the owner and a friend were beaten severely, and the inside of the barroom was vandalized and looted.[51]

The racial issue placed the liquor dealers' association in an awkward position. On one hand, it had to maintain peaceful relations with city hall; there were literally dozens of ways that city officials could use to seek vengeance if they did not. The association had also featured Abraham Lincoln's experience at barkeeping at New Salem in its anti-temperance propaganda. But saloonmen wanted the right to serve whomever they wanted, and in the long run, the association ended up supporting the idea of racial exclusion. Although it was never a public-ly stated policy, its own lawyers defended members in discrimination suits. And when Chicago blacks founded their own liquor dealers' group, the Chicago association refused their offer of affiliation. It also remained silent when Oscar DePriest, the city's first black alderman, introduced an antidiscrimination bill in the City Council. This legisla-tion would have required the mayor to revoke the license of any busi-ness, including saloons, that refused service to Negroes. Dealers breathed more easily when the bill died in committee.[52]

An antidiscrimination law had been in operation for years in Massa-chusetts, but it did not end discrimination. As far back as 1710 anyone who held an innkeeper's license was legally bound to receive any trav-eller or lose his license. The same provisions were extended to all vic-tuallers in 1878, and since most saloonkeepers held such licenses and a traveller was defined as anyone who walked in from the street, they technically had no choice of customers. But discrimination was actual-ly common practice in Boston, and a black who tried to integrate an es-tablishment faced arrest for disturbing the peace.[53]

Even if blacks were excluded from many saloons, other barrooms provided them with substantial employment opportunities. Census data for Chicago revealed that they held 116 bartending jobs in 1900 and 137 a decade later. Another estimate claimed that in 1914 about 12 percent of the black men in that city worked in saloons and poolrooms. The number of black proprietors, however, declined after the turn of the century, from forty-eight in 1900 to thirty-three in 1910 and to twenty-three in 1916. The exact cause of that trend is impossible to es-tablish, although racial prejudice undoubtedly influenced it.[54]

The statistics for Boston indicate a much smaller connection between the saloons and the black population. That city demonstrates quite clearly the national trend away from their employment in domestic and personal service that took place around the turn of the century. White immigrants displaced them as barbers, coachmen, bootblacks, bellboys, and waiters in the downtown district.[55] Within the saloon itself, the number of black bartenders declined from sixteen in 1900 to four in 1910. The independent black saloonkeeper disappeared completely. There were only five in 1900, and by 1914 there were none at all.[56] John Daniels, in a study sponsored by South End House, attributed the trend directly to the License Board which went into operation in 1906: the new authority refused to grant liquor licenses to blacks. While no direct evidence of racial motivation exists, the care and sensitivity to public opinion with which the board selected among applicants adds considerable credence to this allegation.[57]

In Chicago, however, the saloonkeeper was an important part of the black business community. Where white barrooms seldom advertised in the daily press, the *Broad-Axe* carried numerous news stories that told of new openings, remodeled storefronts, and expanded facilities. These not only served to generate revenue for the weekly Negro press, but ads for places like the Elite Cafe and the Railroad Inn also informed readers of where they would be welcome. Business directories aimed at black consumers featured long lists of barrooms interspersed with laudatory self-help biographical sketches.[58] For example, I. C. Harris's *Colored Men's Professional and Business Directory* for 1885–86 proclaimed: "As an enterprising businessman, J. H. Howard [who owned two saloons] can, beyond a doubt, be classed among the most energetic and exemplary colored businessmen in our city. Through tact, energy and perseverance, at the same time dealing consistently with his fellow men, he has been able to make a front rank with other leading men of business and demonstrates by genius and merit what the Negro may accomplish if he is accorded half a chance in his eventful race of life."[59]

Direct appeals to customers on the basis of race were also common where the establishment was a pioneer or a "first." Barrooms that opened in changing neighborhoods were anxious to inform the black community of their establishment. Since most of these areas contained housing that was less densely packed together and in better condition than in the slums, the open-air quality of a few places was a prominent part of the advertising. The Chateau de Plaisance, 5318–26 South State, featured "band concerts, vocal solos, roller skating," as well as food and drink. Noting that "State Street cars pass the door," it called itself a "summer resort" and boasted that "Ladies and Gentlemen . . . will find the desired spot at the only amusement park and pavillion owned and controlled by negroes in the world."[60]

Other saloon advertisements conveyed a defensive tone. Readers of the *Broad-Axe*, for instance, were told that Charles Gaskin "does not permit any kind of gambling . . . and [that] it makes no difference how many times the police raid places where gambling is conducted, it does not interfere with his business." Other places were careful to emphasize that they did not admit women.[61] The reasons for these pronouncements may lie in a growing sensitivity to race pride expressed in some quarters. Not unlike the temperance attitude in many white ethnic neighborhoods, the *Broad-Axe* considered the debauchery usually connected with saloons to be a significant impediment to progress. Although it continued to accept liquor advertising, it frequently criticized parents who sent children to buy their beer or abandoned their families during the evening hours in order to hang around saloons.[62] "Afro-American women in the Town of Lake," it complained, "frequent saloons, fill up with beer and whiskey. Then they enter churches where they hollar [sic] and shout for Jesus!"[63]

Defensive advertising was also employed to counteract the white stereotype of black saloons as dives and criminal establishments. Undoubtedly some of them were lower class, generally reflecting the economic status of their users, and actually were involved in crime. But the local press spared few adjectives in its descriptions; as one Boston story commented: "The door gave admittance to a dark, foul-smelling narrow entry, and passing through this, the ballroom of the establishment was reached. Three sets, composed of white women and colored men, were engaged in a quadrille. . . . In another corner, stretched out on a chair, were several bulky Negroes, sleeping off the effects of liquor. Chromos and cheap prints hung along the wall, and over the piano was a picture of the proprietor of the establishment."[64]

The Non-Participants: Greeks, Jews

Poverty, overcrowded housing conditions, and the resulting use of public space did not automatically result in greater patronage of saloons. A variety of social and cultural factors considerably modified the pattern of leisure and economic mobility that developed among some ethnic groups in both cities. Some neighborhoods had little dependence upon the barrooms and the attractions that they offered. These residents did not necessarily support antiliquor movements, but they remained indifferent. They chose alternate centers of social activity and routes of economic advancement.

The Greeks of Chicago and Boston were no strangers to the street. They engaged in peddling and operated open-air fruit stands in their own neighborhoods and elsewhere. In Boston a few resourceful vendors stationed themselves between the department stores and the streetcar stops, hoping to talk middle-class matrons into purchasing fruit to take home to their children. Similar skills could be found in Chicago's public places. One estimate in 1886 contended that over half of the 200 or so Greeks in that city were sidewalk fruit salesmen.[65]

Boston's Greeks lived in a small section of the South End. Although they dominated the fruit and confection business, the community never reached the size and prominence of the one in Chicago. In the latter city they lived in what became known as the Greek Delta, a triangular block bounded by Halsted, Blue Island, and Taylor streets. This was in the heart of congested Near West Side, the polyglot neighborhood that surrounded Hull House. There were a few saloonkeepers of Greek descent. Grace Abbott and the Immigrant Protective League found fifteen in 1909, a slight increase over those counted in the 1900 census. Their location in the heart of the community would seem to indicate local usage, but it was the coffeehouse, or *kaffeneion*, that functioned as the primary social gathering place. Most of these had the simplest of facilities — a few tables and plain chairs — and the fare consisted of coffee, tea, cider, soft drinks, ice cream, and native confections like baklava.[66]

The social role of the *kaffenia* was not unlike that of the saloons. Fraternal societies, mutual aid, and charity groups used them for meetings. Most Greek immigrants were unmarried males, who lived in crowded rooms, so they escaped the privatizing effect of family life. They were simply places where men met and conversed, and this activity alone probably sustained most of the 138 places in the Delta.[67] As one commentator described it:

There are hundreds of these restaurants standing side by side and all occupying ancient one and two story brick and wooden houses. In many cases, these buildings are very dilapidated and deteriorated. Sanitation on the whole, is not very good. The coffee shops do not have clean appearances and in reality are not very clean. . . .

On the side of social life of the "Delta" is the coffee shops. Each one stands for a district of the "old country," and men go to the coffee house which bears the name of their district. They sit around the tables and talk about conditions — political, social and economic — of Greece and their respective districts, drinking Turkish coffee or inhaling the heavy smoke of a Turkish pipe. Or they play cards — pinochle or "thirty-one" — smoking cigarettes and arguing very vociferously at times. To observe this district at its most picturesque moments, walk down the various streets on Saturday or Sunday night. For the most part the arc lights along the curb supply little illumination, so that the neighborhood has a dingy and shadowy appearance. But the apparently endless row of coffee houses are all brightly lighted and may be seen at their gayest on Halsted Street. One also finds seemingly endless numbers of tables inside these places, most of which are occupied by the dark and mustached sons of Hellas.[68]

Like their Greek neighbors, Jewish immigrants also made intensive use of public areas but not saloons. Peddlers and outdoor stands of every variety were very common. The street, even if muddy and littered, was a welcome refuge from the tenement and the sweatshop, and a lively social life evolved from door sills and steps of buildings. Like other foreign-born residents, many Jewish families took in lodgers to supplement their incomes, and the overcrowding that resulted placed even more of a burden on the limited housing facilities.[69]

But even these conditions did not produce much saloon patronage. That institution meant little to Jewish social life. Barrooms were scarce in Chicago's ghetto, even along the few blocks of busy Halsted Street that ran through the Maxwell Street market area of the Near West Side. Similar conditions prevailed in Boston's South End Jewish neighborhood, where such streets as Genesee, Oneida, Oswego, and Seneca were virtually saloonless.[70]

Instead, most drinking among Jews was confined to religious ceremonies or done in the privacy of the family or the worship service. There was also a wide variety of alternate institutions that provided places for sociability. Cigar stores, soft-drink parlors, and candy shops furnished newspapers and a few tables and chairs for spontaneous and unstructured socializing. A system of private charities removed the need for the philanthropic activities associated with saloons, while lodges and synagogues kept members busy with community welfare projects. Finally, the Yiddish theater, one of the most creative and best patronized of ethnic entertainments, drew potential customers away from saloons.[71]

Changes in this pattern, however, were clearly under way by the turn of the century. Jews exhibited a stronger tendency to move into the retail liquor business in the second generation than in the first. Although statistical precision is difficult because the census made no distinction between Jews and their Russian and Polish gentile conationalists, there is strong indication that only the Italians displayed a stronger intergenerational increase in the number of saloonkeepers. The reasons for this are not entirely clear. Both Jews and Italians saw a permanent store building with one's name over its door as a desired economic goal; indoor businesses were usually considered to be of higher status than the street trades. Also, the fact that Jews occasionally been the public-house keepers in European countries may have been a contributing factor; some, perhaps, were only returning to a traditional family business.[72]

The Yiddish press viewed the growing prominence of the saloon as another sad example of assimilation. American-born children acquired the tastes, habits, ideas, and social institutions of the larger city. Editors blamed the decline of the Yiddish theater on youths who went outside the neighborhood for entertainment. Some patronized saloons elsewhere in the city, but when they found other Jews operating bars near the ghetto, public drinking seemed more acceptable than it had to their parents. It was this tension between assimilation and the need to preserve the community and its customs that led the *Daily Jewish Courier* to support the temperance movement.[73] This was an unprecedented action, but the newspaper's rationale speaks for itself:

> We should not only sympathize with our neighbor, the Gentiles, in their fight against inebriety, but we must also apply all our energies to help them root out this plague, which is so dreadfully contagious. Gradually our young Jewish people are being dragged into this marsh. . . .
> Until now we are still sharing the reputation of being a sober people but this holds good in so far as the immigrant is concerned and it hardly applies to their offspring, the first generation of Americans. The more Americanized we get, the more impreg-

nated we become with the general faults of our neighbors. It is no
uncommon occurrence nowadays to see a young Jew indulging in
liquor, and not exactly in Jewish districts on Purim or Simchas
Torah. . . .

The Jewish neighborhoods have their saloons and wine-joints
where young Jewish people spend their time at the bar or in provi-
sional rooms where one can drink and do everything that should
not be done. There is nothing new in seeing Jewish girls standing
on street corners, waiting for a friend to go to a Jewish saloon to
spend an evening at a table covered with liquors. . . . There is no
excuse for us to stand aloof and witness unconcernedly how the
serpent of inebriety innoculates its poison into the best elements of
our youth.[74]

Bootstraps

The structure of the retail liquor business helped to promote the
ethnic diversity among saloons. Would-be proprietors needed little
capital to open, and so even the poorest among the recent immigrants
could realize the dream of rapid social mobility. The proof was in the
front door key he carried in his pocket. The competition among barrooms, especially in Chicago, also meant that the brewers who bank-
rolled their retail outlets were especially interested in tapping new
consumer markets. The recently arrived immigrant communities,
trapped in the tenement districts, provided rich opportunities. Brewers
had previously concentrated their efforts in those same inner-city districts where they had already secured the necessary buildings. All they
needed were personnel who could speak the language, tell the proper
stories, and prepare the right food for the lunch. The task was made
easier by the high rate of failure, since the constant turnover of proprietors made room for incoming ethnic groups.

Those changes are reflected in what the census statistics tell us about
saloonkeepers and bartenders and how their ethnic backgrounds
changed during the last two decades of the nineteenth century. First,
the figures for 1880 reveal that native-born people still operated a surprising number of saloons. The data does not distinguish between
immigrants and the offspring of immigrants; indeed, some of them
might be the thirty-year-old sons of those who fled the potato famine. In
either case, a clear majority (56.2 percent) of Boston's liquor dealers
and bartenders were born in America, while 59.1 percent of that city's

total work force claimed similar origins. The saloon, however, remained a relatively unpopular vocational choice among all of Boston's native-born, accounting for only 0.7 percent of their total work force. Meanwhile, in Chicago, the native-born were of far less importance, accounting for only 23.1 percent of the saloonkeepers and 44.2 percent of the total city work force. Furthermore, Chicago workers born in America apparently found greater opportunities in other kinds of economic activity. Only .01 percent of Chicago's U.S.-born workers joined the retail liquor business. In other words, an American-born Bostonian was seventy times more likely to work behind a bar than was his or her Chicago counterpart.[75]

The 1880 census figures also lend credibility to some ethnic stereotypes, while revealing significant flaws in others. First, there is the image of the Irish saloonkeeper. While tradition held that every other Celt wore a bar apron, they actually demonstrated no particular affinity for the liquor business in 1880. The Irish were the largest foreign-born group in Boston (23.3 percent of the city total), but made up only 22.3 percent of the liquor retailing employees. Furthermore, that trade claimed only 0.7 percent of the total Irish work force, exactly the same percentage as among the native-born. Meanwhile, Chicago's Irish, though only 12.5 percent of the work force, claimed 14.7 percent of the liquor jobs. What is more important is the fact that they demonstrated well over twice as much interest in the trade as did their Boston counterparts. But even then, only 1.7 percent of all Irish workers in Chicago became saloonkeepers or bartenders.

In both cities the Germans demonstrated the most consistent interest in the liquor business. In Boston they represented only 2.7 percent of the work force, but held 10.4 percent of the retail liquor jobs. And that figure did not even include brewery workers. Furthermore, no ethnic group in 1880 had a greater proportion of its workers in the liquor business; 2.9 percent of all German workers could be found behind the counter, over four times the proportion found among the Irish. Similarly, in Chicago the German-born constituted 21.3 percent of the working population, as compared with 42.8 percent of the bartenders and saloonkeepers. Within the German community the same percentage (2.9 percent) of workers went into the trade in Chicago as in Boston.

Both cities also contained a scattering of less-numerous ethnic groups. The share of the saloon market claimed by the English-born,

English-Canadians, and Scandinavians in both cities was smaller than their population should have warranted. The only exception, and it was a minor one, was Boston's Scandinavians, who were 0.8 percent of the population, but whose saloons made up 1.1 percent of the total. Of greater interest are those groups whose numbers are lumped together in the mysterious category labeled "other." Although their individual identities remain unknown, they probably included those people commonly classified as "new immigrants": French-Canadians, Poles, Russians, Russian Jews, Austro-Hungarians, and Italians. In both cities, this category operated more than its share of saloons, although the figures do not reveal individual ethnic associations. Collectively, they were 1.2 percent of Boston's work force, but together claimed 3.7 percent of that city's saloon jobs. Chicago's newer immigrants were a much more significant factor in the liquor business, making up 7.0 percent of the city's working population and 11.3 percent of its saloonkeepers. Furthermore, their attraction to the saloon trade was even more significant, since 2.3 percent of the population classified as "other" went into the liquor trade. That meant that only among the Germans did a larger portion of the group (2.9 percent) choose the liquor trade as their occupation. That figure would prove to be the beginning of an important trend in Chicago.

Unfortunately, the next census did not specify the ethnicity of occupational groups, but the 1900 census did, and the twenty-year interval provides enough time to document some trends. First, there was an apparent decline in the percentage of native-born dealers and bartenders in both cities. Their proportion of all bartending and saloonkeeping positions fell from 23.1 percent to 18.1 percent in Chicago and from 56.2 percent to 23.3 percent in Boston. That decline was only relative, however, in Chicago; the total number of native-born in both job categories actually increased from 642 to 1,931. But in Boston, the U.S.-born suffered a decline in actual numbers as well — 619 in 1880 compared with 562 in 1900. The combined total of the two jobs, however, masked an important contrast between the two cities. While the 1880 census did not differentiate between saloonkeepers and bartenders, the one in 1900 did. The latter figures reveal that Chicago's native-born constituted only 7.7 percent of the former and 32.9 percent of the latter. In Boston, that group accounted for 39.7 percent of the proprietors, and 14.5 percent of the barmen at the turn of the century. In other words, the American-born people left in the liquor trade in 1900 were much more likely to be proprietors in Boston and bartenders in Chicago.[76]

The native-born were not the only group to undergo a relative decline in the retail liquor business. The Germans, for instance, lost considerable ground in Chicago. Where they had accounted for 42.8 percent of all bartender and saloonkeeper jobs in 1880, that figure stood at 36.3 percent in 1900. The actual number of Germans in the liquor trades did increase, from 1,192 to 3,879 in the same period, but that expansion failed to keep pace with the growth of other nationalities in the business. Thus, while the proportion of Germans among the total work force climbed from 21.3 percent in 1880 to 24.7 percent in 1900, their share of liquor dealerships declined. Likewise, statistics indicate that fewer among the Germans entered the liquor business. Whereas 2.9 percent of all Germans in Chicago had gone into the business in 1880, only 2.2 percent found it attractive in 1900.

In Boston, meanwhile, Germans held their ground in the liquor business. Although they became more numerous in that city's total labor force, growing from 2.7 percent in 1880 to 6.7 percent in 1900, their portion of the saloon proprietorships remained nearly stable. The 1880 census did not differentiate between owners and bartenders, but an 1885 Massachusetts state census did. The latter figure lists ninety-seven men and two women as proprietors; they were 7.8 percent of all saloon owners in the Hub. Because of the limitation law and the way the license officials implemented it, there were only seventy-one German proprietorships in 1900. This number still amounted to 7.7 percent of the total, so the proportion of German owners remained approximately the same, a different situation than prevailed in Chicago. Perhaps the most important contrast between the two cities, however, is in the balance between proprietors and bartenders. In 1900 there were 2,298 German saloonkeepers and 1,524 bartenders in Chicago. This meant that Germans either operated one-man businesses or employed other ethnic groups behind the bar. By contrast, however, that same census found more German bartenders (ninety-seven) than owners (seventy-one) in Boston, so there was a greater likelihood that a person of that national origin worked for someone else.

If the native-born and Germans were finding the liquor business less attractive in the last two decades of the century, who was replacing them? Some of the smaller groups among the older nationalities assumed a slightly larger proportion of the trade, but there was no consistent pattern. In Chicago the British-born and English-Canadians held a declining share of liquor jobs, but the share claimed by Scandinavians increased sharply from 0.1 percent in 1880 to 4.8 percent in 1900, a change that was much greater than their population increase would have warranted. In Boston all three groups enjoyed small gains in the liquor trade, but in neither city did they collectively command a major share of the liquor trade (12 percent in Boston and only 8.9 percent in Chicago). Thus, the larger share of the people who were displacing Germans and native-born were representatives of other groups.

In Boston two groups accounted for the bulk of the redistribution. First, there were the newly arrived immigrants. In 1880 they had claimed 3.7 percent of the liquor jobs, while in 1900 that figure had grown to 12.5 percent. Italians (4.9 percent) accounted for the largest share of the new trade. Poles, Russians (probably Jews), and French-Canadians made up only a tiny proportion of the total, while those of "mixed parentage" held 4.2 percent of the retail liquor jobs. The most significant change in Boston, however, was the growing predominance of the Irish among the dealerships. In those same two decades, they managed to increase their share of the trade by nearly two-and-one-half times. In 1880 they had held 22.3 percent of all liquor jobs, while in 1900 they claimed 52.6 percent of the combined total of proprietor and bartender positions. The largest share of the increase came in the subordinate bartender jobs, but the number of Irish proprietors also rose dramatically.

The ethnic pattern of Chicago's liquor trade evolved in a different direction. First, the proportion of Irish in the combined liquor trades declined slightly, from 14.7 percent to 14.4 percent, rather than increasing as had been the case in Boston. Chicago's total Irish working population also remained roughly the same, increasing modestly from 12.5 percent of the total to 14.3 percent; this increase was small when compared to the fact that Boston's Irish increased from 23.3 percent to 33.7 percent of that city's work force. Furthermore, whereas the Irish behind Boston's bars were overwhelmingly employed as bartenders, those working in Chicago tended to be the proprietors; 21 percent of Chicago's proprietors were Irish, but only 5 percent of the bartenders were sons of Erin.

The most significant difference between the two cities was the role that was assumed by the later immigrant groups. Whereas they constituted only 12.5 percent of all saloon employees in Boston in 1900, they were 26 percent of that total in Chicago. That statistic proved to be of great importance, for saloon licenses were widely distributed among Chicago's newcomers. French-Canadians, only a tiny portion (2 percent) of the city's work force, claimed 1.3 percent of the barroom jobs, while Russians held 2.5 percent of these jobs and were 2.1 percent of the populace. Those were only the smallest among the groups. Poles got 4.7 percent of the jobs, while Austro-Hungarians got 6.2 percent, and Italians, 5.1 percent. Another 5.6 percent was distributed among a variety of newly arrived people. Moreover, the newcomer in Chicago was more likely to be a proprietor than a mere bartender. The Windy City really was a place of great opportunities.

Two important factors accounted for the differing ethnic distribution in the liquor trade of the two cities. First, the saloon was a reasonable reflection of the ethnic patterns of the working populations. Chicago was a much more heterogeneous place. Whereas Boston continued to be home for a substantial number of Irish immigrants (33 percent of the total in 1900), it had few Slavic peoples. The Hub had only 2,404 Poles and 1,012 Austro-Hungarians in 1900, and to service their needs, there were only three Polish saloonkeepers, no Polish bartenders, and no Austro-Hungarians at all in the liquor trade. The Scandinavians that year numbered only 5,129, and even the famous Italian colonies totaled only 8,616 residents. By contrast, Chicago's largest foreign-born group, the Germans, made up only 24.7 percent of the working population in 1900, and the remainder was scattered among a wide variety of nationalities. The greater the diversity of people, the greater the need for saloons to service the needs of each group.

Second, the regulatory and financial situations differed markedly in the two cities. Boston remained a tightly controlled town, where a license was difficult to obtain and cost over $10,000. Brewery competition was less strenuous, and so the brewers were not as anxious to open new markets by subsidizing neophyte immigrant businesses. As a result, the liquor business in Boston appears to be far less responsive to the changing ethnic structure of the city. Instead, Boston liquor wholesalers, many of the larger of them being Irish, installed fellow countrymen behind the bars of their small chains of saloons.

In Chicago the opposite conditions prevailed. Until 1906 the license fee remained at $500, quite moderate compared with Boston's soaring rates. Prior to that date there also was no limit on the number of licenses issued in Chicago and no premium to drive up the value of the annual permit. Brewers could establish as many outlets as they could afford, and the resulting overcompetition brought their agents into the newest and poorest neighborhoods in search of entrepreneurial talent.

That fact was reflected in the way that young men in ethnic neighborhoods turned to the liquor business to seek their fortunes. In every one of Chicago's ethnic communities, a greater proportion of the working men entered the liquor business than did their counterparts in Boston. The Italian communities provide the most dramatic contrast. In 1900 the Hub had only 24 Italian proprietors and 72 Italian bartenders to quench the thirst of 7,694 Italian working men and 922 Italian working women. This meant that 2 percent of all employed Italian-born males were in the liquor business. On the other hand, Chicago's 213 Italian saloonkeepers (including one woman) and 313 bartenders served 8,830 Italian men and 810 women. Thus, 6.2 percent of all Italian men in Chicago entered the liquor trade, making it the largest proportion of any ethnic group to concentrate in the retail liquor business at any time in the history of either city. Not even the Irish or the Germans could equal that record.

Conclusion: A Mirror of City Life

The story of the saloon as an ethnic institution in Chicago and Boston was shaped by three basic factors. First, and perhaps most obvious, was the fact that the saloons of some ethnic groups were more open and more accessible to the general population than were those of other nationalities. Irish and German places, dispersed and assimilated, were often located to be convenient to an anonymous stream of traffic, although some bars representing both ethnic groups drew their customers from a narrow neighborhood base. Other ethnic groups, including Scandinavians, Bohemians, Italians, and Poles, were divided from fellow drinkers by language, food, and internal customs. Greeks and Jews, meanwhile, generated their own substitutes for saloons. Finally, blacks suffered discrimination that all but eliminated their participation in the Boston liquor business. Black Chicagoans became saloonkeepers in much greater numbers, operating both Levee district dives that drew "sports" of all races and nationalities and ethnocentric bars to serve the emerging Black Belt.

Second, the heterogeneity and social class of the street life surrounding the saloon had an obvious impact on the activities inside. Bars in the "portal of entry" neighborhoods, where the most recently arrived immigrants lived, serviced customers who were most often poor, clung most tightly to ethnic customs, and seldom spoke English. The migration of ethnic groups outward led to more homogeneous areas, where fewer of the customers depended on the barroom for the necessities of life or emergency relief. Ultimately, the free lunch on the sideboard became more Americanized. Thus, in part, the status of the Irish and German saloons as ethnic universals came from the economic mobility and assimilation of those two nationalities.

A third factor in shaping ethnic saloons was the nature of the licensing system and the manner in which this allowed outside economic interests to bankroll individual barrooms. In Boston high license fees and prohibitive premiums severely limited the access by newcomers to the liquor business. As Irish entrepreneurs gained more money, they took over a larger share of the business from the native-born, who moved into other activities. The nonethnocentric type of bar that resulted from Irish domination fitted the goal of Boston license authorities: located on major streets and devoid of as many ties to dependent tenement populations and ethnic customs as possible.

Quite the opposite happened in Chicago. Cheap beer, comparatively cheap licenses, the lack of a premium, the domination by aggressive breweries, easy entry into the business, and the tendancy to allow overcompetition among too many outlets all allowed great flexibility in responding to the heterogeneous immigrant tide. Native-born, German, and Irish barkeeps gave way to an increasing number of the so-called new immigrants. None of the latter nationalities made up more than a few percent of the trade, but as a group they claimed an important share of the business. Thus, the saloon in Chicago became an important avenue of social mobility for the newcomer.

CHAPTER 6

The Saloon in
a City of Strangers

T HE URBAN TRANSPORTATION revolution of the last quarter of the
nineteenth century transformed the metropolis and the lives of the people within it. The omnibus, followed by the horsecar, cable car, electric
streetcar, elevated, and subway, reduced commuting time and dispersed the city.[1] The new mobility also remade neighborhoods. Just as
work and home became separated, other areas assumed more specialized functions: industrial, wholesale, retail, vice, entertainment, and
culture, to name a few. And the widening range of movement also
helped to create an anonymous city that was increasingly mobile and
rootless.

The city of strangers tested the malleability of the saloon. Barrooms
that catered to an endless flow of people who were sometimes far from
home competed to develop services and attractions that often differed
from those in residential neighborhoods. In the case of the rooming
house districts the anonymity was there without the daily travel. In
either case the constant movement of the city crowds made new demands and created new opportunities for such semipublic places as
saloons.

The Commuting City

The rise of the mobile worker was one of the most important developments in the last half of the nineteenth century. There are many indications that there was a growing distance between the two places
where most men and a substantial number of women divided their daily lives. There were "cordon counts," or measures of traffic passing a
particular point. This movement of people daily into the mid-city
choked its streets and helped make them impassable. But traffic into the

downtown also contained the middle class and the wealthy; measures of population movement along streets that ran primarily through working-class neighborhoods provide a more credible measure of the rise of the commuting worker.[2]

There are many other indications that the journey to work was becoming an important part of blue-collar life. Complaints about poor transit service came not only from middle-class riders, but also from working-class patrons. People in South Boston grumbled about the infrequency of service to other parts of the city, especially for night workers.[3] And in Chicago one angry person wrote to the editor of the *Herald* to reveal the discomforts encountered on the Halsted Street car line during the winter of 1893. Signing the letter "A BRIDGEPORTER, BY NECESSITY, NOT CHOICE," the individual was indignant: "It is true our people are poor and working, most of them, in the packing houses, but the south side railway ought to remember that we are not pigs; and yet the cars they give us cannot be compared in cleanliness with the cars the railroads furnish for their shipment of hogs. . . . And the men employed as drivers and conductors, surrounded by nothing but filth and dirt, they cannot but get rough and uncourteous and treat their passengers in a way that at times makes a man's blood boil. . . ."[4]

A number of observers became interested in the working-class commuter. In 1903 a Harvard University student named Roswell Phelps conducted a major study of journey-to-work patterns in the South End. He found that the gradual expansion of the downtown district and encroachment by industrial facilities were steadily displacing the South End's residents. His survey of 2,000 workers disclosed that only 33.5 percent lived within a mile of where they worked. Another 20.8 percent commuted one to two miles each direction, and no fewer than 31.4 percent traveled more than four miles round trip each day. Nearly all of these journeys were taken on street railways and on foot, and the distance usually had a direct correlation with the workers' economic status; the more money they made, the greater the separation between home and work.[5] The principal exception to that rule were Boston workers who lived in city tenements and worked in the suburbs. Boston housing was cheaper, and if they lost permanent employment, it would be easier to find new work, part- or full-time, in the city than in the suburbs. Because they could neither afford to live near their jobs nor pay carfare, this portion of the "Tin Bucket Brigade" walked several miles in each direction between home and work.[6]

Chicago's Special Park Commission, which was empowered to investigate tenement congestion, noted a similar movement each day of people in the slums. The Sixteenth Ward on the Near Northwest Side was not only the city's most crowded district, but also housed one of the largest groups of working-class commuters:

> One can only realize what it means to be an American when he has walked with that great army of toilers — men, women and children, which shoulder to shoulder, makes a steady stream of moving figures from five to eight o'clock on the morning and again from five to eight in the evening, marching to and from their labors along that great artery of traffic — Milwaukee Avenue. When one has walked five miles or ridden in the packed cars with men and boys, fastened like barnacles all over the platform the crowd begins to disappear.[7]

And a little further out that same street, Graham Taylor of Chicago Commons settlement could later observe that "a few steps away Milwaukee Avenue's trams and trucks roared by this corner, while down in the morning and back at night surged such tides of workingmen as were to be seen on only two or three other thoroughfares in Chicago. Such traffic as passed through our unpaved street to and from the factory freight yards at the other end of the block raised clouds of dust which rose as high as our roof."[8]

The first government response to commuting was a gradual improvement in public amenities. Slowly, both cities repaved mud and wooden block streets with stone, then brick, and finally with a smooth macadam surface.[9] Cities also began to improve their municipal lighting systems. Streetlights were once so poor that store owners regularly illuminated their own sidewalks, but the introduction of electric lights signalled a significant improvement for the convenience of commuters and shoppers.[10] Similarly, the elevation of railway tracks through residential and commercial areas not only removed a serious hazard, but also eliminated constant traffic jams that once plugged busy grade crossings.[11] None of these improvements corrected the major wrongs of urban life, and each one by itself was of no great significance. But together they do indicate that city officials were becoming aware of the increasing geographical mobility of the urbanite and concerned with the citizen who traveled some distance to work each day. And, as was so often the case, the saloon played a prominent role in shaping their plans for a convenient city.

The politics of Boston's Police Board helped to bring saloons to locations where they could profit from this mobile trade. When the limitation law went into effect in 1889, the board rejected applications for bars in residential areas in favor of those on heavily traveled streets. Moreover, it also centralized liquor licenses into distinct clusters at specific points, usually at a major intersection which in later years also became an elevated or transit stop. By creating what amounted to saloon districts, the board attempted to quiet the complaints of temperance interests that the saloon was too ubiquitous. The policy was also designed to facilitate police patrol by concentrating the potential trouble spots, but it probably had its greatest impact on drinking practices. The Boston saloon habitué had to make a conscious effort to travel from his home, often blocks away, to a bar. But the mobile drinkers who used the major streets or rapid transit found saloons to be convenient.[12]

The pattern of saloon locations remained remarkably haphazard in Chicago before the turn of the century. The mayors continued to proclaim that no licenses would be granted where they were not wanted and that churches and schools would be safe, but vigilant citizens continued to issue an unending stream of complaints. There was no trouble in obtaining a license for one of the congested tenement neighborhoods, but getting permission to open in an outlying district was usually a matter of trial and error modified by political considerations. Even then, there were hundreds of saloons in or very near to districts of single-family homes.

The appearance of Chicago saloons on major thoroughfares was, with the approval of the mayor, primarily an economic decision based on the conscious effort to locate where crowds passed by. This was especially true of the larger places. Employment studies conducted between 1903 and 1912 by the Illinois Department of Factory Inspection indicate that virtually all of the larger bars with hired help could be found either downtown or along major streets.[13] Furthermore, *Chicago's Thousand Dollar Book*, a privately printed compilation of people owning at least that amount of personal property, indicates that there was a distinct geographical pattern to success. Every one of the saloons in its listings was downtown or on a major section line or diagonal street. Each move away from the quieter neighborhood corners to busy streets demonstrated a conscious effort to take advantage of the new patterns of intraurban travel.[14]

The commuting workers usually made their daily trek on a particular street. Some were wider and had better sidewalks and superior illumination. The development of mass transit further accentuated the concentration of traffic because horsecars and streetcars drew pedestrians away from side streets to major arteries. Rapid transit again altered the pattern of rush-hour crowding. The elevated and subway created new layers of urban space in the most crowded sections of town, but at some point along the line the passengers had to return to ground level. The stations functioned as funnels, concentrating the riders through entrances and exits. This tended to raise commercial property values near the stations and depress those of locations that the trains bypassed. Most important of all, the new traffic pattern aroused an intense desire on the part of small businesses, including saloons, to locate themselves directly in front of the transit entrances. And so, in many parts of Boston and Chicago, it was no longer sufficient merely to be on a major street; the choice spot was directly in the path of the mobile drinker.[15]

Physical barriers also narrowed the selection of commutation routes. For instance, not all of Chicago's streets that encountered branches of the river had bridges, nor were there rail crossings on all of them. A similar pattern apeared in the Hub. South Boston was all but cut off from the downtown by South Bay; Dorchester Avenue, Broadway, and Dover streets became the prominent lifelines of commerce and transportation.

Irregularities in the urban topography further influenced the distribution of saloons. Barrooms clustered around bridges, where passersby might find it appealing to "lift the suds" while waiting for a passing ship. There were always several saloons at the ends of the streetcar lines, offering a shot before finishing the homeward journey on foot. And finally, many bars found it advantageous to locate at major intersections in outlying commercial districts. Many of these locations, which developed into major shopping districts after 1910, began as streetcar transfer corners. These were especially important in Chicago, where the multiplicity of transit companies blocked the introduction of universal free transfers until 1907. This meant that riders had no specific limits on their waiting time and could easily enjoy a drink between cars. Intersecting schedules never were fully coordinated, and the misfortune of a long wait on a street corner befell many nighttime commuters. Needless to say, the bright lights of a saloon sign attracted many stranded wintertime travelers.[16]

According to one humorous New York observer, the conditions of Chicago's streets also affected the drinkers' affinity for saloons:

There is one thing that is peculiarly Chicagoese. If a man wants a drink, rather than wade through the mud and over various pitfalls which abound in the streets, he gets a drink at the nearest saloon, no matter what or where it is. In consequence, a sort of "drink-where-you-are-at" system prevails. The average Chicago man is a martyr and don't know it. When he walks he plods through mud and slush, climbs over piles of stone and other defenses which would make one believe that he was in South Africa among the Boers. During the rush hours he rides, perfectly content to be stuffed into a street car or hang, cheerfully, on the outside thereof. "Comfort" is a word your true Chicagoan knows nothing of and cares less for.[17]

In effect, the saloon benefitted from the inefficiencies of the public space outside its front door. When the transportation system seemed on the verge of a breakdown and the sidewalks became impassable, the customers poured in. Ironically, the growth of the street trade and the occasional customer led to the search for greater efficiency in the use of space inside the barroom. Proprietors learned that tables and the stand-up bar each appealed to a different kind of customer. Ethnic spe-cialities accounted for part of the preference, but the mobility of the customers was also an important factor. Tables allowed drinkers to face each other and encouraged them to tarry. That practice was im-portant in neighborhood places, but it was less successful for those that drew upon massive streams of mobile people, especially strangers. The stand-up "mahogany," equipped only with a brass rail, could handle large crowds with relative efficiency. Conversations could be carried on comfortably between only two people—the bartender in front and the person to one side. Most important of all, the lone drinker would not feel uncomfortable, as he might if he were occupying a whole table by himself.[18]

The question of interior design came up during the debate over the repeal of Massachusetts' Public Bar Law. Liquor dealers were unhappy about having to serve customers at tables. Not only was it inconvenient to provide food, but the comfort of the tables and chairs lowered the turnover of drinkers and decreased profits. It took more waiters and bartenders to serve fewer people, and the customers complained when asked to buy another drink or leave. Finally, the liquor dealers sided with temperance people in arguing that the antibar law also promoted treating, since it was easier to buy rounds when drinkers were assem-bled around a table. These arguments helped sway public opinion, and

when the General Court finally repealed the hated law in 1891, most of
Boston's downtown drinking spots quickly converted their facilities to
accommodate stand-up customers.[19]

The Saloon and the Mobile Workers

There were several ways in which saloons adapted their social functions to serve the needs of the mobile working class. The same place
often served the neighborhood folks during the evening and the outside
workers all day. Both kinds of trade were crucial to the proprietor's
economic survival, and many of his defenders were quick to point out
how important the saloon was in the lives of the workers. When the
Chicago City Council debated the merits of enforcing its own midnight
closing law in 1904, the liquor interests enjoyed the support of one of
the city's leading social reformers. Raymond Robins, who managed the
Municipal Lodging House, eloquently defended the interests of the
night toilers, who depended on the free lunch to brighten their homeward journey. The council agreed. Instead of retaining the law, which
they never enforced, they simply extended the legal closing hour to
1:00 A.M.[20]

Saloons also welcomed the early labor unions, which had encountered great difficulty securing meeting places elsewhere. The fear of
radicalism, especially after 1870, made it almost impossible for labor
groups to use publicly owned facilities. Many who owned nonsaloon
halls were suspicious of the trade union movement, and most labor organizations were too small or impecunious to build their own places.
Massachusetts lawmakers banned the combination of liquor licenses
and rentable halls, and so the union members had to go down the street
to purchase drinks. But in Chicago the same man who operated the
free lunch counter where the workers ate would also allow the union
men to have his upstairs hall for little or nothing. In return, the proprietor expected each member to pay at least one visit to the bar. This
provided a regular home for the union and a predictable trade for the
owner. Neither the whims of fickle neighborhood customers nor the unpredictable weather conditions could ruin his business. Having one's
name circulated among the workers could not hurt business either.[21]

The adaptability of the saloon as a social institution helped it bridge
the ethnic divisions that fragmented the labor movement. Immigrant

groups frequently dominated particular skilled trades in the same manner in which they developed specialties among street businesses. Factories that drew upon work forces from relatively homogeneous neighborhoods strengthened that tendency. This placed a saloonkeeper who spoke the workers' language at a distinct advantage.[22] But when the union included a mixture of nationality groups or attracted residents from several parts of the city, the ethnic orientation of the meeting place was of little significance. In Chicago few of such larger halls as Martine's, Ulich's, Baum's Pavilion, Greenbaum's, and Yondorf Hall attracted city-wide unions. The typographers, telegraphers, conductors-drivers, and other cosmopolitan groups turned to the daily press to announce the times of their meetings, while the sheer size of their membership narrowed the choice of halls.[23]

A saloon was also the logical location for a central headquarters during a strike. If located near a factory, its hall was useful for mass meetings needed to rally support. On the other hand, downtown places were best situated to coordinate city-wide walkouts, such as that staged by Chicago's carpenters in 1887. Strikes, however, associated saloons with a movement that many people in the community considered dangerous and disruptive, even though some labor leaders and the whole Knights of Labor organization opposed liquor.[24] In commenting on walkouts by horsecar drivers in Cleveland and Chicago, the official publication of the Massachusetts Law and Order League complained: "The headquarters of these turbulent men who drive inoffensive workingmen who desire to continue their labors away from their tools, who destroy property, and with the reckless disregard for the rights of others go about terrifying the community, is always in the liquor shops."[25]

The fear of disorder emanating from working-class saloons took many forms. The railway strike of 1877 had indirectly been responsible for the formation of the law and order movement in Chicago. Police frequently closed all barrooms during strikes, claiming that temperance was the best preventative against violence. The long-standing hostility against labor turned to hysteria during the 1880s. In 1882 the Village Board of suburban Hyde Park refused to renew the liquor license held by a man named Colehour because his picnic grove and roadhouse hosted many "Socialistic" outings and was therefore "a tough place." For the next few years the daily newspapers continued to publish un-

favorable accounts of various radical meetings in saloon halls, but the
Eight-Hour movement and the anarchists brought the greatest amount
of difficulty to the saloons involved.[26]

One especially noteworthy bar was located at 54 West Lake Street,
near the West Side vice and flophouse area. From the time that
Thomas Grief opened his place, he had played host to a variety of labor
and radical groups, including the furniture makers, cigar makers, boil-
ermakers, and the Chicago Labor Union. But the most important con-
clave that took place there was no mass gathering. Rather, it was a
quiet meeting around a table in the back room that would create headlines across the world, for it was in Thomas Grief's saloon that a small
group of men planned the meeting at which the Haymarket Riot took
place. For most of a decade after that event, Grief and several other
dealers paid for their affiliations with labor agitation. Police staged
continuous raids, roughed up Grief's daughter, and closed the place
several times for minor violations. But despite the harassment, some
twenty unions continued to meet there until well into the next decade.[27]

This aftermath of the Haymarket affair lasted for several years and
speeded the gradual disassociation of labor and the saloon. Saloonkeepers realized that affiliations with labor unions could bring unwanted
trouble from the police. At the same time the more successful unions
began to accumulate enough money to build their own halls, some of
which had liquor licenses. In other cases, various unions composed primarily of one nationality group shared in the construction or rental of a
single building in the neighborhood where they lived, instead of where
they worked. And so, by the turn of the century a great portion, if not a
majority, of Chicago's labor unions had left the saloon. The workingmen themselves had found a substitute.[28]

However, another custom that brought the workingman into the saloon was much more difficult to break—its role as a labor exchange.
Men out of work gathered in particular saloons, often located near the
jobs they wanted or once had; employers in search of labor knew where
to look. East Boston bars, for instance, were near the shipbuilding
yards, while a man could obtain a job in the forests of New England by
going to saloons near the docks where the lumber boats unloaded.
There were also specialized areas in Boston where employers could find
unskilled workers for casual jobs. Drinking spots along the transient
areas of Eliot, Kneeland, Causeway, and Washington streets served the
city's floating population and proved to be the best places to find strong

backs.[29] Police officials in Boston kept tight control over employment bureaus and subjected their books to careful inspection.

By contrast, Chicago's saloons operated with few regulations. One place on the Northwest Side called itself the Stonecutters' Exchange, and several bars in the Italian neighborhoods north and west of the Loop were owned by men who supplied *padrone* labor. Many of these operations were informal, with the proprietor benefitting only from the drinks that the men purchased. But in Chicago a large portion of the commercial employment agencies operated either inside the saloon or in the rooms upstairs. In 1889, for instance, the *Lakeside Directory* listed eighteen agencies. Of these, eight (44 percent) shared a building with a saloon, and four more (22 percent) were within two doors of one. Generally, these were located near the lumber, wholesale, and warehouse districts where large numbers of unskilled men found employment, but several others operated in Chicago's large skid row area.[30]

Not every labor group enjoyed this relationship. In 1881 the Chicago Bakers' Union complained loudly to the *Illinois Staats-Zeitung* that the unemployed among their numbers who hung around saloons actually diluted the power of the union by providing an accessible pool of "scab" labor. As an alternative, the union offered a registration system that cost the job seeker only a quarter, which he paid only after obtaining employment. The plan apparently did not work well; three decades later cooks and bakers were still going to four saloons in search of employment.[31]

Chicago social reformers made numerous attempts to correct the situation. In 1899 they opened three free employment agencies to compete with the commercial offices. This experiment supplied thousands with jobs, but it still did not loosen labor's tie with the saloon. In 1903 the coalition of settlement and temperance workers broadened their efforts from finding substitutes to enacting strict regulation of existing agencies. The new law banned unfair practices and specifically prohibited labor agencies from operating in "or in connection with" saloons.[32] Its supporters held high expectations, but the new law had little impact. A study made five years later revealed that of the fifty-six agencies supplying men, twenty-three were either above, below, or next door to saloons. Two others operated directly across the bar.[33]

Antisaloon forces were also upset over the custom that brought workers into the saloon to cash their paychecks. For a variety of reasons, many companies chose not to pay their employees in cash. It made their bookkeeping system more complicated and created obvious security problems in dangerous neighborhoods. But payment by check created a serious problem for the worker — finding a place to cash it. Nearly all of the banks were in the downtown districts of both cities, often a considerable distance away. And many workers felt self-conscious about their attire amidst the marble and onyx banking rooms. Instead, the workingman was forced to find alternative places, preferably somewhere between work and home, and the saloon was the logical choice. The proprietor's reputed wealth made many people think that he always had sufficient money on hand for such an operation, and a few probably did. But help came from the brewers, who dispatched large sums of money to their tied outlets. At the end of payday, the saloonkeepers merely signed over the checks to the beermaker.[34]

The practice was a great inconvenience for the saloonkeepers and the brewers, but it attracted many customers who also purchased a drink as a token of appreciation. One saloon at Ashland Avenue and Forty-third Street in Chicago cashed over $40,000 worth of paychecks each month because it was adjacent to the Union Stockyards. Saloons near police and fire stations were unofficial partners in handling the city payroll. That fact greatly disturbed temperance advocates, who openly wondered how the citizenry could trust police regulation of saloons which provided this convenience for those who supposedly enforced the liquor laws.[35]

Not everyone cashed their checks in saloons. A study conducted in 1898 by the United States Department of Labor indicates that ethnicity played a significant role in the worker's decision to take his check to a barroom or to a grocery. Of the Chicago workers whose payday habits came under scrutiny, the Polish, Hungarian, Irish, German, and "American" men went to saloons, while the Swedes and Norwegians, perhaps reacting to ethnic temperance pressures, chose the alternative.[36]

The custom of cashing paychecks in saloons disturbed many interests in the community. Temperance spokesmen complained that Saturday night's paycheck seldom made it home intact. Some antiliquor people finally persuaded a few employers to distribute their wages on some other day of the week. And after 1910 other firms began to pay their employees in cash once again, and the Chicago, Burlington and Quincy Railroad even ordered its workers to take their checks to a more temperate merchant. The company examined all third party signatures for the names of liquor dealers.[37]

Such companies as the Burlington presented the only real challenge to the workingmen's bar. Where a few industries, such as the foundries and breweries, had actually furnished liquor to their employees, the vast majority of businesses appreciated a sober worker. Near the turn of the century the employers began to see the nearby saloon as a direct threat to efficiency and profits. The railroads led the way. Faced with intense public concern over the incidence of wrecks and passenger injuries, the carriers tightened their rules on employee sobriety. They had banned drinking on the job many years earlier, but after 1890 workers were directly ordered to stay away from bars. The Burlington discharged anyone found to "frequent drinking places."[38] And the Chicago Great Western "served notice on employees that it would be necessary for them to secure boarding places without saloons attached, if they wished to remain in the service of this company."[39] Two lines, the Burlington and the Santa Fe, even went so far as to establish recreation halls near their shops, in order to keep their employees contented as well as sober.[40]

Perhaps the most extreme case of an employer attempting to regulate his workers' drinking habits took place in Chicago. Aaron Montgomery Ward, the cantankerous owner of the mail order house, had long been disturbed by noon-hour drinking. When the firm was located downtown on Michigan Avenue, he had agonized over the way that hundreds of employees were using the anonymity of the Loop crowds to slip away for a drink. And so, when the plant relocated along the North Branch of the Chicago River in 1908, he had the Chicago City Council vote the territory immediately surrounding his company dry. Then he forbade workers from visiting bars within half a mile of the dry district. Company spies photographed saloon crowds, and any employee identifiable in a picture was subject to instant dismissal. Meanwhile, one of the most prominent items in Ward's mail order catalog continued to be liquor.[41]

Most companies installed their own lunchrooms and encouraged workers to remain in the building during mealtime. Labor groups later condemned these white tile cafeterias as corporate paternalism and complained that the real purpose was to destroy the fledgling union movement, but the companies were initially interested in industrial

efficiency. Not long after Frederick Taylor began to publicize his efficiency ideas, the temperance publicists began to tie the liquor problem
to the scale of industrial output. Alcohol, they claimed, was responsible for Monday absences, work-place accidents, shoddy craftsman-
ship, and a generally poor state of health among the workers. Thus, the
search for efficiency and profits brought many businessmen to an antiliquor viewpoint.[42]

Downtown Drinking Spots

Although saloons were both numerous and important in tenement
neighborhoods and along major streets, they were most heavily concentrated in the downtown shopping districts. Virtually every street and
most of the intersections had at least one bar, and some blocks seemed
to be given over completely to drinking purposes. This omnipresence
confirmed the formless flexibility of the saloon as a social institution.
Any semipublic place would have its most severe test for flexibility
amidst the confusing mixture of people, yet here the saloon seemed to
thrive.

The downtown proprietors also had to contend with the growing
specialization of land use. This evolutionary process transformed jum-
bled patchworks of warehouses, retail stores, financial institutions, and
residences into relatively specialized districts. New buildings, such as
banks, office buildings, and department stores could be more easily designed for specific rather than general uses, since succeeding tenants
would continue the same kind of trade.[43] The specialization of downtown public space had been a major factor in the growing concern over
the urban environment. Congestion made it obvious that many types of
land use were incompatible with each other and were best kept in
separate areas. Warehousing, offices, retail trade, cultural activities,
and financial institutions each created a separate district.

The spatial reordering of downtown areas brought many changes in
the social structure of urban street life. People in search of particular
services could be found in the appropriate districts, rather than scattered throughout the downtown. More important, the process of specialization brought a new temporal rhythm to the central area. The
removal of residential areas from the downtown, accomplished largely
by the Chicago Fire of 1871 and the one in Boston the following year,
meant that most activities took place during the daylight or early even-

ing hours. Within the central district each functional area operated according to its own time schedule, attracting workers at a given time and making its unique demands on the public and semipublic places, saloons included, around it.[44]

Perhaps the first to awaken were the market areas. The rural green-gardeners arrived before dawn. They unloaded their wagons early, so that wholesale dealers could make their sales to retailers before the latter opened at mid-morning. This brought a large number of customers to saloons near Chicago's Haymarket and Boston's Faneuil Hall and Quincy markets before 7:00 A.M. For some barrooms it was one of the busiest hours of the day.[45]

Then came the commuter rush hour, with its thousands of people arriving on foot, in carriages or cabs, and on streetcars. This traffic also displayed a distinct temporal pattern, since the social standing of the individual determined the time of arrival. According to one visual survey by a *Boston Globe* reporter, those who worked in the wholesale drygoods and warehousing areas appeared on the streets at the earliest hour. The clerks and secretaries were next. and the executive-level workers and professional people were last. Of course, the barrooms that they might frequent adjusted themselves to the status of their customers.[46]

The morning activity in the streets and saloons was sporadic, but the noon hour poured thousands of people from offices, factories, and stores. Some pedestrians used their free time to wander about looking at store windows, but the vast majority had time to do little else but eat. Lunch was the most public meal of all. Citizens developed a series of social customs and semipublic places that allowed them to secure varying amounts of comfort and privacy at their noon-time repast. Thousands carried their lunches. Working-class men employed a tin bucket whose purpose was obvious, but those who aspired to higher social standing tried to conceal their edible cargo. As one popular account from Boston reported, "A dainty miss bearing an alligator music roll fell down on Berkeley street at 7:30 o'clock one morning, and the music roll bursting open it was found to contain three Frankfurter sausages, two cream tartar rolls and a bottle of mustard. . . ."[47]

Box lunches were available at the curb, but the weather limited the number of days when they could be enjoyed outdoors. Instead, thousands of people chose to frequent some type of eatery. The variety was endless, everything from fancy hotel dining rooms to small cafes. The wealthy could afford to take leisurely lunches in their private clubs, but most diners demanded inexpensive meals and fast service. The result was the "hash house." Service was impersonal, and the diner often had to stand or perch upon an uncomfortable stool that had no back. He gave his order in front of patrons seated nearby and consumed it in an equally public fashion. The necessity for speed, induced by the brevity of the lunch break and impatient customers who were waiting behind him for a seat, caused etiquette to be cast aside. "Sixty-two pairs of jaws beat to the music," observed a *Globe* writer. "Sixty-two water glasses and coffee cups clink against hardwood. Higher, carrying the air, rise the shrill nasal sopranos of the garrison [of waitresses]."[48]

Many women also ventured into food shops. The exact extent of their female patronage is impossible to determine, especially among the more "respectable" people. But their mere presence in public places, doing the things that men did, was such an emotional issue that details of their drinking habits were either sensationalized or suppressed altogether. The appearance of women in "cheap restaurants"—probably ones that served liquor—raised many Boston eyebrows in 1890. This concern with the well-being of lunching women had fostered a rapid increase in the number of tearooms near the turn of the century. Even the name of these light-fare restaurants distinguished them from places serving alcohol. The tearooms were usually located near the major retail and department store districts but seldom were found on the ground floor. Their gross revenue probably limited their ability to pay high rents, but contemporary descriptions also stress the semiprivate nature of their location. Women who had a special dislike of liquor could also choose among several temperance dining rooms, either operated independently or in conjunction with a temperance hotel.[49]

The vast collections of downtown saloons attracted much of this noon-hour trade. There was a barroom lunch to suit the taste of every customer. Many skyscraper office buildings contained drinking spots, but these were usually small, stand-up places that drew their patronage from the young male clerks and secretaries who worked in the nearby financial district. Their bosses dined at better places, such as the Berghoff or Vogelsangs, that combined a bar with a regular restaurant and contained numerous cozy and semiprivate dining rooms. The restaurant bars, of course, did not want to compete with the food they had for sale, so their free lunches tended to be rather small and Spartan. The best free meals could be found in the larger saloons. For instance, Chicago's Tacoma Arcade provided "baked beans, hot roast beef, white and brown bread, salads, crackers, and cheese."[50] According to one hungry Northwestern University student, "The quality of food at the lunch counters in most of the downtown bars is equal to that served in any of the first class restaurants."[51] Some bars were even equipped with booths and dining rooms so that business transactions, often involving large sums of money, could be made over food that cost only the price of a drink.[52] The downtown district also generated enough patronage to support several types of bars that attracted a specialized clientele. There were "newspaper bars," where an assemblage of reporters and editors hung out, and political places near City Hall.

The free lunch cost proprietors great amounts of money, so they often tried to minimize the labor costs by spreading the service thin. Like the sullen waitress at the coffeeshop counter, the bartender or "lunchman" in a large place could be taciturn, or even unfriendly. He dressed in a formal uniform, served mixed drinks — an unmasculine taboo in working-class bars — and acted aloof. "The bartender does not have to listen to the fellows' stale jokes," remarked one observer, "and the men do not drink enough to get drunk."[53] The friendliness of the neighborhood tap had clearly given way to the efficiency of numbers, and by 1915 at least seven Loop saloons had replaced the sideboard man with "free lunch machines." Slicers sheared off razor-thin portions of meat—"untouched by human hands"—while coin-operated machines dispensed crackers and cheese that had once been free.[54]

As the hours passed, the afternoon patronage became highly mixed. Casual passersby accounted for a few nickels, while a clerk from the financial district found ways to sneak out for a drink during a lull in business. The *Chicago Tribune* even went so far as to blame drinking for the excessive speculation on the Board of Trade. "There is a constant rush from the wheat pit to the saloon and back again," warned its editorials. "Is it any wonder that the followers of that perilous business think that it is a dull day when there has not been a failure or someone 'hurt' in his deals."[55]

The late afternoon patronage was especially large near the transportation terminals. Drinkers were apparently afraid to change altitude without a bracer, as they stopped at bars near the steps leading up to Chicago's elevated loop and down to Boston's subways. Also, a substantial number of those who worked downtown rode commuter trains home each evening. As early as 1849 there were already 118 daily arrivals and departures connecting Boston with eighty-three suburban stations within fifteen miles of the city. Each subsequent decade brought an increasing number of commuters to the streets. Meanwhile, the simultaneous consolidation of railroad stations into huge terminals meant that by the turn of the century both Chicago and Boston witnessed enormous crowds of people who poured forth from the trains in the morning and toward the station at night.[56]

As was the case in intraurban transportation, the railroad commuter chose specific routes to the depot as his favorites. Saloonkeepers realized the opportunity to draw a large and predictable trade and promptly moved into every available storefront nearby. Many other businesses had abandoned these locations because of the noise and smoke, and their departure opened up many vacancies unwanted by most kinds of commerce. The result was a temperance worker's nightmare. Saloons lined the streets leading to Chicago's depots, so that no one heading for a train or emerging into a street could avoid passing in front of a pair of swinging doors. In the mid-1880s, there were 175 bars near Boston's northern depots, eighty of them within 650 feet of the Albany and Old Colony terminals alone. Nearly every storefront for blocks around was a saloon, meaning, in the words of one liquor foe, that "every traveler in that region passes through a gauntlet of rum."[57] The choice was endless. A thirsty man could spend months sampling the bars, eventually finding one that served the best snacks or liquor. There was no compelling need to become a regular or know the bartender. If the drinker returned day after day, he did so because of the service or convenience rather than because of any ethnic or social loyalties.

This situation angered the antisaloon forces. The availability of liquor at a time when the commuter was weary only compounded the temptation of convenience. Many erstwhile good family men could not resist. Furthermore, the concentration of the bars in that locale meant that "respectable" people, including middle-class suburban women on shopping expeditions, could not help but encounter streets lined with saloons.[58] In order to alleviate the problem, temperance interests in the Massachusetts General Court tried to enact laws that would place limits on how close a saloon might be to a depot. Those attempts failed, and the Boston license officials maintained that it was still better to

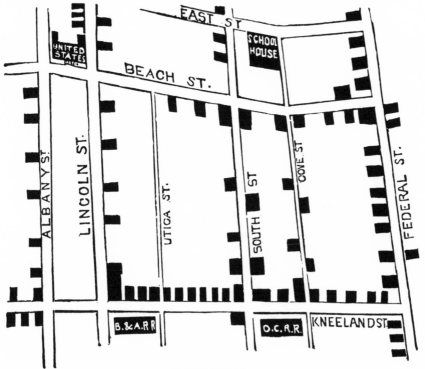

SALOON MAP.

A temperance organization found dozens of bars in an area just 650-by-650 feet. Nearby rail stations provided the customers for these Hub bars. (Reprinted from *Temperance Cause* 6[Jan. 1884]:n.p.)

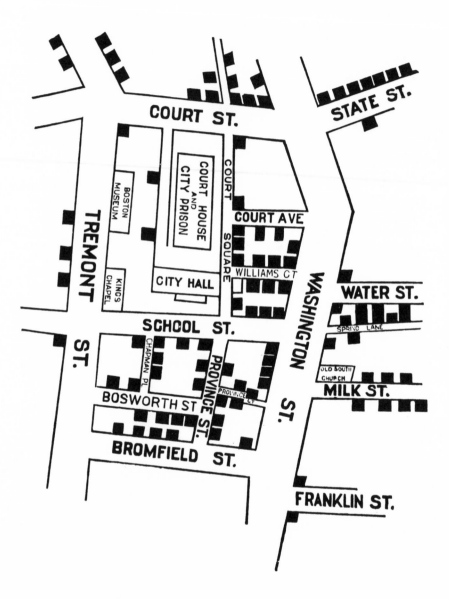

Near the commercial and governmental center of Boston there were ninety-five saloons "from the gilded gin mill to the dive." (Reprinted from *Temperance Cause* 8[Sept. 1886]:n.p.)

locate a bar in the midst of commuter areas than it was to place it in a residential neighborhood.[59]

When the last of the workaday commuters had departed, the focus of saloon activity shifted to the amusement districts. The development of specialized "bright light" areas accompanied the growth of the legitimate theater. These entertainments varied considerably in their quality and moral tone, and they tended to cluster with others of their own level. In Chicago they could be found on side streets leading from Dearborn Street. Monroe, a block south of Madison Street, was the site of Haverly's Theater. The McVickers was on Madison just east of Dearborn, and there was a cluster of cheaper, though respectable, theaters a few blocks to the north. The lower-class places could be found on major transportation lines to the north, south, and west edges of the Loop. In any of these cases, theatergoers need never worry about thirst. Every marquee shed its light on an adjoining saloon that beckoned the homeward bound in for a nightcap.[60]

Boston's primary entertainment district was located along Washington Street, where the Boston, Park, Globe, and Bijou theaters attracted huge crowds every night. Their numbers, attire, and joviality gave the district a deceptive appearance of showy prosperity. "The great thoroughfares, as the public meeting place and exchange, have the effect of keeping up the economic tone of the district," commented social worker Robert Woods. "One would hardly imagine from a walk out Washington Street, that there was a large amount of actual poverty on both sides."[61] The theater crowds had been both the cause and the effect of the South End's decline, for as the commercial areas, theaters, and saloons moved in, middle-class families moved out.

After midnight the small amount of street life that survived was concentrated into a few small districts. All-night industries provided patrons for all-night restaurants and illegal saloons. After the turn of the century all of Boston's "night car" service terminated at Adams Square, at which the last of those on their way home greeted the newspaper workers, bakers, and others on their way to work. Only a few others, such as watchmen, police, or cab drivers, could be found working in dispersed locations at that hour.[62] By 1903 the temporal specialization of Chicago had become so great that when the *Tribune* sent reporters to find "the loneliest spot in Chicago," their selection was a downtown office building at night.[63]

Public Comforts

The obvious presence of the saloon in this daily cycle disturbed the temperance supporters. As early as 1867 their spokesmen in Chicago began to call for public drinking fountains as a means of combating the attraction that saloons held for passersby. Calling it "practical temperance," the *Tribune* called on the city government to "put up two or three score of hydrants at street corners and at all public places where it is needed."[64] But the city built few fountains outside of parks, and so the private antiliquor groups like the Women's Christian Temperance Union eventually had to provide construction funds. The municipality was supposed to maintain them, but it did a very poor job. By 1908 the City Club found that many had gone dry or had been vandalized by removing the hand-held drinking cup. The club demanded that the city erect many more fountains and selected several potential locations where large crowds of pedestrians passed by. But only a few more were ever erected, and these, of course, by private donation.

In stark contrast with Chicago's municipal negligence, Boston began a conscientious effort to build and maintain fountains. The city government constructed a few, while the WCTU and other temperance organizations built others. A third category were really memorials, self-glorifying monuments donated to the city at the directive of a wealthy person's will. Many objections were raised to using public space to commemorate private individuals, especially when tax money had to be used to lay water pipes and supply maintenance. After 1889, however, the city found a new source for maintenance funds; by diverting money formerly set aside to provide soup for the poor, it could provide practical aid for the poor without the appearance of charity. By 1893 the aldermen had willingly accepted over thirty fountains and saw to it that the Street Department kept the drinking cups in order and packed the cooling coils daily with ice.[65] Boston that year was so well supplied with fountains that one charitable journal could boast that "Florence Street became a thoroughfare for large teams simply because it was known that cold water was to be had. Drivers, known to have been patrons of neighboring saloons, now use cold water instead of beer."[66]

The drinking fountain demonstrated that city governments could provide convenience that indirectly competed with the saloon for patronage. Another municipal facility that was designed to give people an alternative to the barroom was the public restroom. Again, Boston led

the way. In 1866 its City Council appointed a commission to investigate the matter, and within a year public toilets for both men and
women were under construction at three busy locations, including a
corner of the Public Garden. A decade later the new Boston Health
Department contributed its support to the idea, noting the backward-
ness of American cities compared to those in Europe.[67] During the last
two decades of the nineteenth century Boston led the nation in the
number of public restrooms. Ward politicians were anxious to provide
some visible evidence of service to their constituents. Councilmen and
aldermen from the better sections of the city heard speeches claiming
that the need for relief affected all levels of society. "I met a gentleman
the other day," intoned Mr. Keenan of Ward Eight (West End), "a millionaire, who said he walked twenty minutes before he found a sanitary."[68] Finally, such antiliquor groups as the Church Temperance
Society kept up a petition campaign demanding additional facilities.[69]

While Boston officials expressed concern over the commuting
public's comfort, Chicago did nothing to compete with the semipublic
places that provided the only existing toilet facilities in the downtown
area. Women flocked to department stores, which opened ladies'
lounges equipped with overstuffed chairs as well as "convenience stations." But men enjoyed few luxuries. A workingman's clothes made
him feel self-conscious in such opulent surroundings. Railway terminals were inconveniently located on the periphery of the Loop, while
the restrooms of office buildings were never located on the ground floor
and were not meant for public use. Instead, men in distress were
thankful for the swinging doors of a saloon.[70]

This attraction brought many customers to the brass rail. The saloon
restroom was free, usually clean, open on Sundays and at night, and it
could be found almost everywhere. Most men followed the unwritten
rule and bought a drink as a token of appreciation, a custom which disturbed temperance people. In 1907 the City Club of Chicago sponsored
a survey of the situation. The investigator, an engineer named V. C.
Hart, found that "the saloon men regard this privilege as bringing in
more trade than their free lunch counters."[71] The club gathered the
support of other civic groups and formed the United Associations of the
Committee of the City of Chicago on Public Comfort. "With very little
expense," advised one member, "Chicago can be relieved from the absolute stigma of being barbarian in respect to this matter."[72] Chicago's
toilet crusade, however, met with limited success beyond a few token

efforts. When the new city hall building opened in October 1911, the press gave as much coverage to the basement restrooms as to the massive entrances and elaborate hallways upstairs.[73]

Chicago officials did little else to appease public opinion. They merely enlarged the employee restrooms in the Public Library and opened them to the public. Then they called attention to existing comfort stations that the complainers had overlooked. After 1913, however, the reformers concentrated their efforts on correcting the lack of facilities at elevated stations. Saloons that were strategically located at entrance stairways gained additional patrons because of their restrooms. Reformers were disturbed because the city had failed to use its franchise powers to force the elevated companies to provide for the public comfort while feasting on public profit. Outlying stops had no conveniences at all, while those at downtown Loop stops were located inside the turnstiles; only those who could afford the fare could use them.[74] After three more years of complaints, the transit companies reluctantly altered their coin booths and entranceways, and city officials began to talk about opening more convenience stations.

Alone in the City

The welfare of thousands of single people who moved to the metropolis in the late nineteenth century troubled many reformers. Young and unmarried men and women had always been there, but after the 1880s, they appeared to be more visible and the subject of more frequent comment. Their working and living conditions dominated many of the earliest reports of state bureaus of labor statistics. Moral reform groups expressed fears about the potential for sin, fearing that the location of housing frequented by unmarried people placed them in great moral danger.[75]

The dwellers of the better boarding houses almost defied social classification. Most of them made little money. But they managed to survive, as their contemporaries tell us, because they saw their position as temporary. The women hoped to be married, and the young men saw their humble status as the first step toward ultimate financial and social success. But meanwhile the reality of low wages and the desire for respectability placed a severe strain on their life-style.[76]

Most were also native-born. Some among them had grown up in the city and continued to live at home. Their income supplemented their family's budget, and their social life was little more than an extension of childhood. But the young people who attracted the most attention and concern were those who resided in the rented rooms and boarding houses, the single people alone in the city. In 1900 in Boston fully two-thirds of them were the sons and daughters of old stock, rural and small-town New Englanders and upstate New Yorkers. Chicago, too, attracted the same type of people, the upwardly mobile young who saw little opportunity in the country towns. In both cities large numbers of them were also students; since many small colleges and trade schools offered no housing facilities, the rooming houses became quasi-dormitories.[77]

The areas where they lived were clearly on the decline. In both Chicago and Boston these neighborhoods were characterized by sharp changes in population and land use. Normally, these were areas where the wealthy had once lived in spacious townhouses and detached dwellings close to the central business area. These districts were not the transient flop-house areas, although the two were often near each other. Aside from being far more unsanitary and run down, the "flops" were always on business streets, while the respectable places were more residential in character. Furthermore, the tramps were able to exist because the owners of buildings, confident that central business districts would expand, suspended maintenance and improvements on buildings they expected to tear down shortly. But the roomers, who were more middle class, arrived in a neighborhood because someone wealthy had fled.

The boarding house districts — areas contiguous to Chicago's Loop and in Boston's West and South Ends — were usually located on or near major transportation lines, and the daily ebb and flow of hurrying commuters gave them a sense of constant motion. This feeling of impermanence was also reflected in the residential mobility of the lodgers. They rented by the week rather than by the month or year. Some remained for years in the same building, but most were as transient as the families in the tenement districts. In part this was due to their life-style; they had no family or furniture to limit their mobility. But the constant mixing and clashing of personalities also contributed to the instability. Noise, nocturnal revelry, or vice could invade even the most respectable house with relative ease.[78] *Moran's Dictionary of Chicago* advised: "Strangers . . . would do well to carefully avoid engaging their rooms longer than from week to week, as the presence of disagreeable people or other contingencies frequently make it desirable to change, and an arrangement for a longer term is more sure to result in trouble."[79]

The rooming house district also included the largest share of both cities bohemian population. The furnished rooms attracted young artists and writers who blended with the old-line socialists, syndicalists, communists, and others on the intellectual fringe of radicalism. They gathered at particular bars, especially on Clark and State streets just north of Chicago Avenue, where they argued politics, religion, and free love into the early hours of the morning. These bars, which often had artists' studios upstairs, usually had few physical attractions and made no effort to draw trade from strangers. The barroom was often dingy and dirty and distinguished by the total absence of a free lunch counter. The bar, seldom used, seemed almost a vestigial reminder that a more typical saloon had once been housed there. Instead, the small round table and the bentwood chair became the standard equipment, for these surroundings encouraged the heated debates and intellectual probing that were the real entertainment of the place.[80]

Because their personal dwellings were small, the residents of the rooming house districts spent much of their time in public or semipublic places. Few rooms had any cooking facilities, and those that did offered only makeshift stoves fitted into the once elegant marble fireplaces. Nearly all of the single dwellers had to dine outside their rooms. Some chose the common boarding table provided by the resident landlord, but this had its limitations. The fare frequently was rude, and at mealtime not everyone turned out to be an Oliver Wendell Holmes. The rigid mealtime schedule also limited their personal freedom and the dining choices available to the otherwise footloose residents; they paid for the week's fare whether they ate it or not. These disadvantages contributed to the decline of the boarding house after 1880 and its replacement by the rooming house, sans meals.[81]

Instead, nearly all of the residents ate out. At noon they dined downtown or near their place of employment, but in the evening they usually chose a cheap restaurant in their neighborhood. Dining rooms appeared in the basements of some of the rooming houses. They sold tickets to be punched at each meal; lodgers whose lack of banking facilities forced them to take their weekly earnings in cash welcomed the opportunity to purchase a ticket in advance. But many of the roomers found these places to be dreary and unsanitary, and so they patronized the dozens of cafes and small restaurants that thrived along Clark Street in Chicago or Columbus and Washington avenues in Boston. There was a wide selection that included bakeries and delicatessens selling precooked foods that could be consumed in one's room. A 1912 survey of Chicago's North Side rooming house district revealed that there were sixty-two such bakeries and ninety-three restaurants in an area two miles long and half a mile wide.[82]

Entertainment posed another problem for the lodgers. The confines of their rooms were especially oppressive after a day's work. In summertime the men occasionally sat on the front steps and conversed, but this practice lacked widespread acceptance among the middle class and was totally improper among the more respectable women.[83] Moreover, the family that owned the rooming house faced another problem when they allowed tenants to use the parlor. As one study commented:

> In another house were seven or eight young men lodgers. The landlady had quite a family of her own — a husband, a married son and his wife, and an unmarried son. Nevertheless, before long the family circle had widened to admit the seven or eight young men as friends of the sons.
>
> The piano was always going in the evening. There was no privacy for either mother or father. And there was no chance for anybody to nap until the party came to an end. For in these houses the allotment of a room for a public parlor would entail a critical money loss.[84]

There were many entertainment alternatives open to men, including the saloon. Nearly all of the downtown drinking places were accessible to them after working hours, especially if their employment and status required them to be well dressed. In addition, there were a number of drinking places along the transportation routes between where they lived and where they worked. This was especially the case on the North Side of Chicago, where the influx of liquor dealers coincided with the transformation of the area into a rooming house district. In 1880, for instance, there were relatively few saloons along North Clark Street, other than a few German beer gardens. But nine years later, there were seventeen bars in the five blocks of the main rooming house district between Elm Street and North Avenue. The number remained relatively stable until World War I, when there were only two blocks in the two miles between the river and North Avenue that did not have at least one saloon.[85]

The mobility of these young single men may have brought them near poolrooms and thousands of saloons, but they were less dependent upon the barroom's services than men from the transient or tenement neighborhoods. In the latter the saloon functioned as a quasi-welfare institution, providing numerous services to people who had few realistic alternatives. But the unmarried and upwardly mobile young men went to saloons less out of need than desire. The free lunch remained an attraction, but the most humble clerk could purchase a cheap meal. Likewise, other features of a clerk's situation opened up alternatives to the saloon. He did not belong to a union, so there was no mandatory need to visit the saloon hall. He worked downtown and could cash his check at a bank rather than at a bar. He could spend an evening in a billiard hall. He was reasonably well dressed; he and his female counterpart were, in fact, so well attired that their supposed extravagance disturbed settlement reformers. But their appearance also admitted them without comment to libraries, museums, and even restrooms where a shabbily clothed workingman might have felt self-conscious.

During decent weather groups of young single women took walks in the parks, but that was a seasonal activity. Financial considerations limited other opportunities, including decent seats at the theater or orchestra. Even then, there was widespread suspicion of women alone in public or semipublic places. As a consequence, many apparently led very lonely lives. The press described "newspaper girls," single women who appeared at the Boston Public Library each evening to read the papers from their hometowns. In maudlin details, reporters described those who wept over each page and then quietly left for their dreary rooms.[86]

In the public's mind, at least, such conditions were fraught with potential immorality. More venturesome women might go to dance halls or, later, to cabarets or the movies. The influence of drink or the temptations of darkness might overcome them and lead to a life of shame. One major study, conducted in 1884 by the Massachusetts Bureau of Labor Statistics, concluded that the majority of women who had become prostitutes had followed just such a downward path. Furthermore, women who had met young men they liked and who did not wish to be courted in public had few alternatives to inviting their male companions to their rooms.[87]

In the case of the immigrant's daughter, the lack of privacy rather than loneliness drove her to the dance hall.[88] To solve that moral problem, settlement house workers Robert Woods and Albert Kennedy noted, "The main source of safety . . . is believed to consist in keeping recreation under the influence of home and neighborhood life. Dancing places under strict supervision should be provided in every community, the clientele drawn from within a few blocks."[89] Among the tenements, then, the revitalized neighborhood provided the answer, but that solution was of little use in the rooming house districts where there was no basis for a community spirit.

The Search for Substitutes

It was obvious to any astute observer that for many urban dwellers the saloon was probably the most important social institution outside of the family and perhaps the church parish. Many people worried about how the forces of moral reform could combat the saloon curse. Temperance pledging had attracted few followers.[90] Nor would such respectable vigilance societies as the Law and Order Leagues stand much chance of success in the slums where dry spies, who were all native-born, could not have maintained their disguises. Before World War I prohibition seemed to be a proven failure and an infeasible dream. Faced with this perplexing problem, reformers turned to what appeared to be the most realistic solution: to provide alternatives to the saloon. By setting up attractive substitutes, the antisaloon forces hoped to give the drinker a choice.

It is difficult to establish exactly when this type of activity started. In 1835 the Boston Seamen's Friend Society expressed its concern about the high rate of drunkenness among sailors, by opening a Sailor's Home. This large boarding house, designed to accommodate wintering mariners, attempted to attract patrons from the cheap dives and rooms adjacent to the docks. Although the society never did eliminate the "low dens," it did preserve the morality of between 400 and 500 sailors each year.[91]

While such institutions as the Sailor's Home appealed to a narrow group of would-be saloon habitués, the temperance coffeehouse was intended to attract a wider variety of clientele. This institution had been imported from England by charity workers, and it made its debut in Chicago in a rather unusual form. Shortly after the Great Conflagration of 1871, the antidrink forces began to experiment with coffee wagons, which they placed near the city newspaper plants. Night workers, who might otherwise have sneaked away to nearby saloons, instead rested from their labors by purchasing a cup of coffee. These wagons, which moved from plant to plant, also provided nonalcoholic drinks for hundreds of news vendors who arrived in the early dawn to fold their papers.[92] It was a popular idea — except in winter — and in later years similar activities moved indoors, opening quarters that resembled restaurants or even saloons. During the 1870s and 1880s charity workers opened several other coffeehouses, and before the end of the century settlement houses had copied the idea.

Meanwhile, Mrs. Annie Adams Fields introduced the idea to Boston. The wife of James T. Fields, publisher of the *Atlantic Monthly*, devoted great amounts of time and money to establishing coffeehouses in tenement districts. During the 1880s her idea was duplicated in several areas of the city. The Oriental Tea Company subsidized one place in the North End, and when it opened in 1881 its proponents claimed that it was "bright and attractive so that it will be visited by those who now spend their evenings in liquor saloons."[93] The Wells Memorial, a large city mission on a decaying part of Washington Street, opened the Casino the following year; fitted with billiard tables and smoking rooms, it even welcomed women without escorts. During the next decade nearly a dozen more Boston temperance centers appeared along with several others that operated in settlement houses. All featured newspapers, nongambling games, and fixtures that were as nice as, if not more splendid than, the nearby barrooms.[94]

Another vital substitute was the YMCA in each city. Founded in 1851 in Boston and seven years later in Chicago, these institutions were aimed primarily at the social and moral well-being of young men. In 1867 the Boston Y noted with anguish that: "formerly clerks and apprentices boarded with and were directly under the eye of their employers. Now, the virtuous and the vicious are oftentimes herded together in the same boarding house, room and bed. Driven to these places by limited salaries, and unable to afford fires in their rooms, they are consequently led to frequent saloons and like places, where they are exposed to the most contaminating influences."[95]

To combat evil, the YMCAs provided direct competition to bars in the form of employment agencies, reading rooms, and wholesome alternatives to the "Sunday Night Frolics." Both the Boston and Chicago associations opened branches near railway shops, and the one in the Hub operated a center at the Navy Yard in an attempt to divert sailors from spending their shore time in the city's sin spots. By the early years of the century, however, even the Y had to bend to the trends of the times to remain competitive with barrooms. Describing its reading room in 1902 as "a loafing place of tramps," the Boston association installed billiard tables and bowling alleys.[96]

The most curious of all of the nineteenth-century saloon substitutes was Chicago's Home Salon. Started in 1895 by the Right Reverend Samuel Fallows, an Episcopal bishop, it was designed to retain all of the features of the barroom except the drink. There were barmaids during the daytime hours, spittoons, and even a nickel lunch on the sideboard. The only thing significantly different from Jerry Sullivan's saloon, which it had displaced, was "Bishop's Beer," a watered-down near-beer. Chicago greeted Fallows's project with great fanfare, and its originator predicted that a chain of Home Salons would drive out the evil saloons. But in a very short time, the place was closed for a most unexpected reason. A Health Department analysis — no doubt instigated by the liquor interests — demonstrated that Bishop's Beer was a bit too authentic. Its alcoholic content was great enough to warrant a regular saloon license, and an embarrassed Bishop Fallows closed up shop.[97]

By the end of the century the search for saloon substitutes had become a major preoccupation among social reformers. Religious missions attempted to duplicate the attractive features of nearby barrooms, while settlement houses expanded their activities designed to appeal to men. They began clubs based on a number of mutual interests. Debating societies discussed topics of current interest, while demonstrations of folk arts and dancing proved to be popular evening entertainments.[98] Settlements even moved into athletics and larger ones such as Hull House erected gymnasium buildings. They also supported the efforts of women's clubs and juvenile reformers to open neighborhood schoolhouses at night. It took several years of lobbying, but finally after 1900 the Open Door movement persuaded school officials to begin turning their buildings into social centers for the people nearby.[99]

These activities received encouragement from a national group of prominent educators, clergymen, lawyers, and physicians. What became known as the Committee of Fifty grew out of periodic informal meetings of noted reform-minded writers who contributed articles on social questions to national magazines. In 1893 they organized a formal group and began to focus their efforts on the liquor issue. During the

next decade they sponsored a number of investigations of the physiological, economic, legislative, and ethical aspects of that problem. But
their most important and widely discussed publication was a volume
entitled *Substitutes for the Saloon*. Written by a young, Harvard-
educated minister named Raymond Calkins, the book was based on a
series of local studies conducted by settlement houses. Its optimism
gave encouragement to the movement, and the descriptions of various
activities provided an interchange of ideas.[100]

But the varied assortment of theaters, clubrooms, schools, lunchrooms, coffeehouses, missions, and other competitors proved disap-
pointing. The barroom survived virtually undamaged for a number of
reasons. First, there was the matter of numbers. At no time did the various substitutes number more than 100 or so in any American city; in
Chicago's congested Nineteenth Ward there were that many barrooms
in less than a mile of Halsted Street. This meant that residents had to
seek out the substitute, which was often poorly marked and located in a
maze of settlement buildings. On the other hand, saloons were located
in the most obvious places. Competition, the business acumen of brewery realtors in Chicago, and the conscious decisions of Boston's police
board had all contributed to the gradual movement of saloons to major
streets. Settlements and missions were outnumbered.[101]

The substitute also presented the reformer with a temptation to uplift and moralize. Idle moments were to be organized and diverted to
educational purposes. One settlement memorandum, for instance, advised that experience had shown that one of the most effective means of
uplifting individual and social morality was through wholesome social
contacts and wisely organized recreational activities.[102]

Critics also complained that the substitutes failed because they continued to be operated as charities. Even when the workingman purchased his coffee or temperance brew, he felt he was being helped, that
someone was doing something for him. In the case of the Morgan Memorial Mission in Boston's South End, the ulterior motive for the substitute was clear. "When men drop in to the Temperance Saloon," noted
one of its publications, "in some tactful, unobstrusive way the claims of
religion are pressed upon them. They are made to feel that real relief,
the help which after all they are seeking, is found in the heavenly
Friend."[103] By contrast, the saloon was strictly commercial; the customer knew that someone was making a profit from the transaction,
but the place lacked the element of paternalism. As one observer put it:

"The tired, over-worked laborer enters unobtrusively. No one meets him at the door with a clammy hand-shake and stereotyped inquiry into the health of his wife and family. No one bustles about to see that he is amused. No one makes any strained attempt at intimacy."[104]

Saloon substitutes were also doomed to failure because their activities were too highly structured. The barroom operated with few rules; the reformers' clubs had constitutions, officers, dues, and agendas. Whereas the barroom drinker chose his companions on the basis of personal reactions and feelings, the settlement club was organized along interests rather than personalities. The barroom's activities were spontaneous, but those in the settlement were carefully planned and timed. Whereas the barroom operated as a shelter from the fast-paced temporal rhythm of the industrial city, almost as a retreat, the settlement club depended on members having a particular interest at a prescribed hour of a certain day. The necessities of scheduling had to precedence over the personal convenience of the members. As a result, no matter how much the missions and settlements opened their doors to the neighborhood, the saloon still seemed to be much more of a public place.[105] As the director of one settlement put it:

> Settlements as a whole are justly suspicious of too much organization; we know that it kills individual initiative and group spirit, both essential to growth. Instead of offering a group a choice of already established activities we meet their appeal for a night in the gym or a social club, in all sincerity, and offer such leadership as shall help them to work out their own salvation, thus putting the responsibility upon the group itself.

> Whatever activities are offered in the form of a definite program are the outcomes of actual requests or vague gropings which the leader discerns. Many times, or course, a group won't know what they do want, and then wise leadership is more than ever needed to suggest and advise.[106]

Finally, saloon substitutes failed because of insurmountable problems of communication.[107] The settlement and charity workers often encountered great difficulty in breaking the foreign language barriers of their communities, especially in older districts near the center of the city. The polyglot patch of a few square blocks near Hull House contained fifteen different nationalities, each with its own language or dialect.[108] This made it virtually impossible for the substitutes to attempt to serve more than one group at a time. If they reserved space for specific nationalities at scheduled times, then they lost the spontaneity necessary to attract the whims and fancies of customers. But if they opened up activities to all language groups at the same time, one group would often predominate. When Hull House inaugurated its new coffeehouse, one of its potential customers shook his head and warned, "Yez kin hev de shovel gang or yez can hev de office gang, but yez can't hev 'em both in the same room at the same toime." In this case, social class reinforced assimilation, and the English-speaking or native-born predominated at the coffeehouse, while the immigrants went to their respective saloons.[109]

Conclusion: Serving the Strangers

The rise of public transportation had a dramatic impact on the way citizens of Boston and Chicago lived. Not only did it allow an increasing separation of home and work, but it brought shoppers and those seeking entertainment out of the neighborhood more often. This allowed a dramatic enlargement of such downtown semipublic places as department stores and theaters, and it also transformed the nature of the street as well. Rush hour traffic reduced the desirability of many public ways as places to socialize. As utilitarian handlers of crowds, practicality and efficiency displaced beauty and friendliness.

The growth of the anonymous crowd also changed the semipublic businesses, such as saloons, tobacco shops, and grocery stores, that were dependent on the street traffic that moved by outside. Although commuting and factory lunch hours tended to produce a predictable group of regulars, there was a new emphasis on finding a replacement for the friendly firsthand knowledge of the customer. "Scientific" choice of location, often a decision made by a brewery real estate department, assured a spot near the flow of pedestrians. In Boston the deliberate policy of the licensing authorities steered license applicants to these locations, while in Chicago it was purely a business decision.

Saloons of this type often depended on the inefficiency of traffic to bring in customers. Owners also had to adjust to the geographic specialization of the city by functions: financial, theater, office, and shopping districts, as well as industrial concentrations. The ebb and flow of customers also moved to the beat of time clocks and lunch hours, rather than to the casual pace of the neighborhood. Saloons dependent on mobile customers were also much less ethnocentric, when customers came from many neighborhoods. Localized work forces supported nearby bars, but many places turned to gimmicks, such as bowling alleys and bicycle races, to draw the crowds. Lunch also became less of a gesture of friendship than a gamble to outdo competitors. The vending machine on the bar was the ultimate symbol of impersonal efficiency.

Both cities also had large numbers of citizens who lived amidst the anonymity of this mobile crowd. Once-fashionable neighborhoods adjacent to downtown declined into rooming house districts, because the encroachment of commercial land uses and traffic congestion rendered them less desirable. Wealthy residents fled to outlying districts, and roomers moved in. Often low-paid, the dwellers of the furnished rooms often left their compact quarters for public and semipublic spaces to dine and pass their idle hours. For the young men the saloon proved an important supplement to the rooming house parlor.

The bars designed to attract both rooming house customers and mobile drinkers attracted opposition from a variety of reform groups. What seemed most dangerous about this type of drinking experience was its anonymity, the absence of pressure to conform to community standards because neighbors were not present. Members of the crowd found a dangerous kind of personal privacy. Besides efforts to enforce the closing hour in Chicago and Boston's Public Bar Law, some antisaloon groups promoted functional substitutes. If the bar kept late hours, so did the all-night coffee wagon; if workers wanted a place to spend idle hours, there was the YMCA or railway employees' recreation hall. The company lunchroom was available instead of the saloon sideboard, and payment of wages in cash made it unnecessary to go to a barroom to cash paychecks. The hiring hall and restroom functions of the saloon found competition from state employment services and public restrooms.

Although the effort to dismantle the saloon's draw through the use of functional substitutes became a national movement through the Committee of Fifty, the barroom survived. As in the case of the settlement house crusade against tenement drinking spots, the "antis" were hopelessly outnumbered. The saloon was both ubiquitous and highly adaptable to the public street life outside its door.

CHAPTER 7

The Triumph
of Moral Geography

D URING THE WINTER of 1893 a citizen from one of the solid middle-class neighborhoods on the South Side wrote a letter to the *Chicago Herald* to complain about something that had been going on for years. The "Alley El," nicknamed because of its off-street route to the World's Columbian Exposition grounds, passed by the rear windows of Appleton's Saloon on South Wabash. Business in that tough Levee district barroom-brothel must have been slow during that afternoon, because the "loose women" employed there were reportedly "exposing themselves" to the riders of the passing elevated trains. One citizen was apparently so shocked by this very personal form of advertising that he had penned an angry demand that the police immediately raid the dive and stop that very visible form of vice.

The incident made no headlines, and there were no reports that the police department closed down Appleton's bar. But it was symbolic of a particular attitude in Chicago, one facet of which had been responsible for the creation of Levee vice districts. That was the belief that certain unpleasant, even immoral, yet inevitable social activities should be segregated into a particular area, where authorities could restrain the excesses. But segregation was also a protective policy designed to keep sin from spreading to places where no one wanted it. The man who wrote to the *Herald* had experienced one of the frequent times when moral insulation had failed.

The growth of the protective idea through the last half of the nineteenth century was one of the most important developments in the social history of urban moral standards. It applied to prostitution and gambling, but it also came to shape much of the debate over the saloon as well. The issue involved not only the reputed sinfulness of liquor, but also questions of the way in which social class shaped the meaning of privacy among the dwellers of cities and suburbs. Affluence and geographical mobility meant that some people could exercise a wider degree of choice in their relationship with the saloon. But what the middle- and upper-classes failed to realize and learned very painfully was the ironic way in which transportation both made moral insulation possible and at the same time insured its eventual failure.

Money and Privacy

After the 1880s even middle-class residents who remained in the central part of the city were still able to obtain a considerable amount of privacy. This was due to the widespread adoption of the flat, or apartment building. In earlier decades there had been a strong social stigma attached to a multifamily building with a shared entrance. This had constituted the popular definition of a tenement, and with it came images of poverty, privy vaults, and disease.[1]

The creation of the apartment building was as much a matter of changing an image as it was a problem in technological design. Basically, its plans resembled those of the tenement except for the privatizing of the interior spaces. As in the model tenements, each room had a special function, with separate spaces for water closets and storage, and the plumbing system was self-contained within each housing unit. The most spectacular changes came in the way the building presented itself to nonresidents. The entrance shared by the tenants was made as attractive as possible. The first "family hotels" in Chicago sported awnings that reached to the curb. A uniformed doorman, who presided over arrivals and departures, along with bells, speaking tubes, and locks on the front doors, assured the family's privacy and protection. Unlike the tenement, where a stranger might walk the hallways, the interior and exterior spaces of the apartment building were clearly defined.[2] The "flat craze" swept the country after 1880. The Hotel Pelham, built shortly after the Civil War, had been Boston's first, but by 1890 there were already 495 so-called family hotels, and in 1900 and 1910 that number jumped to 523 and 659, respectively.[3]

Even the single people of the city were able to partake of apartment life. Specific buildings for gentlemen, or "bachelor flats," combined the best features of the apartment and the boarding house. Three- or four-room suites provided commodious space and privacy unknown in rented rooms, while the management provided services that a bachelor presumably was unwilling to provide for himself. Maids cleaned his quarters; laundrymen made regular calls; valets saw to it that clothes were picked up, cleaned, and mended. And downstairs there was a restaurant where the tenant could take his evening meal.[4]

Money could purchase many things in the Victorian city, including privacy, space, and relative independence from coinhabitants of the urban world. Wealth allowed people to have enough rooms in their homes so that each could have a specialized purpose. The various activities of life, from bathing, to breakfasting, dining, and reading—each had a specific space. Unlike the tenement, where these were all performed in one room, the homes of the wealthy were highly structured collections of functional areas.[5] These amenities were not exclusively limited to the very wealthy. The proliferation of mass transit opened up vast tracts of land on the edge of metropolitan areas. This mobility, in turn, made it possible for large-scale contractors to erect hundreds of look-alike houses for land-hungry urbanites.[6] Those of middling wealth could afford a spacious nine- or ten-room house of stucco or clapboard construction.[7]

The search for privacy created an unusual relationship between the comfortable home and the neighborhood in which it stood. On one hand, the residents attached considerable "sentiment and symbolism" to a particular location. The reputation of Boston's Commonwealth Avenue or Chicago's Prairie Avenue had great social significance and remained a goal for the upwardly mobile.[8]

But the neighborhoods of the most desirable symbolic value were often of the least practical use to the residents. Despite the fact that the poor generally stayed away from prestigious streets, many comfortable homes seemed to look inward, as if their grounds were a buffer against the outside world. For many years walls and ornamental fencing had assumed great significance as a way of dividing one's property from the street. This was as true of people of moderate means as it was of residents of Beacon Hill or Prairie Avenue. Humorist Frank Willkie noted the significance of ornamental fencing in lending prestige to the street: "When ever a man in Westside [Chicago] builds a house and puts up a fence in front of it, he immediately calls the space in front of his lot an avenue."[9]

Some residents went to great trouble to insure their domestic privacy. The John J. Glessner house, Henry Hobson Richardson's contribution to Chicago's Millionaire Row, employed its heavy Roman-esque walls to protect an interior courtyard. Exterior windows were of minimal size, often as little as a slit carved between the granite blocks.[10] Glessner later remembered Richardson's advice: "He maintained that the windows of a city house were 'not to look out of' and should not be large: 'You no sooner get them than you shroud them with two thicknesses of window shades, and then add double sets of curtains.' "[11] But large interior panes flooded the inside rooms with light and provided an unobstructed view of the walled garden. In other houses the grounds of an estate and its shrubbery were often employed to shield the house from the peering eyes of passersby.

Associational life for the wealthy was also closed, voluntary, and private. Both Chicago and Boston witnessed a proliferation of organizations during the postbellum decades. Many were special-purpose groups that studied literature, music, or municipal problems. Others provided men and women with a semiprivate place to dine downtown; even the number of guests was limited, lest the group become too public. And political activity, which ultimately had to depend upon the support of the masses, was planned and discussed amidst oak-paneled privacy in such places as the Union League and Hamilton clubs in Chicago and the Somerset and Algonquin clubs of Boston. James Michael Curley realized that fact when in 1909 he attacked the licensing authorities for allowing nomination petitions to be circulated in the clubs of the wealthy, but not in saloons. The former was a private circle of friends; the latter was a public place.[12]

The wealthy were also able to employ more private means of communication, which eliminated the need for such places as saloons as a center of neighborhood gossip. The calling card announced the visitor, while the ability to write and afford postage allowed people to exchange messages by mail. The telegraph allowed privacy in business communication, but the most significant development of all was the invention of the telephone.[13] Adopted first by the wealthy, this instrument allowed instant contact. No one, aside from a nosey operator, could eavesdrop, and, most important of all, it helped preserve the privacy of the home.[14] The phone companies realized the significance of privacy and security. For instance, an ad in the *South Side Sayings*, a neighborhood newspaper in Chicago's Hyde Park, suggested: "To be within reach . . . by telephone of the police and fire departments, and of your grocery, butcher, druggist and others with whom you have dealings, renders your home life *Safer, More Convenient*, and *More Comfortable*."[15]

When the wealthy did venture into the public areas of the city, they isolated themselves from the urban environment. This was especially true of carriage travel, but the principle also applied to the middle-class rider of a suburban train or an elevated car who had little direct contact with street life. At cultural events or even at church, the family of means sat in private boxes or partitioned pews. Even the summer-time heat, which drove the poor from their stifling tenements, also brought the rich outdoors, but not into common public places. Instead, they left their town houses behind in favor of Nahant or Marblehead, Lake Geneva or Lake Forest. Here they owned estates or rented private buildings or rooms in exclusive resort hotels. Their beaches were private.

Other outdoor pastimes bore the mark of social class. The bicycle craze, which swept the country during the last quarter of the nine-teenth century, brought many people of substantial means into the fresh air. But this did not mean that the cyclists mingled with others. Many outings were under the sponsorship of expensive clubs whose memberships were tightly regulated. Nor did the wheelmen choose routes that led them through slums. The Boston club rejected the city's dangerous hills in favor of a more agreeable suburban terrain. Wealthy Chicagoans could use the large, landscaped parks, which long dis-tances and social custom had virtually sealed off from the poor. In ex-clusive North Side neighborhoods adjacent to Lincoln Park cycling was a popular family recreation. As Edith Ogden Harrison, wife of one of Chicago's most popular mayors, remembered:

> Especially during the lovely summer evenings, before every Astor Street home on our block one could see the trim bicycles awaiting the cessation of an early dinner for the owners inside, for it was just a foregone conclusion that every one took a ride after dinner in the cool of the evening. . . .
>
> Almost at its very appearance, the riders numbered hundreds. Schools opened to teach its riding, and traffic in this really expen-sive sport became a thing of wonder.[16]

Finally, in death the wealthy could also maintain a sense of symbolic privacy. They were buried in family plots, not mixed with the graves of people of lesser means. The larger plots were usually surrounded by enough open space to allow room for later generations and often a fence. Even the particular cemetery assumed a status of its own, as did Chicago's Graceland, which became known as the Prairie Avenue of the dead.[17]

The desire for tranquil privacy, open space, and protection of youthful morality in the suburbs often brought residents in direct conflict with liquor dealers. On occasion the confrontation was rooted in the early history of the town. Many outlying residential districts had begun with a crossroads inn amidst a farming district. Such stagecoach drinking houses hosted farmers on their way to and from market and other travelers, providing beds and meals at night and water and hay for the horses during the day. The countryside surrounding both Chicago and Boston was dotted with these small hostelries, holdovers from the colonial period in their services and operation.[18]

As years passed, some of them fostered the growth of small shopping districts and early service industries, such as blacksmiths. Some country taverns also drew more of their clientele from among the nearby farmers than from wayfarers. Gradually, they became the center of village social life, and on at least two occasions on the fringe of Chicago, the inaugural masses of Roman Catholic churches were said in a saloon hall. Ironically, when many of these little farming communities became towns, when suburban tracts grew up around farmhouses, when the weekend gardener replaced the farmer, and when more exclusive drygoods stores replaced the general store, then the liquor dealer who had been the town founder became the target of local prohibitionists.[19]

Travelers were not the only outsiders who visited the outlying inns. Many liquor dealers positioned themselves conveniently near the entrance to cemeteries. Here the mourners stopped on their way back to the city. If they traveled by train or streetcar, the nearby inn was within walking distance. If the procession came by carriage, there was often shelter, feed, and water for horses. Other rural barrooms opened picnic groves and beer gardens, where urban families could enjoy a bucolic Sunday afternoon. Bicyclers, often traveling in club groups, were regular visitors. Finally, an occasional industry, such as a brickyard, which had to be located near a source of clay, or a city dump might generate enough traffic to support an isolated barroom.[20]

A great portion of these early liquor dealerships survived the beginnings of suburban growth and found themselves unwanted by new residents, many of whom had escaped the city "saloon menace." But in other cases, liquor dealers responded to the changing leisure habits of urbanites. Even with limited victories for shorter hours and work-weeks, workers in the last quarter of the nineteenth century found the time and money for nonessential travel. Hundreds, then thousands, of laborers and their families escaped the heat and unpleasant atmos-phere of the tenements and sought relief in parks and on beaches. While Boston's weekday rush hours in the summer consisted largely of middle- and upper-class men traveling between work and the family summer home, on weekends the urban working class took their places on suburban railroads and streetcars.[21]

Astute saloonists wisely realized that heavy trade on weekends might compensate for slow weekdays. They positioned themselves opposite park entrances, next to suburban rail stops, and near beaches. There the weekend saloonists frequently came in conflict with year-round res-idents. For instance, in 1878 the *Chicago Tribune* carried the letter of an angry German resident of the Wicker Park neighborhood. He com-plained that summer weekends were ruined by noise and "rough char-acters" who patronized dance halls and beer gardens near the park. A few days later, another resident complained that the noise generated by outdoor drinking establishments disrupted church services. In some cases, patrons of these establishments were rowdy, driving residents from the streets and park in the evening. "This is bad enough," wrote a resident of Humboldt Park area, "but worse than this, their sidewalks, their yards, and even their doorsteps and porches, have been defiled by prostitutes and their male companions." Public officials ignored the problem, and an attempt to pass corrective legislation in Springfield also failed.[22]

Suburbanites, meanwhile, faced another problem in the popularity of race tracks. Not only did the tracks create enormous traffic jams on race days and draw undesirable gamblers to outlying residential areas, but the crowds also consumed enormous amounts of liquor. Brewers frequently owned a large interest in a track or in land near it. For in-stance, the Downer and Bemis Brewing Company of Chicago owned the Chicago Trotting Association track on the West Side during the late 1870s, while the Seipp Brewing Company bought large parcels of land near Washington Park and built saloons on them. The liquor consump-tion at Corrigan's Race Track, later Hawthorne Park, near Cicero also upset nearby residents.[23]

Beaches presented yet another problem. Families who paid high rents or purchase prices for places usable only five months of the year sometimes found the most pleasant season marred by "tramp saloons." This was less a problem in Boston, where resort towns were often more restrictive than the city. The public swimming areas established by the city also drained much of the potential profit from private beaches that charged admission. In Chicago, however, there were no public beaches until after 1910, and people who owned property fronting on Lake Michigan were only too willing to make a dollar. Whether a place stayed open or not depended on how the mayor felt. In one notable incident residents of Windsor Park complained loudly about a continuous, six-block stretch of commercial beaches, saloons, and dance halls that marred their lakefront. The publicity that residents generated and their petitions to city officials finally closed the strip during the late 1890s. [24]

While the masses crowded the beaches, wealth brought a more selective and symbolic view of the public places of the city. Urban space might be useful for recreation or civic aesthetics, but little else. Semi-public places, which were rarely found in middle- or upper-class neighborhoods, lacked the same survival-oriented functions they possessed in tenement districts. The saloon was most conspicuously absent. Men of wealth could do their drinking in clubs, fine restaurants, hotel bars, or at home. Because they had little need for the open barrooms, it became easy for them to advocate keeping the barroom out of residential areas and confining it to the inner city. This notion that upper- and middle-class areas must be protected from the saloon first appeared in the suburbs and then gradually spread to the interstitial areas between innercity tenements and the outlying borders. When the idea began to spread during the 1880s, few people realized that its widespread adoption would prove to be a major turning point in the history of the saloon.

Saving the Suburbs

In the Chicago area the development of a ring of dry towns extended back to 1851, when Northwestern University was founded in the village of Evanston. The Methodist institution was deliberately located a dozen miles from the sinful influences of Chicago. To insure the purity of the students, the Illinois General Assembly added an unusual clause to the charter: no liquor was to be sold within four miles of the campus.

Evanston included its own prohibition provision in the town charter of
1853.[25] No one realized it at the time, but a seventy-year war between
liquor sellers and prohibitionists was about to begin. The central issue
was not Evanston, but the outlying fringe of the four-mile limit. Residents of nearby country towns and unincorporated areas challenged
the Northwestern charter, but in 1862 the Illinois Supreme Court upheld the dry clause and kept eight miles of lakeshore settlements saloonless.[26] Blind pigs, however, were abundant, leading Evanstonians to
found various vigilance groups to bring the surreptitious sellers to justice. The success of these investigations, however, was often hampered
by a critical flaw which the dealers employed as a standard defense:
pure-minded prohibitionists had never tasted liquor and could have no
accurate idea of what the accused had been serving.[27]

The dry territory to the north inspired other Chicago suburbs to remove the saloons. Under an old Illinois statute of 1839 any city, town,
or village could hold a prohibition election. Oak Park to the west and
Blue Island to the southwest dried up, as did a scattering of country
towns. To accommodate this temperance movement, the General Assembly passed a law in 1883 prohibiting county boards from granting
liquor licenses within two miles of any town. This not only prevented
the growth of a ring of cheap licenses around a high-license town, but
it also stopped the development of a wet fringe around bastions of
temperance.[28]

Boston also saw itself become surrounded by dry suburbia. In 1881
the General Court enacted a town option law. Unlike a similar statute
in Illinois, it called for annual elections in all towns and cities and did
not require a petition to place the matter on the ballot. The frequency
of the vote made it especially responsive to the social changes in every
community, especially the transformation of country towns into commuter suburbs.[29]

The results of Boston's annual election were never in serious doubt,
but suburban prohibitionists quickly used the law to create a solid band
of no-license towns surrounding Boston. Quincy, Malden, Newton,
and Somerville joined the ranks almost immediately, while Waltham
switched back and forth several times before closing its saloons for
good. Only Chelsea remained wet.[30] The most famous fight, however,
was in Cambridge. In many respects this suburb resembled Evanston.
Both were college towns bordering on major cities. Both contained cot-
tage districts with minority residents as well as the comfortable man-

sions. But several miles of open countryside separated Evanston from Chicago, while Boston's social problems easily spilled over the Charles River. Transients preferred the Cambridge police station to the Hawkins Street Woodyard, and Boston's criminals often sneaked over the bridge to commit crimes in Cambridge and then return to the relative anonymity of the larger city. The shacks of the "Tin Village" on the suburban side of the river duplicated some of the worst tenement conditions in Boston. Even Cambridge's saloons were owned primarily by the brewers and wholesalers of the Hub.[31]

The prospect of annual license elections inspired a concerted effort to dry up Cambridge. The first balloting, in 1882, saw the town remain wet by a mere six votes. During three subsequent campaigns the churches and traditional temperance groups failed against an opposition that included vote buying and tampering with ballot boxes. Finally, in 1886 the dry forces changed tactics and saturated the city with parades, posters, and billboards. The dry forces greeted pedestrians with handbills and made straphangers gaze into ads in streetcars. A special temperance newspaper, the *Frozen Truth*, reproduced arrest blotters and listed kitchen barrooms. The result was a dry victory by 616 votes. To prevent backsliding, the Dry Cambridge Committee, which had coordinated the victory, hired professional political organizers to widen support in the ethnic communities. Cambridge never again produced a prolicense majority before 1920.[32]

The movement that created rings of dry suburbs around Chicago and Boston also stimulated efforts to ban barrooms in outlying middle-class residential neighborhoods. Most of the latter efforts came in areas annexed to larger cities in the postbellum decades. Between 1868 and 1874 Boston added Roxbury, West Roxbury, Dorchester, Charlestown, and Brighton; annexation was the greatest source of population growth. In 1889 Chicago absorbed the townships of Lake, Jefferson, Lake View, and Hyde Park, increasing the city's size from 43 to 169 square miles. Most of the territory in both cities consisted of comfortable single-family dwellings and apartments, with some open farmland included in Chicago's addition. Many of these districts had been added against their will as parts of larger jurisdictions.[33] The promise of improved municipal services had been a major inducement to annex, but many new residents were disappointed. The result was a series of neighborhood improvement associations designed to act as lobbies at city hall. As early as 1880 a City Point Improvement Association had been formed by South Boston businessmen, and within a decade the idea had spread to Orient Heights, East Boston, Washington Village, and Roxbury. Chicago's first group of this type was founded in Wood-lawn, a part of the Town of Hyde Park, soon after its annexation in 1889. Within a decade twenty-four groups were scattered in communities around the periphery of the city.[34]

The interests of the improvement associations were parochial and usually limited to upgrading city housekeeping services. But they also represented a desire to protect middle-class homes from the invasion of such undesirable elements from the inner city as peddlers, prostitutes, and the noise of elevated trains.[35] And after viewing the creation of dry suburbs, outlying city areas began to seek ways of protecting their homes from saloons. In Boston residents began complaining that the abutters' law of 1880, which was supposed to allow adjoining property owners to challenge saloon licenses, was ineffective. Bribes for signatures and the tedious task of examining lists of licensees left most neighborhoods powerless. The presence of a barroom also had an obvious effect on far more than the property immediately adjoining it. Nor were license officials completely trustworthy, despite their promise to keep the saloons on main thoroughfares and principally downtown. By the early 1890s residents of Sullivan Square, Brighton, South Boston, and several other districts were complaining about noisy drinking spots in their midst. By 1902 various church, neighborhood improvement, and temperance groups had joined to form the Boston Temperance Federation. That confederation had a singular goal: passage of a "district option" law.[36]

That proposal was a compromise between total prohibition and total lack of geographical regulation. It was a logical outgrowth of a tradition of internal districting — ward boundaries, school districts — and the notion that laws regulating public morality need not be the same across the entire city. Supporters of the district option proposal assumed that the residential areas would be prohibition territory and the downtown and crowded tenement districts would be left to the saloons. The law, as proposed, created eight license districts, allowing one license for each 500 people in "Boston proper," but only one per 1,000 in Roxbury, West Roxbury, East Boston, Charlestown, South Boston, Dorchester, and Brighton. A majority of the voters in any district could create no-license territory. The General Court approved the measure in 1902, but it required the approval of Boston voters to become law. Generally, anyone opposed to liquor claimed the need for "home protection" and cited the failures of the license officials. Opponents of the bill complained that it would result in the loss of 79 licenses, or $80,000 revenue annually to the city. Moreover, smaller patches of prosaloon sentiment, such as the Germans of Roxbury, would be overwhelmed by the temperance majority of the section. This violated the idea of home rule. After months of debate over the measure, the voters rejected it 45,914 to 35,810. The heavy support it garnered in Dorchester, Brighton, and West Roxbury was not enough to overcome its overwhelming opposition in "Boston proper." Control over the distribution of saloon licenses would remain in the hands of appointed license officials rather than voters for the rest of the years before national prohibition.[37]

The districting idea fared better in Chicago, where vice was segregated. Neighborhood protection took three forms. The first was a peculiarity in the ordinances by which the town of Hyde Park was added to the city in 1889. In order to guarantee support for annexation, Chicago officials allowed the new districts to keep their old liquor laws intact. Seven small areas entered Chicago as dry territory, while Hyde Park and the Town of Lake, whose combined eighty-four square miles made up most of the annexation, were declared "local option" territory. License applicants in the latter had to obtain signatures from a majority of the voters within one-eighth of a mile of the proposed saloon. In Hyde Park dealers needed the approval of a majority of the property owners, tenants, and businesses on both sides of the street in the block where the barroom was to be located. As difficult as it seemed, the petition requirement proved no obstacle in the industrialized Town of Lake or in the South Chicago manufacturing areas in Hyde Park. The great controversy was in the northern portion of Hyde Park, from 35th to 59th streets and Washington Park east to the lake. This section of comfortable single-family homes and luxury apartments had resisted annexation, and its struggle against saloons would capture local headlines for over three decades.[38]

Soon after Hyde Park became a Chicago neighborhood, a fanatic prohibitionist named Arthur B. Farwell founded the Hyde Park Protective Association to root out blind pigs and other license violations. The HPPA, distrusting the police, hired investigators and financed judicial tests of every section of Hyde Park's liquor laws. Saloon interests managed to establish a few beachheads.[39] Several roadhouses survived near Washington Park, relics of the days when open country separated the city from its encircling park system created in 1869. Only after ten years of badgering property owners and pursuing legal tests of the meaning of "a block" and "a resident" was the HPPA able to close these old bars. It was far less successful in its war against Saloon Row, a two-block strip along Lake (now Lake Park) Avenue facing the Illinois Central tracks. The railroad refused to sign prohibition petitions, and since a nearly solid stretch of saloons had developed to serve thirsty commuters, tenant liquor dealers and breweries gladly signed each other's petitions. Saloon Row remained a conspicuous failure in the HPPA's crusade.[40]

The events in Hyde Park were further complicated by its hosting of the World's Columbian Exposition of 1893 and its aftermath. The South Side community was rapidly transformed from a sleepy village to a busy, cosmopolitan district visited by millions in a few months. The HPPA not only tried without success to keep the fair closed on Sundays, but it also lost a more important struggle against an invasion of amusements, cheap hotels, and saloons near the fairgrounds. When the elevated railway was constructed from the Loop to Jackson Park in 1892, it spanned nearly two miles of Sixty-third street. The noise and smoke from the steam-powered trains ruined the street below for residential purposes, and saloons were prominent among the invading businesses.[41] After the fair the street was unable to shake its tawdry image, but amusement developers realized that its location adjacent to Washington and Jackson parks and the elevated might attract crowds. The result was a string of amusement parks, including the Sans Souci, the Chutes, and Dreamland, the giant later renamed White City. Another attraction was Midway Gardens, designed by Frank Lloyd Wright and opened in 1913. It opened as a high-class dining spot, complete with Max Bendix's orchestra. But financial problems after a few seasons caused its sale to the Edelweiss Brewing Company. A cheap dance band appeared, and the Edelweiss gained a city-wide reputation for underage drinking and other license violations. The HPPA tried but never succeeded in having it closed.[42]

Despite the problems involved in keeping Hyde Park dry, the presence of local option territory in the annexed portions of Chicago inspired other middle-class neighborhoods to search for ways to protect themselves from the saloon. The easiest method was found in the City Council. In 1894 it adopted an unwritten policy: all members would respect the wishes of any alderman who wanted a portion of his ward to become antisaloon territory. After the council approved the first such district for a portion of the Buena Park area on the North Side, dozens of requests poured in from churches and neighborhood groups. Each district, usually a few square blocks, required a separate ordinance, but all requests were honored. Even Bathhouse John Coughlin of the Levee admitted, "Ain't it right — all right? I'm not for gin mills in the residence district where there's a roar raised against them."[43]

The third method of drying up neighborhoods was similar to the district option proposal defeated in Boston. Local option, as it was known in Chicago, allowed petitioners in a precinct, ward, city, or county to place a prohibition referendum on any ballot. The struggle focused on Springfield, where such groups as the Illinois Anti-Saloon League took up the cause and proclaimed the virtues of home rule. Opponents claimed that rural areas could vote whole counties dry, including unwilling towns. Furthermore, when the Chicago City Council dried up a district, it was usually careful not to include major commercial streets, only residential sections. The proposed law employed precinct lines that made no such distinction. After an intense lobbying effort by the Anti-Saloon League, the legislature passed the measure in 1907. During the next two years dozens of precincts and wards in Chicago voted themselves dry. Many of the neighborhood barkeeps saw it as a plot hatched by the big downtown saloon owners and the prohibitionists. The "swells" and the middle-class commuters could drink at fancy Loop clubs and bars, but return to their homes in dry districts and carry on the pretense of sobriety. Meanwhile, by 1909 nearly two-thirds of Chicago was dried up, and the remaining licensees were jammed into the slums, working-class neighborhoods, and the Loop.[44]

The creation of dry suburban rings and saloonless outlying districts also proved to be an important factor in the decline of annexation as a means of city growth. By the first decade of the new century residents of outlying towns and farms increasingly saw it advantageous to remain free from the grasp of ward bosses. It was so much easier to resist annexation and remain dry than to plunge into the unknown future of city politics. There was always the danger that redistricting of some kind might result in a wet majority. The concern with open immorality in the form of gambling, prostitution, and license violation made suburbanites proud of the relative purity of their residential areas. These attitudes helped Evanstonians resist intense annexation drives in 1894 and again in 1909; the suburb did, however, give up a small section to Chicago where their common border met the lakeshore. Evanston's temperance groups had carried on an unsuccessful crusade against blind pigs there for years, and it was thought easier to get rid of what later became known as the "Juneway Jungle" than to continue the fight. In one other celebrated fight, Morgan Park entered Chicago in 1914 after two decades of debate and litigation. A villager bitterly complained that he was being annexed against his will to "a city run by red-nosed rum-soaked pot-house politicians."[45]

The liquor question created a similar stir in Boston. The city had made large annexations in the 1860s and 1870s, but by the latter part of the century many Boston officials had begun to believe that the cost of providing services to the new districts outweighed the advantages of annexation. Visionaries, however, noted the need to coordinate the chaotic expansion of the metropolitan region, arguing that some type of unification would make Boston more competitive with other major American cities. The liquor issue proved to be the major obstacle. After the law of 1881 gave each town the right to vote itself dry, saloonless suburbs routinely resisted annexation attempts: Somerville, for instance, in 1893, Cambridge in 1892 and again in 1901. Even Chelsea, which regularly voted wet, retained its independence. The liquor issue also destroyed attempts to create regional governments. In 1891 a utopian writer named Sylvester Baxter envisioned "Greater Boston," a plan to unite twenty-seven towns in a ten-mile radius of the Hub under a single county government. Suburban temperance groups were instrumental in killing the plan. One dry voiced the common fear: "[with annexation] we should have a rum shop on every corner." Advocates of unification argued in vain that local option would be preserved. Finally, the failure of the district option plan in Boston in 1902 further hardened suburbanites in their belief that any political ties with Boston would draw them into a cesspool of rum.[46]

Private Evasion in Chicago

Few who carried the banners of local option would acknowledge anything but success. Even the defeat of district option in Boston was not a complete failure, because it demonstrated to legislators and the police board that there was substantial sentiment in favor of keeping the bar in its place. Yet the idea of districting contained the seeds of its own failure. Local option and dry districts only prohibited open, commercial, public drinking in a barroom. Such liquor laws concentrated on the *place* where people drank, not on the act of drinking. This did not make citizens more temperate. It only changed their drinking habits. There were several ways to evade the law without ever leaving the dry district. Blind pigs and private clubs took on added importance. Membership in a country club became popular in communities where the prohibition sentiment was often the greatest.[47]

Many residents of dry neighborhoods also found the pharmacy a convenient source of liquor without the stigma of the saloon. Liquor sales by druggists in Illinois were entirely unregulated until 1883, when barkeeps pressured the City Council to enact a twenty-five-dollar license in Chicago. Pharmacists complained that any such permit unfairly interfered with their duty to dispense medicine, while some liquor dealers were unhappy at the low rate. In 1894 it was raised to $250.[48]

The central problem, however, was the intent of the sales. In 1883 the saloonkeepers pushed a law through the City Council that was designed to break down the privacy and anonymity of nonprescription liquor sales by requiring the pharmacist to record each transaction in a "well-bound book." The police could then determine who might be selling illegally. In 1904 that law was modified to include all prescriptions containing liquor. But even with registration books the secret liquor trade continued to flourish in the apothecary shops of dry neighborhoods. The growing popularity of the soda fountain introduced new possibilities for evasion. Instead of flavored syrups, the clerk added a portion of claret or even brandy to the soda water.[49]

But the most important threat to the integrity of dry districts was the portability of beer and liquor. The delivery wagon not only continued to become a more troublesome competitor to the saloonkeeper, but each improvement in communications and transportation aided home drinking at the expense of public imbibing. Street railways found it profitable to modify some of their cars to carry small packages, while the proliferation of interurban electric trains just after 1900 reduced delivery time to distant suburbs. And the development of automobile delivery introduced new door-to-door flexibility.

Saloonkeepers were unhappy about bottle delivery, but their anger did not become public until the large department stores entered the home sales competition in the early 1890s. The barkeeps complained both about the deliveries and the counter sales to Loop customers. In 1891 the stores were forced to purchase both retail and wholesale licenses, but this failed to halt the rapidly expanding department store trade. Finally, in 1897 the council passed the Walker ordinance, which prohibited liquor sales in the same stores that sold dry goods and other merchandise. Charles Netcher, owner of the Boston Store, led the court test of the law, and the Illinois Supreme Court declared it unconstitutional. Noting the origins of the department store in the old-fashioned general store, the court failed to find any threat to the community.[50]

While express service had carried liquor to the suburbs for many years, the telephone introduced new convenience to shopping in the home. The phone made it possible to order anything from the comfort and privacy of the parlor: women and "respectable" men did not have to worry about being seen while making an inconvenient trip to a dealer. This fact was not lost upon the wholesaler, whose newspaper ads seldom failed to mention a telephone number. "Call before 11 and delivery before 5" became a common advertising phrase which was usually set in distinctive type to attract the attention of readers.

Prohibitionists found few legal remedies. The laws that regulated liquor deliveries made no special provision for dry districts. Moreover, legal precedents held that any telephone sale technically took place at the dealer's office, even if there was a later cash-on-delivery transaction at the buyer's door. Delivery wagons could cart their liquor into any prohibition district, provided that they were responding to orders. Some Hyde Parkers were pleased when the HPPA's lawyers discovered a loophole. A few years before annexation, the Town of Hyde Park had enacted a high license fee of $500 for each wagon that delivered liquor. Since all of the old alcohol statutes remained in force after 1889, wagons operating in that neighborhood needed the license. Chicago police were not especially anxious to enforce the law, but the Protective Association successfully used it to reduce the number of deliveries in the community.[51]

Meanwhile, the express business into Evanston created its own complicated legal question over the meaning of legal boundaries. Legal tradition held that a municipality might regulate deliveries that originated within its city limits, but it could not erect barriers against commerce coming in from outside. When a judge ordered a jury to acquit a man caught delivering liquor into Evanston, *Mida's Criterion* celebrated the occasion in verse:

> Judge Dunne pronounces it good form
> To peddle beer from break of morn,
> To satisfy the thirst forlorn
> Of Evanston for early horn;
> Once more on prancing palfrey borne
> The beer keg takes the town by storm,
> Assisted by the juice of corn,
> And prohibition is uptorn.[52]

A few years later the Illinois Supreme Court upheld the principle that town boundaries could not be barriers in the path of commerce. Their landmark decision, which disallowed Chicago's attempts to prevent out-of-town brewers from shipping beer into the city as an unfair restraint of trade, also struck down Evanston's attempt to restrict delivery.[53] That decision severely reduced the power of the Evanston police. In 1899 the suburb's city council, alarmed over the way that the Supreme Court's decision gave encouragement to the peddlers, granted a special appropriation of $1,050 to the police. Officers seized any wagon whose drivers looked like they might be soliciting trade instead of responding to it. During the next few years the police showed great imagination. Inspectors on bicycles followed suspicious trucks to their destinations, then demanded to examine the order receipts if liquor was part of the cargo. Finally, they placed the names and addresses of all liquor purchasers on a list kept in the possession of the police. The knowledge that one's alcoholic preferences were no longer completely secret was thought to be a legitimate deterrent to future purchases. There is no accurate way to determine whether the controversial plan worked, but within a few years the Evanston police stopped arresting liquor deliverymen.[54]

Before the century ended, brewers were also promoting delivery sales. Their conversion is evident in the changes in their attitude toward advertising. Earlier, they had been suspicious of promotional activity of any kind except among saloonkeepers. In 1878 the *Western Brewer* had even warned its liquor trade readers that newspapers which solicited such ads were merely trying to extort money under the threat of editorializing in favor of prohibition.[55] But by 1888 Pabst had advertising in ethnic newspapers and was spending $3,000 annually for signboards in 650 Chicago streetcars. Eleven years later Pabst and Schlitz were erecting large billboard posters on city streets. Exposed sidewalls of downtown buildings now carried giant-sized blue ribbons and globes, while signboards dotted the major commuter routes from the city. Even barn roofs along the Chicago-Milwaukee rail lines proclaimed the superiority of one brand of beer over another.[56]

Boston's Portable Sin

Boston suburbanites reacted much like their Chicago counterparts to the drying up of suburban areas. Department stores began a large over-the-counter business, sometimes camouflaged as medicine. Finally, in 1905 the Police Commissioners issued the first clear wholesale license to a department store.[57] But this problem was minor compared with the invasion of surreptitious sellers that crossed the Charles into Cambridge when the suburb banned the saloon.

Throughout most of the nineteenth century Massachusetts had exercised much more careful control over liquor sales by apothecaries than did Illinois. The first license was issued in 1838, and thirty-one years later an amendment required the buyer to reveal his name and the intended use for the spirits. Subsequent laws required the name of the physician and the price recorded. All such records were subject to inspection by police authorities. And because medicine was obviously for private consumption, no imbibing was allowed on the premises.

Customers were thought to be of two types. Some went to the druggist for whiskey because they thought it to be of superior quality to that purchased in saloons or from wholesalers. Antiliquor tracts had stressed the supposed adulteration in saloon whiskey and had inadvertantly driven some drinkers to druggists instead. The fact that so many patent medicines contained alcohol merely made it easy to switch to the straight drink. Other customers, who were treated much more severely in the liquor trade press, were those who wanted to drink but would not go near an honest saloon. These were the true "water bigots," who wanted secret drink conveniently nearby and available at the extended hours of the apothecary, but who wanted to promote a public image of abstinence.[58]

The evasion of the dry law prompted the quick formation of the Citizens' Law Enforcement Association. With the old Law and Order League nearly defunct, the group took over the role of private inspectors that both watched and aided the police. At first, the group was completely voluntary, but soon it hired professional detectives to help. The dry spies had plenty to watch, for the desire to purchase liquor was matched by the ingenuity of those who wanted to sell it.[59] Druggists were even more tempted to give the word *medicinal* a broad interpretation. It was easy to "forget" to record sales properly or to ignore the number of times they refilled the same prescription. The association's investigators uncovered dozens of such violations every week. During January 1888 one Cambridge druggist filled 1,066 liquor "prescriptions," including more than twenty-five pints of whiskey to fifty customers in just one day. Several buildings that had once been saloons now called themselves apothecaries. But despite the mortar sign over the door, no one inside knew much about a pharmacy, and the prescription counter sported a brass rail in front.[60]

The suburban soda fountain presented its own special enforcement problem, for it was really a revival of one of the oldest kinds of illegal dealers. Sodas and sundaes contained fruit mixes and toppings that were an excellent camouflage for liquor. Customers who gave the right signal to the counterman might be able to buy a rather potent concoction without lowering themselves to the task of finding some surreptitious seller. Thus, a "cherry wink" could have all the force of a "shot" without arousing the suspicion of an abstainer seated at the next table. This kind of evasion had been popular during the statewide prohibition of the mid-nineteenth century; now it appeared once again in Boston's dry suburbs.[61]

The druggist problem was especially troubling for the temperance movement, because many of the purchasers were evidently female alcoholics. The few "respectable" women who had been bold enough to drink in public had evoked the expected shock from the press and from the WCTU. But public drinking was much easier to control than private tippling. A growing number of women poured a drink to relieve "female complaints" or boredom. While their husbands were away, they would make the rounds of the soda fountains and apothecaries. This shocked the devout abstainers, and, as they had done during the famous 1867 debates, Bostonians asked themselves whether the private drinking that inevitably accompanied prohibition was worth the price of closing the public barroom.[62]

Meanwhile, within the city Boston never did enact a district option law, and consequently within its borders it avoided most of the delivery problems encountered in Chicago's Hyde Park. But the close proximity of the Hub's downtown district to its dry suburbs created a legal question similar to that found at the Evanston border: a no-license town so

close to a wet one was always subject to frequent forays by liquor delivery teams. The Cambridge case was also complicated by the fact that
the same people who once owned saloons there were the same Boston
wholesalers and brewers who were anxious to retain the trade of their
old suburban customers. Moreover, dealers had been carting liquors of
various kinds across the Charles River for years and were reluctant to
let prohibition stop them.[63]

Almost immediately after Cambridge voted no-license, its city government adopted tough legal standards for the delivery of liquor.
Police, acting with the aid of the Cambridge Enforcement Association,
detained hundreds of suspicious wagons each year. Anyone making
deliveries to an alleged kitchen barroom could expect to have every
parcel searched by police. Finally, expressmen could not deliver liquor C.O.D.; the purchaser had to travel to Boston to make the
transaction.[64]

The Cambridge statutes were somewhat more restrictive than the
state laws. As far back as 1855 the Massachusetts legislators had made
it illegal to carry liquor for sale into a prohibition town, but the law
and its amendments remained unclear about deliveries of alcohol purchased elsewhere. That was a matter for local authorities to decide. By
1897 the amount of intercity liquor traffic had grown so large that the
confusion of conflicting town statutes hindered rather than helped law
enforcement. When the General Court decided that year to enact a
uniform statewide law, it chose the Cambridge regulations as its
model. The new statute required that all deliverymen carrying liquor
be on their way to a specific location that had been entered in an order
book. The place of sale, which was defined as the spot where the money
changed hands, was also required to be in the wet city. The new law
inspired the Boston police board, who were themselves appointees of
the governor, to add restrictions of their own. After 1900 all delivery
teams carrying liquor *from* the city had to obtain special police permits
as well. Boston police were curious about the amount of alcohol being
delivered into the dry zone, and the number of permits — 1,726 in the
first year — revealed the astonishing size of the trade.[65]

Temperance forces were perplexed, because the new regulations
failed to reduce the amount of liquor delivered across city boundaries.
Their next move was an attempt to disrupt the traffic through inconvenience by reducing the number of carriers. The Boston police board
aided this policy by rejecting over two-thirds of applicants for express

permits in 1901. Three years later, the temperance interests went into court and brought a test suit against a Boston wholesaler. They claimed that if a team owned by a liquor dealer made the delivery into the dry town, it was part of an illegal transaction. The state Supreme Court agreed and ruled that only bonafide express companies could make liquor deliveries from a wet town into a dry one.[66]

That ruling meant that suburban officials had a new weapon to use against liquor deliveries, but some individuals who were really in the employ of brewers and wholesalers masqueraded as legitimate express companies. Suburban police found it difficult to uncover the real ownership of each one. Finally, in 1906 the General Court passed the Pony Express law. This controversial act allowed the police in dry towns to require the registration and disclosure of ownership of all teams that brought in liquor from wet towns. Suburban officials could now regulate the incoming commerce more easily, but the real significance of the bill lay in the new emphasis it placed on the meaning of municipal boundaries. Unlike Illinois, where Evanstonians could control intercity liquor deliveries only by intimidation, a Massachusetts town had broad powers to license and inspect commerce originating outside its borders. Moral geography had won a major victory.[67]

While the Massachusetts temperance people did battle with the express wagons, they found themselves combating another form of portable sin — drunkenness among commuters. It was an old problem. As early as 1843 Harvard students reportedly had begun descending on Boston for liquor. Years later the few wet suburbs had to contend with saloonkeepers rushing to set up their businesses along the boundaries of neighboring towns where prohibition had already triumphed.[68]

Thousands of suburban people took advantage of the convenience and drank themselves into intoxication, or "let out," as one early observer put it.[69] They piled into saloons located at the Boston ends of the suburban bridges. People staggered across the lonely spans or crawled aboard public transportation. One commentator, writing from the prohibition viewpoint, called it a "river of tipsiness sluggishly flowing over that Craigie Bridge from Boston into Cambridge," and went on to describe a ride on a night car: "The car rolled on; saloons to the right and to the left, each filled with a half-tipsey crowd; and in all of them the horrible work of drunkard-making going on. That car, on its short circuit of about a mile before it gets back to the bridge, passes fifty or sixty open drinking places. And, as that motley crowd changes continually from five o'clock till eleven, from five thousand to twenty thousand men there taste the poison every night."[70]

After Cambridge voted itself dry, its police department began to station officers at the suburban ends of the bridges. By checking all horse-cars and pedestrians they arrested most of the disorderly drunks before they even had a chance to make a disturbance. Watertown officials inspected debarking passengers at the first car stop in their town and at the railway depot.[71] But commuting inebriates caused the greatest amount of trouble for the Boston police. In 1887 that department began to tabulate the residence of the intoxicated people it arrested. An astonishing 40.8 percent were from out-of-town. Over the next twenty-five years that portion seldom fell below 40 percent and climbed gradually from 38.5 percent in 1900 to 47.9 percent a decade later. A special analysis of Boston arrests in 1907 revealed the expected residential distributions. That year the police detained 35,728 people on intoxication charges. Of these, 19,781 (55.4 percent) were Bostonians, while 15,957 (44.7 percent) were "strangers." Among the total, 408 (1.1 percent) were visiting seamen, 1,557 (4.4 percent) were from out-of-state and 2,454 (6.9 percent) were homeless drifters. That left a total of 11,528 (32.3 percent) from Massachusetts towns, nearly all of which were dry suburbs within ten miles of Boston. Further computation revealed that 2,100 (5.9 percent) of them came from Cambridge alone. This meant that on the average Boston police were arresting fifty-eight intoxicated Cambridge residents each day.[72]

Suburbanites also complicated the disposal of inebriate cases in Boston. It was difficult to investigate the background of each offender and decide on whether or not to grant parole or probation. Bondsmen were also wary of nonresidents; before the widespread use of driver's licenses or selective service cards for identification, it was easy to conceal one's true identity, never to return again. All that the police could do was to carry out well-publicized crackdowns. In May 1903, for instance, inebriates on downtown sidewalks received jail sentences rather than lectures, and officers boarded suburban trains in the depots and hauled away anyone even suspected of being tipsy. But all that a tougher attitude toward inebriates accomplished was a gradual increase in the percentage of nonresidents among those arrested.[73]

Another form of portable sin that temperance forces and police tried unsuccessfully to control was the ease with which thirsty people could personally carry liquor bottles from Boston to their dry suburban homes. This, too, was an old problem. During the long period of state prohibition, obtaining liquor had always been easier in the anonymous atmosphere of Boston than in the outlying towns. As one Hub merchant commented in 1867: "There are three or four liquor shops in Merchants Row, and I have noticed, on Saturday afternoon, the large number of demijohns that go into these stores where liquors are sold, to be filled and carried out of town for the comfort of the people of the neighboring towns during Sunday and the following week."[74]

The development of a ring of dry suburban towns came close to duplicating that earlier situation. Expressmen handled the bulkier crockery, but the parched commuter could still carry a smaller quantity home with him. Saloons adjacent to the rail depots and streetcar terminals were always happy to sell a bottle or fill a pocket flask. The wholesalers, who already owned many of the retail licenses, opened bottle goods departments for the convenience of hurrying commuters. Although many dealers profited from that trade, some proliquor observers could not help but point out the moral ambiguities that were involved in selling to "the hand-bag brigade, that ever flowing army of individuals who combat prohibition along scientific lines." The Boston correspondent to *Mida's Criterion* noted:

> They know where and how to "get it" and nothing is more commodious and plausible than a hand-bag. To it the genuine, unadulterated Bostonian is wedded. Down on Blackstone Street, toward North Station the dignified procession comes tripping along to his or her favorite establishment and the attendant behind the counter (not bar, if you please) nonchalantly pulls from the aforesaid hand-bag a two-gallon pitcher, the kind mother used to have on the washstand and with a most dignified mien proceeds to fill requirements and incidently, the pitcher. But this is only a "demand for immediate requirements," the great bulk of the counter trade is bottled goods . . . and each package, neatly wrapped ready for quick delivery is limited in size only to a man's pocketbook.[75]

The Irony of Moral Geography

The cities of Chicago and Boston differed dramatically in their official reaction to the encroachment of saloons into residential areas, although the final result in both cities was the protection of middle-class homes from the influx of liquor licenses. In the Hub regularized control through the abutter's law functioned relatively well to protect the immediate areas of homes and public institutions, while the policies of the police board reinforced neighborhood protection by carefully restricting most liquor licenses to major commercial streets and the downtown. Although the system was open to some fraud, Bostonians had enough faith in it to reject the idea of district option, which would have placed control of neighborhood prohibition in the hands of the voters. There was also the belief that decentralization of such policy making might play into the hands of ward bosses. Meanwhile, suburban voters created a ring of prohibition around the city to prevent Boston liquor dealers from invading middle- and upper-class residential areas. Industrial Chelsea provided the only major exception.

Meanwhile, corruption and controversy surrounded Chicago's neighborhood liquor control. Mayoral discretion and an ineffective frontage consent rule in Hyde Park left property owners in constant fear of a saloon invasion. The first mechanism of protection was the aldermanic ordinance that dried up small districts. This, however, placed residents at the mercy of politicians and provided no guarantee against instant reversal at a future date. It was not until the passage of the Local Option Law of 1907 that the power of protection reverted from the City Council to the neighborhood electorate.

This notion of moral geography — making something illegal merely because it took place on the wrong side of an abstract line — proved ironic in two ways. First, many of the same middle-class areas that fought so hard for local control of the liquor issue also supported municipal reform movements that disdained such parochialism on other issues. Political reformers attacked bosses for their small-scale pork barrel projects, their control of small fiefdoms, and their apparent concern with only the interests of their particular constituents. When police applied the law differently in various parts of the city, reformers viewed it as unprofessional; the same law demanded application everywhere. Reformers talked tirelessly about city planning, the need to coordinate neighborhood growth, and the organic nature of the city as an economic unity.[76] However, the question of saloons and such nuisances as peddlers and noisy cable cars evoked arguments in favor of parochialism. The liquor interests cried hypocrisy, demanding to know why citywide standards should apply in some areas of legislation and not in others. The answer from the drys would, of course, eventually be an effort to ban liquor from city and suburb alike through national prohibition.

The second irony that grew from moral geography was that the ulti-

mate effect of neighborhood protection was not to reduce liquor consumption but merely to privatize it. The semipublic saloon disappeared,
but in its place was a parade of delivery wagons, a growing concern
about alcoholic housewives, and the stumbling phalanx of homeward-
bound commuters. The social problems rising from excessive drink had
also been privatized. In a strange turn of events, the same arguments
that had been used against statewide prohibition in 1867 — that drinking behind closed tenement doors would be purified by placing it under
licensing and public observation — now applied to the wealthy as well.

CHAPTER 8

Saloon Crime:
From Wide-Open
to Underground Vice

AT EACH UPWARD STEP along the social scale the saloon became of less value as an institution of everyday survival and more of an unnecessary intrusion into private lives. For those who either did not want it near them or could afford deliveries to the private sideboard or the closed society of the club, the saloon was an unpleasantness to be shunned, except perhaps near the downtown train station. In impoverished areas it had been an institution central to neighborhood life, but in many affluent enclaves residents drew together just to keep it out.

The image of the saloon as a criminal institution was often at the core of the local option movement. As the decades passed the average saloonist bore an increasingly heavy burden of ill repute that had been generated by a minority in the trade. The weakest links endangered the whole chain. Thus, the barroom became part of the old neighborhood that was left behind when the upwardly mobile family could finally afford the tract house on the urban fringe; in the new setting it was viewed as a threat to property values, and the words *no saloons* were set in large type in subdivision ads.

The public nature of the business was a critical factor in its criminal image. The disorderly activities inside poured out onto the sidewalk. And as urbanites across the country became increasingly concerned about the unpleasantness of the streets, the saloon and vice were classified with garbage, billboards, smoke, noise, skyscraper "canyons," and peddlers as nuisances. The streetwalker was a peddler of sorts, while saloon disorder allowed vice on private property to make the public environment around it unwholesome, much as a careless housekeeper might spill garbage on the sidewalk. To reformers it was often necessary for authorities to invade the private property of the bar and brothel to insure a safe and moral public place outside.

There is no accurate way of determining what portion of saloons were involved in crime. To many citizens, the Devil's workshop lay behind the swinging doors. The Cook County Grand Jury of December 1900 claimed that "at least 90 percent of all criminal cases . . . have some saloon connection." But defenders, such as Chicago Mayor Carter Harrison I, believed that only about 5 percent of his city's barrooms were involved in wrongdoing.[1] In either case, the public nature of the retail liquor business, the openness of the wrongdoing, and the citizens' willingness to tolerate obvious lawbreaking made the career of the criminal taproom so notable. As the decades passed, the wide-open conditions which reached a peak in the 1880s gave way to the suppression of gambling by 1894 and set the stage for driving the world's oldest profession underground some twenty years later. The old debate over whether society's sin should be public or private was finally won by the latter; saloon vice would be driven from sight.

Covert and Public Crimes

Crime was an occupational hazard for the saloon owner. The temporal specialization of cities virtually depopulated many neighborhoods at night; after the rush hour, the sidewalks were silent. When clerks succeeded in closing stores at an earlier hour, the saloon was in many places the only business open late. Racks of gas lights were common fixtures, and barrooms were among the first eager owners of electric lamps. Late hours meant that the barroom could become a haven from the dangers of the streets, a place where the injured were taken to await the arrival of the ambulance. Or it was ideally adapted as a hangout. For many customers it was an institution of the night in an era when dozens of popular books warned of the evils of the dark hours: *Darkness and Daylight, Sunlight and Shadow*, and other contrasting pairs that symbolized sin and purity. The Massachusetts Total Abstinence Society pointed out the peril in 1884:

Night is sin's harvesting time. More sin and crime are committed in one night than in all the days of the week. This is more emphatically true of the city than in the country. The street-lamps, like a file of soldiers with torch in hand, stretch away in long lines on either sidewalk; the gay-colored transparencies are ablaze with at-

tractions; the saloon and billiard halls are brilliantly illuminated;
music sends forth its enchantment; the gay company begins to
gather to the haunts and houses of pleasure; the gambling places
are ablaze with palatial splendor; the theaters are wide open; the
mills of destruction are grinding health, honor, happiness, hope
out of thousands of lives.

The city under the gaslight is not the same as under God's sunlight.
The allurements, and perils, and pitfalls of night are a hundred-
fold deeper, and darker, and more destructive.[2]

There were many other explanations for the involvement of saloons
in crime. A common belief held that the predominantly male clientele,
lacking the moral restraint of women and family, lapsed into automatic immorality symbolized by the nude paintings over the backbar.[3]
Some barrooms were undoubtedly forced to supplement their revenue
through crimes of various sorts in order to survive economically.
Brewers were also capable of ignoring misdeed in the bars they controlled. For instance, an 1889 guide to Chicago's brothels, the *Sporting
House Directory*, contained numerous advertisements for the Seipp
Brewing Company. And years later, when a prominent black gambler
named Pony Moore declared bankruptcy, his largest creditor was
Anheuser-Busch.[4] Finally, some bars were involved in crime because
their owners were criminals before they obtained their liquor licenses.
This was less likely to happen in Boston, where applications had to be
advertised and reformers could object. But in Chicago there was nothing to prevent the worst criminals in the city from opening saloons except a veto by the mayor.

While these general explanations are important, barroom-related
crimes were much like legitimate social life. Both involved the distinction between public and private urban environments. But the various
kinds of saloon misdeeds also differed in the degree to which the citizenry supported the venture, whether or not there was a clear victim,
the degree to which the location could be ubiquitous, and the amount
of secrecy necessary to make them successful.

Some misdeeds were covert. These depended on perpetrators remaining anonymous and being able to seek out victims from crowds of
people; those who lost money—or their lives—stumbled onto the
crime. They did not seek it; it sought them. Often, it was a matter of
robbing someone who flashed a hefty wallet or money clip in a bar.
The growing geographical mobility of commuters assured a steady flow

of strangers, as did Chicago's rise as a rail center. Farmers who patronized barrooms on the way home from selling their crops often lost the
proceeds to pickpockets. The city, in fact, added a word to the American lexicon through the exploits of the real Mickey Finn, a dive owner
who robbed his patrons after serving them knockout drops. From 1898
through 1903 Finn and his wife, "Gold Tooth Mary," operated the
Lone Star amidst a row of brothels just south of the Loop. Hundreds of
out-of-towners and "slummers" from better parts of the city and
suburbs helped make Finn famous, though his place had no monopoly
on murder and abduction.[5]

Other rustics and an occasional commuter fell prey to bunco schemes.
Crafty operators patrolled railway terminals and hotel lobbies, where
they met an endless stream of victims. The crook played on the stranger's ego and desire to make easy money, and after the operator and victim had become friends, they retired to a nearby saloon. Drinking and
a bit of gambling usually followed. Then came the sure-bet business
deal in which the sturdy yeoman of the plains or New England woods
left without his money. Chicago became far more famous for this type
of activity than Boston. By 1859, when the city on the prairie had only
93,000 people, its reputation warranted the publication of *Tricks and
Traps of Chicago*. Nine years later *Chicago after Dark* made similar
warnings to visitors: do not talk to strangers and avoid saloons.[6]

A second broad category of saloon-related misdeeds were genuinely
public crimes that were well known to the city as a whole. Such widespread infractions as Sunday- and midnight-closing violations were
relatively ubiquitous rather than dependant on a particular location,
as were covert crimes. Nor were public wrongdoings easily concealed.
They were as widespread as they were tolerated.

Public crime was uncommon in Boston. Sunday closing was generally enforced because it had been a tradition; and because virtually all
businesses were closed, an open barroom was conspicuous. Nor was
nighttime closing a controversial issue. Drinkers with an extraordinary
thirst could find liquor in hotels. But in Chicago unpopular liquor laws
were subject to a silent veto by the people and their government.

The oldest issue in the prairie metropolis was Sunday closing. Although the Illinois legislature passed a statewide closing law in 1841, it
was almost universally ignored in Chicago before 1915. The two mayors
who tried to enforce a dry Sabbath provoked political upheavals.
Nativist Levi Boone ordered saloonkeepers to comply in 1855 and also

raised the license fees. This was his way of punishing the German community for supporting his opponent. The street brawl known as the Lager Beer Riot was the result.[7] Boone's successor, Thomas Dyer, returned to a policy of nonenforcement, as did the other mayors before 1872. In that year, shortly after the Great Fire, Joseph Medill came to power in a sweep of reform. As publisher of the *Tribune,* the new mayor thought he could lead Chicago to a new era of morality, and Sunday closing was prominent among his plans. But his temperance tendencies helped drive him from office the following year, and the new chief executive, Harvey Colvin, pushed a new law through the City Council which he hoped would resolve the Sunday issue forever. The 1874 law required dealers to close their front doors and windows on the Sabbath, but allowed them to open the back or side door and operate as usual inside. Subsequent litigation upheld this moral compromise: if violations of a state law were hidden from public view, they were not infringements of city law.[8]

Violations of Chicago's eleven o'clock closing ordinance aroused much less controversy. Drinkers of the late hour were often somewhat suspect; compliance also inconvenienced fewer people and did not appear to be an ethnic insult. Yet as a practical matter, both the mayor and the City Council knew that strict enforcement was difficult. Again, Joseph Medill unwittingly prompted the first change in the law. When he dispatched officers to compel observance, his police chief refused to carry out the order, calling it impossible. Rather than risk a governmental crisis, the aldermen merely amended the ordinance to allow an extra hour of drinking. But even the new time commanded little respect. Mayor Carter Harrison I tried in vain to introduce a special category of all-night licenses. The aldermen, responding to corrupt elements in the liquor trade, reasoned that in some areas of the city there were already *de facto* twenty-four-hour bars. Why charge extra for the privilege?[9]

Saloons and Segregated Vice

Crimes relating to prostitution and gambling were the most controversial of the saloonkeepers' infractions. These deeds shared the characteristics of both the covert and public variety. They were clearly illegal, but they were thought victimless, "crimes of human weakness" which were widely believed inevitable and resistant to abolition. Like public crimes they were voluntary, requiring a conscious effort on the part of a customer to seek out "the action."[10] For this reason saloon gambling and prostitution were highly dependent on being in a particular location and on the rise of geographical mobility in the city to bring in customers.

Segregated vice was a moral compromise. While churches and reform groups expressed shock at the idea, there was a strong movement to legalize both gambling and prostitution through the late nineteenth century. The former had actually enjoyed legitimacy in the form of lotteries, while the proposal to license brothels and inspect inmates was hotly debated in Illinois during the 1870s and in Massachusetts two decades later.[11] Although gambling and prostitution remained illegal, both Chicago and Boston adopted various forms of a policy commonly known as "segregated vice." This was a geographical compromise that allowed vice to operate in a restricted locale. Thus the improving transportation system allowed customers to frequent low resorts, while they fought to preserve the purity of residential neighborhoods.

The policy of segregating sexual vice fell into official disfavor much earlier in Boston than in Chicago. Before 1870 the principal resort district in the Hub was along Ann Street (renamed North Street) in the North End. Over half of the city's bordellos were said to be concentrated there. Just off of that street, which connected the wharves and Faneuil Market, was a nest of tough drinking halls, sailors' boarding houses, and whore houses known as the Black Sea. Ministers and leading citizens were especially disturbed at the openness of the solicitation and carousing. The dens opened their doors and lured customers with loud music, even in coldest weather. Because the inmates were in court so often, the Black Sea was its own advertisement. Meanwhile, in the words of an antivice pamphlet of 1846, "the more genteel brothels and houses of assignation are unmolested" in their secluded locations. With wealth came discreet privacy.[12]

Public opposition occasionally led to violence. In 1825, 200 Bostonians attacked and burned the Beehive, a notorious bar and brothel in the Ann Street area. But most antivice action consisted of police raids, especially against streetwalkers. Attacks against brothels were less common and usually followed a loud public outcry. But by 1870 the official attitude had changed, and all open vice resorts were subject to suppression, not just those who plied their trade in the street. The dramatic climax came in 1870, after numerous incidents of respectable women being insulted on the street, and residents of areas adjacent to

Ann Street complained that noisy crowds were spilling into more respectable areas. In one night Chief Edward Savage rounded up 183
prostitutes because, in his words, "the houses of ill fame had become
too open and bold in their proceedings."[13]

Savage's raid proved more symbolic than damaging, because vice
was already in transition. Streetwalkers had left the public places for
solicitation in saloons and other semipublic places. Similarly, the open
bordello, whose location was stable and well known, had given way to
the privacy of quarters in the rooming house districts of the West and
South ends, with the latter police district recording the largest number
of prostitution arrests. By 1871 Savage also claimed that the kept
woman, a semipermanent and private relationship, was also becoming
more common.[14]

Chicago's sexual vice flourished more openly than did Boston's, and
it was more confined to specific districts. As was the case with the Black
Sea, the Illinois city's earliest prostitution areas were centrally located
and predominantly lower class, but not on major transportation lines.
The Sands was on the north side of the Chicago River and virtually in-
accessible because of poor bridges. This shanty town was destroyed by
Major "Long John" Wentworth on April 20, 1857.[15] The resorts then
moved to the southwest part of what later became the Loop, with
lower-class houses on Wells Street and the better ones on Clark and
State streets to the east. By 1870 there were estimated to be as many as
7,000 inmates in 250 bordellos.[16]

Two major conflagrations and the development of rail transportation helped shape the Levee district as it emerged by the late 1870s.
The Fire of 1871 and a smaller blaze that burned over ninety acres
three years later pushed vice to the far southern border of downtown,
while the construction of new passenger terminals during the 1880s
made a narrow north-south section of buildings undesirable for residential purposes. Major streetcar lines from the South Side passed
through the area, making it convenient for out-of-town "slummers."
Convenient location and the cooperation of city officials encouraged
the development of two smaller vice areas, one on West Madison Street
just beyond the river and the other on Clark Street just north of the
river. Improved bridges and tunnels under that stream had made
transportation easier. At that same time specialized districts of department stores, wholesaling, culture, finance, offices, and entertainment
were emerging downtown; in its purely economic aspects of land use,

vice was no different.[17] When brothels moved in near one depot, the *Tribune* bristled, "It is especially bad to have this depravity exhibited in LaSalle Street, for the reason that it is a street much used by passengers for the suburban trains of the Rock Island Road, and it is not pleasant for a gentleman with a lady companion to have to listen to all of the filth he will have to encounter and hear on his way."[18]

The size of the vice business shocked reform groups. In 1881 the Citizens' League of Chicago stationed observers in five tough saloons in the South Side Levee and saw, by their count, 11,608 men and 1,007 women enter and leave in less than five hours. Another survey conducted a year later concluded that within twenty square blocks were 500 saloons, six "variety theaters," more than 1,000 "concert halls," fifteen gambling houses, between fifty and sixty poolrooms, and fully 500 houses of ill fame harboring over 3,000 women. The police patroled only the borders, carrying out raids when public opinion demanded it or when a murder or some other extraordinary event made the need for a visible corrective obvious. Public officials made little effort to stop what many viewed as an inevitable outgrowth of human weakness. Exposés also revealed that many of Chicago's elite were, in fact, major property holders in the district. Such investors as Potter Palmer, E. O. Gale, and Mayor Harrison himself purchased land on the fringe of the vice area because they eventually expected to raze the rundown buildings and sell the land to developers. Everyone expected the Loop to expand southward; instead, the skyscraper pushed it upward, and the Levee survived.[19]

Chicago was not only a wide-open town compared with Boston's secretive and somewhat more dispersed vice, but the Midwest city also welcomed the "concert saloon," which was banned in the Hub. This mixture of musical showmanship, liquor, and sex was thriving in most major East Coast cities by the 1860s, but an 1858 General Court statute forbade local authorities in Massachusetts from issuing liquor licenses to any "theatrical exhibition, public show, concert or dance hall exhibition of any description." In later years the courts interpreted it to mean that customers could dance where drinks were sold, but they could not imbibe while watching others dance.[20] By contrast, when Chicago's first concert saloon opened on West Madison Street in 1873, it started a fad. Within a few years they numbered in the dozens: the Alhambra, Tivoli Gardens, the Garden, the Park, and the Foxhall, to name a few.

The concert saloon was a department store of vice. The earliest ones, which operated in basements, gave way to multistory palaces with a different specialty on each level. Typically, the main bar stood near the front door, and patrons were expected to buy a drink before they visited other attractions. "Grisettes," or waitresses functioning as modern "B-girls," also circulated everywhere soliciting drinks. The stage and theater section, complete with private box seats, satisfied the voyeur, while the more daring sexual exhibitions were on display in the basement. Prostitutes circulating among the crowd took "tricks" to small cubicles on the upper floors.[21]

To drum up business, concert saloons advertised themselves with posters on telegraph poles and vacant buildings across the city. Newspaper exposés with maps and lurid descriptions also inadvertantly attracted customers. The concert saloon quickly became the most visible feature in the Levee areas, while various massage parlors, opium dens, pornographic bookstores, and sporting houses crowded into nearby storefronts and employed bells, flashing lights, and signs to draw in passersby. There was no room for an honest saloon.[22]

Gambling was the other segregated vice in Boston before the mid-1880s and in Chicago prior to 1894. But its concentration was more a matter of economic convenience than a response to moral pressures; the degree of segregation depended primarily on the type of game. For instance, although such moral reform groups as the New England Watch and Ward Society fumed over petty gaming near schools, beaches, and amusement parks, small games of poker or dice drew nowhere near the wrath that a streetwalker might encounter. These forms of gambling were often camouflaged by saloons, grocery shops, cigar stores, barbershops, and other businesses where large numbers of men entered and exited. If raided, it was easy to conceal the equipment or absorb the confiscation of petty cash.[23] But the larger gambling houses were another matter. Faro, Keno, and other sophisticated games requiring tables and wheels were in larger houses, more often centrally located, which drew a clientele from a wider area. Considerations of transportation and location were much more crucial. Although the mobile urbanite might be willing to travel miles to play in one of the famous houses, the more successful ones established themselves amidst a steady flow of patrons. And as the larger houses clustered, their existence as a district was their own best advertisement.[24]

Chicago's Gamblers' Row grew up on Clark Street, near the emerging LaSalle Street financial district. Here one could find such places as the Store, operated by Michael Cassius McDonald. By the early 1870s he had purchased an interest in a saloon and gaming house, and he soon parlayed his friendships with Democratic politicians into protection from raids. The Store had a saloon on the ground floor and wheels and table games upstairs. The bar, however, was merely a front; professional gamblers seldom touched liquor. McDonald retired to ownership of a newspaper and the Lake Street Elevated line, and the Store closed in 1888, but Gamblers' Row continued to thrive.[25] Down the street was a row of gaming halls that included one owned by the Hankin brothers; it was best known for its use of "ropers," who lured amateurs inside with promises of free liquor. Varnell's, which catered to a higher-class crowd, underwent a spectacular refurbishing during 1891. Some $40,000-worth of Mexican onyx, Florentine mosaic, mahogany, and silver greeted its visitors.[26]

By 1871 Boston's gambling had also become concentrated in a limited district; near Dock Square there were twenty-five houses. City officials carried out occasional raids, leading some places to install iron doors and alarms activated by sentries on the street to give warning when necessary. At other times gambling bars opened directly into the street, where the bright lights of one competed with those of another for the attention of passersby. An angry citizen signing his letter "E.P." complained to the *Transcript* in 1884 that "every day and every night Bostons gambling halls are in full blast, and [they are] as well known by all who desire to play as is the Boston State House."[27]

The most notorious place in the Hub belonged to a black gambler named Bose Cobb. Born in Natick, by the late 1870s Cobb turned a series of small crap games into a large gaming house on Norman Street. Cobb's place included a dance hall, bar, faro bank, and a "sweat [shell] game." His place operated openly and had become so famous during the early 1880s that the Chicago press said it compared quite favorably with anything in the Midwest. Within a few years his racially mixed clientele had provided him with a comfortable fortune.[28]

The operation of such gamblers as Bose Cobb, Mike McDonald, and the others depended heavily on the cooperation of the police and the judicial system. Even the most honest of saloonkeepers could be vulnerable to shakedowns and tempted by bribes. An officer might claim that the lights burned past the legal closing hour or that a child had been seen drinking there. In the quiet of the nighttime, it was the dealer's word against the policeman's. The complex regulations that limited what could be sold, to whom, how, where, and when meant multiple opportunities for money to negate law enforcement. And that was just the beginning.[29]

"Inflooence" and Shakedown

Semipublic crimes were the most profitable for saloonkeepers, but the concentration of gambling and prostitution in specific districts and the open nature of the attractions made them especially vulnerable. Survival depended on an elaborate system of payoffs, usually beginning with the patrolman on the beat and often reaching to the higher ranks of the department. The sketchy evidence surviving indicates that bribes were charged according to the size, type of vice, and vulnerability. The most famous estimate, published in Chicago in 1912, revealed a range of twenty dollars a month for a cheap brothel to as much as fifty times that amount for luxurious houses. Some gamblers turned over half their take.[30]

Influence, however, could work in both directions. The bribe and the extortion were essentially the same thing. The police could force saloonkeepers to contribute to many supposedly benevolent causes. Joseph Kipley, Chicago's police superintendent during the late 1890s, condoned a scheme to hold illegal prize fights to aid the "Police Relief Fund." When that idea fell through, he announced plans for the department to publish an official history to which saloonkeepers would be expected to subscribe. Various yearbooks, directories, and tickets for political and police dances could always attract at least a "fiver" from the till. It was often impossible to differentiate between benevolence and shakedown.[31]

The bar owner was also subject to the whims of politicians who wielded "inflooence," as the Boston press called it. In that city controversy swirled around the police commissioners, whom city politicians routinely attacked because of state control of the force. One series of scandals revolved around William Osborne, who had been appointed one of the inaugural members of the metropolitan police board in 1885. A few years after taking office, he secretly organized the New England Printing Telegraph Company. Brewers, anxious to avoid trouble, became the principal stockholders and kept Osborne's involvement secret. He then persuaded his fellow commissioners to reequip the department's communication system with one produced by his company. With that accomplished, he proceeded to extract contributions from saloonists for testimonials, and in one stroke of business efficiency, he had the license list rearranged by street address to facilitate collections.[32]

These extortions were small when compared with his quest for the "*Globe* Sword," a circulation-building gimmick of the newspaper. This popularity contest asked readers to clip a coupon and send it in to vote for their favorite fireman, policeman, store clerk, or other public personality. Osborne was carried away by his ego and dispatched a squad of officers to make the rounds of liquor dealers. The police hinted that barkeeps should buy the newspapers by the hundreds and submit the coupons on Osborne's behalf. Dozens of licensees were involved, some acting as organizers for the others. M. H. Curley, whose bar stood on Green Street in Charlestown, put an employee to work clipping coupons and applying a rubber stamp with the commissioner's name. Curley then distributed them to other saloonists who submitted them in their names. Despite this Herculean effort to satisfy his vanity, Osborne finished far down the list. When word of his scheme leaked, the Democratic Boston City Council conducted an extensive investigation of the Republican police commissioner, but Governor William Russell allowed Osborne to finish the remaining two years of his term and to retire quietly in 1893.[33]

Influence and extortion also became a fine art in Chicago. A licensee who angered the mayor or an alderman could be put out of business within hours, but politicians also regularly interceded on behalf of their liquor-selling constituents. The alderman who also owned a saloon faced a mild dilemma. On one hand, his indirect control over the other sellers could earn him tremendous profit in bribes. But other dealers were also potential competitors. As the *Liquor Trades Review*, a New York publication, put it, "You may see . . . how important it is for anyone in the business to attend to the voltage of his pull and not to locate a liquor establishment near the one owned by the Alderman or even the faro bank in which he is interested."[34]

If the saloonkeeper's arrangement with police and politicians failed him and he was arrested, each step in the judicial process provided ample opportunity for extralegal manipulation. The justice of the peace, who was easy to bribe, handled minor cases without a jury. For a con-

victed saloonkeeper a minor fine was frequently smaller than the pay-
off, but the latter left a clear record and allowed the justice to pocket
the extra money.[35]

More serious saloon-related cases, including gambling and prostitution, were the concern of the grand juries. They could be unpredictable. When the press warned of crime waves, the grand jury led the
call for strict enforcement of all laws. But when times were less tense,
they were lenient. For example, in 1880 the liquor dealers in Chicago
complained about the grand jury's "present inquisitional and star
chamber techniques," but a few months later the Citizens' League
claimed that the jurors were "largely foreigners and saloonkeepers."[36]

A grand jury might return an indictment, but the district or state's
attorney was responsible for moving the judicial proceedings to a con-
clusion. He might act promptly on the findings or do nothing. He could
launch his own investigations or use his office to hide wrongdoing.
There were more arrests among Boston's 2,000 saloons in 1885 than
among Chicago's 6,000, but the office in Massachusetts as well as in Illinois was elective and open to influence exercised by liquor interests.
Oliver Stevens, Suffolk County district attorney, proved to be a fast
friend of saloonkeepers after his election in 1880. During his first five
years in office there were nearly 300 liquor cases commenced each year,
mainly involving complaints brought by the Law and Order League.
But few were ever pursued to a verdict: 3 percent in 1881, and 3 percent, 9 percent, and 4 percent, respectively, during the next three
years. The rest were appealed, *nol. pros.*'d, or continued. In a four-
year period ending September 30, 1884, 986 cases were started, but only nineteen resulted in guilty verdicts. The Law and Order League and
the press blamed Stevens; he blamed the juries. Stevens's critics tried
unsuccessfully to persuade the state supreme court to remove him. Attempts to persuade the General Court to enact legislation that would
require state's attorneys to dispose of cases within a time limit also
failed, largely because that body was debating the Metropolitan Police
bill and was not interested in reforming prosecutors as well as police.
Four years later, however, the issue was largely eliminated when the
law limiting the number of licenses reduced not only the number of
dealers but also the docket of liquor complaints.[37]

But in Chicago the practice of using the court system to protect rather than prosecute saloonists continued unchanged. Those with the best

connections could have their cases rotated to a safe judge. Those accused of violating nighttime and Sunday closing laws and other unpopular statutes stood a good chance of automatic acquittal. A prosecutor in such cases knew he was defeated if Germans appeared on the jury. Thus, the more open and ubiquitous the crime, the greater the likelihood that it enjoyed widespread public support and the more substantial the chance that prosecution would fail.[38]

By the early 1880s the liquor interests had learned how to manipulate the jury system in other cases as well. The crucial achievement was control over the selection of reliable jurors. In Boston the process was supposed to be public, and except for a few years during the mid-1880s court officials regularly published the names in the jury pool. But even the Law and Order League, which assumed the self-appointed duty of examining the rosters for liquor men, found it difficult to ferret out all of the objectionables. The attitudes of the other jurors were also unknown to the league, and a number of unfavorable verdicts in the mid-1880s led to serious discussion of a plan to replace juries altogether with judicial panels. Justice Robert C. Pitman of the Massachusetts Supreme Court, a leading prohibitionist, was the principal architect of that plan. The jury reform movement in the state reached a climax in 1888, when the Law and Order League tried unsuccessfully to have the General Court ban the seating of saloonkeepers on juries hearing liquor trials. But after the limitation law of 1889 decimated the ranks of dealers, that issue also faded into obscurity.[39]

In Chicago, however, politicians continued to select veniremen from the so-called "jury saloons." In 1883 there were reported to be fourteen such bars located conveniently within 400 feet of the Cook County Criminal Courts Building. The constable in charge of juries dispatched youthful runners to summon the faithful, some of whom made their living as professional jurors and saw duty several times each week. During the spring of 1888, when a jury-bribing scandal erupted in Chicago, the *Tribune* grumbled that "jurors not kept under the custody of the courts . . . are frequenters of rumshops in the immediate neighborhood of the Court House. Every appointment with corrupting middlemen was laid in a saloon."[40]

Attempts to reform the system in Chicago failed. William Onahan, city collector during the 1880s, championed the idea of random selection of jurors. But even when Cook County adopted that plan in 1897, saloon interests secured copies of the lists and questioned the neighbors of prospective candidates. Lawyers defending dealers could thus know in advance which prospective jurors to challenge.[41]

Closing Down Segregated Vice

Beginning in the mid-1880s in Boston and a half-dozen years later in Chicago, a gradual change took place toward the segregated and highly visible crimes of gambling and prostitution. Casual tolerance gave way to persistent attacks by private reform groups, and the comfortable arrangements between vice interests and politicians dissolved. The transition first appeared in a war against gambling and later evolved into a spectacular crusade against prostitution. In both cases the weakening of toleration first took place in Boston, where a more restrictive attitude toward "human weakness" crimes already existed. But wide-open Chicago eventually began to close down as well.[42]

The morals crusade in Boston was led by the New England Watch and Ward Society. Organized in 1878 as the New England Society for the Suppression of Vice, its initial concern was the sale of obscene literature. During the next decade its activities broadened to include a war on gambling. The society adopted the techniques of the Law and Order League, which continued its war on illegal saloon sales. Volunteer and professional sleuths, under the direction of Henry Chase, carried out the league's work of collecting evidence, filing complaints, and waiting for the police to execute a warrant. Most important of all, Boston had for the first time a permanent antivice organization; Chicago would have to wait.[43]

A second major factor in the Hub's moral awakening was the work of two major reform publicists of the early 1890s. The Reverend Louis A. Banks preached from the press as well as from his pulpit at St. John's Methodist Church in South Boston. Monday newspaper readers learned of sweatshops, transients, and the dens of immorality near the business district. Benjamin O. Flower published scholarly, yet shocking, exposés in his monthly, the *Arena*. Both crusaders blamed such social problems as industrial violence and slums on the failures of the industrial system and such "parasitic" agencies as the saloon, which Flower labeled the "capital curse of the Nineteenth Century." Both men produced shocking books. Flower's *Civilization's Inferno; or, Studies in the Social Cellar* (1893) and Banks's *White Slaves; or, The Suppression of the*

Worthy Poor (1892) both made it hard to contend that Boston was much better than evil Chicago.[44]

The third factor in the revival of Boston moralism was the growing number of complaints against its police department. The bad publicity surrounding the Osborne scandals, along with reports of inefficiency, had left the force in a demoralized condition. But a dramatic shift in leadership brought the Watch and Ward Society into a close alliance with local officials. In June 1894 Governor Frederick Greenhalge appointed former Boston Mayor Augustus P. Martin to the chairmanship of the metropolitan police commissioners. Martin renewed strict discipline in the department, even ordering officers to shine their shoes and wear white gloves for the first time in years. His leadership survived a major scandal involving a dive keeper's bribe of a sergeant and a captain; Martin tried to remove the men, but he was outvoted by the other two commissioners. He did convince them to reorganize a special liquor squad based in headquarters rather than scattered throughout the precincts. This reduced the chance of tip-offs of impending raids. With this new arrangement in place, Martin began a long series of attacks on brothels, kitchen barrooms, and gambling houses.[45]

Compared with the gradual growth of indignation in Boston, Chicago's transformation resembled a religious revival. Excitement over plans for the World's Columbian Exposition had made the citizenry self-conscious about their town's image; at the same time vice interests were planning on a bonanza. Such exposés as Vivia Divers's *The Black Hole*, an account of the work of a religious missionary in the slums, and the report of a special committee of the Woman's Christian Temperance Union, *Chicago's Dark Places*, painted an evil picture. These works were joined by several visitors' guidebooks, such as *Chicago by Day and Night*, a reveler's Baedeker. The police response was a few symbolic raids.[46]

But there was also a growing sense of uneasiness in Chicago. The severe national depression brought thousands of homeless job hunters to the nation's rail center. The assassination of Mayor Carter Harrison I in the closing months of 1893 provided a numbing shock, as did the arrival of a famed British journalist, William T. Stead. He had come to the city to study the Levee district, where he roamed the streets and dives talking to their habitués. He also used the occasion of the mayor's demise to call a mass meeting on November 11, 1893. That assembly proved to be the greatest exercise in municipal soul-searching in the city's history. Speakers dramatically described Chicago's evils, linking such diverse problems as dirty streets, political corruption, the exploitation of labor, and vice as all part of an atmosphere of civic neglect.[47]

Stead's visit accomplished two things. In 1894 he published *If Christ Came to Chicago!*, perhaps the most vitriolic exposé of vice and municipal malfeasance written about any city. More important, his mass meeting led to the formation of the Civic Federation of Chicago, a large and diverse assembly of business, religious, educational, and reform leaders. Shocked into existence by Stead's mandate for civic reformation, it confronted a variety of problems ranging from unemployment to street maintenance. Soon, however, a crusade against vice would occupy its attention, and Chicago would join Boston in a reform of segregated vices. Activities that had been centralized and protected in a location known to all gradually began to disperse and become private.[48]

The End of the Saloon Casino

The problem of open gaming attracted the most immediate attention in both cities. Since gambling houses were often located downtown, where they were most visible, and wagering seemed a more surmountable vice than the oldest profession, the "green felt" houses fell first. On September 21, 1894, the Civic Federation engineered the largest "pull" in the history of Chicago gambling. Plans were concealed from police officials until the last minute, because federation lawyers had discovered a seldom-used law that allowed justices of the peace from anywhere in the county to order police to execute warrants. At the appointed hour several buggy-loads of suburban magistrates, each armed with writs, arrived on Clark Street. Seventy-eight games fell that night, while raids later in the month netted dozens more. Symbolically, the era of centralized and protected gambling was over in Chicago.[49]

Reform in Boston evolved rather than exploded. There were individual crusades, such as that of a local captain against Bose Cobb; in 1886 the gambler was driven from his Norman Street den to spend his final years managing a hotel in Brighton. The Watch and Ward Society pursued other violators, but the enactment of a pair of laws by the General Court proved even more important. One made it illegal even to be a bystander where there was gambling. The other ordered police to seize all furniture and liquor, as well as gaming equipment. Thus a saloonkeeper might lose his fixtures and stock. The limitation law of 1889 had already made dealers wary of anything that might imperil their precious licenses; the new gambling laws of 1894 and 1895 made the potential loss even more serious.[50]

The result of the raids and new legislation was essentially the same in both cities. Wide-open saloon gaming gave way either to the closed gambling club or to forms of wagering that were dispersed and harder to detect. After 1889 Boston police noted a sharp increase in the number of young men's "social" or "literary" clubs, whose state charters made their quarters into private places where friends gathered. Although magistrates routinely refused to issue warrants against such clubs unless someone, usually a "member," filed a complaint, tight security prevailed. Raiders would have to cut through an iron door and plates bolted to the insides of the windows. Similar armament could be found in Chicago after 1894.[51]

While the more complicated table and wheel games became private, poorer and more amateur gamblers such as clerks patronized "poolrooms," or betting rooms equipped with direct wires to baseball parks or race tracks. The "bucketshop," a specialized type of poolroom, centralized wagers on the fluctuations of the agricultural market prices. These spots were often located downtown, largely for the convenience of customers, but also because it was easy to camouflage the arrival and departure of hundreds of bettors.[52]

Little evidence exists to connect liquor sales in Boston with poolrooms and bucketshops, but in Chicago some of the largest operators were saloonkeepers. Horse race betting was rare in the latter city before the 1880s. Varnell's place partially filled that void after 1891, but after the gambling raids of three years later, the poolroom spread rapidly across the city. Some places remained hidden downtown, but the telegraph and telephone allowed it to invade the neighborhoods. Communications technology made protected gambling virtually unnecessary. Any business with a high volume of customers could conceal backroom activity from honest police as well as the public.[53]

The most important saloon gambler was "Big Jim" O'Leary, son of the Mrs. O'Leary of Chicago Fire fame. He had spent much of his youth working for other gamblers, and in the early 1890s he took over a storefront on Halsted Street opposite the entrance to the Union Stockyards. It was an ideal location. After selling their livestock, the cattlemen had money to spend and no wives along to keep their pleasures legitimate. The Horn Palace featured an ornate barroom, baths, barbershop, billiard parlor, and a concert hall that seated a thousand. A $20,000 orchestrion furnished the music. But the heart of the business was an impenetrable gambling room, connected by wire to every major sporting event in the country. Because of the fortifications O'Leary was also able to offer faro and roulette for high-stakes players.[54]

Meanwhile, the pressure to close down gambling drove the poor to games that were cheap, mobile enough to escape police raids, and required few skills to play. The Louisiana Lottery was still operating in Boston during the 1880s. Early in the decade patrons could purchase tickets at a downtown building and watch the newspaper for results. By mid-decade the Society for the Suppression of Vice had forced dealers into mailing the ticket to patrons, thus avoiding the legal definition of placing a bet by personal transaction. Changes in the postal laws, however, soon forced lottery dealers into the streets and saloons of tenement neighborhoods. Headquarters was secretly located, while betting transactions were carried on in the anonymity of the crowd.[55]

Many of the urban poor also invested their nickels and dimes in the policy game, or "the numbers." Agents sold the slips in bars and on the sidewalks and announced the winners of lottery-type drawings in policy shops. An import from the South, it was first played in black neighborhoods in both cities. But by 1892 there were an estimated 100,000 daily players among the Hub's poor and some 500 policy shops in saloons, grocery stores, barbershops, and other small businesses in the slums of Chicago.[56]

Still another game popular among the poor shared the characteristics of portability and cheap investment. The principal equipment of craps consisted of dice, which could be rolled either on the curbstone or on a special table. Sugar cubes with dots inked on were a sufficient replacement for real dice, especially when the possibility of police interference made it convenient to swallow the evidence. Most of the games were small, although such protected places as Alderman Johnny Powers's saloon hosted large games that were well attended by blacks, Chinese, and lower-class whites.[57]

Finally, as the newspapers and antigambling reformers continued their crusade against the open casino in segregated districts, many saloonkeepers turned to slot machines. Frequently disguised as vending machines, these devices were scattered through all parts of both cities. Police raids in Chicago during 1898, along with exposés revealing the failure of Boston officials to prosecute violators, merely drove manufacturers to more ingenious methods of camouflage. The appeal of profit was hard to resist, even for dealers who had never allowed card games.[58] One manufacturer, the Conrad Jackson Desk Company of Cincinnati, wrote to George E. Bowen, a prominent Chicago businessman, offering its "Game O' Skill" in 1902. Describing it as "lawful everywhere," the company quoted a Boston distributor's claim that: "my earnings on a machine placed on the bar of a hotel were $38.70 for five days, after which the hotel manager refused to allow it to run on commission, but purchased it. I also had two machines at another hotel, one on the bar and the other on the cigar stand, but as the earnings for my share were too large for the first four days ($33.35 for both) the manager decided to buy them or not to operate them anymore." The manufacturer suggested that the distributor hire a porter to carry a sample Game O' Skill from saloon to saloon, offering the house a 65 percent cut of the proceeds.[59]

By 1902 there were estimated to be between 10,000 and 20,000 slot machines in Chicago alone. Because of its numbers, the petty nature of the bet, and the cloudy definition of what was or was not a gambling device, mechanical gaming was a burgeoning business. Like policy, craps, and the lottery, it was dispersed and represented a replacement for the old-fashioned casino. The player no longer had to travel far to the game; it almost literally came to him. Places such as bucketshops and wirerooms had to resort to secrecy and fortification to survive.[60]

The War against Segregated Prostitution, 1894–1906

While the crusades against gambling resulted in its rapid dispersal and concealment, antiprostitution reformers had to battle the widely held notion that the "weakness of the flesh would always plague humanity." Efforts were also hampered by the unwillingness of the New England Watch and Ward Society (formerly Society for the Suppression of Vice) to send agents into vice dens to obtain evidence. But 1894 proved to be a major turning point in these antivice efforts, especially in Boston, where the business of sex adopted venerable provisions in the liquor laws to conceal vice. Chicago officials, meanwhile, tried to create an illusion of reform.[61]

The year 1894 initiated an era of frenetic reform interspersed with periods of self-congratulatory complacency. When Augustus Martin became chairman of the metropolitan police board, he encouraged the Watch and Ward Society to aid in a series of raids that closed down the last remaining bordellos. The *Globe* noted that "signs of 'To Let' are to be found in the windows of houses that for many years have borne a bad reputation, and there is scarcely a day that does not bring to light some new resort where the occupants are moving out."[62]

But by the end of the century Bostonians had lapsed into an attitude of smug contentment. The press proudly reprinted the remarks of a New York clergyman that Boston was "too good." Judge Henry Dewey of the municipal court blamed what few problems the Hub had on suburbanites looking for a good time. Robert F. Clark, who replaced Martin as head of the police board, measured the success of his department in the declining arrest rate for vice activities. John E. Hendsey, who ran a rescue mission in Dover Street's transient district, noted that fewer "outcast women" applied for help than in past years. And Robert Woods, head of South End House settlement, noted that "there is no such flaunting of immorality as was evident here a few years ago." What Bostonians soon discovered, however, was that the absence of open vice did not mean that civic virtue was pure.[63]

Two problems destroyed that tranquility. One involved an unexpected consequence of a police board policy. Beginning in 1895 its members decided to combat the growing problem of illegal kitchen barrooms, estimated at 400 to 500, by expanding the ranks of innkeeper's licenses. During annual renewals, licensees were encouraged to establish small hotels and convert their "paper." Police officials hoped that legal liquor available during extended hours would drive unlicensed places out of operation.

Instead, the new hotel licenses played into the hands of the vice interests, which had already moved into the rooming house districts by the mid-1890s. Prostitutes used amusement spots to find their "tricks" and took them to their rooms nearby. Many of the women had also adopted the technology of the telephone, allowing them to stay in their rooms and receive customers sent them by bartenders. But the growing ranks of small hotels provided the most convenient arrangement of all, since the operation was entirely under one roof. The innkeeper's license legitimized liquor sales at late hours and added an aura of legality to the place.[64]

By the early months of 1901 the "small hotel" had become a major scandal. Newspaper features described "twelve-room hotels" that were nothing more than saloons with sleeping cubicles upstairs and empty guest registers. A Watch and Ward Society investigator described one resort on Tremont Street: "It was crowded with young men and girls, and some of the girls, I am sorry to say, were rather affectionate. There were no women downstairs, but in such of the upstairs rooms as we were allowed to enter, there were a great many women sitting at the tables with men, and drinking. The man who had charge of the register here would not show it to me when I went to find out how many had registered for the night. . . . The sandwiches which we saw at all these places . . . were not touched. They were hardly fit to eat. You could pick them up and drop them on the table and they would rattle like rocks. . . ."[65]

The legitimate hotel interests were correctly worried that the bad publicity would hurt them as well. When the General Court launched an investigation, a representative of the innkeepers reminded legislators that even the smallest places served thousands of meals each year. He also revived the old issue of public observation. Police could gain access to the small hotel and discover wrongdoing much more easily than they could in the secret kitchen barroom, which was the inevitable alternative. Despite this powerful defense, the metropolitan police board began to reverse its distribution policy the next year.[66]

It was a cruel bit of irony, but as the two sides debated the merits of small hotels, a printer's error eliminated one of the innkeeper's most cherished privileges by accidently omitting a semicolon from a line in a new compilation of state statutes. The mistake, which was not discovered until weeks later, had the effect of stopping all liquor sales at eleven o'clock, including those made at hotel bars. The state supreme court upheld the error, because the General Court had voted to adopt the volume as the official code. Attempts to repeal what became known as the "semi-colon law" failed, largely because of the adverse publicity generated by the small hotel scandal.[67]

The other crack in Boston's moral complacency was produced by the dance hall issue. During the first few years of the new century the Hub and its young were swept up by a new craze. Thousands of youth flocked to commercial dancing facilities during the evening hours. Often, various social clubs sponsored regular gatherings, but many dancers created their own informal associations connected with particular halls. While most dance halls were legitimate, others appeared to be a threat to youthful virtue. The fact that many halls were connected with saloons meant that there was a constant temptation to sell liquor to minors; some licensees resisted, but others did not. Revelations that prostitutes had moved into dance halls as places of assignation revived the old image of the "sailors' jilt shops" of the mid-nineteenth century. The worst fears were realized when, during the early weeks of 1901, Officer George McCaffrey swooped down on the toughest resorts in the North End. Not only did the raids prove that vice was not confined to the rooming houses of the West and South Ends, but his raids sent so many syphilitic prostitutes to the Deer Island jail that officials had to open a new venereal disease ward.[68]

The small hotel and dance hall issues were only the beginning. The scarcity of licenses created by the limitation law not only created a premium value for the right to hold one, but it also gave rise to a political gold mine. One state legislator grumbled that the permits were being "hawked about by local politicians at $5,000 to $6,000 each, and it is virtually impossible to secure one [even] through the medium of one of these license brokers and at the premium named." In addition, the press reported an increase in the number of charges of police shakedowns, including several by imposters who were so successful before their apprehension that saloonkeepers appeared to expect to pay extortion money. Since many of the shakedowns involved prostitutes, the *Globe* asked whether or not the old red-light districts had returned to Boston.[69]

The police board withstood the criticism for two more years, but then Dr. George W. Galvin, a prominent surgeon, released a list of twenty-two specific charges. These ranged from shakedowns and payoffs, to giving brewers preference in reassigning licenses, to the annual renewal of a hotel within 400 feet of a school and a saloon that was notorious for selling to drunkards. After months of denying that anything was wrong, Governor Curtis Guild responded by installing a new chairman of the police board, Judge William Henry Harrison Emmons of East Boston. Emmons first sought to educate himself. Almost every night he wandered Boston's streets, visiting tough saloons, anonymously visiting the parlors of suspected vice resorts, and talking with the Hub's lowlife on the streets.[70]

At first, the new police chairman merely revived the old idea of select liquor squads and raids. But early in 1904 he changed his approach, issuing an order banning women from all places serving liquor except hotels. The "Emmons rule" never stood the test of a legislative vote, and it soon proved as unenforceable as it was unconstitutional. Prostitutes simply moved into massage parlors, bookstores, and other places without liquor licenses, or they moved in even greater number into cheap hotels, such as the Piscopo Hotel in the North End. Almost immediately, the owners of large restaurants applied political pressure on Emmons and gained exemptions. Faced with growing newspaper criticism, he quietly withdrew the rule. But although it was in effect for only a few months, the "Emmons rule" raised a basic question: could women drink in public without being labeled prostitutes? The controversy left its mark. Many respectable women refused ever again to return to their favorite drinking places. Dealers near railway stations, for instance, reported the loss of thousands of dollars of trade from suburban women who formerly came to Boston to drink or stopped on their way home from a day of shopping in the city. Those drinkers instead went to such wet suburbs as Chelsea or had liquor delivered to their homes.[71]

While Boston officials tried with great difficulty to keep the city's vice concealed and maintain the "too good" image, Chicago's Levee district remained one of America's top low-life attractions. Newspapers flailed away at civic indifference, but to no avail. The Civic Federation lost interest in the issue, and there was no organization to parallel the work of the Watch and Ward Society. On occasion, even ethnic tradition interfered with antivice measures. Several times between 1899 and 1905 Mayor Carter Harrison II bent to the wishes of church groups who were sure that the sensuous strains of live music promoted promiscuity and banned performances where liquor was sold. Downtown restaurants immediately installed phonographs, but German saloons on the North Side refused to silence their beer garden bands and plugged the courts with lawsuits. Levee resorts gradually drifted back to live music.[72]

The dance hall also became more of an open problem in Chicago than in Boston. The fad grew with enormous speed in the Midwest, and saloon owners who had lost their union meeting business when workers constructed their own halls jumped at the opportunity to install profitable activities in their large rooms. The 1898 bar permit law worked to their advantage by allowing them to purchase a one-day special license for only $2.50. There was no mandatory closing hour. Some barkeeps even found it more profitable to drop their regular license in favor of bar permits for only the nights they wanted to be open. It was easy to evade the rule limiting the number of the special licenses issued to one person by creating fictitious organizations to place on the application. The opportunities for underage imbibing, casual sex, late hours, and other problems connected with rebellious youth were obvious. Church and temperance organizations complained, but the mayor and aldermen resisted change.[73]

The response of the city's leadership to the vice issue occasionally included sham reforms. In 1901, for instance, Mayor Harrison urged the city council to outlaw "winerooms," or small, partitioned compartments in saloons. Once legitimately used to sample wine or drink privately, these areas had come into wide use in Chicago for assignation, acts of prostitution, or seduction. Harrison's ordinance prohibited private rooms or curtained cubicles and forbade serving liquor to groups smaller than four in the private rooms of hotels and restaurants. Although saloonkeepers complained that their poker games would be ruined, they were given only fifteen days to comply. But the law was quickly ignored. Virtually every report on Chicago vice issued before national prohibition mentioned the wineroom as a standard feature in Chicago's low saloons. In blocking another attempt at reform, Chicago aldermen were more direct when they voted down the abolition of side doors. The so-called "family entrance" or "ladies' entrance" was of obvious convenience to prostitutes as a short cut from the street to the back room. But side doors gave corner saloons an important competitive advantage on Sundays, since the front door could be closed and the side door open in compliance with Chicago's Sabbath liquor law. Customers had to tread through the city's filthy alleys to get to bars in the middle of the block.[74]

The Revolutions of 1906

The years between 1894 and 1906 were an era of transition in both cities. Segregated gambling districts disappeared in Chicago, much as they had a few years earlier in Boston. The latter tried to destroy the moral compromise of red-light districts, but performance did not always measure up to the reputation. Even Chicago officials were having a more difficult time convincing the press and civic reform groups that the Levee was the answer to keeping neighborhoods pure. The rapid adoption of ordinances drying up dozens of square miles of the city was obvious testimony of the doubts that many middle-class homeowners harbored. By keeping saloons out of the new neighborhoods, families sought to escape the dance hall and prostitute as well.

Those were also the years of great civic doubt and questioning. The Massachusetts Civic League, the Twentieth Century Club, and other reform groups brought in a new park system and elected reform aldermen. In Chicago, the Municipal Voters' League was successful in bringing a number of honest votes, mainly from the outskirts, to the City Council. Charles T. Yerkes's attempt to freeze his monopoly of streetcar and elevated service for most of the next century was defeated, and the election of Edward F. Dunne to the mayoralty meant that Chicago put its first true reformer in office in 1905. But these changes were an accompaniment to a revolution that took place in the regulation of the liquor trade in both cities in 1906.[75]

The change in Boston took place amidst a six-year period of political upheaval that began as a reaction to the dramatic increase in city expenditures of Mayor Josiah Quincy. Although he was a Brahmin and scion of a famous family, Quincy had the support of the Irish ward bosses and embarked on an ambitious plan to build new schools, parks, and public bathhouses for the poor. Elected in 1895 as the first mayor with a two-year term, he was reelected in 1897. Quincy spent the city heavily into debt, but his successors, Thomas N. Hart (1899–1901) and Patrick A. Collins (1901–1903), did little to slow the growth in the budget. The next mayor, John F. Fitzgerald, however, accelerated the pace of spending. The son of a barkeep and a loyal son of the "Dearo" North End, "Johnny Fitz" found himself under constant attack from the Good Government Association. Formed in 1903, the GGA was an offshoot of the Chamber of Commerce and represented Beacon Hill families and suburbanites who owned businesses within the city. Although it also tried to promote the election of "clean government" candidates, it was most interested in reducing taxes by lowering city budgets.

The Good Government Association hounded Fitzgerald until 1906, when he boldly accepted the call of the reformers for the creation of a finance commission to investigate the budget. The mayor expected to control the commission, but he could not, and its detailed exposés contributed to his loss to George A. Hibbard in 1907. That was only the beginning. The commission and the GGA also pushed a new Boston Charter through the General Court. Voters approved a new electoral system that abolished party labels and converted the old bicameral

City Council into a single board of nine, who were elected at large rather than by wards. Mayors served four-year terms, unless recalled after two. In 1909 Fitzgerald overcame this effort to smash the ward machines and won reelection.

In Boston the issue was power. The state and the city had struggled over its centralization for decades, and in 1885 one system of distribution had been erected by the General Court: a board of police commissioners, appointed by the governor, would oversee the distribution of liquor licenses and the enforcement of all laws. That system had withstood scandal, but it could not survive William Henry Harrison Emmons. His regular appearance at temperance meetings drew criticism from saloonkeepers, who thought that he should at least be neutral. He was also a strict disciplinarian with his men, denying them a trip to the free lunch table and dismissing several officers caught in uniform within the swinging doors. By late 1904 even the newspapers that had supported him earlier had begun to portray him as a crank, overzealous about liquor law enforcement to the neglect of other duties.[76] Even more important were the persistent rumors that Boston was a major link in a panders' circuit. Young girls were seduced by "cadets" in the Hub and then shipped to New York brothels. Some ended up in vice dens on Commercial Street. Without criticizing Emmons directly, the Watch and Ward Society began emphasizing the problem of "social evil" in its reports, noting that "though more harmful, [it] is different from the drink evil, in that the signs of an impure life are generally concealed."[77]

The problem of what to do with Emmons was finally resolved early in 1906, when the General Court enacted a new law which divided the work of the police commissioners. A new license board of three, appointed by the governor, handled liquor permits and regulated the street trades. Actual enforcement of all laws remained in the hands of the police department, but the General Court used the opportunity to replace the old board of three with a single police commissioner, whom the governor appointed to a five-year term. And since the new system replaced the old, Judge Emmons lost his job despite the two years remaining on his commission.[78] In an apparent exchange for their support, the liquor interests finally obtained a modification of the hated "semi-colon law." A small number of Boston hotels, in a ratio of one-per-twenty-thousand population, could purchase the privilege of staying open an extra hour for an additional license fee of $500. By a wide margin Boston voters approved the new late-night license, while the press praised the wisdom of dividing Emmons's old office.[79]

The new system, however, created problems of its own, because it divided authority among three governmental entities without an adequate system of checks and balances. The mayor retained the authority to approve the quality and morality of musical and theatrical acts, a fact that would become more significant when the cabaret fad reached Boston, but the new license board actually issued the permit. The latter also granted liquor and innkeeper licenses, but it depended on the police to report chronic violators of the statutes. When the licensing commissioners approved the applications of several vice-ridden small hotels, the police commissioner complained that he could not enforce the statutes if lawbreakers gained such quick approval. Finally, there was no legal provision for any of the three municipal powers to establish new liquor laws; only the General Court could do that.[80]

The reorganization of 1906 left a vacuum of initiative into which both the police commissioner and the license board tried to maneuver. The former, Stephen O'Meara, was editor of the *Boston Journal* before his appointment by fellow-Republican Governor Curtis Guild. At first reluctant to accept the five-year term, O'Meara wisely used his talent for leading public opinion and promoting the reputation of his department. His reappointments in 1911 and 1916 gave him unusual longevity in a state where mayors and governors held office for short terms. His good name also enhanced the persuasive powers of his office.[81]

The license board also found a way to increase its power and, in effect, generate new liquor legislation. Within six weeks of taking office, the commissioners had issued the first "License Circular," a periodic announcement which "suggested" means by which licensees should mend their ways. The first informed the barmen that they "should not" display any type of political portrait, poster, or advertisement anywhere on their premises. Because the commissioners could revoke licenses, their word was law. Thus, the regulation of saloons and hotels in Boston was largely out of the hands of the police for the first time since 1885.[82]

The year 1906 also brought a major realignment of power in Chicago in which the political influence of saloonkeepers' associations and aldermen was eroded amidst the continuing furor over the vice issue.

The problem was the dance hall and the failure of municipal authorities to respond to growing pressures for reform. As stories of seductions and underage carousing continued, law-abiding German and Bohemian organizations became fearful that their weekend dances might be curtailed in a sweeping abolition of the one-night bar licenses. During 1904 such groups as the German Citizens' Union and the Union of Bohemian Associations joined in circulating petitions against altering the law; they called for improved police enforcement of existing statutes instead. When the Chicago City Council began discussing reforms, the ethnic organizations created a permanent United Societies for Local Self-Government under the leadership of Anton Cermak. Chicago politics would never again be the same.[83]

The new group was a confederation of 319 singing societies, athletic clubs, and nationalistic associations totalling over 100,000 members. By drawing upon an existing organizational framework the United Societies avoided long years of membership building, and it could count on some support in almost every part of the city. It made aldermen sign a pledge to gain its support for reelection, and in 1906 it achieved its first legislative victory. German and Bohemian aldermen who had no direct financial ties to the liquor business directed the saloon interests in the council in preventing major changes in the law. The fact that "outsiders" were organizing the barkeep legislators indicated an erosion of traditional politics, the importance of which would become increasingly clear.[84]

The United Societies appeared at a critical time, just as the regular political parties were being discredited by a series of scandals. During the early months of 1903 the newspapers revealed that police officers were collecting payments from saloonkeepers in exchange for evasion of the closing ordinances. This was hardly news, except that it launched a continuing series of exposés over the next few years that revealed almost total corruption in City Hall. Jobs, city contracts, court decisions, licenses, elections, protection from prosecution — every function of government had its price. The calamitous Iroquois Theater Fire of December 26, 1903, which resulted from unenforced fire and building codes, added to the distrust of government. In an attempt to rescue his reputation, Mayor Carter Harrison II appointed a special graft committee, which found no evidence of an organized ring. The investigators did complain that a few police districts had allowed open gambling to return, and when discussing the relationship between the Levee and graft, their report endorsed segregated vice as long as authorities suppressed "all solicitation by disreputable women on the streets or in public places of any kind, including saloons."[85]

The graft committee failed to quiet the criticism, especially after it was revealed that Harrison had ordered it to be a whitewash of his administration. The incumbent was forced to step aside for a fellow Democrat, Edward F. Dunne. Although he had risen through the regular party ranks, Dunne was a reformer elected on the promise of municipal ownership of mass transit, but even he could not clean up government fast enough to avoid being tainted by Chicago's corrupt reputation. By mid-1905 the declining confidence of the citizenry in its police led to near hysteria over "crime in the streets." Yellow journalists switched stories of routine street crimes to the front page and added glaring headlines. "Scoreboards," often printed in colored ink, kept account of the murders and muggings.[86]

Chicago's 7,600 saloons were blamed for much of the wrongdoing, and by the early months of 1906 a familiar suggestion was emerging: raise the license fees. Proponents of the idea pointed to the huge number of liquor outlets that made intoxication convenient. Chicago's license fee had been stable for two decades, and a dramatic increase would not only provide more funds for police, but it would reduce the number of barrooms to patrol. The arguments were old, but the focus of the debate was Chicago's City Hall rather than the General Assembly. The aldermen were fearful that an increase dictated by Springfield might be many times the current $500, and they were anxious to make some sort of gesture toward reform, especially after their failure to abolish the one-night bar permits. A new $1,000 license fee passed the council by a 37-to-31 vote.[87]

The new high license took effect on May 1, 1906, and 1,354 bars closed, mostly in poorer neighborhoods. There were the predictable grumbles from smaller saloonists, but the $1,000 was only the beginning. A few months later Daniel Harkin, a LaSalle Street lawyer representing a silk-stocking ward, introduced an ordinance freezing the number of liquor licenses until the population grew to a ratio of 500 to each permit. The proposal passed easily. It looked like a reform, but it was actually a trade-off for the passage of the high license. It imposed no harsh reduction in the ranks of saloons, as had happened in Boston in 1889, and it gave current holders preference at renewal time. Most importantly, for the first time the right to hold a Chicago saloon license promised to accrue in premium value because of future demand. This pleased the brewers, who began taking out additional licenses, even if they had no immediate need for them. By July 31, 1906, the last quarterly renewal date before the Harkin Law went into effect, 1,951 new licenses had been purchased, pushing the total to 8,097, or one for every 239 men, women, and children. The city treasurer rejoiced at the windfall revenue, but many of the vocal advocates of the $1,000 license were angry because limitation neutralized the impact of their reform.[88]

What would prove to be the most effective opponent of the saloon had also begun to emerge. The Anti-Saloon League had been founded in 1893, but because of close affiliation with church groups and unimaginative leadership, it had languished for nearly a decade. Early in the century a new generation of lawyers and publicists forged a new policy of multiple means toward a narrow goal. The league absorbed the remnants of the old Law and Order movement in Illinois, became involved in the drive to furnish saloon substitutes, started its own temperance pledge drive, and began an enormous production of temperance literature. League attorneys drafted legislation and defended it in the courts.[89]

By 1906 the Anti-Saloon League was clearly the most dangerous enemy to the liquor dealer's associations in Massachusetts and the United Societies in Illinois. Both the league and the Cermak group forced legislators to make promises of cooperation in exchange for political support. Although the league was careful to focus its attack on the saloon and the commercial liquor traffic rather than on the individual drinker or the act of imbibing in privacy, the United Societies tried to catch the league in statements that would reveal the true purpose: prohibition of alcoholic beverages altogether. The United Societies complained that the "personal liberty" of the drinker was in danger, that abolition of the Sunday beer garden was only the beginning of an attack on all freedoms. The league, meanwhile, accused Cermak's organization of protecting the evil saloon, even though the Bohemian's rise to power was symbolic of the decline of saloon influence in politics. As time would reveal, both bitter opponents symbolized the rise of the politics of mass manipulation, the advertisement, the "monster parade," the dramatic show of indignant, protesting strength.[90]

SUNNYSIDE PARK

S. FREUDENBERG, Prop'r.

CLARK STREET AND MONTROSE BLVD.

The Finest Resort for Cyclers in the City.

Meals Served at all Hours.

Eight Acres of Shady Grounds.   Thirty Private Dining-rooms, with Cuisine, Wines and Liquors Unsurpassed.

CONCERT BY
ROSENBECKER'S ORCHESTRA **EVERY EVENING**

And Matinees Saturday and Sunday Afternoons.

Sunnyside Park was an old Ravenswood (Chicago) roadhouse that survived until the end of the nineteenth century. (Reprinted from the *Official Entries and Handicaps of the Tenth Annual Road Race, May 30, 1896*)

The first Edelweiss, which opened in the mid-1890s, stood at the edge of Washington Park and did battle with the Hyde Park Protective Association. (From the author's private collection)

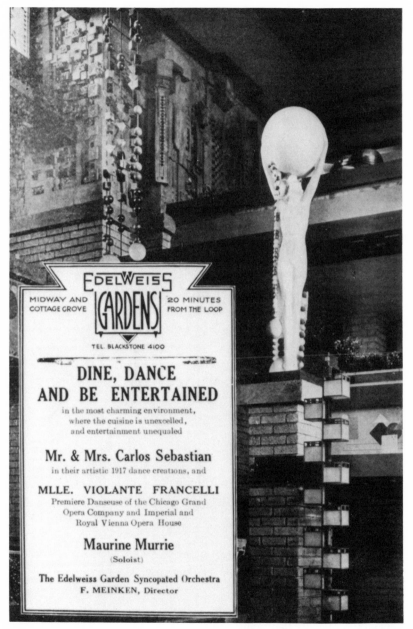

The second Edelweiss was actually the new name of Frank Lloyd Wright's famous Midway Gardens during the teens. (From an Illinois Theater program, March 4, 1917)

The Suburban Wards of Boston are
Cesspools ^{FOR}_{THE} Drunkards

of the surrounding towns, who surge in daily, littering the sidewalks with filth, tainting the lives of the youth, and lowering the moral tone of the communities.

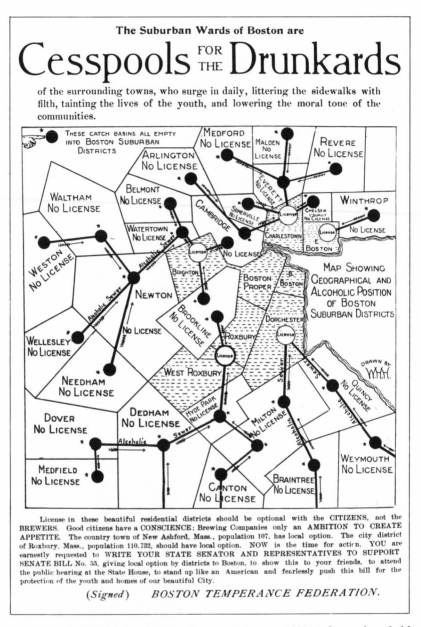

License in these beautiful residential districts should be optional with the CITIZENS, not the BREWERS. Good citizens have a CONSCIENCE; Brewing Companies only an AMBITION TO CREATE APPETITE. The country town of New Ashford, Mass., population 107, has local option. The city district of Roxbury. Mass., population 110.732, should have local option. NOW is the time for action. YOU are earnestly requested to WRITE YOUR STATE SENATOR AND REPRESENTATIVES TO SUPPORT SENATE BILL No. 55, giving local option by districts to Boston, to show this to your friends, to attend the public hearing at the State House, to stand up like an American and fearlessly push this bill for the protection of the youth and homes of our beautiful City.

(*Signed*)　　*BOSTON TEMPERANCE FEDERATION.*

This handbill favoring local option districts in Boston, 1903, indicates fears held by many suburbanites that liquor was easily transported in bottles and flasks from wet outlying areas to dry suburbs. (From the author's private collection)

Antisaloon groups played heavily on the theme that barkeeps sold liquor to youths in order to trap them in the "saloon habit." The use of postcards to tell this story was an innovation in publicity. (From the author's private collection)

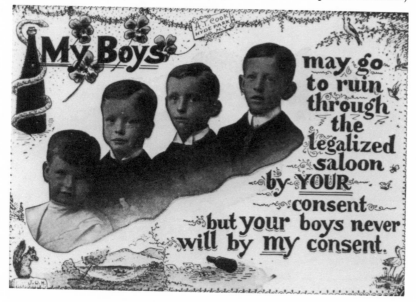

REFORMER'S CLUB ON SUNDAY. ALL SALOONS CLOSED.

To liquor advocates, the closed club was a hypocrisy. (Reprinted from *Mida's Criterion* 15[March 1, 1909]:18)

Through the operation of the Harkin Ordinance, limiting the number of saloons, licenses in Chicago have become negotiable paper and are quoted in the open market at a premium. Doubtlessly it will not be long before quotations on certain locations will be bid on by the howling mob of the stock exchange at exceedingly high prices.

When Chicago's City Council limited the number of barrooms, this liquor trade cartoon depicted the result: the license premium rose as if it were a valuable stock. (Reprinted from *Bar and Buffet* 2[Oct. 1906]:16)

Antivice interests turned out dozens of books on the white slave trade. This posed view shows the innocent woman about to go to her doom in "the fatal wine room." (Reprinted from F. M. Lehman, *The White Slave Hell; or, With Christ at Midnight in the Slums of Chicago* [Chicago: Christian Witness Co., 1910], facing p. 252)

Chicago writer and publisher A. C. Anderson warned of Chicago street and saloon dangers in his *Chicago After Dark* and helped generate Chicago's criminal image (Chicago: A. C. Anderson, 1868). (Courtesy Library of Congress)

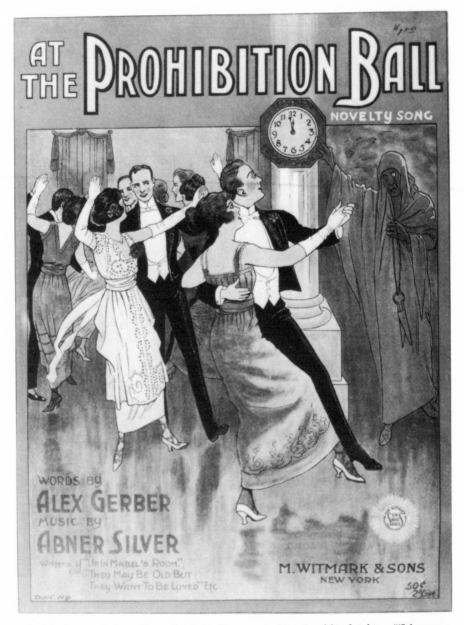

This 1919 sheet music reflects the dismal last year of legal public drinking ("It's gonna take til early morn/ to say goodbye to Barley-corn"). (From the author's private collection)

Yet another factor in the realignment of power in Chicago also grew out of the graft investigations and the crime waves of 1903–1906: the creation of what would become the city's most effective antivice organization, the Chicago Law and Order League. It was similar in both name and methods to the antidramshop crusade of a quarter-century earlier. Formed in 1903 by the anticigarette reformer, Lucy Page Gaston, it hired its own sleuths to investigate moral crimes, badger laggard police officials, and initiate court cases. At first, fund raising was slow, but the event that catalyzed support was the extension of saloon drinking hours to 1:00 A.M. Coming amidst the graft investigations of 1903–1904, Gaston and her followers became convinced that crime was now beyond all control. Under its first president, the Reverend Johnston Myers, the league assembled support from churches, neighborhood improvement associations, philanthropists, youth workers, and others concerned with the infiltration of vice into respectable communities. The Law and Order League lost its first major battle when it failed to repeal the one-night bar permit law in 1905. But during the next seventeen years the two leagues would compete for legislative victories and popular support.[91]

The final element in Chicago's revolution of 1906 was the reform of its court system. After years of complaints about the inefficiency and corruption of the "justice shops," the Chicago Bar Association helped draft a proposal to reform the courts. The graft scandals virtually assured passage by the General Assembly in May 1905 and by Chicago voters the following November. When the new system went into operation in January, it centralized most of the cases handled by the justices of the peace and created specialized branches to deal with such specific problems as juvenile delinquency.[92] The Municipal Court of Chicago considerably diminished the influence of neighborhood ward politicians, while enhancing the power of the mayor and party politicians because judges stood for city-wide election. Anton Cermak also realized the political power of the courts and in 1912 was elected chief bailiff. Because that office was responsible for selecting juries, Cermak accumulated many political debts for empaneling veniremen holding the "right" opinions. Thus, the municipal court reform constituted more of a realignment of power away from individual aldermen than a reform. And whereas the revolutions of 1906 had brought a schism of influence among the mayor, police commissioner, and licensing board in Boston, the principal political result in Chicago had been centralization.

The Vice Crusades, 1906 – 1912

The turmoil of 1906 was only the beginning. During the next half-dozen years the vice issue would reach a jarring crescendo. Despite the involvement of only a small percentage of barrooms in crime, all would suffer a declining status that would contribute to their gradual displacement by the delivery truck, the home sideboard, and, eventually, the Volsted Act. The vice situation in the two cities differed dramatically — the brazen Levee versus the quiet "buffet flats" of the Hub. But before America's entry into World War I both would be subjected to a searching investigation of the causes and operation of prostitution, and both would see a series of sensational charges made against officials.

The most emotional issue of the crusade was the question of how young women became involved in vice. According to Chicago reformers the dance hall was still the major villain. Clearly, efforts to reform the one-night special licenses were doomed. Officials made no effort to investigate applicants, and such groups as the Juvenile Protective Association even failed to have the words No Minors Allowed posted in the dance halls. The JPA expressed shock at the ease with which youngsters could purchase liquor, nor were police present to prevent such sensuous activities as the "barefoot can dance" and the masquerade dances which allowed unsavory characters to operate in the hall under cover. Furthermore, the lack of a drinking fountain in the crowded and often overheated room brought dancers back to the bar repeatedly. White slavers were ready to pounce on their innocent prey, and many young women were reputedly dragged off intoxicated to rooming houses nearby.[93]

The restlessness of youth was central to the involvement of Boston women in vice, but the issue also involved questions of public versus private conduct. For instance, when the Watch and Ward Society turned its attention to the commerce in flesh, it blamed crowding and the lack of privacy in tenements for driving the indigent young to seek amusement in dance halls and cheap theaters. From there it was an easy step to involvement in vice. But the society stressed its belief that conduct at public recreation spots demanded more strict standards than in private homes. Suggestive paintings, songs, dances, and similar artistic activities might be both moral and legal in private, but not in a public place. Barefoot dancing, an avant-garde art form in 1909, was acceptable as private culture "in its own home and screen[ed] . . . in the privacy of its own chambers." But if allowed to operate in public, it would be difficult to justify denying the uncultured the same form of dance. As Frank Chase, the secretary of the Watch and Ward Society, exclaimed: "We have to distinguish in our work between public and private immorality. Private immorality is vice as diversion. Public immorality is vice as business, or the systematic promotion of vice for *mercenary ends*. The general method of our work is the legal suppression of the business in vice, because the law makes this possible."[94]

Bostonians were especially upset over the so-called "bohemian resorts." These saloons catered primarily to college-age students and were ideally equipped for seduction. According to Frank Chase they were "attractively furnished, supplied with delightful music, . . . provided with comfortable chairs and tables, and . . . a measure of seclusion not, in some cases, foreseen by the powers of the law."[95]

The danger for young women seemed to be everywhere. Robert Woods of South End House joined with New York social worker Albert Kennedy in writing *Young Working Girls*, a perceptive treatise on the moral problems of single women in the city. Monotonous work, low pay, and lonely, unattractive quarters left them searching for excitement to replace their fatigue. Frequently, they accepted the offer of an evening's entertainment from men they hardly knew. A night of drinking left the women defenseless. Even those who shunned tawdry entertainments could fall prey to downtown resorts that appeared to be respectable cafes. Thinking that the privacy of dining in a separate compartment would also be safer, the young women found themselves trapped. As the Watch and Ward Society described it: "We found several places where the private dining rooms were fitted with lock and key. . . . The room to all appearances was only fitted with table and chairs and a mirror, but behind this full-length mirror was a folding bed which could be taken down easily, and the girl was in reality in a bedroom with the door locked and no means of summoning a waiter."[96] These dens were located in the business district. In 1913, after three years of lobbying by the society, the license board finally issued a new rule: parties of fewer than four people could not occupy a private dining room.[97]

Local seduction was only the beginning, for newspapers and popular books emphasized the development of national and international white slave rings. In 1910 a Chicago antivice crusader named Clifford Roe

gave an explosive speech entitled "The Boston Hypocrisy" at several
Hub locations. His most shocking charge was that the city had become
a recruiting center whose victims were shipped to several cities along
the seaboard. The accusations so shocked the General Court that it
quickly passed a new white slave law that clarified definitions of seduction and detention that were unclear in previous kidnapping statutes.
The Watch and Ward Society immediately used the new law to break
up a gang recruiting for Panamanian bordellos and to rescue several
girls from Boston bars and opium dens.[98]

A spate of sensational books described similar conditions in Chicago.
*Panders and Their White Slaves, War on the White Slave Trade, From
the Dance Hall to Hell*, and similar volumes exploited the facts revealed
by settlement house workers, physicians, and other civic reformers. But
the publicity did help the Illinois General Assembly decide to pass a
revised white slave law in 1908. The previous year the *Inter-Ocean* had
uncovered a "syndicate" to kidnap girls from dance halls and other
amusement places. Headquartered at 2252 Wabash in the Levee district, its organizer posed as the son of a wealthy packer, lured the
women to his place, trapped them, and sold them to other brothel
keepers. The Springfield legislators responded with a new law clearly
defining the illegal act and prescribing stiff penalties.[99]

But such state laws were clearly limited. Not only was there an east
coast ring, but Chicago's location at the center of America's rail network facilitated the interstate shipment of women. In 1909 federal
officials broke up the notorious Chicago-St. Louis Gang. Maurice Van
Bever, its organizer and the owner of a Levee saloon, implicated several members of the Chicago police in the plot to circulate victims between the two cities. While Van Bever and his wife spent a year in
prison, their junior partner, "Big Jim" Colosimo and his assistant,
Johnny Torrio, kept watch over their Levee resort. The latter two
would gain experience and later create what became the Capone organization. One of the most important results of the Van Bever affair was
a visit by Law and Order League officials to Congressman James R.
Mann of Hyde Park. They proposed legislation making it a federal
offense to take females across state lines for immoral purposes. In June
1910 what became known as the Mann act became federal law.[100]

The problem of pandering and white slavery continued to capture
headlines after 1910, but the issue also focused attention on the vice resorts that ultimately used the women. In the quickening swirl of

events, "wide-open" Chicago would begin to adopt the policies of Boston. Police officials in the latter city could boast that it was the only major metropolis in America without a red light district, and that claim became a standard feature of each annual report. Careful gathering of evidence resulted in a high rate of convictions. Longer jail terms had kept the courts from becoming a "revolving door," or quasi-licensing system so common in cities with minimal fines and frequent arrests. Fear of conviction had all but driven prostitutes from the ranks of the street trades and brought vice indoors and under cover.[101]

But private prostitution continued to flourish. Clifford Roe's 1910 crusade described upper-class brothels whose customers were known and trusted. Arrangements were made by telephone. Buffet flats, operating for a slightly less affluent clientele, used the same methods of communication. The closest thing to open vice could be found at hotels. Reforms promised after the small-hotel scandal of 1901 had never been executed. In desperation, the license board in 1907 adopted its version of the "Emmons rule" of four years earlier. A License Circular restricted drinking by women to places where food, rather than liquor, made up the greatest portion of the business. In practice intoxicated women could be found in many drinking spots. In 1909 the board revealed that seventy-nine hotels and ninety-one cafes could legally admit women.[102]

The image of "too good" Boston was clearly wearing thin when muckraker Carl Hovey published his account of American police departments the following year. He attacked the smug Bostonian, who could see no evil, as being more of a problem than corrupt officers. "Let him first go a block or two south of Boylston and look over the 'hotels' on Eliot and the neighboring streets, which cater to thieves and prostitutes, and are filled with them every evening—'hotels' without a kitchen, where a call for food would be a joke, without a single sleeping room, but with boxed-off 'private dining rooms'. . . ." These bars were used by women who took their "tricks" elsewhere, but such places as the Piscopo Hotel in the North End saw a rapid turnover of guests each night in its rooms. Proprietors easily evaded the food requirement by allowing patrons to purchase a five-cent meal check which was exchanged for a beer. Police officials meekly admitted that the tiny amount of legitimate trade in these places probably would not even cover the cost of taxes.[103]

By 1911 the license board found itself under personal attack by antivice groups, which followed the commissioners to their offices and homes shouting taunts and insults. But the policies of the board remained unchanged. It would not institute segregated vice, nor would it attempt to exclude women from licensed houses altogether. Judge Emmons had failed to do it earlier, and the board doubted the constitutionality of such a measure. Meanwhile, members felt that it was better to have women drink in open, licensed hotels and cafes, "larger places on public thoroughfares," than in "homes and kitchen barrooms" or "small places on back streets." Despite official intransigence, the idea of excluding women altogether refused to die, and during the winter and spring of 1912 the Boston Social Union, an association of settlement house workers, lobbied unsuccessfully in the General Court for the ban.[104]

Meanwhile, Police Commissioner O'Meara managed to avoid most of the criticism. When he took office in 1906, he immediately blamed immoral women themselves for their situation, claiming that they did it because of "longings for luxuries, excitement and 'good times.' " The Watch and Ward Society shared those attitudes at first, but between 1907 and 1912 the moral reformers shifted the blame to social rather than personal factors: apartments replacing single-family homes, relaxed divorce laws, the lure of commercialized leisure, and a widening freedom of movement in an anonymous city that opened the weak to new temptations. O'Meara, however, remained unconvinced. His annual reports on vice were reprinted as pamphlets, and rather than deal with the cause of vice, he complained that the only alternative to the present system was the red light district. He complained that the source of the problem was the license board's lax investigation of applicants and willingness to tolerate a certain amount of vice. The privacy of prostitution in Boston was a source of frustration to O'Meara. Police could not even examine hotel registers, and judges could issue warrants to search only for gambling or liquor violations, not for prostitution. Furthermore, a public hearing was required before issuing each warrant, and eavesdropping vice agents had plenty of time to warn their cohorts.[105]

While the vice crusades were clearly building toward a climax in Boston, the attack on Chicago's Levee district had already become frenzied. The defenders of segregated vice reiterated the familiar points that concentration and observation were preferable to scattering and secrecy. Writing in 1909, Graham Taylor, founder of Chicago

Commons settlement house, warned, "If they [the police] drive it away from sight, it is simply driven below the surface only to reappear after doing untold damage in secret . . . [and] disease, demoralization and death . . . will grow beyond all control."[106]

The principal opposition came from churches, temperance groups, and the Law and Order League. They claimed that the Levee promoted the white slave trade and corrupted the local political system. With no fear of arrest, young men were attracted to licentiousness and domestic relations were imperiled. The location of the Levee on the edge of a poor, largely black, neighborhood raised questions of social class. The Illinois edition of the *American Issue*, the Anti-Saloon League journal, asked:

> Shall it [segregated vice] be located in the region of the rich? Surely, they by their wealth and home surroundings are better fitted to protect themselves and their families from evil. They live comparatively isolated from their neighbors and so they could more defend their children from the proposed contamination of the herding together of a large number of known criminals to openly flaunt their evil living in the face of the community. No one for a moment supposes that this would be permitted. . . . Yet could wealth make any more despicable use of its power than to force by the side of the poor man and his family the evil that it will not permit in its own section.[107]

The debate over the future of the Levee was largely an academic question, since between 1900 and 1912 brothels and tough saloons were already beginning to spread beyond the borders of the original districts at the north, south, and west edges of the Loop. Clearly, the efforts to declare neighborhoods dry, either by acts of the City Council or through the 1907 state Local Option Law, were an effort to keep vice as well as liquor out of residential districts. Keeping the saloon away was essential to local purity.

But vice was on the move. The construction of the new terminal of the Chicago and North Western Railway scattered the West Madison Street district into the declining rooming houses a mile or more west of downtown.[108] The seedy hotels of North Clark and parallel streets saw respectable tenants displaced by prostitutes.[109] But the dispersal of vice to the south was most dramatic. As early as 1899 there had been reports of vice as far south as Thirty-ninth Street, and seven years later, Twenty-second Street had become the center of the Levee. The older district immediately south of the Loop had fallen to the expansion of railway stations and commercial buildings. A new network of communications involving the telephone, saloonkeepers, taxi drivers, and prostitutes housed in rooming houses and buffet flats was displacing the streetwalker and the bordello whose location was known to almost everyone.[110]

Antivice reformers won a few symbolic victories at first. The English evangelist "Gypsy" Smith staged a well-publicized march and prayer meeting through the heart of the district in 1909, and later that year Mayor Fred Busse forced the cancellation of the annual First Ward Ball, an orgy put on by the denizens of the Levee. But by 1910 it was clear that the sermons, sensational books, parades, and lobbying by antivice groups were overpowering the defenders of wide-open Chicago.[111]

The first change in policy came on April 28, 1910, when Chief LeRoy Steward issued orders designed to push prostitution from public view. He outlawed "short skirts, transparent gowns or other improper attire" in such places as barrooms. Open solicitation "from doorways, from windows or in saloons" was to cease, as was the use of "signs, lights, colors or devices, significant or conspicuous, indicative of the character of any premises occupied by a house of ill-repute." Brothels were ordered to move at least two blocks from any streetcar line, and finally, Steward directed resorts to replace any "swinging door that permits . . . easy access or a view of the interior from the street" with "double doors which shall be kept closed." Chicago police had obviously decided to follow Boston's philosophy of driving vice from public view.[112]

By 1910, however, neither the superficial reforms in the Windy City nor the license board's policies and O'Meara's public relations efforts in the Hub would satisfy the growing crusade against vice. One demand was for reliable information collected from sworn testimony and reliable investigators. That year, Chicago officials were the first to accede, when Mayor Busse appointed a special Chicago vice commission composed of settlement house workers, clergy, physicians, educators, and lawyers. This was the first publicly funded vice study, and it inspired dozens of similar investigations across the country, including one started in 1913 by the Massachusetts General Court.[113] In both studies the role of liquor and the question of the public versus private aspects of vice were of considerable importance, although the copious detail about prostitution revealed in the Chicago report was considered so salacious by the Chicago postmaster that he banned it from the mails.[114]

The reports reflected the degree to which Chicago vice had become similar to that in Boston, especially after Chief Steward's orders driving prostitution from public view. The commerce in sex had largely followed the same pattern of scattering and dependence on electronic communication that had transformed gambling two decades earlier. Old-fashioned direct solicitation was less frequent and more limited to the lowest classes; the Chicago study found more of it outside the Levee than in. The "call-house flat" and the telephone were the most commonly used arrangements because of their convenience and privacy. Chicago vice operators were careful not to keep women who had been in large bordellos or streetwalkers because they "will never do in a quiet place. They love excitement, the music, lights and large business at small prices." Such noise was not compatible with sedate residential surroundings. Both reports also confirmed the role of saloons and dance halls in white slave seductions and warned officials to increase the patrol of commercial amusements frequented by young girls.[115]

Liquor was also central to the differences between the cities and their vice problems. The Chicago report placed greater emphasis on the role of the saloonkeeper in putting customers in contact with prostitutes and with providing the money needed to bail the women out of jail. The liquor interests were more visible than in Boston, while the hotel continued to be a special problem in the Hub. The Massachusetts investigators wanted new laws to open registration books and provide search warrants quickly and more secretly from the court.[116]

The most shocking recommendation in Chicago, however, called for an end to the Levee district. Reportedly, Mayor Busse had expected the commission to favor continuing segregated vice, but its report appeared after Carter Harrison II had once more become mayor. It would be his decision, and he received plenty of advice. Another series of lurid books summarized the report and retold the evils of the Levee and its ties with evil saloons.[117] Meanwhile the young Walter Lippmann wrote a widely quoted analysis warning that raids and suppression simply drove vices underground and into the home; it had already happened with gambling. Unsure of what to do, Harrison made the symbolic gesture of closing the Everleigh sisters' place on October 24, 1911. The following March he ordered yet another inquiry, this one conducted by the Chicago Civil Service Commission. It reaffirmed the Vice Commission's findings and went on to complain about "half-naked sirens" displaying themselves in the windows of tough bars along a mile and one-half stretch of West Madison Street.[118]

Finally, Harrison could stand the public pressure no more, and on November 20, 1912, he ordered an end to segregated vice. Denizens of the districts were predictably angry, and a mysterious group calling itself the United Police distributed 100,000 copies of a circular that warned, "Would you rather have it [vice] where your wife and children would come into contact with it and see it daily and hourly, or would you rather have it where those who want it know where to find it?"[119]

The Law and Order League promised to shield neighborhoods from vice and applauded Harrison's decision. The local option law of 1907 was supposed to protect residential areas, because the absence of saloons would make it more difficult for prostitutes to solicit. But while the closing of the Levee came to be regarded as a milestone event in Chicago's history, it was an illusory victory, much as the gambling raids of 1894 had been. What had disappeared from sight had not ended, but was flourishing underground.

The saloon was, ultimately, like a chain — no stronger than its weakest link. Despite the warm memories shared by thousands of happy evenings in friendly, neighborhood barrooms, it was the evil saloon that did the fatal damage. The gambler and the white slaver caught the attention of the press. In part, it was a matter of coincidence. The growing concern about pandering and the invasion of gambling into the neighborhoods took place roughly at the same time that municipal political reform reached its peak. And finally, various temperance strategies — Scientific Temperance Instruction, abstention pledges, supporting dry candidates, helping apprehend erring barkeeps — joined to form the Anti-Saloon League movement. By 1906 that coincidence had pushed the saloon to what would prove to be a fatal end.

The attacks on saloon-related vice were part of a larger impulse toward urban moralism that swept Victorian America and reached its peak in the 1890s. From the WCTU to the religious revivals to the "civic awakening" of the National Municipal League, the notion of moral rebirth was everywhere. But during the last decade of the century these attacks on sin and corruption changed from persuasion and character building among the poor to a more coercive stance in the form of antigambling and antiprostitution campaigns.[120]

Finally, the saloon became mixed in the popular mind with the rise of commercialized leisure. Baseball, amusement parks, commercial beaches, cheap theater, and vaudeville represented the creation of semipublic places where individuals made profits from the leisure time of others who were often adventurous youth or the poor. The concern expressed over the rise of the dance hall was but a reflection of a larger feeling that these activities were somewhat tawdry and frought with potential immorality. Eventually, the attack on semipublic amusements would claim a victim — the saloon.

Conclusion: Criminal Saloons and Dirty Politics

No matter how honest he was, the average saloonkeeper was constantly burdened by a tainted image. Some crimes were so open and public that most citizens did not really regard them as infractions. Closing-hour and Sabbath-breaking violations were virtually universal in Chicago, but much more rare in Boston. Covert misdeeds, such as harboring murderers, pickpocket rings, or bunco games were another problem, for they involved few places that gave a bad name to all. Covert crimes were also transitory, contributing to hysteria over crime waves and danger in the street, but fading after a few months to newspaper stories that drew only limited attention. Finally, there were semipublic crimes. Classified as victimless, they were a more serious threat to the legitimate saloonkeeper because the issues of gambling and prostitution were permanent controversies. Semipublic crimes also required some sort of police cooperation and could greatly supplement the income of the barkeep. Those who did allow games and loose women on the premises drew drinkers away from "clean" places nearby.

The first response to semipublic crime had been segregation. Much like local option to ban saloons from residential neighborhoods of the upper- and middle-class, segregated vice was a moral and geographic compromise: allow the unwanted activity to thrive, since it was deemed an inevitability rooted in human weakness, but keep it in a restricted area. This accommodation required a delicate balance of forces. The activities had to be public enough for customers to find them, but not so outrageously open that undue publicity resulted. Vice required excellent transportation convenience and usually prospered where there were few legitimate land uses that were more profitable. The need to seek police protection also made clustering more convenient for pay-offs.

Segregated vice, however, was always an uneasy compromise. Many citizens objected to the way in which it seemed to place government sanction on immorality. The misspent paychecks and venereal disease prompted others to question whether gambling and prostitution really were victimless. As a new moralism swept America in the 1890s, attacks on sin and corruption changed from persuasion and character building among the poor to attacks on the brothel keepers and gamblers themselves through the courts. Ultimately, these semipublic crimes became entwined in larger complaints about incompetent and dishonest government. Failure to halt open vice was an affront to moral sensibilities, much as failure to clean streets or pick up garbage was an affront to the senses. Such reform groups as the Civic Federation of Chicago or the Massachusetts Civic League saw crime and bad government as parts of the same problem.

The world of segregated vice unraveled in stages, with Boston leading the way. By the end of the 1880s police officials and the Watch and Ward Society had closed down the gambling district and begun the attack on prostitution; by the mid-1890s the latter would be scattered. Closing down wide-open Chicago took a much greater effort, but the shock of W. T. Stead's exposé and the Civic Federation's importation of suburban justices of the peace finally brought down Gamblers' Row.

The reform efforts reached a second peak from 1906 to 1909 in both cities, as charges of corrupt and incompetent government, a new fear of crime on the streets, and a growing concern about white slavery combined to produce a restructuring of licensing and policing powers within reformed city governments. Chicago saw the emergence of the Anti-Saloon League and the Law and Order League, a remodeled court system, and the Local Option Law. The $1,000 license and the limitation law were sham reforms, which merely introduced license premiums into the city. Boston, by contrast, restructured its licensing and policing powers just before passage of a new city charter changed all of city government.

There was also a dramatic difference in the way the two cities handled the vice issue during its emotional peak from 1909 to 1912. The Hub exhibited a smug sense of superiority at its lack of a segregated district. Even occasional exposés could not deflate the city that was "too good." In Chicago, meanwhile, the Levee became the target for a dramatic crusade that finally brought an official ban on the red light district in 1912. In reality, vice in the Windy City was governed by the laws of laissez-faire economics. Just as the advantages of telegraphic and telephonic communications made secretive replacements for the open casino possible, the new technology of the telephone and automobile allowed call girls and buffet flats to displace the old semipublic bordello.

In both cities the saloon-vice issue was also tied to an emotional reaction to the inability to control youth. While older people were involved, the innocent young girls from the country and the "young sports," often barely old enough to grow their symbolic mustaches, were the victims and customers of the vice system that drew most of the attention. Thus, the image of the saloon entered a new era. In earlier years concern over young people in barrooms had focused on rushing the growler. But the appearance of dance halls at the turn of the century began a new, insidious intrusion of immorality into the leisure of both girls and boys. The "saloon menace" was no longer confined to adult males. In part, the limited profitability and fierce competition in the saloon business, especially in Chicago, had driven some barroom owners to add dances and other amusements to supplement revenues. Soon, however, they found themselves swept up in an emotional crusade. The adaptability of the saloon as a social institution had gotten them into trouble.

CHAPTER 9

The Long, Slow Death
of the Saloon

Henry barrett chamberlin sensed the change. As editor of the *Chicago Record* and the *Record-Herald* since 1898, chief investigator for the Chicago Vice Commission, and publisher of a magazine of political commentary, he was well aware of the fact that the saloon was dying even before World War I. Writing in 1915, he described the decline of public drinking and the bitter contest between "The Public Bar and the Private Sideboard." Through an imaginary debate between "Mr. Saloon Fan" and "Mr. Anti," Chamberlin made his point: the return of the decanter to the sideboard meant, unfortunately, that the saloon was becoming passé. This was happening not only among the wealthy, but also among those of lesser means. This was unfortunate, for drinking in the home lacked the restraint of public observation, infected the family, and more easily led to solitary overdrinking. "A man would be ashamed to get as drunk in public as he does in the privacy of his own home," snorted Mr. Saloon Fan, who went on to say, "As the saloon is today, it means segregated drinking. Those who drink go inside, others do not. They have all the rest of the town for themselves."[1]

The arguments were essentially the same used back in 1867 when the Massachusetts General Court debated the merits of repealing statewide prohibition. The antidrink forces replied, as did Mr. Anti, "Close the saloon and liquor cannot advertise itself." Drinkers would not waste idle hours in saloons, where the sociability of the situation led to drunkenness. Chamberlin realized that the latter attitude was winning ground rapidly, that drinkers were abandoning the barroom for the living room. Indeed, by 1915 not only the idea of segregated vice was dead; segregated drinking in such separate places as saloons, hotel dining rooms, and dance halls was terminally ill. There are many explanations for the change. The activities of criminal bars and vice resorts had tarnished the reputation of the legitimate liquor trade. The ease with which the disloyalty stigma attached itself to a business that was no longer really a Germanic institution seems to indicate that the citizenry was eager to discard a habit for which it had little use. Fashion, rumor, and technology were conspiring to lead drinkers away from the swinging doors.[2]

Crime and the Image of Public Drinking

The closing of Chicago's Levee in 1912 and the inquiry by the Massachusetts white slave commission the following year were landmarks in the growing public indignation over the criminal saloon, but they were by no means the end of the issue. The safety of young women in public places, the dispersal of vice into residential neighborhoods, and the growing fear that commercial amusements frequented by youth were increasingly dominated by the evil liquor interests — all continued to generate controversy. And even the most respectable barrooms suffered a marked decline in public image that ultimately contributed to national prohibition.

Because of its reputation as a wide-open town dominated by criminal elements, Chicago continued to be the target of antivice reformers. Where the Watch and Ward Society was predominant in Boston, the Windy City was crowded with investigators. Besides the Law and Order League, the Committee of Fifteen dispatched its investigators to the streets in search of blind pigs, prostitutes, and gamblers.[3] At the time Harrison closed down the Levee, a City Council vice committee was beginning its investigation, and in February 1913 Lieutenant Governor Barratt O'Hara convened yet another vice inquiry, this one sponsored by the Illinois State Senate. The following May, Alderman Charles Merriam talked his colleagues into funding an investigation of the causes of crimes, but the innocuous study soon expanded into a sensational exposé of Chicago vice and the politicians who protected it.[4] Meanwhile, such groups as the Juvenile Protective Association continued to collect information and publish pamphlets describing the downfall of youthful purity. Finally, in 1914 the Chicago City Council created a permanent morals commission to study all phases of immorality in the city and cooperate with the police department in eradicating it.[5]

The inquiries produced volumes of information, but most of it confirmed trends that had been developing for a decade or more. The dispersal of vice, for instance, had clearly reached the neighborhoods. In Boston lottery and policy were found in many parts of the city, but always quietly hidden. By 1914 the Watch and Ward Society had begun to complain about the "automobile gaming nuisance." Road houses on the edge of Boston featured casino gambling and sold liquor to underage women at all hours of the night.[6] Chicago gambling also scattered, as saloonkeepers installed slot machines and allowed a card game called "26" to flourish. In neighborhoods where prohibition was in effect, cigar stores and local restaurants welcomed small-scale gaming.[7]

The dispersal of prostitution, on the other hand, was more pronounced in Chicago than in Boston. Every study of vice in Illinois ignored the old Levee area and described in detail the influx of immoral women into apartment houses miles from the Loop. The nightly rounds of detectives working for the Committee of Fifteen took them to all parts of the city. In 1913 the Chicago South Side Women's Club conducted a survey of women drinking in saloons and found over half of the tough resorts in residential areas, and Alderman Merriam's City Council committee on crime found criminal bars in many scattered locations.[8] While not segregated, Boston prostitution was less widely distributed. There were a few road houses in such districts as Brighton, while the toughest hotels and saloons were in the North End. And winerooms were reported to be in operation in a few downtown resorts in 1915.[9]

The contrasting situations in the two cities produced different strategies. In Boston the problem was solicitation in saloons — legally "cafes" — prompting the Watch and Ward Society to complain that a particular business rather than a designated location was harboring prostitutes. Society officials called it "cafe segregation." The police were powerless. Although the screen law of 1880 allowed officers to view saloon interiors from the street, the mixing of people in a crowded room made it easy to conceal assignation transactions from them. And since Police Commissioner O'Meara refused to allow his men to enter a bar even to collect evidence, some exterior means had to be found to prevent illicit liaisons from happening. The answer was the License Board's new policy announced May 1, 1915, which was simply a modified version of the old segregation-of-sex rules imposed several times earlier: "Whenever in a room that is in use by any innholder or First Class Victualler chiefly for the sale of liquor and women are allowed, no men patrons unaccompanied by women shall be permitted to enter or remain."[10]

The rule, which applied only to the sixty-five places admitting both sexes, placed the blame for prostitution on the men seeking it rather than the women offering it. The license board expected that the "jealousy of the women" would keep the men they were with pure of action. Police officers stationed on the sidewalks could intercept lone males before they entered or on the way out, and although these patrons had broken no laws, the licensees could face suspension. The board did bend a bit, however, allowing bars to serve single men if they were kept in a separate room or on the other side of a curtain or partition.[11]

The effort to stop saloon vice received another boost in 1915, when the General Court enacted a law specifically banning solicitation for prostitution anywhere liquor was sold or consumed. The New England Watch and Ward Society heralded the development as an important step in drawing vice out of its hiding places, especially the protective cover of the saloon. When forced to become streetwalkers, prostitutes were much more vulnerable to arrest. The society claimed a 60 percent reduction in prostitution in Boston.[12]

In Chicago, where vice was more scattered because saloons and buffet flats were sprinkled over a hundred square miles of neighborhoods, even an honest police force equipped with automobiles could not have benefitted from a segregation-of-sex rule. Chicago had never tried to cluster saloons or even to keep them on major thoroughfares. Instead, reformers turned to an ancient precedent. The "injunction and abatement law" allowed adjacent property owners to sue the operators of any brothel, blind pig, or any other illegal activity for damages because property values had declined. The saloon could be ruled a common nuisance. Chicago antivice groups, led by the Law and Order League, tried to convince the General Assembly to pass similar legislation, but they failed. Finally, in 1913 the league successfully sued one brothel owner in a civil suit. Calling the decision the "Appomatox of Open Tolerated Vice," the reformers renewed their efforts in Springfield, and the following year the lawmakers yielded to the pressure. But even this law proved ineffective when police officials failed to cooperate in proving that defendants had actually broken the law. By the time Massachusetts enacted its injunction and abatement law in 1915, the idea had become a reform fad across the country, but in most instances it was of limited value in fighting clandestine vice.[13]

Chicago's antivice reformers also noted another disturbing trend that was directly related to the breakup of segregated vice. This was the rise of new organizations to coordinate criminal activities. When the Levee district and its smaller twins north and west of the Loop had contained the vast majority of the city's vice, local aldermen had used their influence over the police precincts as a tool to organize the assorted brothels, streetwalkers, gamblers, liquor licensees, and pornographic bookstores. The chain of command was direct and political. But when gambling was driven underground and prostitution moved far beyond the Levee, crime crossed ward borders. Before the rise of the power machine of the 1930s and later, aldermen were independent powers, cooperating with each other when necessary, but independent heads of fiefdoms. When vice dispersed, they were ill-equipped to keep control, and new criminal organizations appeared. Unwittingly, the crusade against the Levee had helped initiate the criminal gangs that would terrorize Chicago during the 1920s.

The signs of the change were everywhere. The "26" game was scattered in saloons across the city, but a Merchants Protective Association appeared in 1913 to collect tribute from barkeeps for a "trust fund" to pay off city officials. This group reportedly tried using force to extort money from brewers that owned chains of saloons. Graham Taylor, the settlement house worker, realized the growing complexity of the white slave and prostitution networks and warned that "either those who are in the business" or the police were "syndicating" crime. The Merriam crime committee found that saloons were widely used as headquarters for professional criminals highly organized into "rings." And the following year, Henry Barrett Chamberlin published "50–50" an examination of several of the criminal "trusts." He investigated arsonists, wiretappers, pickpockets, horse thieves, and other criminals and described their organizations and ties to politicians. While none approached the sophistication of the next decade, these gangs did represent the primordial forms of syndicate mobs.[14]

The crime-laden images from the vice crusades made all liquor dealers sensitive about their reputations. Trade journals were distressed to tell of barkeeps who were asked to resign fraternal and church memberships in increasing numbers. Saloonkeepers began to form their own lodges. The dealers also looked for ways to improve their standing.[15] After 1912 the *Champion of Fair Play*, the Chicago saloon paper, began featuring articles on the importance of good grooming and courtesy. That same year President Thomas Fuller of the Massachusetts Liquor League proclaimed the need to "encourage a sound public sentiment in favor of our trade." A year later the group adopted a credo suggested by James Nicholson, president of the Harvard Brewing Company: courtesy, honesty, "neatness and wholesomeness" of the premises, and a promise not to sell to inebriates or to heads of needy families. In 1914, in a pamphlet entitled *The Cooperation of the Retail Trade in Saloon Regulation*, that prescription for good conduct was expanded to include discussions of sports without obscenities, clean pictures and jokes, and the discouragement of profanity among the patrons.[16]

The problem of reputations also prompted the liquor interests to resort to a special investigatory commission in Chicago. On July 12, 1915, the City Council established a panel of six aldermen and three private citizens to collect information about saloons and recommend ways to improve them. When the Chicago commission on the liquor problem issued its report eighteen months later, the purposes of the investigation became clear. One was to impress the citizens with the vast size of the liquor industry and the severe economic consequences of eliminating it through prohibition. The huge investment in real estate, the thousands of employees and their families, and the enormous share of the city's revenue — estimated at one-third — from licenses could not easily be replaced. The other purpose was to identify problems that could easily be corrected.[17]

The commission's remedies were obvious, but stood little chance of being adopted. It suggested that licensing be divorced from politics, that care be taken in the choice of licensees, that bartenders be licensed, and that the city adopt something like Boston's screen law. Critics called the report a whitewash, noting that the chairman, Alderman John Toman, was a leader of the United Societies. This commission's report had hardly appeared before the City Council established yet another. Fifteen aldermen junketed to New York and Boston to learn how other cities regulated public drinking. Their exhaustive report proclaimed the Hub to have the most orderly, least criminal, and best operated license system in the United States. But the aldermen made no specific recommendations, and neither investigation resulted in any changes in the Chicago licensing system.[18]

The Roots of Political Betrayal

The year 1906 probably marked the beginning of the end in both cities. Not only was the vice issue heating up to a frenzied crusade, but the massive changes in the relationship between saloons and governments that were enacted that year ultimately weakened the political influence of the liquor interests. The restructuring of the licensing system in Boston and the rise of the United Societies, the $1,000 license, and the limitation law in Chicago set the stage for dramatic political betrayals in both cities during the following decade. At crucial moments officeholders elected with the help of saloonkeepers made decisions that hurt the saloon business precisely at the time when it was becoming more vulnerable for other reasons.

The signs of weakness were everywhere. Reform in Boston left a serious power vacuum because the police commissioner, the license board and the mayor shared authority. While most Boston mayors after 1906 were content to license "amusements" and leave saloon regulation to the other two bodies, James Michael Curley was not. He constantly tried to undercut the authority of Police Commissioner Stephen O'Meara. In 1914 Curley teamed with Martin Lomasney, the Ward Eight "Mahatma," to apply pressure in the General Court to strip the commissioner of the power to establish salaries and promote officers in his own department. Another unsuccessful Curley-Lomasney bill would have given the mayor power to remove the commisioner.[19] A few years earlier, when the Massachusetts Equal Suffrage Association for Good Government had asked O'Meara to establish a special force to watch over unchaperoned girls in public places, the commissioner had refused. But Curley, with great publicity, created a small unit whose presence conflicted with the state police. The colorful mayor also attempted to undermine the license board's authority by sponsoring legislation in the State House that would have given Boston all, not just 75 percent, of the liquor license revenue and left the board without funds to operate. Curley also cheered when the reform-oriented Boston Finance Committee revealed that Louis Epple, secretary to the license board, had illegally placed recording fees in the state treasury. With great flourish, Curley reclaimed the funds for the city coffers. It was increasingly clear that even though he had little actual authority, the mayor of Boston was becoming an influential factor in liquor matters. [20]

Chicago was afflicted with a similar vacuum of power. Although the mayor continued to hold almost absolute authority, the combined impact of the Harkin limitation law and the rapid turnover of officeholders confused matters. On one hand the new law generated a premium value for the right to hold the license. While it remained quite small compared with the $15,000 that a permit could bring in Boston, a Chicago license was worth $750 in 1909 and $1,800 to $2,500 in 1912 beyond the annual fee. Independent entrepreneurship was all but dead, but the limitation and shortage also redirected the politics of obtaining "the paper." The ward leader's recommendation to the mayor had been of great importance in pre-Harkin days, but with the premium value climbing, the brewers decided to take a more active hand in license politics. The Illinois courts were allowing the license premium to become part of the estate of the deceased, thus assuming automatic renewal unless the holder committed a crime. The fact that Edward F. Dunne remained in office for only a single two-year term (1905–1907) and took little interested in licensing matters also detracted from the mayor's power.

Dunne's successor, Fred Busse, tried to reverse the trend, and a new four-year mayoral term helped. By 1910 the number of disputes between retailers and brewers had become so large that Busse set up a "license court" composed of the city collector and two assistant corporation counsels. Since Busse was known to be a friend of saloonkeepers, most of the time the tribunal sided against the brewers. In 1911 the mayor circulated rumors that brewery interests were trying to purchase influence so that the police would harass independent dealers. An angry City Council made the license court an official agency. [21] Busse might have been able to consolidate all power once more in the mayor's hands, but numerous scandals, the vice issue, and confusion over the new primary election law drove him from office. Charles Merriam, the Hyde Park reformer, took the Republican nomination, but Carter Harrison II rode back into office with the help of the United Societies. Anton Cermak's group defeated the man who, as alderman, had sponsored the bills to end the one-night bar licenses. [22] But even Harrison fell into disfavor when he closed the Levee district in 1912. Three years later party chieftains, reportedly at the direction of "Bathhouse John"

Coughlin and Michael "Hinky Dink" Kenna, denied "our Carter" re-
nomination. Harrison I and II had occupied the office for a total of
twenty-one of the previous thirty-six years, and they had reliably
served the interests of the saloon. Now that tradition was gone.[23]

Underlying the change was the fact that the proliquor movement in
Illinois was headed by the United Societies, not the saloonkeeper-
aldermen, who numbered only three in 1910, or the liquor dealers' associations. Cermak's organization focused on protection of the Sunday
saloon tradition, where the city law allowed side or rear doors to open
in defiance of state statutes. This proved to be the single most important factor in the defeat of the new Chicago Charter in 1907. Gigantic
parades, posters, and protest meetings rallied ethnic voters around the
cry that a change in Chicago's form of government might mean an end
to home rule on the Sabbath question. The United Societies could not
stop the General Assembly from enacting the charter, but the city's voters did defeat it at the polls.[24] The following year Cermak's group created the Liberty League along legislative district lines and attempted
to move into suburban and downstate areas to combat the growing influence of the Anti-Saloon League. The immediate result was the reelection defeat of Cook County State's Attorney John J. Healy, who
had unsuccessfully tried to prosecute Sabbath breakers. His replacement, John E. W. Wayman, was a friend of Cermak.[25] Finally, in
1910 the local courts reportedly responded to pressure from the United
Societies and threw out thousands of signatures collected by the Anti-
Saloon League in an effort to place the whole city on a local option
ballot.[26]

Woman suffrage was another unsettling element in liquor politics.
For decades it had been assumed that because women had played such
a prominent role in temperance organizations, their entrance into the
electorate would lead eventually to prohibition. The WCTU and various total abstinence societies had been led by women. Both states had
allowed equal suffrage in school elections, Massachusetts in 1879 and
Illinois in 1894, but the vote in local option elections and for representatives was another matter. Predictably, old-line political bosses fought
any change, as did some upper-class conservative women; in 1895 a
group of the latter formed the Association Opposed to the Further Extension of Suffrage to Women. The Massachusetts Liquor League,
along with brewers' and wholesalers' associations, hired the brilliant
young attorney Louis Brandeis to state their case before the General

Court. Chicago retailers did similar lobbying in Springfield.[27]

But not all of those with an interest in the liquor issue lined up as expected on matters of woman suffrage. Anton Cermak's United Societies opposed it at first, then realized that many women would vote along ethnic lines and strengthen the wet ranks. By the time the Illinois legislature granted political equality in 1914, Cermak had already created a women's auxiliary.[28] In Massachusetts, leaders of local town efforts to maintain dry majorities at annual elections were fearful that woman suffrage might upset the status quo. The lineup of wet and dry towns had remained essentially stable, and such local leaders as Frank Foxcroft of Cambridge believed that the votes of "foreign-born women of the slums and saloons" might offset female dry support. Also, many temperance leaders felt that by linking the no-license vote to women, too many male voters would lose interest in the dry movement.[29]

Woman suffrage was also a central issue in the actions of two politicians accused of betraying the liquor interests. When Carter Harrison closed the Levee, he was responding in part to the expected victory of equal suffrage in Springfield; by shutting down open immorality, he hoped to gain female votes in 1915. But he never got the nomination.[30] Similarly, James Michael Curley had been elected Boston's mayor in 1914 with the help of saloon interests. As an alderman he had attacked the license board's edict against political signs and campaigning in saloons, complaining that if wealthy members of the Somerset and Algonquin Clubs could circulate petitions and hear speeches, why were poor men forced to remove politics from their "clubs"? But after he was installed as mayor, he took a neutral position on the suffrage issue. This disappointed the liquor dealers who backed his candidacy, and when he was nearly removed from office in a 1915 recall election, political insiders said that it was because of his stand on women and the vote.[31]

The actions of Curley and Harrison against the saloonkeepers were minor compared with the antics of the traitorous Eugene Foss and William Hale Thompson. Foss was a Republican-turned-Democrat who had first been elected Massachusetts governor in 1910. Liquor dealers had given him their undivided support, and he, in turn, had lobbied on their behalf in the General Court. His appointment of Samuel Hudson, a former Boston alderman, to the license board had angered church leaders, who wanted Robert A. Woods of South End House instead. During his first three years in office Foss, however, began to change. Labor troubles in a factory he owned turned him against the Democratic party, and in 1913 he returned to the Republicans. His efforts to obtain signatures for his nomination papers failed, and Gene Foss found himself a lame duck.[32] His only hope for reelection was the prohibition party, and when license board member Fred Emery died on July 28, 1913, Foss saw an opportunity to impress his new antiliquor colleagues. He turned to Robert Woods to finish the remaining eighteen months of Emery's term.[33]

The South End House settlement worker proved to be the most controversial appointment ever made to the license board. He managed to alienate prohibitionists by refusing to take an adamant antisaloon stand. Like many other social workers he saw some social function in the saloon and viewed his role on the board as similar to regulating a public utility. He thought dealers should have a fair profit. But he also attacked the idea of the license premium, claiming that it benefitted the creditors from whom dealers had to borrow in order to start a business. Those statements, however, upset dealers who already had a large investment in their licenses. They were also angry over his longtime affiliation with the Watch and Ward Society.[34]

Woods quickly became the dominant personality on the board. That body had already begun to respond to the complaints of antivice crusaders by issuing more stringent circulars and revoking larger numbers of licenses. New edicts appeared against refilling bottles, failing to display a license and a name on an outside sign, and giving away free samples. A few months before Woods joined the board, it ordered a halt to treating and buying rounds. Enforcement, however, was less than vigorous, and Woods's first official act was to complain to Commissioner O'Meara. The latter, in turn, openly questioned whether the police were required to carry out policies established by another state agency rather than the General Court. Reportedly, O'Meara also felt that it would undermine the morale of his men to arrest people for so minor an offense. But because Woods felt so strongly that treating was a major source of drunkenness, he pressured the license board into upgrading its inspection force and using suspensions and revocations to force dealers into compliance.[35]

Woods attracted headlines whenever he commented on the saloon situation, and in January 1915 he was further emboldened by the appointment of Charles Gow as the new chairman of the license board. Governor David I. Walsh, the Democratic successor to Foss, had resisted pressure from Mayor Curley and former Mayor John F. Fitzgerald to pick Gow, an engineer from West Roxbury. Most early observers saw the appointment as a shift to more liberal license policy, but Walsh wanted someone who was independently wealthy and able to resist bribes. What the governor got, however, was a maverick who quickly sided with Woods to outvote the other board member, Josiah Dean. [36]

The Gow appointment also contributed to the temporary demise of Walsh, once the most promising young man in the state Democratic party. Both Curley and Fitzgerald were angry, but prohibitionists became upset because Walsh refused to back their call for a statewide dry law. The fact that his law firm had numerous liquor men among its clients also angered the drys, as did his veto of a bill that would have outlawed the transport of liquor through no-license towns. [37]

Thus, David I. Walsh tried to be a compromiser at a time when the middle road was disappearing. By 1915 the state Anti-Saloon League had merged with the Massachusetts No-License League, a group that had been trying to coordinate annual dry campaigns on the local level since the 1880s. Together, the pro groups finally formed a respectable statewide political party, and Eugene Foss had become its candidate for governor. Although not strong enough to win, the prohibitionists managed to drain enough votes away from Walsh to assure the election of a moderate Republican, Samuel McCall. It was rumored that saloonkeepers actually preferred the winner because they thought both Walsh and Foss to be traitors and because they were concerned that prohibitionists might try to take over the Republican party if McCall went down to defeat. [38]

By the middle of 1916 Woods was too controversial to remain in office for a second term, and Governor McCall replaced him with Fletcher Ranney, who also became the new chairman. Angered because Ranney's law firm represented several saloon owners, Charles Gow resigned a few weeks later. For months afterwards the press pondered the reasons for Woods's dismissal. Years later, Eleanor Woods's biography of her husband blamed the "criminal element," although the real reason was problably the fact that the settlement worker had become too much of a political liability. In either case, after Robert A. Woods left the license board, he became one of Massachusetts's leading proponents of both statewide and national prohibition. His appointment, however, was a sign of the declining influence of liquor and the work of a maverick. [39]

The departure of Woods was definitely related to the success of the segregation-of-sex rule, an idea which he had promoted. Soon after he and Gow had gone, their replacements, Fletcher Ranney and William Prest, issued a license circular warning that while there had been a change of personnel on the board, there had been no alteration of its general policy. But on April 2, 1916, the board quietly dropped the Woods plan of separating men and women, replacing it with a policy too vague and unrealistic to be enforceable: men and women were not allowed to sit at tables together unless they had entered together, nor were they permitted to move from table to table. Where possible, men and women were not even to be allowed to sit together. The new rules, if followed closely, would have made parties rather dull affairs. Instead, the restrictions were largely ignored. The dozen worst dens in Boston regained their reputation as assignation spots, and Frank Chase of the Watch and Ward Society complained that Boston seemed to be moving backwards toward more open vice.[40] When he visited a hotel bar nicknamed "Purgatory," he found that:

> the Revere House has a room, a large place, where . . . three hundred men and women can go in and sit down; and after a certain hour of the night one or two out of a hundred couples will be ordering a club sandwich while all of the rest are purchasing liquor. . . . And in the processes [sic] of purchasing liquor they are picking up men, making their acquaintances there; and then you can go right upstairs and get a room in that place—register right there. . . .
>
> Now, then, that is used constantly for "picking up" purposes. It is the biggest fast house. It is as big as any twenty fast houses that we have ever had in the City of Boston—as big as any twenty of them.[41]

Eugene Foss's perfidy had been deliberate, while David Walsh had simply failed to check Charles Gow's opinions before appointing him. But neither managed to defy the shrinking power of the liquor interests as dramatically as did Chicago Mayor William Hale Thompson. In 1915, as the Republican candidate, he had agreed to sign the United Societies' pledge not to close Chicago saloons on Sundays. After his April victory he began to have second thoughts. The Chicago Citizens' Committee, a coalition of temperance and church groups, was sponsoring a legal test of bond that a saloonkeeper had to purchase along with his license. City officials were fearful that thousands of licenses could be voided because their owners failed to comply with their bonded oath not to break any laws; technically, they were still in violation of state law. Thompson was also nervous about rumors of a grand jury investigation of his nonenforcement of the Illinois Sabbath statute. By mid-September the mayor seemed to be hinting that there might be a change in policy.[42]

That day came on October 4, 1915. Thompson and his entourage boarded a train bound for the San Francisco exposition, and as he sped across the prairies, the City Council heard his aide read the most shocking news regarding Chicago saloons in decades. By mayoral proclamation, all saloons would remain completely closed on Sunday, rear and side doors as well as the front entrances.

The aldermen were stunned. Stories about Big Bill's betrayal filled the newspapers for weeks. The saloon trade papers began recalling the Lager Beer Riot and wondered aloud whether mobs would once more roam the streets. Buttons proclaiming "Personal Liberty" appeared on thousands of lapels, while signs in barroom windows asked, "Don't ask us what we are going to do next Sunday. What in hell are you going to do?" Hinky Dink Kenna, always thinking of practical problems, reminded reporters that 7,000 comfort stations would no longer be available for people traveling about the city on their day of leisure.[43]

The most serious damage, however, was to the reputation of the United Societies as a political force. Cermak had copies of Big Bill's pledge mass-produced, but it only made the Bohemian leader look more powerless. Thompson was perhaps looking toward the governorship and campaigning in all of those downstate counties dried up by the Anti-Saloon League, or perhaps he was looking toward the presidency. But one purpose of the closing order became obvious a few months later. Selected saloons that reportedly agreed to pay tribute to Thompson's organization were allowed to reopen on Sundays. Cermak could only stand by helplessly, because the mayor not only controlled the revocation of licenses, but also could direct the police to ignore certain violators.[44]

After Thompson's dramatic action Chicago antisaloon efforts focused on ways to vote the city dry. Since 1907 temperance legislators in Springfield had been attempting to amend the state local option law to allow counties as well as precincts, townships, and cities to eliminate saloons. The strategy, once the amendment passed, called for suburban Cook County to join with dry districts of Chicago to form a voting majority. But when the efforts in the General Assembly failed because of the influence of the United Societies, the Anti-Saloon League strategy switched to a campaign to place a city-wide prohibition vote on the ballot. As early as 1910 the temperance workers began collecting signatures on the required petitions, but the numbers on the lists always proved insufficient. Finally, in 1914 the Anti-Saloon League, the Law and Order League, and more than a score of church groups united for the first time in a Dry Chicago Federation, modeled on the United Societies. But parades, prohibition sermons, and over a million campaign buttons still produced only 90,000 of the required 171,000 signatures. Not even Big Bill's betrayal of saloonkeepers could inspire sufficient support to dry up Chicago.[45]

In Boston, where the prohibition election was mandatory each December, antisaloon forces attracted national attention by importing evangelist Billy Sunday to campaign in 1916. But the brewers, wholesalers, and dealers brought trade unionists, allied businesses, and "enlightened" civic leaders together to form a Liberty League. "Yes" labels appeared on merchandise all over town, and licenses survived by a wide margin. As in Chicago, the majority of citizens still opposed prohibition even though individual politicians were now brave enough to defy the liquor interests.[46]

The Declining Importance of the Saloon

The continuing vice scandals and the loss of political power were indications of another, larger fact: citizens in both Boston and Chicago were less willing to tolerate the old-fashioned saloon because they had discovered substitutes for it. For decades temperance organizations had attempted to oust the barroom by promoting functional replacements. Those efforts had failed, but broad changes in social habits and the evolution of the saloon itself accomplished the same goal. These changes were gradual and subtle, but they hastened the demise of the public drinking place and the arrival of national prohibition.

One basic change was the dispersal of population outward from tenement districts near the center city toward less congested neighborhoods nearer the periphery. Despite the arrival of new immigrants, the encroachment of industry and commerce destroyed some housing stock, while increasing numbers of workers were migrating to better homes as fast as their economic security permitted. Such districts as the

North, West, and South Ends of Boston and Chicago's Bridgeport, "Back of the Yards," and Near North, West, and South Sides were all declining steadily by 1910. The following decade would perpetuate those trends.

What the population shift meant for the saloon was a loss of neighborhood clientele. The bars that attracted the more anonymous commuter business were less directly affected than others, but one type of dealer profited by the change. Those who sold bottled goods or made deliveries to the home both benefitted from the trade of drinkers who had foresaken the barroom and were in the best position to adapt. Both cities witnessed a gradual shift toward wholesale dealerships at the expense of retailers. In the case of Boston it was part of a calculated policy on the part of the license board. In 1906, when that body was created, 173 of a total of 976 licenses were allotted to Fourth Class Wholesalers. In subsequent years that ratio grew to 212 of 972 in 1910, to 279 of 978 in 1911, to 301 of 971 in 1915. Most of the losses came in the common victualler, or saloon, category, which accounted for 694 licenses in 1906 but only 550 in 1915. In Chicago the number of wholesalers grew from 198 to 1910 to 251 in 1914.[47]

The expansion of the bottle trade in Boston created a much more intense controversy among Boston's antiliquor groups than it had among their Chicago counterparts. Part of the uproar began with disappointment over the failure of the license board to reduce the Boston alcohol traffic. Robert Woods, then serving a term on the governing board of the state's alcoholics' asylum, expressed concern at the ease with which "handbag liquor" could enter middle-class homes by the bottle or case. In the summer of 1909 Woods joined with Anti-Saloon League officials and other settlement workers to draft a proposal to place before the General Court. It was a simple measure that required a dealer to operate either wholesale or retail, but not both, at a single location. Wholesalers had traditionally dominated bars, two-thirds of whose owners held both types of permits and sold both by the bottle and the drink on the same premises. Woods and his followers were sure that if the trade were divided dealers would not be able to afford to rent separate locations for each part of their business. Given the choice, most dealers would prefer the greater profits from retailing and, according to Woods, "almost unanimously select the bar license." The existing law also allowed dual licenses in one place to count as a single "licensed place" under the limitation law, but Woods's bill defined the limit as applying to the total number of *licenses*, not locations. This meant that the actual number of licenses would decline sharply.[48]

The "bar and bottle bill" promised many reforms. Saloonkeepers would no longer be able to sell bottles or growlers to retail customers. This would reduce the amount of drunkenness in the home. Although Woods was willing to concede that there was little inebriation in the barrooms themselves, he did complain that drinkers who finished their libation from a growler in the tenement or a bottle on a suburban train were the source of misery for themselves and their families. And women, who were not welcome at the bar, were toting pitchers into lower-class places and taking them home to drink.[49]

The liquor interests realized the threat and complained that prohibition was the real object of the bill. Limit the licenses further, and old-time problems related to secret drinking and unlicensed dealers would return. The Dramshop Act already provided a way to punish dealers who sold to drunkards of all classes. Finally, the Massachusetts Wine and Spirits Dealers' Association complained that dealers would lose thousands invested in real estate, stock, and fixtures. And since the law would make licenses good for only one branch of the trade, the premium value would decline.[50]

After a heated series of debates the General Court approved the bill. Last-minute attempts to amend it did manage to delay its passage until May 3, 1910, three days after the licenses for the following year had been issued. That helped ease the transition, as did a fortunate ruling by Boston licensing authorities that a firm could purchase a second license to be used in a separate building. Thus, wholesalers could still operate saloons, but the new demand for licenses touched off a bidding war that pushed the premium value of a license as high as $15,000 by the end of the following year.[51]

The liquor business did not collapse, but the retail end of it was hurt. The ranks of retailers began to shrink, because there was more profit from wholesaling. More important, the surviving saloonists who were located in poorer neighborhoods were now anxious to generate maximum profit from their precious licenses. The result was a strong pressure to move licenses to locations with less competition and a potential clientele that was both larger and more affluent. By 1913 the license board was under great pressure to break the tradition of protecting middle-class residential neighborhoods from an influx of barrooms. In

1914, for instance, Boston proper had 334 retailers, or one to every 558 people, but the ratio in Roxbury was one to 877, in West Roxbury it was one to 2,246, and in Dorchester, one to 9,925. When Robert Woods joined the license board, he was determined to reverse the pattern. In his experience at South End House, he had decided that the poor bore an unfair "saloon burden" and that if the middle class was willing to patronize liquor dealers, then the licenses should be located in better neighborhoods. In the spring of 1916 Woods finally convinced the other two commissioners to back a policy of dispersal. The protest from expected quarters was instant and loud. Residents of the outlying districts complained that they had rejected the district option bill a decade earlier because license officials had promised to confine the saloons to Boston proper and a few heavily traveled commercial streets. The policy, however, was never really implemented. Both Robert Woods and Charles Gow left the board a few months later, and perhaps their replacements believed the threats to vote the city dry at the next license election if liquor dealers opened where they had not been before.[52]

In Chicago prohibition districts created by the City Council or dried up by the action of voters, along with territories still under preannexation laws requiring permission of nearby property owners, were hardly dry. Whereas in Boston the source of alcohol had been bottles, primarily of whiskey, carried home or delivered, in Chicago the favorite beverage was beer and the principal source was the brewers' teams. By 1910 the beermakers had begun to advertise extensively in the daily press and particularly in publications read by the more affluent. Theater programs and fashionable local magazines included telephone numbers and promised prompt delivery. What had been a profitable service to the suburbs turned into a booming business in dozens of parts of town.[53]

More perceptive members of the saloon trade realized that the brewers were also siphoning off potential business, eliminating the saloon middleman, and pocketing the profit directly. By early in the century a few retailers had begun to predict that the brewers would eventually save themselves time and money by closing down the public saloons they owned and making all of their sales directly to the drinkers' homes. By 1911 that bitterness had produced an open rift, when the Schlitz Brewing Company failed to renew its long-standing advertising contract with the *Champion of Fair Play*, the official journal of the

Chicago Liquor Dealers' Association. The beermaker had lost interest in attracting saloons to its fold and had been angered by the number of disputes with retailers that had ended up in court. The *Champion* used the occasion to launch a vendetta against the Milwaukee brewer that lasted for two years. Schlitz had begun using brown bottles, claiming in its ads that its superior beer would never be spoiled by sunlight. The saloonkeepers' paper labeled the claims "bosh" and called Schlitz's product "skunk beer" that was capable of "rotting the bartender's fingers." The break between Schlitz and the newspaper would be final.[54]

Antisaloon forces also realized the impact of home sales. During 1913 and 1914 it pressured two major daily papers, Hearst's *Chicago American* and the respected *Record-Herald*, into refusing to take any liquor advertising, despite the obvious loss of revenue. And in another landmark battle a Chicago billboard company fought all the way to the Illinois Supreme Court before winning the right to erect beer signs in dry territory.[55]

While drinking in the home was becoming an important substitute for the saloon, the liquor industry as a whole had to contend with the impact of technology on leisure time. The major social attraction of most barrooms, especially the neighborhood variety, had been the joys of conversation and the congenial diversions of pool and cards. But the rise of the automobile and the nickelodeon presented a new challenge. Both could be more thrilling, and both could also bring families together during the wage earner's spare time. The central difference between the two was a matter of social class, since automobile owners tended to be very affluent at the beginning of the century and gradually less so as mass production reduced the price. But even as early as 1910 the Boston correspondent to the New York-based *Bonfort's Wine and Spirits Gazette* complained that an important reason for the dullness of the trade was "the automobile craze, which has induced people of large and medium means to invest and ride off into different parts of the country and scatter their spending money away from home. This may all come back some day through other channels, but for the time being it leaves many people short and unable to promptly meet their bills. What is now needed is for the masses of the people to resume their regular avocations, and normal conditions will soon be restored."[56] Not only did the auto steal customers from barrooms near parks and other leisure spots, but automobile commuting also reduced the patronage of

streetcar stops and transfer corners. By 1913 the rates of drunken driving were described as shocking, and saloon journals found another
reason to condemn the automobile.[57]

While the horseless carriage eliminated a portion of the middle-class
patronage, the nickelodeon posed a more serious threat because of its
wide social appeal. The automobile was a private space that isolated its
riders from others on the street or on mass transit, but the movie theater was as much a semipublic place as the saloon. Both appealed to
casual passersby, with nickelodeons frequently employing "ropers" to
lure in customers. But at a time when saloons were losing popularity,
the movie houses were enjoying their most spectacular growth. From a
handful of converted storefronts in 1900, eight years later the number
of theaters had grown to eighty-eight in Boston and 320 in Chicago.
Saloon journals agonized over the problem, cheered when antivice reformers attacked immoral films, and discussed ways to attract trade
back to the swinging doors. But a number of barkeeps joined the
enemy, some buying nickelodeons in adjoining buildings so that they
could watch both enterprises. One Chicago survey taken in 1910 indicated that, except for clerks and salesmen, saloonkeeping constituted
the largest occupational group of those entering the theater business.[58]

In Boston the increasing demand for licenses for movie theaters became a replacement for the saloon licensing power that the mayor had
lost years earlier. When James Michael Curley held office, there were
constant complaints about graft; those who had found a building and
set up the seats and projector often discovered that an extra payment
was necessary to secure a license. There were also charges that politicians distributed the permits as favors. And, finally, Curley alienated
residents of Dorchester, Roxbury, and East Boston by allowing theaters
to open over the objections of those who equated movie audiences with
saloon patrons.[59]

The decline of the saloon was not entirely the result of outside competition. Changes within the retail liquor business were also responsible
for transforming the weakened remnant of public drinking institutions.
In a desperate effort to adapt to new demands and survive, many saloons turned into cabarets or cleared tables to create dance floors. The
cabaret was both a tradition and a fad. Its roots went back to the old
music halls of the 1880s and to the dance halls that had become popular
just after the turn of the century. Yet the word *cabaret* and its unique
internal arrangement arrived in Chicago early in 1913, and within

months hundreds of saloons added live entertainment on small stages. There was a sudden demand for chairs and tables, and a few places even tore out the bar if it got in the way.[60]

The Windy City's antivice reformers were upset with the cabaret. Sensuous dances, torrid songs, and revealing costumes seemed fraught with moral danger, while the innovation of having the entertainer, usually a woman, mingling with the crowd while performing seemed little more than indoor streetwalking. Finally, the cabaret also introduced public dancing among patrons who were often perfect strangers. Even the one-night bar permits provided at least a semblance of a private group. The dancing was an excellent cover for solicitation, while the sudden demand for singers made it easy for panders to travel the neighborhoods as "theatrical agents," while actually recruiting future prostitutes. And because the cabaret was patronized more freely by women than the saloon had been, it was harder for the police to detect assignation. Finally, the table system made violations of the closing hour ordinance easier, because crafty proprietors concealed ice buckets and bottles under the tablecloths to keep drinkers supplied for hours after closing.[61]

Antivice groups, led by the Juvenile Protective Association and the Chicago Law and Order League, urged immediate regulation, and on July 30, 1913, the City Council complied. Reportedly, the United Societies helped draft the law to avoid any conflict with the special permit statute, and the legislation ordered entertainers up on a stage, outlawed tights, and ended "public dancing." The Drake Hotel, however, was so angered when police threatened to arrest its wealthy patrons who wanted to dance that it challenged the city law. In 1916 the Illinois Supreme Court found the city law unconstitutional. Because the hotel had not charged admission, its dance floor was more public than private and was therefore exempt from amusement licensing of any type.[62]

While the cabaret was generating controversy in Chicago, Boston's strict amusement law and limited number of barrooms kept the fad out of the Hub. But a few of the outlying dealers did introduce "bungalow dancing," much to the anger of neighbors. Mayor Curley stepped in, using his license power over entertainments, and closed down several places. Then he also tried to apply the same rule to posh hotels. During 1914 the "dinner dance" became very popular among the affluent. Couples would stroll from their tables to the dance area, most quite unaware that they were violating a law because they were eating and drinking alcohol in the same room with live music and dancing. Curley threatened to shut down the American and the Copley Plaza, which he denounced as little better "than a South End dance hall." When the license board realized that the mayor was trying to usurp their powers, they ordered immediate enforcement of the ban. Soon, however, "the better class of hotels," as the press called them, applied pressure, and the board allowed the dinner dance to return. Curley also compromised by requiring all such festivities to end at 2:00 A.M., unless the dancers had been issued formal invitations.[63]

While drinking at home, Sunday motoring, and the movies represented a rejection of the saloon, the cabaret and dinner dance indicated an attempt on the part of the liquor trade to adjust to changing society. This upset old-timers and purists, who also complained about a distressing trend toward impersonality and greed that had infected many of the surviving saloons. The new "candied" mixed drinks, for instance, masked the taste of the whiskey so that the quality of the ingredients was no longer as important. Haste and efficiency seemed to be displacing sociability. When a bartending school opened in Chicago in 1913, it stressed that it would teach "economy . . . language, cleanliness and the mixing of all drinks correctly." The *Champion of Fair Play* scoffed at the idea, but another trade journal, *Bar and Buffet*, quietly advised that the image of the business was now of crucial importance; neatness and courtesy, along with advertising, might prevent prohibition.[64]

Drury Underwood, a columnist in the *Champion*, remembered the portly barkeep of old, never rushed and more concerned with "the prestige of his trade rather than the volume of it." Writing in 1915, he noted:

> Drinking . . . had little of the hurrah in it. There was far less haste and none of the stuffing of the pockets at the behest of some newly dilated buyer. . . . The waiters were men of fifty or more; some of the bartenders were grandfathers. There was a discreet piece of cheese, a cracker or an olive for consumption upon exit. . . .
>
> The old bartender . . . was bound to pass just as surely as the trade was to crumble before modern notions. Somebody discovered, for instance, that for the attraction of the younger dollars there was an appeal in gaudy food. Another man came along with the mechanical banjo and another with a metallic piano that gorged itself in nickels.

All this was revolutionary. Horseshoe mustaches began to unfurl
and ruby fronts to become pallid. Portly persons shrank. Some of
the old-time barkeeps progressed into proprietorships, but the majority slipped into county or city jobs or passed as the cab horse has
faded into the glare of the taxi.[65]

Rumor and the growing consciousness of hygiene among the citizenry also generated distrust of the venerable saloon. In Boston the question was the purity of the whiskey served across the bar. Adulteration
was an old issue that had surfaced every few decades. Dishonest barkeeps laced their barrel stock with water, prune juice, and brown sugar
to alter its flavor and stretch a few more shots from the stock. Passage
of the federal pure food and drug act started the rumors anew, and by
1914 claims that Boston saloon whiskey was unsafe had reached the
point that the General Court had to reestablish public confidence by
making the state health board responsible for the quality of liquor consumed in the Commonwealth. Meanwhile, wholesale dealers escaped
the problem because the sealed bottles they delivered had been filled at
the distillery.[66]

In Chicago the main issue was the free lunch. For decades this venerable institution had been unpopular for economic reasons. Restaurant
owners had lobbied since 1903 for an end to the competition, while the
Chicago Liquor Dealers' Association polled its members and learned
that they were overwhelmingly in favor of shutting down the sideboard. But those who thought the free lunch was good publicity for the
bar trade had blocked attempts to legislate it out of existence. After
1910, however, sanitary conditions became the main issue. Since 1900
the dealers' groups had promoted a voluntary cleanup of foul smelling
iceboxes, dirty mustache towels, and even the brass footrails that
trapped manure tracked in from the street. But other problems seemed
unavoidable because of the public nature of the saloon. The swinging
doors allowed free access to flies as well as patrons, while the heavy use
of the restroom created another cleanliness problem. Then, during
1910 stories began to circulate around Chicago that the lunch plates
contained horsemeat or spoiled beef that was highly seasoned to kill the
bad taste. Dirty serving forks and flies were reportedly spreading
disease on the uncovered food. Finally, the aldermen began listening to
the city's health commissioner, who recommended a series of reforms.
Glass domes began to appear on the serving tables, and the common
fork disappeared along with the mustache towel. Inspectors also closed

places that did not change the water used to rinse glasses and ordered that toilet vents be changed to open into the street rather than the barroom.[67]

By 1917 the free lunch was widely viewed as an anachronism. Various dealers' associations asked members to cease the spread, and stink bombs sailed through the windows of intransigents. But it was the high cost of bread during wartime and food conservation programs that convinced the Chicago City Council to go along with the ban. Although cleanliness rumors had not been a significant factor in Boston, its city officials also ordered a halt to the free food to preserve supplies for the defense effort.[68]

The most important symptom of the decline of the saloon was, of course, the economic health of the business. During the long, downhill slide after 1910 conditions became difficult in Boston. Winters that were supposed to bring higher whiskey consumption became so severe that barroom traffic dwindled. Hot summers only intensified the growing popularity of beer instead of hard liquor. Since the brewery product produced somewhat lower profit, retail outlets began to feel the pinch. The disruptions caused by the European war not only made it difficult to secure imported liquor, but talk of American involvement reportedly increased religious activity among Bostonians, who then reduced their drinking. As a result of declining sales, retailers allowed their stock to dwindle in order to minimize their investment, while wholesalers and brewers tightened their credit arrangements. The number of court cases between suppliers and sellers rose steadily.[69]

But Boston was not Chicago. The limited number of licenses in the Hub and the tradition of only moderate competition among brewers kept the decline gradual. The only casualty among the beer makers was the Kinney Brewing Company, which closed in 1918. The other major indicators of trade conditions showed no precipitous fall: Boston licensees rarely appeared in lists of bankruptcies in trade journals, and the premium value of the Boston license paper remained stable. The business was troubled, but the close tie between retailing and wholesaling allowed increases in the latter to absorb much of the slack.[70]

In the Windy City, however, the ravages of change took their greatest toll. Between 1910 and 1917 six major brewers folded, and the leaders of two of them, W. C. Seipp and Otto Tosetti, committed suicide. Two of the big syndicates, the Chicago Brewing and Malting Company and the City of Chicago Brewing Company, had required reorganiza-

tion by 1916. The lists of closings in *Mida's Criterion* and other wholesale journals began to include scores of Chicago saloons after 1914,
while the license premium fell from a peak of $2,800 to $1,400 in a year
and disappeared completely by 1915.

Retailers were openly depressed about the future. Their organizations seemed powerless. Of the 664 victuallers and innkeepers in Boston, only 238 belonged to the Massachusetts Liquor League. Chicago
groups were rent by the old disunity among ethnic groups and between
large downtown dealers and those in the neighborhoods. The ranks of
local groups began to dwindle, and reductions in initiation fees and
dues failed to attract new members. Perhaps the most telling sign of the
loss of optimism was the legislative drive for government compensation
when businesses were forced out by prohibition or restrictive laws.
Since 1912 Illinois dealer groups, with the blessing of the United States
Brewers' Association, had argued that when government outlawed or
crippled a business, the owners had a right to reimbursement. Those
efforts failed, and hundreds of proprietors saw their investments shrink
in value.[71]

The World War

The traumatic final turning point in the history of the saloon was, of
course, World War I. But barkeeps in both cities sampled what the
future would be like long before American troops were mobilized. The
federal tax on barrelage, enacted in 1915, brought open conflict between dealers and suppliers. This was especially true in Chicago,
where wholesalers raised the price. Tied houses had little choice except
to pay, while smaller independents suffered because their profit margins were so small. Their Boston counterparts were more fortunate,
because the higher wholesale price made Hub brewers more willing to
share the burden. The Bunker Hill Brewery, in fact, took out an ad in
the *North American Wine and Spirits Review* sympathizing with the
hard-pressed Chicago retailers. A few dealers in the latter city also
failed to pay a special tax on wine and cordials, leading to a series of
raids during the fall of 1915.[72]

The controversy over aliens and German nationalism had also been
debated for nearly a decade in Chicago. Back in 1908 parades and petitions had attempted to close the Sunday saloon through a referendum.
When that failed, temperance lawyers managed to convince several

judges that a violation of the closing law, even if not proven in court, still constituted enough of a crime to prevent an applicant from completing the naturalization process. The courts upheld the principle, and hundreds of men rushed to become citizens, lest they find themselves trapped. In Boston, meanwhile, that problem did not arise, since proof of citizenship was necessary in order to obtain a saloon license.[73]

By the time of the outbreak of the European war in 1914, many liquor dealers and their associations were striving to create an image of neutrality. That was often difficult to do, with the headquarters of the National German-American Alliance located in Chicago's Schiller Building. Its press releases tied German nationalism directly to the antiprohibition movement, while the United States Brewers' Association supplied the alliance with funds. Percy Andrae of Chicago served as chief publicist for both groups. But, nonetheless, fancy restaurants and barrooms removed the German, French, and Russian names from menus, while the bartenders' union in Chicago conducted an antialien crusade. Noting that 5,000 of the 14,000 servers in the city were not citizens, union officials reminded them that they could not vote against prohibition and that their foreignisms did not create a good image for the trade.[74]

As American involvement became a possibility, liquor dealers grumbled that "preparedness" was actually a front for prohibition. But after the United States mobilized and declared war, saloonmen became as visibly patriotic as possible. German and foreign names disappeared from hundreds of barrooms, while ethnic dealers' organizations became merely "locals" of the city association or adopted neighborhood names. War posters filled windows and flags draped the entranceways. Saloonkeepers in Massachusetts contributed over $1.5 million in Liberty Bonds and chided the Anti-Saloon League for moving its fundraising effort to an earlier date in a selfish attempt to grab donations before the defense drive got under way. Chicago brewer Peter Theurer chaired one local bond campaign, while John Cervenka of the United Societies served as an auctioneer at one benefit.[75]

While Chicago bars became the target of some anti-German hostility, the actions of the city's mayor contributed to the problem. This was especially ironic, given the liquor dealers' hostility toward him. William Hale Thompson not only refused to welcome the French and British missions to the United States, but his refusal to support the Liberty Loan effort earned him the nickname "Kaiser Bill." When he failed to function in his mayoral capacity as local registration and draft chairman, the War Department named Governor Frank Lowden in his place. The antics of Thompson angered many dealers, who saw their patriotism tarnished by a non-German.[76]

The war affected the saloon business in less direct ways as well. By December 1917 the federal fuel administration had ordered schools, libraries, and other public facilities to shorten their hours and lower their temperatures to conserve coal. Saloons and other privately owned places were exempted from the order. Temperance interests complained, and by the end of the year the Boston license board and the Massachusetts Liquor League had asked saloonmen for voluntary compliance. Early in 1918 the Boston fuel committee, under the direction of James Storrow, ordered the bars to close at 7:00 P.M. Even this was not enough to satisfy antisaloonists, who demanded a halt to all bars and breweries. The Boston school committee and the United Improvement Association wanted saloons shuttered at sundown. Although that extreme measure never was enacted, Storrow did order saloons, nickelodeons, and other "nonessential" services to shut down on Mondays. Similar restrictions in Chicago left bartenders and customers in coats and gloves, pouring and consuming drinks in near darkness.[77]

Wartime also meant the induction of tens of thousands of young men and a growing concern over their moral well-being. With the antivice sentiment still alive and liquor sales on military bases still prohibited, attention focused on what the young men did in nearby towns and in the major cities during leaves. With the passage of the selective draft act in 1917 the president and the secretary of war gained new powers. Soon, orders went out to close bawdy houses near military installations and all bars within half a mile of urban bases and five miles of rural bases. All consumption of alcohol "except [by] civilians in private homes" was forbidden. Soon, the loose definition of *private* prompted a new order suppressing all drinking by the military, even in homes.[78]

Most legitimate saloons had little trouble complying. The Boston license board could report few instances of liquor sales to men in uniform. There were some illegal bottle sales, but nothing serious. The only genuine hardship was suffered by dealers who were forced to close because they were too close to the Boston Navy Yard. Similarly, the only civilians inconvenienced by the rules were residents of cities near Fort Sheridan and the Great Lakes Naval Training Station. For several months during 1918 federal officials prohibited the delivery of bottle goods to their homes.[79]

Some of the less respectable barrooms and dance halls, however, could not resist attracting clientele from the military. On their nightly rounds inspectors from the Committee of Fifteen spotted many soldiers and sailors drinking, while some prostitutes stationed themselves near train stations, parks, or other places where men on leave gathered. The ultrapatriotic and antiimmigrant group, the American Protective League, sent its agents in pursuit of illegal sales. The dealers' associations, meanwhile, reminded members that the draft card was the easiest way to tell the age and military status of a potential customer.[80]

Predictably, prohibitionists used the war as a tool against the saloon. With worldwide economic dislocation came food shortages in Europe and the call for Americans to conserve grain at home. Viewed as a nonnecessity, alcoholic beverages became a vulnerable target. The inevitable came in the food control bill of 1917. As initially proposed, it would have outlawed the manufacture of all fermented or distilled liquors except those used for scientific, sacramental, or medicinal purposes. The threat of a filibuster resulted in a compromise shutting off the manufacture or importation of hard liquor but giving the president the power to reduce the alcoholic content of beer. Woodrow Wilson exercised that option during the fall of 1917. Meanwhile, as the state legislatures pondered the national prohibition amendment, dry interests in the Congress pushed through a wartime prohibition bill that passed both houses on November 21, 1918. The new legislation was designed to go into effect the following year, but only nine days after its passage the federal food administration exercised authority granted by another law and ordered a halt to brewing. Soon, however, the maneuvering and appeals to the public to preserve "personal liberty" were meaningless. On January 6, 1919, the thirty-sixth state ratified the Nineteenth Amendment. The whole world knew that on one year from that date, all of America would become prohibition territory.[81]

The national amendment and the Volstead Act meant that the manufacture, sale, and transportation of liquors would be outlawed, but the provisions of the wartime prohibition law moved the date of the last legal retail sale back to June 30, 1919. It was an act of cruelty. Not only was the war, in effect, over, but with the saloons already doomed, it merely deprived them of their last six months of business.

President Wilson's decision to allow 2¾ percent beer did little to appease the angry dealers. Their license premiums, which represented their life's savings for many, and their fixtures were worthless. The real estate industry braced for a sharp increase in the amount of rental property on the market, while only the slow demise of the barroom eased municipalities into a saloonless fiscal system.[82]

The last few weeks were sheer agony. The head of Boston's bartenders' union confidently predicted that the 2,100 Hub servers would have little trouble finding employment as salesmen. Those who were less optimistic posted signs reading, "Don't Ask Us What We Are Going To Do After July." For days, auctioneers gaveled off the stock of wholesalers. By June 22, George F. Monahan's place was so crowded that the police had to be called to untangle the crush; another dealer sold $15,000 worth in a single afternoon. Prices fluctuated wildly, some buyers convinced that they had to fill their cellars to last a lifetime. At other times, bidders realized that vast quantities were available and kept the prices low.[83]

The only hope rested with Woodrow Wilson. He retained the power to revoke the wartime prohibition law, and with victory so near, optimists were sure that he would grant a reprieve. When a few dealers took out the next year's license in Boston, there was a stampede at the license board office. In Chicago, the City Council had done the saloonkeepers a special favor by establishing the next official license period as only two months. When, at the last minute, Alderman Anton Cermak discovered that, should Wilson change his mind, there would be no legally licensed saloons after June 30, the leader of the wets pushed a special extension ordinance through the City Council. The new law would also allow the sale of near beer.[84]

But Wilson disappointed them all. When it became obvious that the end was near, a strange mixture of revelry and melancholy settled over the last night crowds. Celebrants jammed every place that accepted reservations, such Chicago beer gardens as the Green Mill, the Marigold Room, the Sheridan Inn and the Rainbow, and the downtown hotels. The same was true in Boston, where the Copley Plaza and the Parker House were filled beyond capacity. They drank toasts, sang sad songs, and, a few minutes before midnight, they said farewell. Although similar scenes would be repeated the night of January 5, 1920, the latter celebrants had to bring their own bottles. This fond wake of July 5 represented the end of the saloon as an American institution, the temporary demise of public drinking. Those who alternately cheered and wept that warm summer night realized what they were losing. After they left and the empty barrooms were left to echoes until other uses could be found for them, all over Boston and Chicago and hundreds of other places proprietors turned out the lights and locked the entrance. The swinging doors were closed forever.

Comments on Primary Sources

This work was assembled from literally thousands of small sources rather than from a few large manuscript collections. Because of space limitations, the following notes include only the most important references. Those who desire fuller documentation should consult my Ph.D. dissertation, "The Saloon and the Public City: Chicago and Boston, 1880–1920" (University of Chicago, 1975), available on microfilm.

Manuscripts. There are few relevant collections that deal directly with liquor. The papers of the Committee of Fifteen and the Anti-Saloon League of Illinois at the University of Chicago Library, the Charles Schaffner and Hyde Park Protective Association collections at the Chicago Historical Society, and the Anti-Saloon League of America Collections at the Ohio Historical Society are the most useful. Settlement house papers are rich in neighborhood observations. Collections at the Houghton Library at Harvard University, the Schlesinger Library at Radcliffe College, the State Historical Society of Wisconsin, and several Chicago area institutions are too numerous to mention specifically. The Stephen O'Meara papers at the Boston Public Library proved to be a small but useful find, while the turn-of-the-century seminar papers and a few early student theses preserved at Northwestern University are little-used gems.

Trade Publications. Industry and retail liquor trade journals were a critical source, especially on the economic health and legal battles of saloonkeeping. The fact that many libraries found the subject matter a bit tawdry and tossed out what they had when Prohibition arrived in 1920 has left a legacy of frustration and travel for the contemporary scholar. The Library of Congress, Cincinnati Public Library, and Ohio Historical Society maintain the best files of such journals as *Champion of Fair Play, Fair Play, Bar and Buffet, American Brewers' Review, Mida's Criterion, Liquor Trades Review, New England Trader,* and

Western Brewer. Temperance and prohibition publications, on the other hand, were much less useful.

Newspapers. While papers cannot always be accepted uncritically, the local press in both cities was an especially useful tool in understanding the saloon in the urban context. A reading of the *Boston Evening Transcript, Boston Globe,* and *Chicago Tribune* during the time period of the study was time-consuming but worthwhile. The lack of decent newspaper indexes for both cities made comprehensive reading necessary, while a few scrapbooks — the large Ambler Collection at the Chicago Historical Society, for instance — supplemented the basic papers with stories from other newspapers. No current sociological theory imposed on the past can substitute for the sound base of information provided by the press. Constant reference to the public nature of the saloon provided one of the inspirations for the public-private interpretation contained in this book.

Government and Court Documents. The other major source of the public space idea was the frequency with which the word *public* appeared in liquor law. Trial transcripts from lower courts, deposited as part of the record at the two state supreme courts, were a critical source of fact as well as argument. When brewers and saloonkeepers sued each other, they both revealed details of their operations that were normally hidden from the public. Federal bankruptcy records and disputed election cases provided similar information.

Local government documents were much more useful in Boston, whose City Council *Proceedings* were not only verbatim but thoroughly indexed; city records in Chicago were, by contrast, disorganized.

Notes

ABBREVIATIONS

A. and R.	Acts and Resolves	C.R.-H.	Chicago Record-Herald
A.B.R.	American Brewers' Review	C.T.	Chicago Tribune
A.R.	Annual Report	C. Times	Chicago Times
B. and B.	Bar and Buffet	C.T.-H.	Chicago Times-Herald
B. Ad.	Boston Advertizer	F.P.	Fair Play
B. Am.	Boston American	H.C.S.	History of Chicago and Souvenir of the Liquor Interests
B.G.	Boston Globe		
B.J.	Boston Journal		
B.M.	Brewer and Maltster	H.P.P.A.	Hyde Park Protective Association
B.P.	Boston Post		
B.T.	Boston Transcript	L.O.	Law and Order
B.W.S.G.	Bonfort's Wine and Spirits Gazette	L.T.R.	Liquor Trades Review
		M.C.	Mida's Criterion
C.C.	Chicago Chronicle	M.D.	Mixed Drinks
C.D.D.	Chicago Daily Democrat	M.S.	Mixer and Server
		N.E.T.	New England Trader
C.D.N.	Chicago Daily News	N.Y.T.	New York Times
C.E.	Chicago Examiner	S.H.S.W.	State Historical Society of Wisconsin
C.F.P.	Champion of Fair Play		
		T.C.	Temperance Cause
C.H.	Chicago Herald	U.C.	The University of Chicago
C.H.S.	Chicago Historical Society		
		U.I.C.C.	University of Illinois at Chicago
C.I.-O.	Chicago Inter-Ocean		
C.J.	Chicago Journal	W.B.	Western Brewer
C.P.	Chicago Post		

INTRODUCTION

1. George Ade, *The Old-Time Saloon* (New York: Ray Long & Richard R. Smith, 1931).

2. Recent studies include Jack S. Blocker, Jr., *Retreat from Reform: The Prohibition Movement in the United States, 1890–1913* (Westport, Conn.: Greenwood Press, 1976); Lewis Gould, *Progressives and Prohibitionists: Texas Democrats in the Wilson Era* (Austin: University of Texas Press, 1973); Allan Everest, *Rum across the Border: The Prohibition Era in Northern New York* (Syracuse, N.Y.: Syracuse University Press, 1978). Excellent studies during the 1960s include Norman H. Clark, *The Dry Years: Prohibition and Social Change in Washington* (Seattle: University of Washington Press, 1965); Paul E. Isaac, *Prohibition and Politics: Turbulent Decades in Tennessee, 1885–1920* (Knoxville: University of Tennessee Press, 1965); C. C. Pearson and J. Edwin Henricks, *Liquor and Anti-Liquor in Virginia, 1619–1919* (Durham, N.C.: Duke University Press, 1967. The classic sources on the movement include Ernest Cherrington, *Standard Encyclopedia of the Liquor Problem*, 5 vols. (Westerville, Ohio: American Issue, 1926–29); George Faber Clark, *History of the Temperance Reform in Massachusetts, 1813–83* (Boston: Clarke & Carruth, 1888).

3. The reform studies that best indicate an understanding of the saloon are John D. Buenker, *Urban Liberalism and Progressive Reform* (New York: Charles Scribner's Sons, 1973) and James Timberlake, *Prohibition and the Progressive Movement, 1900–1920* (Cambridge: Harvard University Press, 1963).

4. Jon Kingsdale, "The Poor Man's Club: Social Functions of the Urban Working-Class Saloon," *American Quarterly* 25(Oct., 1973): 472–89, forces the findings of a turn-of-the-century saloon investigation into an interpretive scheme taken from Ned Polsky, *Hustlers, Beats, and Others* (Chicago: Aldine, [1967]).

5. Sherri Cavan, *Liquor License: An Ethnology of Bar Behavior* (Chicago: Aldine, 1966); Howard Bahr and Theodore Caplow, *Old Men Drunk and Sober* (New York: New York University Press, 1973); E. E. LeMasters, *Blue-Collar Aristocrats* (Madison: University of Wisconsin Press, 1975); Francis Snider, "The Neighborhood Tavern as a Social Institution" (M.A. thesis, University of Chicago, 1951). The study of alcoholism and its treatment is not included in this book, except for a discussion of dramshop and other sumptuary laws.

6. The literature on individual semipublic places is a mixed lot. The best includes Steven Riess, *Touching Base: Professional Baseball and American Culture in the Progressive Era* (Westport, Conn.: Greenwood Press, 1980), pp. 85–120; Robert Twyman, *History of Marshall Field & Co., 1852–1906* (Philadelphia: University of Pennsylvania Press, 1954); Lloyd Wendt and Herman Kogan, *Give the Lady What She Wants: The Story of Marshall Field & Company* (Chicago:

Rand McNally, 1952); Albert F. McLean, *American Vaudeville as Ritual* (Lexington: University of Kentucky Press, 1965). General studies of such spaces include Gunther Barth, *City People: The Rise of Modern City Culture in Nineteenth Century America* (New York: Oxford University Press, 1980), which ignores differences between cities. See also Perry Duis, "The Saloon and the Public City," pp. 8–174, on public and semipublic spaces, and Burton J. Bledstein, *The Culture of Professionalism* (New York: W. W. Norton, 1976), pp. 53–65.

7. Department store novels include Rupert Hughes, *Miss 318 and Mr. 37* (New York: Fleming H. Revell, 1912). Barth, *City People*, has as its central theme the idea that such institutions helped assimilate immigrants and lessen class tensions.

8. James P. Sizer, *The Commercialization of Leisure* (Boston: R. G. Badger, 1917).

9. Duis, "The Saloon and the Public City," pp. 165–70.

10. Allan H. Spear, *Black Chicago: The Making of a Negro Ghetto, 1890–1920* (Chicago: University of Chicago Press, 1967), pp. 29–49; John Daniels, *In Freedom's Birthplace: The Study of the Boston Negroes* (Boston: Houghton Mifflin, 1914), pp. 106–33.

11. Andrew King, "Law and Land Use in Chicago: A Prehistory of Modern Zoning," (Ph.D. diss., University of Wisconsin-Madison, 1976).

12. Elliott West, *The Saloon on the Rocky Mountain Mining Frontier* (Lincoln: University of Nebraska Press, 1979); Larry Engelmann, *Intemperance: The Lost War vs. Liquor* (New York: Free Press, [1976]), which is largely based on the Michigan experience. See also the southern studies cited in n. 2.

13. Barth, *City People*.

14. Edward Hungerford, *The Personality of American Cities* (New York: McBride, Nast, 1913), pp. 1–17.

15. Harriet Ropes Cabot, conversation with author, Boston, Ja., 1970.

16. Lloyd Lewis and Henry Justin Smith, *Chicago: The History of Its Reputation* (New York: Harcourt, Brace, 1929).

17. David Ward, "Nineteenth Century Boston: A Study in the Role of Antecedent and Adjacent Conditions in the Spatial Aspects of Urban Growth," (Ph.D. diss., University of Wisconsion, 1963), pp. 159–75.

18. Ethnic differences detailed in chapter 5, below.

19. John Sanders, *The Education of an Urban Minority: Catholics in Chicago, 1833–1965* (New York: Oxford University Press, 1977), pp. 24–25, 42; Charles Shanabruch, "The Catholic Church's Role in the Americanization of Chicago's Immigrants, 1833–1928" (Ph.D. diss., University of Chicago, 1975), chapters 1 and 4.

20. Barbara Solomon, *Ancestors and Immigrants: A Changing New England Tradition* (Cambridge: Harvard University Press, 1956).

21. Hungerford, *Personality*, p. 1.

22. Ian R. Tyrrell, *Sobering Up: From Temperance to Prohibition in Antebellum America, 1800–1860* (Westport, Conn.: Greenwood Press, 1979), p. 22; Alice Morse Earle, *Stage-Coach and Tavern Days* (New York: Macmillan, 1901), pp. 10–11, 17–19; Elise Lathrop, *Early American Inns and Taverns* (New York: Tudor, 1935), pp. 77–90. William W. Woolen and W. W. Thornton, *Intoxicating Liquors: The Law Relating to the Traffic in Intoxicating Liquors and Drunkenness*, 2 vols. (Cincinnati: W. H. Anderson, 1910), and Frederic A. Johnson and Ruth R. Kessler, "The Liquor License System—Its Origin and Constitutional Development," *Contemporary Law Pamphlets* (New York: New York University School of Law, 1938), ser. 1, no. 6, both provide an excellent overview of American liquor law. Louis Epple, *Liquor Laws of Massachusetts and Digest of Cases Thereon* (Boston: City Printing Dept., 1912) and H. H. Faxon, *Laws of Massachusetts Relating to Intoxicating Liquor* (Boston: Faxon Political Temperance Bureau, 1908) guide the reader through the Bay State's liquor laws, but there are no parallel volumes for Illinois. A. Mathews, *Retail Liquor Dealers' Manual of the United States Internal Revenue Laws, Decisions, and Instructions*, rev. ed., (Omaha: n.p., 1902) is the best work on the minimal federal regulation.

23. Frederick Sawyer, *Hits at American Whims* (Boston: Walker, Wise, 1860), pp. 258–62; R. Vashon Rogers, *The Law of Hotel Life: or the Wrongs and Rights of Host and Guest* (San Francisco: Sumner, Whitney, 1879), pp. 8, 67; Woolen and Thornton, *Intoxicating Liquors*, 1:1148–54.

24. Nathaniel Shurtleff, ed., *Records of the Governor and Company of Massachusetts Bay*, 4 vols. (Boston: Press of William H. White, 1853), 1:100, 106, 213, 221, 258, 271; 2:100; 3:245; 4:463; Gallus Thomann, *Colonial Liquor Laws* (New York: United States Brewers' Association, 1887), pp. 6, 7, 8, 10, 13, 19, 27–29; *Charters and General Laws of the Colony and Province of Massachusetts* (Boston: T. B. Wait, 1814), pp. 314–18; Wendell D. Howie, *Three Hundred Years of the Liquor Problem in Massachusetts*, Appendix B, Mass. House Doc. 1300, 1933, pp. 1–111; Henry B. Parkes, "Morals and Law Enforcement in Colonial New England," *New England Quarterly* 5 (July, 1932):448–50.

25. Paton Yoder, *Taverns and Travelers: Inns of the Early Midwest* (Bloomington: Indiana University Press, 1969), pp. 13–14; Bessie Louise Pierce, *A History of Chicago*, 3 vols. (New York: Alfred A. Knopf, 1937, 1940, 1957), 1:34, 49–50; *History of Chicago and Souvenir of the Liquor Interests* (Chicago: Belgravia, 1891), pp. 88–98.

26. Mass. *A and R., 1786*, ch. 68; Ibid., *1832*, ch. 166; Ibid., *1837*, ch. 242. (See Abbreviations). Cherrington, *Standard Encyclopedia*, 1:373–75, 4:1710–12; Oscar Handlin, *Boston's Immigrants*, rev. ed. (Cambridge: Harvard University Press, 1959), pp. 65–66.

27. *C.D.D.*, Oct. 9, 1849 (see Abbreviations); *Chicago Literary Budget* 4(Jan. 27, 1855):1; *Hall's Business Directory of Chicago* (Chicago: Hall, 1856), pp. 47, 67–69.

28. Cherrington, *Standard Encyclopedia*, 4:1714; Howie, *Three Hundred Years*, pp. 122–35.

29. Ibid., pp. 136–46; *Reports on the Subject of a License Law*, Mass. House Doc. 415, 1867, p. 3.

30. Theodore Voelckers, *Suggestions for a Law to Regulate the Sale of Spiritous and Malt Liquors* (Boston: Rockwell & Vollins, 1867), pp. 1–10; Mass. *A. and R.*, *1840*, ch. 1; Ibid., *1852*, ch. 322; Ibid., *1868*, ch. 141; Ibid., *1869*, ch. 191; Ibid., *1875*, ch. 99; Howie, *Three Hundred Years*, pp. 147–202.

31. *Reports on the Subject of a License Law*, especially the 900-page appendix, contains a wide spectrum of views.

32. Herbert Wiltsee, "The Temperance Movement, 1848–71," *Papers of the Illinois State Historical Society, 1937* (Springfield: Illinois State Historical Society, 1937) pp. 82–92; *H.C.S.*, pp. 98–102 (see Abbreviations); Pierce, *A History of Chicago*, 2:436–37; A. T. Andreas, *History of Chicago*, 3 vols. (Chicago: A. T. Andreas, 1884–86), 1:517–18.

33. Samuel E. Sparling, "Municipal History and Present Organization of the City of Chicago," *Bulletin of the University of Wisconsin*, 23(May, 1898):40–58; Pierce, *A History of Chicago*, 1:320–21, 3:319–20; the 1819 statute is in Illinois, *Revised Laws, 1833*, p. 595; Illinois, *Laws of 1823*, p. 148; Ibid., *1835*, p. 154; Ibid., *1839*, p. 71; Ibid., *1841*, p. 178.

34. Sparling, "Municipal History," pp. 40–58.

35. Roger Lane, *Policing the City* (Cambridge: Harvard University Press, 1967), pp. 87–90, 164, 212–13, 216–17; Solomon, *Ancestors and Immigrants*, pp. 48, 53; John Koren, *Boston, 1822 to 1922* (Boston: City Printing Dept., 1923), pp. 47–48; *W.B.* 9(Apr. 26, 1884):1024; *B.T.*, Sept. 16, 1884, Jan. 30, Feb. 3, 24, Mar. 12, 16, 1885 (see Abbreviations); Clement M. Sites, *Centralized Administration of Liquor Laws in the United States* (New York: Macmillan, 1899) pp. 48–49, 81.

36. Mass. *A. and R.*, *1880*, ch. 239, par. 2; Ibid., *1881*, ch. 225; *B.T.*, July 21, 1880, May 27, Sept. 28, Jan. 18, June 29, Aug. 19, 1885, Feb. 17, 1886; *W.B.* 6(May 15, 1881): 576.

CHAPTER 1

1. There are no comprehensive studies of the history of the American brewing industry as a whole. Thomas Cochran's history of Pabst is the best, but it covers the activities of only one company (note 11, below). W. J. Rorabaugh, *The Alcoholic Republic* (New York: Oxford University Press, 1979), pp. 106–10, 173–76, discusses beer as part of

America's enormous thirst for alcohol before 1840. A standard source remains *One Hundred Years of Brewing: Supplement to the "Western Brewer"* (Chicago: H. S. Rich, 1903), pp. 191, 197.

2. American Brewing Academy of Chicago, *Tenth Anniversary Reunion* (Chicago: Blakeley, 1901), p. 119.

3. E. M. Bacon, *King's Dictionary of Boston* (Boston: Moses King, 1883), pp. 140–41.

4. *One Hundred Years of Brewing*, pp. 207–9, 310–11.

5. Ibid.

6. [Paul Angle], "Michael Diversy and Beer in Chicago," *Chicago History* 8(Spring, 1969):321–26.

7. *A Business Tour of Chicago* (Chicago: E. E. Barton, 1887), p. 160.

8. *Der Westen* (Sunday ed., *Illinois Staats-Zeitung*), June 20, 1875, June 2, 1880; *W.B.* 3(Sept. 15, 1878):588.

9. *One Hundred Years of Brewing*, pp. 488, 497, 498, 501; *W.B.* 2(Dec. 15, 1877):514, 2(June 15, 1878):433; *The Economist* 6(July 11, 1891):62; on Boston, see *W.B.* 1(Aug. 15, 1876):5–7, 1(Sept. 15, 1876):29, 2(Sept. 15, 1877):337, 12(July 15, 1887):1474, 12(Oct. 15, 1887):2172.

10. *Smith and DuMoulin's Chicago Business Directory, 1859* (Chicago: Smith and DuMoulin, 1859), p. 19; *C.T.*, Jan. 1, 1880, May 25, 1896.

11. *W.B.* 1(Oct. 15, 1876):66–67, 2(May 15, 1877):152, 2(June 15, 1877):202; Jonathan Land, *Chicago: Trade, Commerce and Industry* (Chicago: J. Land, 1883), pp. 84, 96, 100; Thomas Cochran, *The Pabst Brewing Company: The History of an American Business* (New York: New York University Press, 1948), pp. 31, 79, 80, 237; Stanley Baron, *Brewed in America: A History of Beer and Ale in the United States* (Boston: Little, Brown, 1962).

12. Cochran, *Pabst*, pp. 77–79; *W.B.* 2(Apr. 15, 1877):94, 4(Apr. 15, 1879):311; David Choate, *The Refrigeration Industry* (Boston: Bellman, 1946), p. 10; Ronald Plavchan, "A History of Anheuser-Busch," (Ph.D. diss., St. Louis University, 1969), pp. 55–60.

13. *B.T.*, May 17, 1883, Aug. 9, 1884; *P.G.* 2(Nov. 28, 1886):1; *B.G.*, May 29, 1901; *M.C.* 18(Nov. 1, 1902):51, 28(May 16, 1912):63.

14. Cochran, *Pabst*, p. 146; *W.B.* 2(Aug. 15, 1871):303; *Illinois Staats-Zeitung*, June 2, 1880; *C.T.* Apr. 10, May 2, 1880.

15. *C.T.*, May 1, 2, 1880, Jan. 5, 1883; *Der Westen*, Aug. 10, 1879.

16. *C.T.*, May 2, 1880.

17. Ibid., June 2, 1901; *W.B.* 6(June 15, 1881):712.

18. *C.T.*, Jan. 1, 1883; *W.B.* 8(Jan. 15, 1883):91–92; Ibid., 8(Apr. 15, 1883):667; Herman Schluter, *The Brewing Industry and the Brewery Workers' Movement* (Cincinnati: International Union of United Brewery Workmen of America, 1910), pp. 95–204.

19. *C.T.*, Jan. 1, 1883.

20. *M.C.* 2(July 8, 1886):1.

21. Cochran, *Pabst*, pp. 139, 142; *C.F.P.* 29(Dec. 22, 1906):1.

22. *C.T.*, Jan. 25, 1880; *W.B.* 3(Dec. 15, 1878):838.

23. *M.C.* 3(Oct. 15, 1887):8; Cochran, *Pabst*, p. 139; Plavchan, "Anheuser-Busch," pp. 92–96; *L.T.R.* 6(Feb. 7, 1899):12.

24. *C.T.*, Apr. 4, 1880; F. E. Coyne, *In Reminiscence* (Chicago: privately printed, 1941), pp. 31–36.

25. *W.B.* 2(June 15, 1877):202, 6(June 15, 1881):703; *L.T.R.* 5(July 12, 1898):6, 5(Aug. 23, 1898):13; *M.C.* 20(June 1, 1904):81, 89; *B.A.B.* 1(Aug., 1906):6, 7, 19.

26. *W.B.* 4(Dec. 15, 1879):1084.

27. Plavchan, "Anheuser-Busch," p. 35; Gerald Holland, "The King of Beer," *American Mercury* 18(Oct., 1929):172–73.

28. Illinois Appellate Court, First District, Abstract of Record, *Phil J. Sommer v. Gottfried Brewing Company*, Oct. term, 1909.

29. *W.B.* 5(Jan. 15, 1880):84; *M.C.* 2(June 21, 1886):1.

30. *C.T.*, July 28, 1883.

31. Letter dated July, 1879, quoted in Cochran, *Pabst*, pp. 142–43.

32. John Vaizey, *The Brewing Industry, 1886–1951: An Economic Study* (London: Sir Isaac Pitman & Sons, 1960), pp. 6–7, 9–12, and Peter Mathias, *The Brewing Industry in England* (Cambridge: Cambridge University Press, 1959), pp. 117–38, are the best of several studies.

33. *Smith and DuMoulin's Chicago Business Directory, 1859*, p. 130.

34. *W.B.* 5(Jan. 15, 1880):46, 8(Oct. 15, 1883):1803; *C.D.N.*, Jan. 14, 1884; United States Commissioner of Labor, *Economic Aspects of the Liquor Problem*, 12th Annual Report, 1893, p. 86; W. S. Asher, "The Norwegian System in Chicago," Seminar in Political Science, Contributions, III, 1895, Northwestern University, p. 2.

35. *Eric Anderson v. South Chicago Brewing Company*, 173 Ill.213(1898).

36. Transcript of Record, p. 28, *Anheuser-Busch v. Fred Rahlf*, 213 Ill. 549 (1905), Illinois State Archives.

37. Woolen and Thornton, *Intoxicating Liquors*, 2:1815–18.

38. *B.T.*, Mar. 1, 20, 31, June 20, 1883; Citizens' Law and Order League of Massachusetts, *A.R., 1884*, pp. 6–7; *C.T.*, Feb. 18, 1880, Sept. 11, 17, 18, 1881, Nov. 26, Dec. 3, 1882, Mar. 4, 1883; *The Curse of Chicago* (n.p., [1883]), *passim*, pamphlet at C.H.S.

39. *B.T.*, May 2, 1883, Feb. 12, 15, 20, Mar. 1, 1884, Jan. 21, 24, Mar. 3, 1885, Mar. 8, 1886; *B.G.* Apr. 6, 27, May 5, 1887; *N.E.T.* 1(Mar. 1, 1885):4–6; *The Public Good* 1(Dec. 31, 1885):4; *L.O.* 1(Jan.–June, 1885) and 2(Mar.–June, 1886) have many stories.

40. Cherrington, *Standard Encyclopedia*, 4:1541–47; *Illinois Staats-Zeitung*, Dec. 5, 1882; *C.T.*, Feb. 18, 20, 1880, Jan. 25, Apr. 2, Sept. 11, 16, Dec. 11, 1881, Jan. 21, 24, 28, Feb. 14, 19, Nov. 25,

1882, Jan. 13, 24, Feb. 1, 4, 9, 14, 15, 19, 20, 21, 22, 24, 1883; *W.B.* 8(Mar. 15, 1883):475.

41. *B.T.*, Feb. 21, 1884; *N.E.T.* 1(Mar. 15, 1884):4; *C.T.*, Feb. 26, 27, June 13, 22, 1880, Oct. 8, Dec. 17, 1881, Jan, 11, 13, 17, 18, Feb. 4, 7, 8, Dec. 3, 1882, Jan. 6, 7, 16, 23, 1883; H. H. Austin, "High License," *The Statesman* 3(July, 1888):307–16; *Cyclopedia of Temperance and Prohibition* (New York: Funk & Wagnalls, 1891), p. 215.

42. *C.T.*, June 10, 1883. See other Chicago papers, June 10–12, 1883. Frank McElwain, "The Saloon Question in Chicago from a Financial, Administrative and Political Standpoint," Seminar in Political Science, Contributions, III, 1895, Northwestern University, pp. 31–33.

43. *Abendpost*, July 8, 1891; *Chicago Daily Drovers Journal*, June 30, 1883.

44. John E. George, "The Saloon Problem in Chicago," *Economic Studies* 2(Apr., 1897):60–64; *C.F.P.* 28(June 24, 1905):4; *M.C.* 6(Dec. 31, 1890):21.

45. *Hannah and Hogg* (n.p., n.d.) pamphlet, C.H.S.; *Old Jim Gore* (Chicago: n.p., 1906); *M.C.* 18(Sept. 1, 1902):71.

46. Based on Boston Police Department, *A.R., 1875–85*; Boston, License Commissioners, *A.R., 1875–78*; Boston, Police Commissioners, *A.R., 1885–1900*.

47. *B.T.*, Apr. 18, May 4, 1882, Mar. 4, 1884, May 2, 9, 1888; *B.G.*, Mar. 30, Apr. 21, 1887, Feb. 28, May 2, 9, 1888; *N.E.T.* 1(Apr. 26, 1884):1; *W.B.* 13(June 15, 1888):1285; Mass. *A. and R., 1888*, ch. 340.

48. *B.G.*, May 1, 8, 1889; *M.C.* 5(May 16, 1889):12; Mass. *A. and R., 1899*, ch. 248; on Chicago, *M.C.* 2(Nov. 12, 1886):1.

49. Citizen's Law and Order League of Massachusetts, *A.R., 1890*, pp. 4–5.

50. Mass. *A. and R., 1897*, ch. 227; Ibid., *1902*, ch. 171; *M.C.* 11 (Mar. 16, 1895):49, 18(Apr. 16, 1901):85.

51. *M.C.* 9(June 16, 1893):20, 11(Mar. 16, 1895):49, 16(Oct. 1, 1900):40.

52. Massachusetts, Licensing Board for the City of Boston, *A.R., 1912*, pp. 8–11.

53. Bill of Exceptions of Lawrence J. Killian, *Harvard Brewing Company v. Lawrence J. Killian*, 222 Mass.13(1915), for example.

54. *B.G.* and other newspapers carried the advertisements regularly.

55. "A Retired Boston Merchant's Opinions," *B.W.S.G.* 71(Jan. 10, 1909):277–78; for biographies of prominent wholesalers, see series "Old Boston Houses," *B.W.S.G.* 38(May 10, 1892) and 39(Nov. 10, 1892).

56. *W.B.* 1(Oct. 15, 1876):66, 6(Sept. 15, 1881):1161; *M.D.* 2(Jan. 15, 1890):1, 2(June 15, 1890):1.

57. Holland, "King of Beer," pp. 171–73; *C.T.*, Oct. 3, 5, 1889.

58. Ibid., Apr. 18, 1872; George, "The Saloon Problem," p. 76; ad in *C.F.P.* 30(July 6, 1907): 6; *Best Brewing Company* v. *Klassen*, 185 Ill.37(1900); Epple, *Liquor Laws of Massachusetts*, pp. 72–74.

59. Mass. *A. and R.*, *1895*, ch. 388; *B.G.*, Jan. 24, 1889; *N.E.T.* 2(Sept. 13, 1884):3; *Boston* v. *American Surety Company* 217 Mass. 508(1914).

60. *N.Y.T.*, Dec. 15, 1888, Feb. 15, 21, Mar. 8, Aug. 18, 1889; *Chicago Securities, 1899* (Chicago: The Directory Company, 1899), pp. 195, 266; George, "The Saloon Problem," pp. 69–70; *The Economist* 2(Oct. 15, 1889):890, 21(May 27, 1899):642, 24(July 14, 1900):40.

61. *N.Y.T.*, Mar. 8, June 3, Aug. 20, Oct. 26, 1889; *The Economist* 1(June 8, 1889):471; *M.C.* 8(Feb. 15, 1892):35, 8(Mar. 16, 1889):87.

62. *M.D.* 8(Oct. 4, 1893):4.

63. *B.G.*, June 19, Aug. 1, 1889, Apr. 12, 1890; *Moody's Manual of Securities, 1900* (New York: Moody's Manual Company, 1900), p. 825; Ibid., *1904*, pp. 1442, 1569.

64. *A.B.R.* 6(Mar. 16, 1893):595; *M.D.* 3(Jan. 15, 1891):1; *The Economist* 6(Nov. 28, 1891):889, 20(Oct. 1, 1898):390.

65. *A.B.R.* 6(Aug. 18, 1892):116–18.

66. *The Economist* 15(Jan. 4, 1896):12, 15(May 9, 1886):569, 15(May 30, 1896):66.

67. Transcript of Record, *Henry Kiel* v. *City of Chicago*, 176 Ill.137(1898), pp. 1–17, Illinois State Archives; *M.C.* 16(June 16, 1900):67.

68. *One Hundred Years of Brewing*, pp. 609–11; *A.B.R.* 9(Aug. 20, 1895):51; *The Economist* 17(July 17, 1897):67, 20(Dec. 17, 1898):703, 21(Apr. 1, 1899):387, 22(Dec. 16, 1899):712–13.

69. *Chicago Securities, 1899*, pp. 195–96, 213–16, 249–54, 280–81; *A.B.R.* 6(Oct. 27, 1892):277–78; story of syndicates pieced together from articles in *The Economist*, Jan., 1893–Dec., 1897.

70. *M.C.* 15(Mar. 16, 1899):87; *L.T.R.* 6(Apr. 25, 1899):12.

71. Ibid., 5(July 25, 1898):1, 6(Aug. 23, 1898):3; *One Hundred Years of Brewing*, pp. 497–50. *C.F.P.* 54(June 15, 1922):8 has retrospective view.

72. *The Economist* 21(May, 1899) and 22(Dec., 1899) has several articles; *B.G.*, May 21, 1900; *Commercial and Financial Chronicle* 67(July 9, 1898):73.

73. *The Call Board Bulletin* 12(Dec., 1898):194–95; *B.G.*, Apr. 15, 1901.

74. *The Call Board Bulletin* 12(Dec., 1898):194–95.

75. Boston, *Permits for Areas under Streets*, City Doc. 69, 1905, lists property owners; *C.T.*, Dec. 31, 1881.

76. Cochran, *Pabst*, pp. 143–44; *C.T.*, Mar. 21, 1880; *M.D.* 2(July 16, 1890):1; *Chicago Securities, 1909*, p. 284; *A.B.R.* 6(Aug. 18, 1892):114; George, "The Saloon Problem," pp. 73–76; *The Economist* 9(Sept. 10, 1892):369; Citizens' Association of Chicago to Pabst Real

Estate Company, Milwaukee, May 27, 1892, Ambler Scrapbooks, LXIV, p. 115, C.H.S.

77. George Kibbe Turner, "The City of Chicago," *McClure's* 27(Apr., 1907):578; Cochran, *Pabst*, p. 198, 212–13; *The Economist* 14(Nov. 30, 1895):668; *L.T.R.* 8(Jan. 19, 1900):6; *Milwaukee Sentinel*, Feb. 28, 1901.

78. *The Economist* 20(July 9, 1898):51. That journal carried bi-weekly lists of building permits from which brewery ownership data was computed.

79. Ibid.

80. Ibid., 29(Feb. 28, 1903):287.

81. Ibid., 32(Oct. 10, 1904):475.

82. Ernest Shideler, "The Chain Store: A Study of the Ecological Organization of a Modern City," (Ph.D. diss., University of Chicago, 1927).

CHAPTER 2

1. *L.T.R.* 8(Feb. 23, 1900):10.

2. *C.F.P.* 15(Nov. 15, 1902):4.

3. *L.T.R.* 8(Feb. 23, 1900):10.

4. Charles Schaffner Papers, C.H.S.

5. Raymond Calkins, *Substitutes for the Saloon* (Boston: Houghton, Mifflin, 1901), p. 7; Jane Addams, *Twenty Years at Hull House* (New York: Macmillan, 1910), p. 222; *W.B.* 9(Mar. 15, 1884):453; Albert Pick and Company, *1912 Catalog.*

6. Ibid., pp. 318, 473; *C.F.P.* 36(Feb. 24, 1912):1; *W.B.* 11(Jan. 15, 1886):106; Ibid., 32(June 17, 1909):5.

7. Albert Pick and Company, *1912 Catalog*, pp. 220, 221, 238–42, 245.

8. *W.B.* 8(Nov. 15, 1883):1994.

9. *C.F.P.*, 29(Apr. 28, 1906):4; Daniel J. Boorstin, *The Americans: The Democratic Experience* (New York: Random House, 1973), pp. 200–203.

10. Chicago Commission on the Liquor Problem, *Preliminary Report* (Chicago: City of Chicago, 1916), p. 16; *M.C.* 7(May 15, 1882):706.

11. "Study of Prohibition," Chicago Commons-Lea Taylor Papers, C.H.S.

12. *W.B.* 7(May 14, 1882):706; *C.F.P.* 36(Feb. 10, 1912):4; *M.C.* 11(Aug. 1, 1895):65, 12(May 16, 1896):59, 61; *Proceedings of the Chicago City Council*, Apr. 8, 1896, p. 2392.

13. Matthew Josephson, *Union House, Union Bar* (New York: Random House, 1956), pp. 3–12.

14. Ibid.

15. *C.T.*, quoted in *B.T.*, May 7, 1886.

16. *M.D.* 1(Dec. 1, 1889):1.

17. *C.T.*, May 16, 1882, Feb. 10, 1893; *Abendpost*, Mar. 12, 1890, Jan. 5, 22, May 4, 1891; *Arbeiter-Zeitung*, May 5, 1884, Aug. 27, Nov. 12, 1888; *Illinois Staats-Zeitung*, Jan. 9, Apr. 12, 1892; *L.T.R.* 5(Nov. 22, 1898):15; *Wage Scale of the Central Council of German Waiters and Bartenders Union* (n.p., n.d.), copy in C.H.S.

18. *M.S.* 12(Jan. 5, 1903):34; *L.T.R.* 9(Nov. 16, 1900):9.

19. Josephson, *Union House, Union Bar*, pp. 38, 43; *T.C.* 10(Nov., 1887):4.

20. *M.S.* 12(Apr. 15, 1903):45; *B.G.*, Dec. 11, 1888, Dec. 10, 1889, June 21, 24, July 21, 26, 1901; *B.T.*, Apr. 21, 1880; *M.C.* 17(Jan. 16, 1901):71, 24(July 16, 1908):74; *C.F.P.* 29(Feb. 3, 1906):1.

21. *M.S.* 12(Apr. 15, 1903):33, 13(Jan. 5, 1904):48, 14(June 15, 1905):25, 31, 14(July 15, 1905):26, 14(Nov. 15, 1905):10; *C.F.P.* 26(Aug. 29, 1903):5, 27(June 4, 1904):4, 28(Oct. 15, 1905):4, 29(Mar. 17, 1906):4, 29(Apr. 28, 1906):4; *M.C.* 20(Apr. 16, 1904):67, 20(July 16, 1904):73.

22. *C.F.P.* 27(July 2, 1904):4.

23. Boston, "An Act to Regulate the Sale of Intoxicating Liquors," City Doc. 63, 1875.

24. *B.T.*, May 13, 1878; Mass. *A. and R.*, 1878, ch. 21.

25. *B.T.*, July 29, 1878.

26. *N.E.T.* 2(Sept. 6, 1884):3.

27. Ibid.; Boston, Police Commissioner, *A.R., 1884*, City Doc. 92, 1885, p. 28.

28. *N.E.T.* 2(Sept. 13, 1884):4; *L.O.* 1(Oct. 11, 1884):14, 1(May 2, 1885):1; *B.T.*, May 2, 1885; *B.G.*, Apr. 29, 1890.

29. *B.P.*, May 9, 1890.

30. *B.G.*, Apr. 26, 29, May 7–16, 1890; *B.P.*, May 9–12, 1890.

31. *B.G.*, May 18, 1890.

32. Ibid., May 17–21, 1890.

33. *M.C.* 6(June 16, 1890):32; Citizens' Law and Order League of Massachusetts, *A.R., 1890*, pp. 6–7.

34. Ibid., *1891*, p. 15; Myles O'Donnell, "The Administration of William Eustes Russell, 1891–1893," (M.A. thesis, Clark University, 1958), pp. 17–20.

35. *The Anti-Bar Law: The Twenty-five Feet Law: Argument of Louis D. Brandeis before the Joint Committee on Liquor Law of the Massachusetts Legislature* (n.p., 1891), p. 2.

36. Ibid., pp. 9–15; quote from p. 13.

37. Ibid., pp. 16–17; *M.C.* 7(Apr. 16, 1891):22.

38. Citizens' Law and Order League of Massachusetts, *A.R., 1891*, pp. 14–15; *M.C.* 7(Apr. 30, 1891):21, 7(May 31, 1891):20, 7(June 30, 1891):21.

39. William I. Cole and Kellogg Durland, "Report on Substitutes

for the Saloon," in Calkins, *Substitutes for the Saloon*, pp. 321–27.

40. *C.F.P.* 30(Dec. 21, 1907):8, 36(Dec. 7, 1912):1.

41. Royal Melendy, "The Saloon in Chicago, I," *American Journal of Sociology* 6(Nov., 1900):296.

42. *C.F.P.* 41(Dec. 13, 1913):7.

43. *M.C.* 12(June 1, 1896):44, 25(July 16, 1909):27; *The Economist* 23(Feb. 3, 1900):135; *The Restaurant Bulletin* 1(Mar. 1904):11; Cook District, Liquor Dealers' Protective Association, *Bulletin Number 10* (n.p., n.d.), pp. 6–7.

44. George, "The Saloon Problem in Chicago," p. 87; *Live Articles on Special Hazards, No. 5* (n.p., n.d.), p. 20.

45. Marie Hall Ets, *Rosa: The Life of an Italian Immigrant* (Minneapolis: University of Minnesota Press, 1970), p. 216; *B.T.*, July 28, 1883; *C.T.*, Sept. 11, 1882; *C.F.P.* 30(May 18, 1907):4.

46. *C.T.*, Jan. 17, 1913; "Occupations and Health of the Mercantile Classes," *Scientific American* 35(Dec. 16, 1876):393.

47. *M.C.* 29(Mar. 16, 1913):28; *C.T.*, Dec. 27, 1880; *C.F.P.* 37(July 19, 1913):5, "Report of the Joint Police Investigation Committee to the Committee on Public Order and Policing," Civic Committee Minutes, V, 1910–11, pp. 103–4, City Club Papers, C.H.S.

48. *M.C.* 13(Dec. 1, 1897):28a; *B.T.*, Oct. 9, 1882.

49. *C.F.P.* 43(Nov. 13, 1915):5.

50. Ibid., 26(Aug. 1, 1903):4; *L.T.R.* 7(Nov. 10, 1899):7; *C.T.*, Jan. 24, 1884, Jan. 31, 1913.

51. George Steinbrecker, Jr., "Inaccurate Accounts of *Sister Carrie*," *American Literature* 22(Jan. 1952):490–93; *C.T.*, Feb. 16, 17, 1886; *The Restaurant Bulletin* 1(June, 1904):23; *C.T.*, Sept. 12, 1882, Sept. 15, 1884. Case of "Joe B-," in Supplement I, Folder 7, June 26, 1897, Juvenile Protective Association Papers, U.I.C.C.

52. *M.C.* 8(Jan. 31, 1892):33; President's Report, *Proceedings of the 1905 Convention of the Illinois Liquor Dealers' Protective Association*, p. 14.

53. William N. Gemmill, "Crime and Its Punishment in Chicago," *Journal of Criminal Law and Criminology* 1(July, 1910):35; *L.T.R.* 5(July 19, 1898):5.

54. *C.T.*, June 3, 1896; *C.F.P.* 30(Aug. 24, 1907):4; 34(Sept. 16, 1911):4.

55. *W.B.* 2(Jan., 1877):13.

56. *L.O.* 1(Apr. 18, 1885):230.

57. *M.C.* 9(Apr. 1, 1893):21.

58. *M.D.* 1(Aug. 2, 1893):1; *M.C.* had lists of openings, bankruptcies, sales, and other changes as a regular convenience to salesmen-readers.

59. *M.D.* 1(Aug. 2, 1893):1; *A.B.R.* 7(Jan. 4, 1894):431; *C.E.J.*, Oct. 25, 1894; *M.C.* 13(July 1, 1897):37; *C.R.-H.*, Sept. 11, 1905.

60. Report of Superintendent and Attorney, Jan. 22, 1909, p. 3,

and Nov. 26–Dec. 31, 1909, p. 3, Supplement I, Juvenile Protective Association Papers, U.I.C.C.; *Chicago Daily Drovers Journal*, Feb. 9, 1884; *C.R.-H.*, Jan. 1, 1905.

61. *Anti-Saloon League Yearbook, 1912*, pp. 28–29; Ibid., *1901*, p. 27; *B.G.*, June 28, 29, 1901; *C.T.*, June 28, 1901.

62. *M.C.* 9(June 16, 1893):20; *Milwaukee Free Press*, Aug. 1, 1901.

63. Cherrington, *Standard Encyclopedia*, 4:1472.

64. *L.T.R.* 9(Sept. 14, 1900):9.

65. *C.D.D.*, Jan. 26, 1849, Jan. 21, 1854, June 26, 1850; Edward Savage, *Police Records and Recollections; or Boston by Daylight and Gaslight* (Boston: John P. Dale, 1873).

66. *Address of H. H. Faxon before the Seventh Annual Meeting of the Citizens Law and Order League of Massachusetts, May 1, 1889* (Boston: n.p., 1889).

67. *Illinois Staats-Zeitung*, Aug. 2, 1879; *C.F.P.* 26(Feb. 28, 1903):4, 26(Aug. 22, 1903):4, 30(May 4, 1907):8; *F.P.* 2(Jan. 17, 1894):1.

68. *C.T.*, Jan. 11, July 28, 1882; *The Emancipator* 1(Aug., 1900):8, 2(Jan., 1901):3; *C.D.N.*, Feb. 13, 1906.

69. Ernest Gordon, *When the Brewers Had the Stranglehold* (New York: Alcohol Information Committee, 1930), p. 100.

70. *W.B.* 1(Aug. 15, 1876):9; *B.G.*, May 13, 1888, May 16, 1887, Feb. 6, June 15, Sept. 30, 1901; *B.T.*, Sept. 8–10, 1885, June 19, 1886.

71. *C.T.*, July 21, 27, Aug. 27, 1880, May 17, June 20, 24, 1881.

72. Ibid., July 21, 24, 1887; *M.C.* 8(Aug. 16, 1892):26.

73. Numerous ads in early city directories.

74. *M.C.* 1(Oct. 16, 1885):1, 2(Nov. 12, 1886):13.

75. Ibid., 1(Oct. 16, 1885):1, 2(Nov. 12, 1886):13; *C.F.P.* 32(Dec. 18, 1909):4.

76. *C.T.*, June 19, 1881; *M.C.* 4(May 31, 1888):12.

77. *B.G.*, Feb. 9, 1885.

78. Christina Campbell, "Memoribilia, or the Street Where She Lived," manuscript [c1888–90], C.H.S. about Leavitt-Van Buren area.

79. *Milwaukee Journal*, July 2, 1901, Nov. 24, 1903; *Chicago's Prosperity as Advanced by Its Brewing Industries* (Chicago: n.p., n.d.), in C.H.S.; Hyde Park Protective Association, *A.R.*, *1902*, p. 6; *C.C.*, July 7, 1896; *C.I.-O.*, July 23, 1896; *Proceedings of the Chicago City Council*, January 16, 1896, pp. 1617–1618; *M.C.* 6(Mar. 17, 1890):23, 6(May 31, 1890):32.

80. *C.F.P.* 29(July 7, 1906):1.

81. *The Public Good* 2(Jan. 20, 1887):4; *B.G.*, Feb. 2, 1890.

82. *C.F.P.* 29(July 7, 1906):1.

83. Ibid. 26(Apr. 18, 1903):1; *The Emancipator* 3(Oct., 1902):3.

84. *M.C.* 22(Aug. 1, 1906):46; *C.F.P.* 33(June 11, 1910):5.

85. *The Economist* 44(Nov. 20, 1915):947.

86. J. B. McClure, ed., *Stories and Sketches of Chicago* (Chicago: Rhodes & McClure, 1880), pp. 88–90.

87. "Faces on the Barroom Wall," *Chicago* 3(Apr., 1956):4–5; *C.T.*, Sept. 2, 1881; *W.B.* 9(Apr. 15, 1884):654. The Chicago Historical Society maintains a collection of the Chapin and Gore paintings in its museum.

88. *C.F.P.* 26(Dec. 14, 1912):4, 32(Dec. 25, 1909):5, 34(May 27, 1911):1; *M.C.* 9(Dec. 1, 1893):25; *H.C.S.*, pp. 149–52; [Charles Hermann], *Recollections of Life and Doings in Chicago* (Chicago: Normandie House, 1945), pp. 63–64.

89. Heinegabubeler's business card, Barton Museum of Whisky History, Bardstown, Kentucky; Calkins, *Substitutes*, p. 23; Robert Casey, *Chicago Medium Rare* (Indianapolis: Bobbs-Merrill, 1952), p. 296.

90. *C.F.P.* 37(Sept. 6, 1913):1; *H.C.S.*, p. 169; *C.T.*, Oct. 23, 1883.

91. R. F. Bibble, *John L. Sullivan* (Boston: Little, Brown, 1925), pp. 14–43; *T.C.* 5(Aug., 1883):3; *C.T.*, Apr. 16, 1883; [Hermann], *Recollections*, p. 51; *F.P.* 2(May 23, 1894):1; *L.T.R.* 7(July 11, 1899):11.

92. *C.F.P.* 36(July 13, 1913):2.

93. Jack Johnson, *Jack Johnson — in the Ring — and Out* (Chicago: National Sports, 1927), pp. 66–67.

94. *C.F.P.* 26(July 13, 1912):5, 26(Dec. 14, 1912):1; *C.R.-H.*, Oct. 21, 31, Nov. 2, 1912.

95. George, "The Saloon Problem," p. 85; *C.T.*, Nov. 11, 1883; *M.C.* 1(Dec. 3, 1885):6, 16(Aug. 16, 1900):75, 25(Jan. 16, 1909):42; *C.F.P.* 34(Aug. 16, 1911):5.

96. Epple, *Liquor Laws of Massachusetts*, p. 19.

97. *B.G.*, Sept. 27, 1902.

98. *C.F.P.* 27(July 30, 1904):1, 27(Nov. 12, 1904):4, 41(Nov. 8, 1913):4.

99. *L.T.R.* 8(Feb. 23, 1900):10; *C.F.P.* 27(Dec. 27, 1903):1, 27(Sept. 7, 1907):5, 30(Mar. 30, 1907):1, and numerous ads in journals.

100. Albert Pick *1912 Catalog*, pp. 414–15; George Moran, *Moran's Dictionary of Chicago* (Chicago: George Moran, 1891) p. 204; *B.G.*, June 19, 1887.

101. Albert Pick, *1912 Catalog*, pp. 378, 379, 409, 413; *American Beverage and Food Journal [B. and B.]* 6(Nov., 1908):21, 7(July, 1909):8; Albert Webster, "The Relation of the Saloon to Juvenile Delinquency," (Ph.D. diss., University of Chicago, 1912), p. 5.

102. *Illinois Staats-Zeitung*, Aug. 2, 1879; *C.T.*, Sept. 12, 1880; Melendy, "The Saloon," pp. 448–50; Calkins, *Substitutes*, pp. 156–57; *M.C.* 25(Apr. 1, 1909):24.

103. Cole and Durland, "Report on Substitutes," pp. 321–26.

104. McElwain, "The Saloon Question in Chicago; *M.C.* 3(Jan. 21, 1887):9; *L.T.R.* 8(Apr. 27, 1900):5; *Chicago's Dark Places* (Chicago: Craig Press and Women's Temperance Publishing Association, 1891), p. 31.

105. *H.C.S.*, p. 142, and *C.F.P.* 26(May 17, 1903):5, for example.

106. *M.C.* 9(July 16, 1893):41, and *C.F.P.* 43(July 31, 1915):4, for example.

107. *C.T.*, Feb. 18, 1880, Apr. 10, 1881, Dec. 14, 1890; *C.F.P.* 26(Oct. 24, 1903):1.

108. *Illinois Staats-Zeitung*, Apr. 16, 1881; *M.D.* 2(June 16, 1890):1; *C.T.*, Dec. 14, 1890.

109. *The Restaurant Bulletin* 1(June, 1904):22.

110. *C.T.*, Sept. 12, 1881.

111. Pierce, *History of Chicago*, 3:271, n.6; *F.P.* 2(May 23, 1894):1.

112. *B. and B.* 3(July, 1907):16.

113. *L.T.R.* 4(Mar. 15, 1898):6, 4(Apr. 5, 1898):13, 4(June 21, 1898):5, 5(Nov. 8, 1898):8, 5(Dec. 13, 1898):11, 5(Jan. 3, 1899):8; *The Economist* 20(Sept. 24, 1898):36; Stephen O'Meara to Henry Cabot Lodge, Jan. 2, 1902, Henry Cabot Lodge to Stephen O'Meara, Jan. 4, 1902, Stephen O'Meara Papers, Boston Public Library; Coyne, *In Reminiscence*, pp. 204–5; *Proceedings of the Illinois Liquor Dealers' Protective Association Convention, 1905*, p. 13.

114. *C.T.*, June 4, Oct. 22, Nov. 5, 1881; Transcript of Record, *Lawrence Killian v. Harvard Brewing Company*, 222 Mass.13(1915).

115. *C.T.*, Nov. 6, 1867, Mar. 1, 14, 17, 1868, Jan. 26, 1869, Apr. 21, 22, June 5, 1886; *W.B.* 13(Oct. 15, 1888):2263; *M.C.* 7(Feb. 16, 1891):23, 11(Aug. 16, 1895):55; *C.D.N.*, Mar. 9, 1896.

116. *Illinois Staats-Zeitung*, Aug. 2, 1897; *C.T.*, July 20, 1882; *Chicago Daily Drovers Journal*, Sept. 28, 1883; *C.F.P.* 42(Aug. 29, 1914):5.

117. *W.B.* 30(Aug. 15, 1878):54; also, Ibid.

118. Clipping, "official brewer's paper," March 4, 1903 in Pabst Scrapbook, XXIII, p. 89, Milwaukee County Historical Society.

119. President's Report, *Proceedings of the Sixteenth Annual Convention of the National Liquor League*, p. 2; *C.F.P.* 27(June 4, 1901):1, 29(Sept. 23, 1906):3, 36(Dec. 28, 1912):1.

120. Adolph Keitel, *Government by the Brewers?* (Chicago: Appersly, 1918), p. 46; *W.B.* 5(Mar. 15, 1880):266; *M.C.* 2(Mar. 4, 1886):2–3.

121. *M.C.* 2(Dec. 17, 1885):1–2, 2(Mar. 18, 1886):2–3.

122. "The Problem of the Saloon—the Clean-up Movement," in *United States Brewers' Association Yearbook, 1909*, pp. 148–51; *W.B.* 5(Feb. 15, 1881):185; *M.C.* 3(Mar. 16, 1887):8.

123. Ibid. 2(Dec. 17, 1885):1–2, 2(Oct. 28, 1886):8.

124. *L.T.R.* 8(Jan. 5, 1900):15.

125. *C.T.*, Sept. 15, 1881, Aug. 19, 22, 26, 1882.

126. *H.C.S.*, pp. 102, 122–23; *C.T.*, Apr. 12, 19, 1872, May 8, 1873.

127. *H.C.S.*, pp. 104, 106; *C.T.*, Apr. 20, 25, 1873, Sept. 4, 1880, Jan. 8, 9, 21, 22, Feb. 5, 18, 19, 1881.

128. *H.C.S.*, pp. 110–12, 188, 124; *C.F.P.* 29(Sept. 22, 1906):1; *C.T.*, Jan. 17, Mar. 20, Apr. 3, Aug. 27, Sept. 4, 18, 1880, Apr. 12, 1882.

129. *H.C.S.*, pp. 126–32; *C.F.P.* 24(Feb. 25, 1911):4; *C.T.*, Oct. 10, 29, 1881.

130. *B.T.*, Jan. 8, May 31, 1883; on Chelsea, *N.E.T.* 1(Aug. 30, 1884):4; on Charlestown, Ibid. 1(May 10–24, 1884:)1; on South Boston, Ibid. 1(May 17, 1884):4; *L.T.R.* 8(June 22, 1900):3; on Germans, *L.O.*, 1(Nov. 29, 1884):3, 2(Jan. 10, 1885):4; *B.T.*, Sept. 13, Oct. 14, 19, Nov. 19. 1882.

131. *N.E.T.* 1(Apr. 12, 1884):4, 1(May 4, 1884):5; *B.T.*, May 6, 7, 1884.

132. *L.O.*, 2(Apr. 3, 1886):212; *B.T.*, Apr. 1, 3, 9, May 1, 1886.

133. Cherrington, *Standard Encyclopedia*, 3:1046–50.

134. *L.T.R.* 8(Mar. 30, 1900):3–4. That journal chronicles the group's history through its short, one-year existence.

135. *M.C.* 9(Feb. 16, 1893):44B, 10(Sept. 1, 1894):55; *1899 Convention Program of the National Retail Liquor Dealers' Association*, pp. 81–87; *C.F.P.*, 26(May 16, 1903):1.

CHAPTER 3

1. Harvey Zorobaugh, *The Gold Coast and the Slum* (Chicago: University of Chicago Press, 1929) is the classic study of nearby contrasts.

2. John H. Bogue, *Chicago's Cheap Lodging Houses and Their Lodgers* (Chicago: Improved Housing Association, 1889); Chicago, League for the Protection of Immigrants, *A.R., 1909–10*, p. 27; *C.D.N.*, Aug. 28, 29, 1893; *C.H.*, Sept. 2, 1893; *C.P.*, Aug. 28, Dec. 6, 1893; "Tramps and Wayfarers," *Publications of the American Statistical Association* 7(Sept., 1900):10–20; J. J. M'Cook, "The Tramp Problem," *Lend-a-Hand* 15(Sept., 1895):167–83; "Wayfarers and Tramps," *Report of the Massachusetts Board to Investigate the Unemployed*, pt. 2, House Doc. 50, 1895.

3. Th. Bentzon, *Les Americaines Chez Elles* (Paris: Librairie Hachette et Cie, 1904), pp. 50–52; *B.G.*, June 17, 1887, May 26, June 16, 1889, Jan. 14, 1900, May 6, 1901; *B.P.*, Apr. 25, 1902; Benjamin P. Eldridge and William B. Watts, *Our Rival the Rascal* (Boston: Pemberton, 1897), pp. 1–14.

4. *The Boston Common* 1(July 16, 1910):20; *B.G.*, July 12, 1889, Feb. 4, 12, 1900; *C.T.*, Mar. 29, 1903, Dec. 29, 1907.

5. *B.G.*, July 17, 1888.

6. *C.T.*, Feb. 21, Dec. 15, 1880, Nov. 22, 1882, Jan. 26, Feb. 3, 1883; W. P. England, "The Lodging House," *The Survey* 27(Dec. 2, 1911):1313–17; "Fifty Cheap Lodging Houses in Chicago," *First Semi-Annual Report of the Chicago Department of Public Welfare, 1915*, pp. 66–73; Edward Kirkland, "Among the Poor of Chicago," in Robert Woods et al. *The Poor in Great Cities* (New York: Charles Scribner's Sons, 1895), pp. 234, 236; Calkins, *Substitutes for the Saloon*, p. 292; Alvin F. Sanborn, *Moody's Lodging House and Other Stories* (Boston: Copeland and Day, 1895), pp. 1–96; *B.G.*, July 17, 1888, Feb. 15, 1900.

7. "Tramps," typescript, Ben Reitman Papers, supplement II, U.I.C.C.; Sanborn, *Moody's Lodging House*, pp. 39–43; "Notes on Municipal Lodging Houses Visited by F. Almy," Raymond Robins Papers, box 1, S.H.S.W.; *T.C.* 1(Jan. 15, 1879):35.

8. *C.T.*, Dec. 30, 1882.

9. "Research Notebooks," XI, pp. 495–96, Committee of Fifteen Papers, U.C.; Calkins, *Substitutes for the Saloon*, p. 293; *C.T.*, Feb. 3, 1883; J. H. Greer, *The Social Evil* (Chicago: J. H. Greer, 1911), p. 117.

10. *C.T.*, Oct. 28, 1880, Feb. 3, 1883, on William Dwyer, a politician.

11. *L.T.R.* 7(Dec. 1, 1899):4.

12. *C.F.P.* 30(May 25, 1907):1; Sanborn, *Moody's*, pp. 22–32; *C.T.*, Dec. 15, 1880, Feb. 3, 1883.

13. *B.G.*, Aug. 15, 1889.

14. Sanborn, *Moody's*, pp. 17–18; "Brotherhood Welfare Association — ARE THE CLERGYMEN CHARITABLE AND KIND? ARE THE PRIESTS AND MINISTERS AS CHARITABLE AS THE SALOON-KEEPERS AND GAMBLERS?" typescript, Reitman Papers, U.I.C.C.

15. Lloyd Wendt and Herman Kogan, *Lords of the Levee* (Indianapolis: Bobbs-Merrill, 1943).

16. *The Evanston Press*, May 28, 1904.

17. Robert Woods, *City Wilderness* (Boston: Houghton, Mifflin, 1898), pp. 91–93, 157; Frances Embree, "The Housing of the Poor, with Special Reference to Conditions in Chicago," Seminar in Political Science V, 1896, Northwestern University; *C.T.*, Feb. 3, 1883; *North End Mission Magazine* 2(Oct., 1873):111.

18. Chicago Bureau of Charities, *Fifth A.R., 1898–99*, pp. 31–33, 36–37; *Proceedings of the Boston Common Council*, October 17, 1878, p. 578.

19. *T.C.* 1(Jan. 15, 1879):35; *A Municipal Lodging House: Details as to Cost and Operation* (Chicago: City Homes Association, [1900]); Massachusetts Civic League, *A.R., 1903*, pp. 21, 23–25; *Charities* 9(Nov. 15, 1902):482–85; *B.G.*, Dec. 14, 1902.

20. Richard W. Schwarz, "Dr. John Harvey Kellogg as a Social Gospel Practitioner," *Journal of the Illinois State Historical Society*

67(Spring, 1965):5–22; Kellogg Papers, Michigan Historical Collections.

21. Allan Bosch, "The Salvation Army in Chicago, 1885–1914" (Ph.D. diss., University of Chicago, 1965), pp. 249–56, 266–90.

22. *Proposed Mills Hotel for Chicago* (n.p., n.d.); *C.T.*, Dec. 12, 1899; *C.I.-O.*, Dec. 10, 1899; Bascom Timmons, *Charles G. Dawes: Portrait of an American* (New York: Henry Holt, 1953), pp. 152–61; Charles G. Dawes Papers, Northwestern University, has folders of clippings.

23. Bogue, *Chicago's Cheap Lodging Houses*, pp. 6–7.

24. Raymond Robins, "What Constitutes a Model Lodging House," *Proceedings of the National Conference of Charities and Corrections, 1904*, pp. 155–66.

25. *B.G.*, Feb. 16, 1902; "The Procession of 22nd Street," *By Archer Road* 3(Nov., 1908):8–9; Sigmund Kransz, *Street Types of Chicago* (Chicago: Max Stern, 1892), p. 22; *B.G.*, July 14, 1901.

26. Milton B. Hunt, "The Housing of Non-Family Men in Chicago," *The American Journal of Sociology* 16(Sept., 1900):145–70; Frederick Bushee, "Ethnic Factors in the Population of Boston," *Publications of the American Economic Association*, 3rd ser., 4(May, 1903):29; Robert A. Woods, *Americans in Process* (Boston: Houghton, Mifflin, 1902), pp. 45, 51–52, 105, 127–28; 135; Woods, *City Wilderness*, pp. 83–84.

27. Thomas Philpott, *The Slum and the Ghetto* (New York, Oxford University Press, 1978), *passim;* George T. Nesmith, "The Housing of Urban Wage-earners in the Sixteenth Ward of Chicago," (M.A. thesis, Northwestern University, 1900), pp. 53, 94, 95–96, 108–9, 131; Robert Hunter, *Tenement Conditions in Chicago* (Chicago: City Homes Association, 1901), pp. 147–50; Frederick Wines, *Punishment and Reformation* (New York: Thomas Y. Crowell, 1895), pp. 275–77; Daniel Levine, *Jane Addams and the Liberal Tradition* (Madison: State Historical Society of Wisconsin, 1971), pp. 111–43; Frank Draper, "The Homes of the Poor in Our Cities," Massachusetts, State Board of Health, *Fourth Annual Report, 1873*, p. 429; J. O. S. Huntington, "Tenement House Morality," *The Forum* 3(June–Aug., 1887):513–22.

28. "The Sweating System in Chicago," Illinois, Bureau of Labor Statistics, *Seventh Bienniel Report, 1892*, pp. 358–99; *B.G.*, Mar. 3, July 6, Nov. 25, 1891.

29. Nesmith, "The Housing of Wage-earners," pp. 50–51, 149–51.

30. Ibid., pp. 44, 141, 148; Massachusetts, Bureau of Labor Statistics, *First Annual Report, 1870*, p. 176; Chicago, Special Park Commission, "Report on Sites and Needs, October 25, 1902," typescript in U.C.

31. Such shortcomings were delineated by features of model tenements and plans, e.g., Robert Treat Paine, "Housing Conditions in Boston," *Annals of the American Academy of Political and Social Science* 20(July, 1902):121–36; David Culver, "Tenement House Reform in Boston," (Ph.D. diss., Boston University, 1972), pp. 129–65.

32. Robert Treat Paine, "Homes for the People," *Journal of Social Science* 15(Sept., 1881):14–15; the same idea is in Alfred T. White, "Better Homes for Workingmen," *Proceedings of the National Conference of Charities and Corrections, 1885*, p. 371. On the Municipal Order League, which left no printed reports, see *C. Times*, Mar. 28, 29, 1892; *C.T.*, Mar. 13, 28, 29, May 24, June 28, Aug. 28, 1892; *C.P.*, Mar. 26, 28, 1892. Caroline Hill, *Mary McDowell and Municipal Housekeeping: A Symposium* (Chicago: n.p., [c.1937]), pp. 1–11; Louise C. Wade, *Graham Taylor: Pioneer for Social Justice* (Chicago: University of Chicago Press, 1964), pp. 129–31; see also the Mary McDowell Papers, C.H.S., and the Graham Taylor Papers, Newberry Library; Louis A. Banks, *White Slaves; or, the Suppression of the Worthy Poor* (Boston: Lee and Shepard, 1891), pp. 17–44.

33. Pierce, *A History of Chicago*, 2:331–33; Hollis Godfrey, *The Health of the City* (Boston: Houghton, Mifflin, 1910), pp. 127–57; Nelson M. Blake, *Water for the Cities* (Syracuse: Syracuse University Press, 1956), pp. 272–73.

34. Reprinted in *M.C.* 8(Oct. 1, 1892):48.

35. Karel Ficek, "Milk: A Type of Study in Social Control," (M.A. thesis, University of Chicago, 1935), pp. 68–108; Godfrey, *Health of the City*, pp. 30–57; *The Neighbor* 1(June, 1900):1–2; *B.G.*, Apr. 28, 1889, Jan. 2, 1901.

36. Finley Peter Dunne, *Mr. Dooley's Philosophy* (New York: R. H. Russell, 1900), p. 149.

37. *W.B.* 5(Mar. 15, 1880):266; *B.G.*, Aug. 9, 1899; Melendy, "The Saloon," p. 462; Ets, *Rosa: The Life of an Italian Immigrant*, p. 222; Woods, *City Wilderness*, p. 72.

38. *B.G.*, Sept. 17, 1901, July 13, 1902; *Harper's Weekly* 40(July 4, 1903):back cover.

39. Ruth Parsons, "The Chicago Department of Health, 1894–1914," (M.A. thesis, University of Chicago, 1939), pp. 27–38, 51–67; *The Neighbor* 1(June, 1900):1–2; handbills, Graham Taylor Papers, Newberry Library.

40. Shurtleff, *Records*, 1:106, 2:100; M.L.V. [Lucius Manlius Sargent], *Licensed Houses: An Examination of the License Law* (Boston: J. Ford, 1833), pp. 19–20; David Flaherty, *Privacy in Colonial America* (Charlottesville: University Press of Virginia, 1972), pp. 195–201.

41. Illinois, *Acts of 1872*, pp. 552–56; Massachusetts, *A. and R., 1879*, ch. 297; John A. Appleman and Marshall Miller, *Illinois Dramshop Briefs* (Indianapolis: Bobbs-Merrill, 1950), pp. 1–15A; *The Civil Damage Law* (Boston, Office of the Police Commission, 1881), pp. 23–34.

42. *B.T.*, Feb. 5, 13, 14, Mar. 5, 1880; Robert Pittman, *Alcohol and the State: A Discussion of the Problems of Law as Applied to the Liquor Trade* (New York: National Temperance Society and Publication House, 1877), pp. 201–3; Robert Bruce, *1877: Year of Violence* (In-

dianapolis: Bobbs-Merrill, 1959), pp. 233–53; *C.T.* Jan. 11, 1882, Jan. 13, 1889.

43. Dexter Smith, *Cyclopedia of Boston* (Boston: Cashin and Smith, 1887), p. 247; L. Edwin Dudley, "The Law and Order Movement — Historical Sketch," *Lend-a-Hand* 8(Mar., 1892):199; *Constitution of the Citizens' Law and Order League of Massachusetts* (Boston: Deland & Barta, 1882), pp. 3–5; *L.O.* 1(Nov. 22, 1884):63, 1(Dec. 6, 1884):1.

44. *N.E.T.* 1(Apr. 19, 1884):3, 1(Apr. 26, 1884):3–5, 1(May 3, 1884):supplement; *B.T.*, Jan. 21, Apr. 28, May 23, 31, June 13, 1884; Citizens' Law and Order League of Massachusetts, *A.R., 1883*, p. 16; Citizen's League of Chicago, *A.R., 1881*, pp. 9, 15, 18, *A.R., 1891*, p. 17.

45. Ibid., p. 30; *C.T.*, Jan. 13, 1889; *N.E.T.* 2(Nov. 22, 1884):5; Cherrington, *Standard Encyclopedia*, 4:1513.

46. Harry Augustus Stoughton, "Preventive Work for Imperiled Children," (B.A. paper, University of Chicago, 1900), pp. 27–29; Gertrude Howe Britton, "Truancy and Home Conditions," *Charities and the Commons* 17(Dec. 22, 1906):523–29.

47. Philip Davis, *Streetland* (Boston: Small, Maynard, 1915), p. 143–71; Myron E. Adams, "Children in American Street Trades," *Child Labor* (New York: National Child Labor Committee, 1905), pp. 25–46; Edward Clopper, *Child Labor on City Streets* (New York: Macmillan, 1913), pp. 83–171.

48. David E. Wishnant, "Selling the Gospel News, or: The Strange Career of Jimmy Brown the Newsboy," *Journal of Social History* 5(Spring, 1972):271–309; Everett Chamberlin, "Boston Newsboys: How They Live and Work," *Charities* 8(June 7, 1902):527–32; Allan Hoben, "The City Street," in *The Child and the City* (Chicago: Chicago School of Civics and Philanthropy, 1912), pp. 451–60; Clopper, *Child Labor*, pp. 52–82.

49. Davis, *Streetland*, p. xvii.

50. Jacob Riis, *The Peril and Preservation of the Home* (Philadelphia: George W. Jacobs, 1903), pp. 71–77, suggests this.

51. Chester Carney, "Truancy in the Tenement Districts of Chicago," typescript, 1905, University of Michigan Library; Woods, *City Wilderness*, p. 198.

52. *B.G.*, Apr. 14, 1902, quotes sermon, "The City's Need of Christ."

53. Ibid., Feb. 7, 1891.

54. Sophonisba Breckinridge and Edith Abbott, *The Delinquent Child and the Home* (New York: Survey Associates, 1916), pp. 175–76; *C.T.*, Aug. 28, 1880, Nov. 7, 1882, Sept. 30, Dec. 20, 1883; *Skandinaven*, Feb. 2, 1889; *C.R.H.*, Dec. 6, 1903, Feb. 5, 1905.

55. Webster, "The Relation of the Saloon," pp. 2–9; *C.F.P.* 27(July 29, 1905):4, 29(Jan. 6, 1906):4; 34(July 29, 1911):1, 36(Oct. 26,

1912):4; *M.C.* 30(June 15, 1914):40; Kimball Young, "The Sociological Study of a Disintegrating Neighborhood," (M.A. thesis, University of Chicago, 1918), pp. 86–87.

56. George Needham, *Street Arabs and Gutter Snipes* (Boston: D. L. Guernsey, 1884), pp. 56–58; Carney, "Truancy in the Tenement Districts," p. 40; Evelyn Boylan Epsey, "The Battle for the Fire Holes," *By Archer Road* 1(Jan., 1907):1–2; Juvenile Protective Association, "Minutes of Quarterly Meeting, May 26, 1911," folder 22, Juvenile Protective Association Papers, U.I.C.C.; Boston, *Proceedings of the Board of Aldermen, March 30, 1885*, p. 235; *C.T.*, Aug. 28, 1890; *B.T.*, Aug. 11, 24, 31, 1885.

57. Woods, *City Wilderness*, pp. 115–18; Frederick Thrasher, *The Gang: A Study of 1,313 Gangs in Chicago* (Chicago, University of Chicago Press, 1927), p. 17; Calkins, *Substitutes*, pp. 47–52; "Extracts from Various Reports, May 1917," Box 7, Gads Hill Settlement Papers, C.H.S.

58. Charles Bushnell, "Some Social Aspects of the Chicago Stockyards, II," *American Journal of Sociology* 7(Nov., 1901):303–4.

59. *M.D.* 1(Dec. 1, 1889):1; *M.C.* 8(July 1, 1892):27; *C.F.P.* 31(Nov. 28, 1908):1; *Milwaukee Sentinel*, Dec. 29, 1906.

60. *M.C.* 7(Mar. 16, 1896):64; *L.T.R.* 6(Feb. 29, 1899):8; the *C.F.P.* 29(Mar.–Sept., 1906) and 36(Apr.–May, 1912), contains many articles.

61. *M.C.* 9(Jan. 16, 1893):19; Humbert Nelli, "John Powers and the Italians: Politics in a Chicago Ward, 1896–1921," *Journal of American History* 57(June, 1970):67–84, gives background information; *C.F.P.* 26(Mar. 7, 1903):1, 26(Mar. 21, 1903):1.

62. *Proceedings of the Chicago City Council, March 15, 1904*, pp. 2248–50; *C.T.*, Mar. 15, 1904; *C.R.-H.*, Sept. 4, 1904; *C.F.P.* 26(June 18, 1904):3, 27(Apr. 23, 1904):4, 27(July 9, 1904):4.

63. Ibid., 30(Jan. 12, 1907):1, 30(May 11, 1907):1, 32(Feb. 27, 1909):4; *M.C.* 25(Mar. 1, 1909):23, 28(July 16, 1912):64.

64. Louise DeKoven Bowen, "Delinquent Children of Immigrant Parents," *Proceedings of the National Conference on Charities and Corrections, 1909*, p. 259, and her *Safeguards for City Youth at Work and at Play* (New York: Macmillan, 1914), pp. 25–29; "Reports on Social Conditions [1910]," folder 16, Juvenile Protective Association Papers, U.I.C.C.

65. "Social Forces in the 17th Ward," in Graham Taylor Papers, Newberry Library.

66. Mary Coynington, *How to Help: A Manual of Practical Philanthropy* (New York: Ronald Press, 1906), pp. 142–43.

67. Benjamin O. Flower, *Civilization's Inferno; or, Studies in the Social Cellar* (Boston: Arena, 1893), p. 36; Massachusetts, Bureau of Statistics of Labor, *Fifth A.R., 1874*, pp. 38–39; Hunter, *Tenement*

Conditions, pp. 147–48, 150; "The Woman and the Beer Pitcher," *T.C.* 18(Feb., 1896):8.

68. *B.G.*, Sept. 11, 1893; "Denison House Diary," Jan. 31, 1893, n.p. Denison House Papers, Schlesinger Library, Radcliffe College.

69. Ibid., Jan. 15, 1893, p. 147, Jan. 3, 1893, p. 43, Jan. 6, 1893, p. 86, Jan. 10, 1893, p. 107, Feb. 11, 1893, n.p.

70. Ibid., July 10, 1894, p. 35.

71. *C.F.P.* 30(Nov. 23, 1907):4, 31(Feb. 8, 1908):5; *The Neighbor* 1(Mar., 1900):3; Mary B. Swain, *A Study in Adult Delinquincy* (Chicago: Juvenile Protective Association, 1911), *passim; Co-operation* 1(June 15, 1901):1.

72. Woods, *Americans in Process*, p. 142; Woods, *City Wilderness*, p. 104.

73. *Chicago American*, June 6, 1906; Addams, *Twenty Years*, p. 438; *Co-operation* 3(Aug. 8, 1903):252–53; *C.T.*, Aug. 2, 1902; Emma Weigley, "It Might Have Been Euthenics: The Lake Placid Conference and the Home Economics Movement," *American Quarterly* 26(Mar., 1974):79–96.

74. Boston, *Report of the Joint Special Committee on Public Bathing Houses*, City Doc. 105, 1860, p. 308.

75. Marilyn T. Williams, "The Municipal Bath Movement in the United States," (Ph.D. diss., New York University, 1972), pp. 111–36; William I. Cole, *Free Municipal Baths in Boston* (Boston: Municipal Printing Office, 1899), pp. 5–23; *B.G.*, Aug. 24, Oct. 16, 1890, July 7, 1901.

76. Williams, "Municipal Bath Movement," pp. 136–50; *C.I.-O.*, Feb. 13, 1889; *Chicago Globe*, Jan. 30, Feb. 6, 10, 1890, in Charles Ambler Scrapbooks, LXIII, pp. 48, 50, C.H.S.; *Chicago City Manual, 1911*, pp. 160–61.

77. Hunter, *Tenement Conditions*, p. 71.

78. "Poor Man's Summer," *B.G.*, July 13, 1890; also Ibid., May 3, 1891, June 17, 1891.

79. Chicago, Special Park Commission, "Report on Conditions, May 24, 1902," p. 7, Raymond Robins Papers, S.H.S.W.; quote in Nesmith, "The Housing of Wage-earners," pp. 167–68.

80. Tyrrell, *Sobering Up*, pp. 55–69, 159–90; Duis, "The Saloon and the Public City," pp. 323–78.

81. Ibid., pp. 299–302, tells the story of Mary Hunt and her crusade, as does Mary H. Hunt, *An Epoch of the Nineteenth Century* (Boston: P. H. Foster, 1897), her autobiography. Her papers are part of the Anti-Saloon League Collection at the Ohio Historical Society.

82. Helen E. Tyler, *Where Prayer and Purpose Meet: The W.C.T.U. Story* (Evanston: Signal Press, 1949), is the official history. Joseph Gusfield, *Symbolic Crusade* (Urbana: University of Illinois Press, 1963), is the most interesting interpretation.

83. *B.T.*, May 3, 1882; *B.G.*, Feb. 12, 29, 1888; Massachusetts, A.

and R., *1888*, ch. 139; *Commonwealth* v. *McCormick*, 150 Mass. 270(1889); *Commomwealth* v. *Ferden*, 141 Mass. 28(1890).

84. *House Beautiful*, 7(Apr., 1900):307–12.

CHAPTER 4

1. Albert J. Kennedy, "The Saloon in Retrospect and Prospect," *Survey Graphic* 22(Apr., 1933):205.

2. *B.T.*, Aug. 27, 1881.

3. John Henry Cutler, *"Honey Fitz": Three Steps to the White House* (Indianapolis: Bobbs-Merrill, 1962), pp. 72–76.

4. Boston and Chicago comptroller's reports, various years.

5. McElwain, "The Saloon Problem in Chicago, p. 38.

6. *N.E.T.* 1(Apr. 19, 1894):4; *B.G.*, Dec. 9, 10, 1888, Dec. 6, 1889.

7. Charles Merriam, *Report of the Investigation of Municipal Revenues of Chicago* (Chicago: City Club of Chicago, 1906), pp. 13, 34, 117, 144; *W.B.* 11(Oct. 15, 1886):2169; *C.R.-H.*, Mar. 1, 1910; *C.T.P.* 33(Mar. 19, 1901):1.

8. *M.D.* 2(Apr. 1, 1890):1.

9. George P. Anderson, "The First Results of Boston's Elaborate Political Reform," *Pearson's Magazine* 23(Mar., 1910):421–28; John F. Connell, "Twenty-five Hundred Miles with Honey Fitz," *New England Magazine* 41(Feb., 1910):700–704.

10. McDonald, who is discussed in chapt. 8, below, evoked excellent obituary retrospectives, such as *C.T.*, Aug. 8, 9, 1907; *C.R.-H.*, Aug., 9, 1907.

11. Nationality maps, residents of Hull House, *Hull House Maps and Papers* (New York: Thomas Y. Crowell, 1895); maps of "Predominant Race Factors" in Woods, *Americans in Process;* Nesmith, "The Housing of Wage-earners," p. 111c.

12. Ibid., pp. 112–13, 175–77; *B.T.*, Aug. 31, 1880; Peter Knights, *The Plain People of Boston, 1830–60* (New York: Oxford University Press, 1971), pp. 48–77, and Stephan Thernstrom, *The Other Bostonians: Poverty and Progress in the American Metropolis, 1880–1970* (Cambridge: Harvard University Press, 1973), pp. 15–38, reach similar conclusions about rapid movement.

13. Quote, *C.I.-O.*, Dec. 3, 1889; *C.D.N.*, Jan. 4, 1884.

14. Sanborn, *Moody's Lodging House*, pp. 97–148.

15. Carroll D. Wright, "The Slums of Baltimore, Chicago, New York and Philadelphia," *Seventh Special Report of the Commissioner of Labor (U.S.), 1894*, pp. 72, 518, 534.

16. Quoted in Norman Hayner, "The Effect of Prohibition in Packingtown," (M.A. thesis, University of Chicago, 1920), p. 17.

17. Immigrant Protective League, *A.R.*, *1911–12*, p. 17; Jakub Horak, "Foreign Benefit Societies," in Illinois, *Report of the Health In-*

surance Commission, 1919, p. 523; "Committee on Immigration, March 26, 1913," Civic Committee Minutes, VIII, 1912–13, City Club of Chicago Papers, C.H.S.

18. Calkins, *Substitutes*, p. 11; Addams, *Twenty Years*, p. 302.

19. E. C. Moore, "The Social Value of the Saloon," *American Journal of Sociology* 3(July, 1897):8; Melendy, "The Saloon," p. 293; Calkins, *Substitutes*, pp. 12–13; Robert E. Park, *The Immigrant Press and Its Control* (New York: Harper and Bros., 1922), pp. 297–98.

20. Webster, "The Saloon and Juvenile Delinquincy," p. 5; Calkins, *Substitutes*, pp. 10, 13–14; and see chapter on crime, below.

21. *The Economist* 32(Dec. 31, 1904):942; *The Emancipator* 2(Jan., 1901):3; Herbert Casson, *The History of the Telephone* (Chicago: A. C. McClurg, 1910), pp. 178–82; *C.T.*, July 19, 1881.

22. Sophonisba Breckinridge and Edith Abbott, "Housing Conditions in Chicago, III: Back of the Yards," *American Journal of Sociology* 16(Jan., 1911):464; Melendy, "The Saloon," p. 295; *C.T.*, Sept. 12, 1882; D. L. Marsh, "The Problem of Polish Immigrants with an Intensive Study of the Polish Colony of Chicago," (M.A. thesis, Northwestern University, 1907), pp. 26–27; *C.D.N.*, Jan. 26, 1884.

23. Addams, *Twenty Years*, p. 131; on institutional churches in general, C. Howard Hopkins, *The Rise of the Social Gospel in American Protestantism, 1865–1915* (New Haven: Yale University Press, 1940), pp. 153–58; Allen F. Davis, *Spearheads for Reform* (New York: Oxford University Press, 1967), pp. 15–25; Emmett Dedmon, *Great Enterprises: One Hundred Years of the Y.M.C.A. of Metropolitan Chicago* (Chicago: Rand McNally, 1957).

24. James Brown, *The History of Public Assistance in Chicago, 1883–1893* (Chicago: University of Chicago Press, 1941), pp. 18–49; *B.G.*, Mar. 25, 1900; Nathan I. Huggins, *Protestants against Poverty: Boston's Charities, 1870–1900* (Westport, Conn.: Greenwood Press, 1971), pp. 70–72, 149, 153–54, 182.

25. Huggins, *Protestants against Poverty*, pp. 69–70; *C.T.*, Feb. 3, 1878; *B.G.*, Feb. 17, 1889, Jan. 1, 24, 1890.

26. *Proceedings of the Boston Common Council*, Oct. 17, 1878, pp. 578–80; ibid., Oct. 31, 1878, p. 595; ibid., Jan., 18, 1883, p. 30; *C.D.N.*, Jan. 12, 25, 1884, tells of a similar debate in Chicago.

27. *B.G.*, Sept. 23, 1888; *C.T.*, Dec. 16, 1882, Feb. 4, Mar. 20, 1883; Chicago Municipal Reference Library, "Analysis and Summary of Replies Received from 66 Pawnbrokers Relative to Sundry Inquiries Contained in a Questionnaire of the Committee on License of the Chicago City Council," mimeo, Apr. 1918; "The Pawnbroking System," *Massachusetts Labor Bulletin* 10(July, 1906):255–73; Woods, *City Wilderness*, pp. 105–6.

28. *Co-operation* 1(Apr. 6, 1901):6–7; William A. Giles, "Pawnbroking," Civic Federation of Chicago, *Federation Papers*, no. 16 (1899), pp. 27–31; W. R. Patterson, "Pawnbroking in Europe and the

United States," U.S. Department of Labor, *Bulletin*, 4(Mar., 1899): 285–89; *C.I.-O.*, Dec. 12, 1899; *B.G.*, Mar. 18, 1899.

29. *Co-operation* 1(Jan. 5, 1901):7, 4(July 23, 1904):234–35; "The Irrepressible 'Loan Shark,' " *The Boston Common* 2(May 27, 1911):4–5.

30. *B.G.*, Nov. 30, 1890; Calkins, *Substitutes*, p. 11.

31. *The Neighbor* 1(Dec. 15, 1899):1.

32. E.g., *B.G.*, Feb. 3, 4, 1890.

33. Marsh, "Polish Immigrants," pp. 28–29; quote, *C.I.-O.*, Dec. 3, 1899.

34. Horak, "Foreign Benevolent Societies," pp. 531–32; "Civic Committee Reports," VI, part I, pp. 24–25, City Club of Chicago Papers, C.H.S.

35. Horak, "Foreign Benevolent Societies," p. 530; *C.T.*, Feb. 7, 1882, Feb. 3, 1883; *C.F.P.* 27(June 18, 1904):1.

36. Carney Hospital [Boston], *A.R.*, *1882*, p. 40; *A.R.*, *1883*, p. 41; *A.R.*, *1884*, p. 40; *A.R.*, *1887–89*, pp. 101–2; *A.R.*, *1890–92*, p. 128.

37. *B.G.*, Dec. 14, 1902; *C.T.*, Feb. 3, 1883; German Aid Society of Chicago, *A.R.*, *1881–82*, pp. 15–21; *1882–83*, pp. 10–19.

38. *C.F.P.* 31(Aug. 29, 1908):8.

39. Cook District, Liquor Dealers' Protective Association, *District Bulletin Ten [1910]*, p. 3; *C.F.P.* 32(July 3, 1909):2, 32(Oct. 23, 1909):4, 33(Mar. 5, 1910):6, 33(Apr. 9, 1910):4.

40. William T. Stead, *If Christ Came to Chicago! A Plea for the Union of All Who Love in the Service of All Who Suffer* (Chicago: Laird and Lee, 1894), pp. 139–43; Melendy, "The Saloon," p. 297; *C.F.P.* 32(Mar. 26, 1910):4.

41. Ibid., 41(Dec. 20, 1913):1.

42. *L.T.R.* 4(Jan. 11, 1898):8.

43. *C.F.P.* 29(Apr. 28, 1906):1.

44. *C.T.*, Feb. 4, Nov. 19, 1883; *C. Times*, Dec. 2, 1894; "Chicago Crime Conditions," Box LXXXVIII, Charles Merriam Papers, U.C.

45. University of Chicago settlement worker quoted in Hayner, "Effect," p. 25.

46. *C.F.P.* 36(Oct. 12, 1912):1.

47. William B. Harrison, "The Social Function of the Saloon," and "Chicago Commons Study of Prohibition," typescripts, Chicago Commons Papers, C.H.S.

48. *C.T.*, Feb. 18, 20, 1881; *Broad-Axe*, Dec. 28, 1901; Calkins, *Substitutes*, p. 10; McElwain, "The Saloon Problem in Chicago," p. 78; *Democracy* 1(Feb. 6, 1916) in William Dever Scrapbooks, IV, C.H.S.

49. Hermann, *Recollections*, p. 137; *C.I.-O.*, Nov. 5, 1899.

50. Quoted in Amy Balcomb, *Our Municipal Government in Its Relation to the Liquor Traffic* (Chicago: Young People's Civic League, [1915]), Part I, p. 36. Busse's brother described in *H.C.S.*, p. 179.

51. Hermann, *Recollections*, p. 212; *Broad-Axe*, Dec. 10, 1904.

52. Hermann, *Recollections*, pp. 137–40.

53. Elmer Ellis, *Mr. Dooley's America: A Life of Finley Peter Dunne* (New York: Alfred A. Knopf, 1941), pp. 65–79; *C.T.*, Apr. 25, 1936; Charles Fanning, *Finley Peter Dunne and Mr. Dooley* (Lexington: University Press of Kentucky, 1978), pp. 23–26; Barbara Schaaf, *Mr. Dooley's Chicago* (Garden City, N.Y.: Anchor Press/Doubleday, 1977), pp. 65–66.

54. McGarry quote in *C.D.N.*, Apr. 25, 1936.

55. *C.T.*, June 25, Oct. 4, 1882; Municipal Court Judge John R. Caverly to Charles Schaffner, Sept. 1, Nov. 27, 1916, Schaffner Papers, C.H.S.

56. *C.F.P.* 29(Nov. 3, 1900):2.

57. *C.T.*, Apr. 2, 1881; Wendt and Kogan, *Lords of the Levee*, pp. 102–4; *B.T.*, Oct. 24, 1881.

58. *C.D.N.*, Oct. 22, 1894.

59. *C.T.*, Oct. 7, 1883; post-election stories, e.g., ibid., Apr. 3, 1883.

60. *L.O.* 1(Oct. 25, 1884):29.

61. *C.T.*, July 22, 1881, Nov. 18, 1883; *C.P.*, Feb. 26, 1895; Sidney I. Roberts, "Businessmen in Revolt, 1874–1900," (Ph.D. diss., Northwestern University, 1960), p. 84.

62. Leslie Ainley, *Boston Mahatma: Martin Lomasney* (Boston: Bruce Humphries, 1949), pp. 47–49; John Buenker, "The Mahatma and Progressive Reform: Martin Lomasney as Lawmaker, 1911–17," *New England Quarterly* 44(Sept., 1971):397–419; A. D. VanNostrand, "The Lomasney Legend," ibid. 21(Dec., 1948):448–49; see *B.G.*, Mar. 2–June 21, 1903 for coverage of an election scandal and information on Lomasney's machine.

63. George Ade, "Some Instances of Political Devotion," *Chicago Record*, Mar. 29, 1894.

64. *C.T.*, Feb. 4, 1883.

65. McElwain, "The Saloon Problem in Chicago," pp. 78–79.

66. Wendt and Kogan, *Lords of the Levee*, pp. 102–8.

67. *C.T.*, Nov. 6, 8, 1892, Feb. 4, 5, 7, 1893, Sept. 13, 1927; *H.C.S.*, p. 197; "Contested Election, Third Senatorial District for State Representative, 1892," typescript, Illinois State Archives (its 1,000 pages contain copious detail about Levee voting practices).

68. Observations drawn from occupations listed in Sampson and Murdock directories.

69. There were also eight wholesalers among the councilmen.

70. By 1902, both retailers were gone from the aldermen; one wholesaler remained.

71. *H.C.S.*, p. 200, on Kowalski.

72. Ibid., p. 161; *C.T.*, Mar. 21, 1886, Apr. 3, 1892.

73. Carter Harrison, *Some Phases of the Municipal Problem*

(n.p.,[1905]), a pamphlet in Carter Harrison Papers, Newberry Library.

74. Lists of aldermen compared with Lakeside and other Chicago directories.

75. Ibid.

76. M. L. Ahern, *The Great Revolution* (Chicago: Lakeside, 1874), p. 218.

77. Wendt and Kogan, *Lords of the Levee*, pp. 40, 43, 44; *C.T.*, Mar. 21, 1886.

78. Joseph Kingsbury, "The Merit System in Chicago from 1895 to 1915," *Public Personnel Studies* 4(May, 1926):162–63.

79. *C.T.*, Feb. 21, 1894, July 15, Aug. 4, Dec. 2, 1905; *C.H.*, May 29, 1895; *C.D.N.*, Dec. 15, 1905; *C.R.-H.*, Aug. 30, 1905; Citizens' Association of Chicago, *Bulletin No. 1*, 1905, pp. 1–2; Roberts, "Businessmen in Revolt," pp. 101–2.

80. Lincoln Steffens, *The Shame of the Cities* (New York: Hill and Wang, 1957), p. 23, a reprint of the 1902 article, "Tweed Days in St. Louis"; Davis, *Spearheads for Reform*, pp. 177–80, 187; Barry D. Karl, *Charles Merriam and the Study of Politics* (Chicago: University of Chicago Press, 1974), pp. 61–83; Joel Tarr, *A Study in Boss Politics: William Lorimer of Chicago* (Urbana: University of Illinois Press, 1971), is a model study of one politician's conflict with reformers.

CHAPTER 5

1. Woods, *City Wilderness*, pp. 85–86; Woods, *Americans in Process*, pp. 106, 118, 125; "Analysis . . . Pawnbrokers," pp. 10–11; Krausz, *Street Types, passim; B.G.*, Sept. 27, 1891.

2. Woods, *Americans in Process*, pp. 224–39; Evelyn Boylan Epsey, "Old World Customs Continued in Chicago," *By Archer Road* 3(Sept., 1909):3–5; "Celebrating a Feast Day," *By Archer Road* 3(Sept., 1909):3–5; *B.G.*, Oct. 4, 5, 1891, on the North End.

3. Woods, *Americans in Process*, pp. 61–70; *C.T.*, Nov. 19, 1883.

4. Ibid.

5. Jacob N. Burnes, *The Story of West End House* (Boston: Stratford Publishing Co., 1934)n.p.; William Foote Whyte, "Race Conflicts in the North End," *New England Quarterly* 12(Dec., 1939):623–42; William Foote Whyte, *Street Corner Society* (Chicago: University of Chicago Press, 1943). The article contains material omitted in the book.

6. Nesmith, "The Housing of Wage-Earners," p. 173.

7. Ulf Beijbom, *Swedes in Chicago: A Demographic and Social Study of the 1846–1880 Immigration* (Upsala: Laromedelsforlagen, and Chicago: Chicago Historical Society, 1971), pp. 258–59.

8. Ibid.; *H.C.S.*, pp. 210–11.

9. *M.C.* 26(Apr. 16, 1910):45; Rocco Brindisi, "The Italian and Public Health," *Charities* 12(May 7, 1904):486; Woods, *Americans in Process*, p. 204; "Chicago Commons Study of Prohibition," p. 7; Frederick Bushee, "Italian Immigrants in Boston," *Arena* 17(Apr., 1897):733; *The Italians in Chicago*, U.S. Commissioner of Labor, Ninth Special Report, 1897, p. 725; Rudolph Vecoli, "Chicago's Italians Prior to World War I: A Study of Their Social and Economic Adjustment," (Ph.D. diss., University of Wisconsin, 1963); Humbert Nelli, *Italians in Chicago, 1880–1930* (New York: Oxford University Press, 1970).

10. Woods, *Americans in Process*, pp. 201–2; Woods, *City Wilderness*, pp. 45–46; Alessandro Mastro-Valerio, "Remarks upon the Italian Colony in Chicago," Residents of Hull House, *Hull House Maps and Papers*, pp. 135–36; Jane Addams, *The Second Twenty Years at Hull House* (New York: Macmillan, 1930), pp. 221–22.

11. *C.F.P.* 42(Oct. 24, 1914):8; *C.D.N.*, Feb. 2, Mar. 19, 1884.

12. Bushee, "Italian Immigrants," pp. 726–28; Woods, *Americans in Process*, pp. 128, 202–6; Vecoli, "Chicago's Italians," pp. 298–301.

13. *L'Italia*, July 20, 1889; Vecoli, "Chicago's Italians," pp. 302–37.

14. Ibid., pp. 245, 253–54, 260, 266–70.

15. Ibid., pp. 91–92; Bushee, "Italian Immigrants," p. 728; Natalie Walker, "Chicago Housing Conditions, X: Greeks and Italians in the Neighborhood of Hull House," *American Journal of Sociology* 21(Nov., 1915):285–316.

16. Robert A. Woods and Albert J. Kennedy, *The Zone of Emergence*, 2nd ed. (Cambridge: M.I.T. Press, 1969), p. 303.

17. Josepha Zeman, "The Bohemian People in Chicago," Residents of Hull House, *Hull House Maps and Papers*, pp. 115–30; Helen Wilson and Eunice Smith, "Chicago Housing Conditions, VIII: Among the Slovaks of the 20th Ward," *American Journal of Sociology* 20(Sept., 1914):145–69; *C.T.*, Mar. 7, 1886; Emily G. Balch, *Our Slavic Fellow Citizens* (New York: Charities Publication Committee, 1910), p. 277.

18. Zeman, "The Bohemian People," pp. 120–21; *C.T.*, Mar. 7, 1886; Pierce, *A History of Chicago*, 3:33–34; Jakub Horak, "The Assimilation of Czechs in Chicago," (Ph.D. diss., University of Chicago, 1920), pp. 1–50; *Denni Hlasatel*, Apr. 23, 1911, Apr. 23, 1913.

19. Ibid., Mar. 13, 1896, Nov. 25, 1907, Dec. 2, 1911; L. O. Cleminson to Victo vonBorosini, Apr. 8, 1913, Civic Committee Minutes, VIII, City Club of Chicago Papers, C.H.S.; Hayner, "Effect of Prohibition," p. 16.

20. *Denni Hlasatel*, June 7, 1901, Jan. 4, 1904, Nov. 23, 1910, Feb. 12, 1912; *C.T.*, Jan. 26, 1880.

21. Justin Galford, "The Foreign-born and Urban Growth in the Great Lakes, 1850–1950: A Study of Chicago, Cleveland, Detroit and Milwaukee," (Ph.D. diss., New York University 1957), *passim;* Woods

and Kennedy, *Zone of Emergence*, pp. 77–78, 102–3, 108, 111, 145, 159.

22. U.S. Census, 1890, *Population*, I, pp. 670–75; Ibid., 1910, *Population*, II, pp. 989, 1007–15.

23. Hunter, *Tenement Conditions*, pp. 26, 41, 54, 59, 64; Edith Abbott, *The Tenements of Chicago, 1908–1935* (Chicago: University of Chicago Press, 1936), pp. 133–34.

24. Joseph J. Parot, "The American Faith and the Persistence of Polonia, 1870–1920," (Ph.D. diss., Northern Illinois University, 1971).

25. *The Public Good* 2(Oct. 28, 1886):6; George, "The Saloon Problem," p. 90; Hayner, "The Effect of Prohibition," p. 76.

26. *Dziennik Zwazkowy*, Dec. 10, 1910; *Narod Polski*, Jan. 17, 1900, Jan. 8, 1913.

27. William I. Thomas and Florian Znaniecki, *The Polish Peasant in Europe and America*, 6 vols. (Boston: Richard H. Badger, 1920), 5:209.

28. *Narod Polski*, Jan. 8, 1913.

29. Ibid., July 6, 1904.

30. Ibid., July 5, 1911; *Dziennik Zwazkowy*, Nov. 30, 1914.

31. *Abstynet*, Nov., 1911.

32. *List of Names of Parties Who Sell or Keep Intoxicating Liquors, 1868*, Boston, City Doc. 140, 1868.

33. Ruth M. Piper, "The Irish in Chicago, 1848 to 1871," (M.A. thesis, University of Chicago, 1936), pp. 47–62; *C.T.*, Apr. 13, 1874.

34. E. P. Hutchinson, *Immigrants and Their Children, 1850–1950* (New York: John Wiley & Sons, 1956), pp. 172–75.

35. *Narod Polski*, Mar. 28, 1900; George, "The Saloon Problem," p. 90; Addams, *Twenty Years*, p. 222.

36. Webster, "The Saloon and Juvenile Delinquency," pp. 3–4; George, "The Saloon Problem," p. 91.

37. *C.F.P.* 30(May 18, 1907):4; George, "The Saloon Problem," p. 91.

38. "Northcenter, Document 5," p. 4 in Vivien Palmer Scrapbooks, II, C.H.S.

39. Unidentified clipping, May 20, 1888, Harpel Scrapbooks, S4–12, C.H.S.

40. *Proceedings of the Boston City Council Board of Aldermen*, July 1, 1878, pp. 427–28, July 8, 1878, pp. 448–50.

41. Ibid.

42. *Public Good* 1(Nov. 26, 1885):1.

43. *M.C.* 8(Mar. 1, 1902):1.

44. *N.E.T.* 2(May 30, 1885):6.

45. *C.T.*, Aug. 15, 1880, March 17, 19, 1881; *C.F.P.* 27(Jan. 9, 1904):5, 31(Mar. 14, 1908):6.

46. Ibid.

47. Spear, *Black Chicago*, pp. 6–7, 41–43; Chicago Commission on Race Relations, *The Negro in Chicago* (Chicago: University of Chicago Press, 1922), pp. 232–34.

48. *M.C.* 9(Feb. 16, 1893):19; Paul L. Dunbar, "The Color Line in Chicago," *The Pilgrim* 7(July, 1903):9–10; *C.T.*, Feb. 7, 1883, is racist in tone.

49. *Cecil v. Green* 161 Ill.265(1896); Spear, *Black Chicago*, pp. 41–43; Chicago Commission in Race Relations, *The Negro in Chicago*, pp. 232–33.

50. *M.C.* 20(Apr. 16, 1904):63; *C.F.P.* 27(Apr. 9, 1904):4; *C.R.-H.*, July 14, 1905; "Douglas, Document 8," p. 4, Palmer Scrapbooks, IV, C.H.S.

51. *Broad-Axe*, May 27, 1905.

52. *C.F.P.* 32(Jan. 30, 1909):4; *Proceedings of the Chicago City Council*, June 12, 1916, p. 648; *Chicago Defender*, June 17, 1916; *C.T.*, June 14, 1916.

53. Epple, *Liquor Laws of Massachusetts*, p. 135; Louis Epple, *Supplement to the Liquor Laws of Massachusetts* (Boston: City of Boston Printing Department, 1917), p. 74; *Bryant v. Rich's Grill* 216 Mass.344(1912).

54. U.S. Census, 1890, *Occupations*, p. 516; U.S. Census, 1910, *Occupations*, p. 544; brewery ads, *Broad-Axe*, Dec. 3, 1904, Sept. 18, 1909; Junius B. Wood, *The Negro in Chicago* (Chicago: Chicago Daily News, 1916), pp. 11–12; Louise DeKoven Bowen, *The Colored People of Chicago* (Chicago: Juvenile Protective Association, 1913). pp. 10–11.

55. Woods, *Americans in Process*, p. 123; *B.G.*, Jan. 12, 1901.

56. U.S. Census, 1900, *Occupations*, p. 494; U.S. Census, 1910, *Occupations*, p. 540. Because of imprecise divisions of ethnic and occupational groups, the Massachusetts State Census is of no use here.

57. Daniels, *In Freedom's Birthplace*, p. 365.

58. *Rhea's New Citizen's Directory of Chicago* (Chicago: Press of W. S. McCleland, 1908), n.p.; Ford S. Black, *Black's Blue Book* (Chicago: Ford S. Black, 1916), p. 32; *Broad-Axe*, Sept. 9, 1905, Aug. 4, 1906, e.g.

59. I. C. Harris, comp., *Colored Men's Professional and Business Directory* (Chicago: I. C. Harris, 1885), n.p.

60. *Rhea's New Citizen's Directory*, n.p.; *Broad-Axe*, June 3, 1905, Aug. 14, 1909.

61. Ibid., Oct. 12, 1907, Oct. 2, 1909.

62. Ibid., Dec. 16, 1905, Mar. 10, 1906, Mar. 5, 1910, Jan. 1, 1911.

63. Ibid., Dec. 16, 1905.

64. *L.O.* 1(Mar. 21, 1885):194–95.

65. Grace Abbott, "A Study of the Greeks of Chicago," *American Journal of Sociology* 15(Nov., 1909):379–93; George Kourvetaris, *First and Second Generation Greeks in Chicago* (Athens: National Centre

for Social Research, 1971), pp. 43–53, 71–77; Walker, "Chicago Housing Conditions: Greeks and Italians," pp. 285–316; Woods, *City Wilderness*, p. 46; Woods, *Americans in Process*, pp. 122–23; William I. Cole, *Immigrant Races in Massachusetts: The Greeks* (Boston: Massachusetts Bureau of Immigration, [1914]).

66. Jeremiah Jenks and W. Jett Lauck, *The Immigration Problem*, 3rd rev. ed. (New York: Funk & Wagnalls, 1913), p. 126; Abbott, "A Study of the Greeks," p. 386; Massachusetts, *Report of the Commission on Immigration*, House Report 2300, 1914, pp. 202–4; Theodore Salutos, *Greeks in the United States* (Cambridge: Harvard University Press, 1964), pp. 78–83.

67. *C.T.*, Mar. 11, 1886; *Salonika*, Nov. 1, 1913, Dec. 19, 1914, Oct. 2, 1915.

68. Quoted in Paul F. Cressey, "The Succession of Cultural Groups in the City of Chicago," (Ph.D. diss., University of Chicago, 1930), pp. 148–49.

69. Immigrant Protective League, *Annual Report, 1909–10*, p. 23; Theodore Sachs, *A Study of Tuberculosis in Chicago, with Special Reference to the Statistics Collected in the Jewish District* (Chicago: Municipal Tuberculosis Sanitarium, 1905); Louis Wirth, *The Ghetto* (Chicago: University of Chicago Press, 1928), pp. 195–240; Hunter, *Tenement Conditions*, pp. 12, 32, 36, 59, 92, 94, 119, 149, 158, 185; Edith Abbott and Sophonisba Breckinridge, "Chicago Housing Conditions, IV: The West Side Revisited," *American Journal of Sociology* 17(July, 1911):1–34; Abbott, *Tenements of Chicago*, pp. 85–92; Woods, *Americans in Process*, p. 240; Ben Rosen, "The Trend of Jewish Population in Boston," *Federated Jewish Charities of Boston* 1(Jan., 1921):12–14; *B.G.*, Apr. 23, 1900, July 14, 1901.

70. Charles Zeublin, "The Chicago Ghetto," in Residents of Hull House, *Hull House Maps and Papers*, pp. 94–95; Late Levy, "Health and Sanitation," in Charles S. Bernheimer, ed., *The Russian Jew in the United States* (Philadelphia: John C. Winston, 1905), p. 320; Melendy, "The Saloon," p. 435; Woods, *City Wilderness*, pp. 40–41; Woods, *Americans in Process*, p. 241; Cole and Durland, "Report on Substitutes," pp. 331–32.

71. Minnie F. Low, "Philanthropy, Chicago," in Bernheimer, *The Russian Jew*, pp. 87–99; *B.G.*, Jan. 28, 1900; I. K. Friedman, "Amusements and Social Life, Chicago," in Bernheimer, *The Russian Jew*; Zeublin, "The Chicago Ghetto," p. 104; Addams, *Twenty Years*, p. 222; Seymour Pomrenze, "Aspects of Chicago Russian Jewish Life, 1893–1915," in Simon Rawidowicz, *Chicago Pinkas* (Chicago: College of Jewish Studies, 1952), pp. 126–29.

72. Hutchinson, *Immigrants and Their Children*, pp. 172–75; Balch, *Our Slavic Fellow Citizens*, pp. 140–41; on Jewish mobility, Thernstrom, *Other Bostonians*, pp. 111–44.

73. Friedman, "Amusements and Social Life," pp. 249–52.

74. *Daily Jewish Courier*, Mar. 6, 1914.

75. The 1880 census did not separate men and women or saloon-keepers and bartenders in each job category.

76. In Chicago the proportion of native-born workers in all fields fell from 44.2 percent in 1880 to 21.7 percent in 1900; in Boston the decline was from 59.1 percent in 1880 to 26.8 percent in 1900. The 1910 census did not break down the foreign-born by nationality, but it did show that in Boston the native-born whites increased their share of proprietorships and bartender jobs from 23.3 percent in 1900 to 41.5 percent in 1910. In the latter year, 49.4 percent of the Hub workforce was native-born. In Chicago, the native-born whites increased their share of the total saloon-related jobs from 18.1 percent in 1900 to 36.8 percent; the total percentage of the Chicago labor force that was native-born white stood at 47.2 percent. U.S. Census, 1910, *Occupations*, pp. 539–40, 544–47.

CHAPTER 6

1. Glen E. Holt, "The Changing Perception of Urban Pathology: An Essay in the Development of Mass Transit in the United States," in Kenneth T. Jackson and Stanley K. Schultz, *Cities in American History* (New York: Alfred A. Knopf, 1972), pp. 324–43; Kate Leipman, *The Journey to Work* (New York: Oxford University Press, 1944).

2. *B.T.*, Aug. 18, 1883.

3. *Proceedings of the Boston Board of Aldermen*, Mar. 14, 1887, pp. 237–39.

4. *C.H.*, Feb. 2, 1893; see also Ibid., Feb. 26, 1892.

5. Roswell Phelps, *South End Factory Operatives and Their Residence* (Boston: South End House, 1903), and Woods, *Zone of Emergence*.

6. "Boston Working Class Homes," Massachusetts, Bureau of Labor Statistics, *Annual Report, 1870*, pp. 175–76.

7. Chicago, Special Park Commission, "Report on Conditions, to the West Park Commissioners, May 24, 1902," p. 2, Raymond Robins Papers, S.H.S.W.

8. Graham Taylor, *Pioneering on Social Frontiers* (Chicago: University of Chicago Press, 1930), p. 280; *The Neighbor* 2(May, 1901):7.

9. Philip R. Mason, "The League of American Wheelmen and the Good Roads Movement, 1880–1905," (Ph.D. diss., University of Michigan, 1957); *C.E.*, July 31, 1903; *B.G.*, Aug. 3, 1901, Sept. 29, 1902.

10. E.g., *Proceedings of the Boston Board of Aldermen*, Sept. 19, 1881, p. 616; *B.G.*, Jan. 27, 1901.

11. *Chicago City Manual, 1910*, pp. 112–14.

12. For references, see Duis, "The Saloon and the Public City," pp. 120–22.

13. Illinois, Department of Factory Inspection, *A.R.*, *1904–12*, contains lists of larger barrooms, their locations, and numbers of employees.

14. *Chicago's Thousand Dollar Book* (Chicago: Thousand Dollar Book Co., 1914), *passim*.

15. Stanley McMichael and Robert Bingham, *City Growth and Values* (Cleveland: Stanley McMichael Publishing Organization, 1928), pp. 81–89; Richard Hurd, *Principles of City Land Values* (New York: Record and Guide, 1903), pp. 89–96.

16. Outlying shopping districts in compact Boston were in the suburbs; on Chicago see Malcolm Proudfoot, "The Major Outlying Business Centers of Chicago," (Ph.D. diss., University of Chicago, 1936).

17. *L.T.R.* 7(Nov. 10, 1899):7.

18. Robert Sommer, *Personal Space* (Englewood Cliffs, N.J.: Prentice-Hall, 1969), pp. 120–31, deals with the design of drinking places.

19. *B.G.*, Feb. 10, 14, Mar. 17, May 8, June 5, Oct. 29, 1891.

20. *C.T.*, Mar. 13–15, 1904.

21. Calkins, *Substitutes*, pp. 55–63.

22. *Zgoda*, Mar. 16, 1887; *Dziennik Chicagoski*, Jan. 2, 1892, Apr. 19, 1893.

23. "City Briefs" column, *C.T.*, during early 1880s gives many examples.

24. Ibid., Apr. 21, 1886, Apr. 6, 1887; Charles Stelzle, *The Workingman and Social Problems* (Chicago: Fleming H. Revell, 1903), pp. 37–52.

25. *L.O.* 1(July 18, 1885):332.

26. Lane, *Policing the City*, pp. 206–7; *C.T.*, Aug. 6, 1883; *Chicagoer Arbeiter-Zeitung*, Sept. 1, 1882.

27. Henry David, *The History of the Haymarket Affair*, rev. ed. (New York: Collier Books, 1963), pp. 220–23, 401–3; *C.T.*, May 4–10, 18, 1886, Apr. 16, 1891; *B.G.*, Nov. 12, 1887, Nov. 11, 12, 1888.

28. *C.T.*, Jan. 23, 1883; *Svornost*, July 18, 1892; *Skandanaven*, Oct. 26, 1890, Jan. 26, 1892.

29. *Boston Almanac and Business Directory, 1890* (Boston: Sampson, Murdock, 1890), p. 306, reveals that eight of the city's twenty-two "intelligence offices" were located along a few blocks of Washington Street and near sixteen saloons; Cole and Durland, "Report on Substitutes," in Calkins, *Substitutes*, p. 326; Massachusetts, Committee to Investigate Employment Offices, *Report, 1911*, pp. 87–89.

30. Melendy, "The Saloon," p. 297; *Chicago Business Directory, 1889* (Chicago: Rand McNally, 1889), is a reverse directory, with listing according to addresses, showing proximity of businesses.

31. *Illinois Staats-Zeitung*, July 1, 1881; Minnie F. Low to Raymond Robins, Jan. 30, 1906, Raymond Robins Papers, S.H.S.W.; Chicago, Mayor's Committee on Unemployment, *Report*, 1914, pp. 116–17.

32. *Murray Mathews* v. *People*, 201 Ill.389(1903); J. E. Connor, "Free Employment Offices in the United States," U.S. Department of Labor, *Bulletin* 4(Jan., 1907):15–28.

33. Grace Abbott, "The Chicago Employment Agency and the Immigrant Workers," *American Journal of Sociology* 14(Nov., 1908): 289–305; Committee on Labor Conditions, Civic Committee Minutes, V, 1910–11, pp. 398–550, City Club of Chicago Papers, C.H.S.; "The 'Vampire' Employment Saloons," *The Survey* 23(Jan. 8, 1910):491–92.

34. Anti-Saloon League, *Yearbook, 1912*, p. 30; Chicago . . . Committee on Unemployment, *Report*, p. 24.

35. Hayner, "Effect," p. 2; Anti-Saloon League, *Yearbook, 1912*, p. 30; *Chicago Sun*, June 14, 1946, tells of a bar near a police station.

36. "Economic Aspects of the Liquor Problem," U.S. Department of Labor, *Bulletin* 3(July, 1898):549.

37. "Chicago Commons Study of Prohibition," p. 1; *C.F.P.* 43 (Oct. 30, 1915):4; see Ibid. 36(Jan. 25, 1913):1, on Burlington.

38. Almon Abel, "The Saloon Question in Chicago from a Financial, Administrative and Political Standpoint," Seminary in Political Science, Contributions, III, 1895, p. 73, Northwestern University.

39. *M.C.* 12(May 1, 1896):56.

40. Ibid., 29(Mar. 1, 1913):36; *Co-operation* 4(July 30, 1904):244; *C.T.*, Mar. 6, 1904.

41. *M.D.* 2(Mar. 1, 1890):4; *L.T.R.* 4(Jan. 18, 1898):15; National Liquor League, *Report of the Annual Meeting, 1908*, p. 15.

42. Paul W. Ivey, "The Liquor Industry and Industrial Efficiency," (M.A. thesis, University of Illinois, 1913); "Welfare Work for Employees in Industrial Establishments in the U.S.A." U.S. Department of Labor, *Bulletin* 250(Feb., 1919):53; George Bevans, "How One Thousand Workingmen Spend Their Spare Time," *Outlook* 106(Apr. 4, 1914):762–66, studies New York; Timberlake, *Prohibition and the Progressive Movement*, pp. 67–99.

43. Earle S. Johnson, "The Natural History of the Central Business District with Special Reference to Chicago," (Ph.D. diss., University of Chicago, 1941), and Ward, "Nineteenth Century Boston," deal with specialization of downtown space.

44. Kevin Lynch, *What Time Is This Place?* (Cambridge: M.I.T. Press, 1972).

45. George Ade, "With the Market Gardeners," *Chicago Record*, May 9, 1894.

46. *B.G.*, Jan. 5, 1890.

47. Ibid.

48. Ibid.; *Among Ourselves* 3(Nov., 1906):72, 3(Feb., 1907):182; *The Restaurant Bulletin* 1(Mar., 1904):22.

49. *B.G.*, May 4, 1890; Frances Willard, *Occupations for Women* (New York: Success Co., 1897), pp. 120–25; *A Business Tour of Chicago*, p. 158.

50. McElwain, "The Saloon Problem in Chicago," p. 52.

51. Ibid., p. 53; "Vogelsang's," *Indoors and Out* 1(Feb., 1906): 247–50.

52. Melendy, "The Saloon," pp. 301–3.

53. Quotes John O'Brien of the Chicago Bartenders Union, *C.F.P.* 26(July 2, 1904):4; *B.G.*, Aug. 22, 29, 1891, makes the same observations about Boston.

54. *C.F.P.* 42(Feb. 6, 1915):1.

55. *C.T.*, Jan. 1, 1889.

56. Charles J. Kennedy, "Commuter Services in the Boston Area, 1835–60," *Business History Review* 36(Summer, 1962):153–70.

57. *N.E.T.* 2(Dec. 13, 1885):156; want ads, *B.G.*, Mar. 14, 1888.

58. *L.O.* 1(Feb. 14, 1885):156; *The Public Good* 1(May 20, 1886):4; Boston, W.C.T.U., *A.R., 1886*, p. 8; *N.E.T.* 2(Dec. 13, 1884):1.

59. *M.C.* 2(Feb. 1, 1904):41, 23(Mar. 1, 1907):53.

60. Johnson, "Central Business District," pp. 490–92.

61. Woods, *City Wilderness*, p. 111; *King's Handbook of Boston*, 5th ed. (Cambridge: Moses King, 1883), pp. 233–37.

62. *B.G.*, Feb. 23, 1890, Aug. 23, 1891, Dec. 1, 1901.

63. *C.T.*, Feb. 8, 1903.

64. Ibid., Mar. 20, 1867; "Report of the Committee on Streets, Alleys and Bridges," Civic Committee Minutes, Nov. 20, 1908, p. 329, City Club of Chicago Papers, C.H.S.

65. Cole and Durland, "Report on Substitutes," p. 326; *Proceedings of the Boston City Council, Board of Aldermen and Common Council*, numerous references, June, 1883–June, 1886; South End House Association, *A.R., 1898; Boston Traveler*, June 28, 1901.

66. *My Neighbor* 2(Oct., 1893):1.

67. Boston Police Department, *A.R., 1867*, p. 13; *Proceedings of the Boston City Council, Board of Aldermen and Common Council*, numerous references, Jan., 1876–Oct., 1879.

68. *Proceedings of the Boston City Council, Common Council*, June 27, 1889, p. 744.

69. *Proceedings of the Boston City Council, Board of Aldermen*, Nov. 30, 1891, p. 1174.

70. Melendy, "The Saloon," p. 299; Calkins, *Substitutes*, p. 19; V. C. Hart, "The Need for Public Comfort Stations," *Domestic Engineering* 39(May 25, 1907):182–92, 217–21, which lists downtown public toilets.

71. Ibid., p. 191.

72. City Club of Chicago, *Bulletin* 1(Nov. 20, 1907):249.

73. "Chicago City Hall Comfort Station," *Domestic Engineering* 57(Oct. 28, 1911):88–90; *C.T.*, Oct. 16, 1911.

74. Benjamin Blinstrub and Eloise Blinstrub, *Survey of Comfort*

Stations on Elevated Railways (Chicago: Juvenile Protective Association, 1916).

75. *Moran's Dictionary of Chicago*, pp. 36–37.

76. Woods, *City Wilderness*, pp. 86, 135; Woods, *Americans in Process*, p. 123; Albert B. Wolfe, *The Lodging House Problem in Boston* (Cambridge: Harvard University Press, 1906), pp. 86–93; Carroll D. Wright, *The Working Girls of Boston* (Boston: Wright and Potter Printing Co., 1889), pp. 6–11, 34, 41–49, 76–118; Robert Woods and Albert Kennedy, *Young Working Girls* (Boston: Houghton Mifflin, 1913); Nell Nelson [pseud.], *The White Slave Girls of Chicago; Nell Nelson's Startling Disclosures of the Cruelties and Iniquities Practiced in the Workshops and Factories of a Great City* (Chicago: Barkley Publishing Co., 1888); "Working Women in Chicago," Illinois Bureau of Labor Statistics, *Seventh Biennial Report, 1892*, pp. xi–l, 1–351.

77. *Report of the Commission Appointed by the Mayor to Investigate Lodging House Conditions in the City of Boston*, Boston, City Doc. 160, 1908, p. 5; "Community Survey of the Twenty-first Ward," [Chicago] *City Club Bulletin* 6(Mar. 13, 1913):89; Wright, *Working Girls*, pp. 22–23.

78. Woods, *City Wilderness*, p. 82; Robert Woods, "Longer and Shorter Retrospects," in South End House, *A.R., 1911*, pp. 7–8; *B.G.*, Feb. 21, 1900; Wolfe, *Lodging House Problem*, pp. 23–24, 110; *Report . . . Lodging House Conditions*, pp. 6–7.

79. *Moran's Dictionary of Chicago*, pp. 36–37.

80. *Chicago Times*, Dec. 2, 1894; Wolfe, *Lodging House Problem*, pp. 52, 155.

81. *B.G.*, Mar. 3, 1901, has revealing fictionalized account; Edith Abbott, "Housing Conditions in Chicago, II: Families in Furnished Rooms," *American Journal of Sociology* 16(Nov., 1910):295; Wolfe, *Lodging House Problem*, pp. 38–51; Woods, *Americans in Process*, p. 140.

82. Wolfe, *Lodging House Problem*, p. 28; "Community Survey of the Twenty-first Ward," p. 94.

83. *B.G.*, Aug. 25, 1889; Wolfe, *Lodging House Problem*, p. 112.

84. Allen D. Albert, *South End House* (Boston: n.p., n.d.).

85. *Lakeside Directory of Chicago, 1880* (Chicago: Chicago Directory Company, 1880), pp. 1461–73; *List of Licensed Saloons in the City of Chicago* (Chicago: Jno. R. McCabe, City Clerk, 1906), pp. 14–15; Young, "Disintegrating Neighborhood," pp. 42, 69; Wolfe, *Lodging House Problem*, pp. 27–29; Henry C. Alley, "Moral Problem of Modern Pool Rooms," (M.A. thesis, University of Chicago, 1915), pp. 7–9; Edith Ogden Harrison, "Bicycles and Billiards," typescript in Carter Harrison Papers, Newberry Library.

86. *B.G.*, Aug. 25, 1889, Sept. 25, 1901.

87. Woods and Kennedy, *Young Working Girls*, pp. 101–11; Elizabeth Westwood, "Working Girls at Play," *Metropolitan Magazine*

33(Oct., 1910):32–39; Nehemiah Boynton, "Working Girls," *The Arena* 2(Aug., 1890):370–72; Wright, *Working Girls*, pp. 118–26; "Working Women in Large Cities," U.S. Department of Labor, *Fourth A.R., 1889*, pp. 14–17; Immigrant Protective League, *A.R., 1909–10*, p. 22; Florence J. Chaney, "The Social and Educational Protection of the Immigrant Girl in Chicago," (M.A. thesis, University of Chicago, 1912), pp. 63–73.

88. Mrs. Charles Israels, "The Dance Hall and the Amusement Resorts," *Transactions of the American Society for Sanitary Prophylaxis* 3(1910):46–47.

89. Woods and Kennedy, *Young Working Girls*, p, 111.

90. Sister Joan Bland, *Hibernian Crusade: The Story of the Catholic Total Abstinence Union in America* (Washington, D.C.: Catholic University of America Press, 1951).

91. Boston Seamen's Friend Society, *A.R., 1830*, pp. 7–8, *A.R., 1845*, pp. 14–20.

92. *C.T.*, Mar. 14, 1880.

93. *B.T.*, Dec. 1, 1881; also, Ibid., Nov. 3, 1881.

94. Massachusetts Total Abstinence Society, *A.R., 1882*, p. 12; *B.T.*, Apr. 30, 1883, May 20, Dec. 2, 8, 1884, Sept. 5, 1885; *L.O.* 1(Apr. 11, 1885):219; *T.C.* 3(Mar., 1881):1, 14(July, 1892):5.

95. *The Necessity for Moral and Christian Effort among Young Men* (Boston: Y.M.C.A., 1867), p. 3; L. L. Doggett, *History of the Boston Young Men's Christian Association* (Boston: n.p., 1901); Dedmon, *Great Enterprises; The Washingtonian* 1(Feb., 1876):11.

96. Boston, Y.M.C.A., *A.R., 1902*, p. 55.

97. Cherrington, *Standard Encyclopedia*, 3:962–63; *A.B.R.* 8(Jan. 31, 1895):373; *M.C.* 11(Feb. 16, 1895):55; Calkins, *Substitutes*, p. 266; Chicago Department of Health, *A.R., 1897–98*, pp. 217–18; John T. Bramhall, "Chicago People's Institute and Home Salon," *Frank Leslie's Weekly* 80(Apr. 11, 1895):240.

98. E. C. E. Dorion, *The Redemption of the South End* (Boston: Epworth League of the Methodist Episcopal Church, 1902); Calkins, *Substitutes*, pp. 148–55; Davis, *Spearheads for Reform*, pp. 82–83.

99. Edward J. Ward, *The Social Center* (New York: D. Appleton, 1915), pp. 134, 135, 138, 255.

100. Its publications include Frederick Wines and John Koren, *The Liquor Problem in Its Legislative Aspects* (Boston: Houghton Mifflin, 1897); John Koren, *Economic Aspects of the Liquor Problem* (Boston: Houghton Mifflin, 1899); and Calkins, *Substitutes*.

101. Moore, "Social Value of the Saloon," p. 6; Calkins, *Substitutes*, pp. 37–41; *C.F.P.* 42(Jan. 2, 1915):1.

102. Allen Pond, "Gads Hill: Its Neighbors and Its Jobs," p. 2, mimeographed, Gads Hill Papers, C.H.S.

103. Dorion, *Redemption*, p. 38; Melendy, "The Saloon," p. 462.

104. Ibid.

105. *Hull House Yearbook, 1910*, p. 29; Melendy, "The Saloon," p. 293; Calkins, *Substitutes*, pp. 9, 46.

106. For instance, Gads Hill Center, *A.R., 1919*, p. 1.

107. Seymour Mandelbaum, *Boss Tweed's New York* (New York: John Wiley & Sons, 1965), is the best study of the city as a communications problem.

108. *Hull House Maps and Papers*, pp. 3–4, found eighty-one saloons in a third of a square mile; on interpreters, Mary Lynn McCree, "The First Year of Hull House," *Chicago History* 1(Fall, 1970):103.

109. Dorothea Moore, "A Day at Hull House," *American Journal of Sociology* 2(Mar., 1897):634.

CHAPTER 7

1. James Ford, *Slums and Housing*, 2 vols. (Cambridge: Harvard University Press, 1936), 1:92, 95.

2. *C.T.*, Mar. 16, 25, 1883; *C.D.N.*, Jan. 5, 1884; *Moran's Dictionary of Chicago*, pp. 9–10; *American Architect and Building News* 1(Apr. 21, 1877):126; *Inland Architect and Builder* 1(Feb., 1883):1; Smith, *Cyclopedia*, pp. 156–57; *Sanitary News* 8(July 31, 1886):169.

3. Boston, Assessor's Office, *A.R., 1890*, pp. 22–24; Ibid., *1900*, pp. 42–45; Ibid., *1910*, pp. 41–45; *B.G.*, Mar. 23, Sept. 28, 1890, Jan. 27, Feb. 17, Apr. 7, 1901, July 6, 1902.

4. *C.I.-O.*, Nov. 13, 1892; *C.T.*, Nov. 18, 1883.

5. Bainbridge Bunting, *Houses of Boston's Back Bay* (Cambridge: Harvard University Press, 1967), pp. 130–32.

6. James L. Davis, "The Impact of the Elevated System upon the Growth of the Northern Sector of Chicago," (Ph.D. diss., Northwestern University, 1970), pp. 103–6.

7. Sam Bass Warner, *Streetcar Suburbs* (Cambridge: M.I.T. and Harvard University Press, 1962); Antoinette F. Downing, et. al., *Survey of Architectural History of Cambridge, Report Two: Mid-Cambridge* (Cambridge: Cambridge Historical Commission, 1967), pp. 76–98; James Marston Fitch, *American Building: The Historical Forces That Shaped It*, 2nd ed. (Boston: Houghton Mifflin, 1966), pp. 118–21.

8. Walter Firey, *Land Use in Central Boston* (Cambridge: Harvard University Press, 1947), is the classic study.

9. Frank Wilkie, *Walks about Chicago*, 2nd ed. (Chicago: Kenney and Sumner, 1869), p. 20.

10. Henry-Russell Hitchcock, *H. H. Richardson and His Times*, rev. ed. (Cambridge: M.I.T. Press, 1961), p. 277.

11. "The Story of a House," a letter from John J. Glessner to his son, John. G. M. Glessner, n.d., reproduced by Chicago Architecture Foundation.

12. Bruce Grant, *Fight for a City: The Story of the Union League*

Club of Chicago and Its Times, 1880–1955 (Chicago: Rand McNally, 1955), *passim*.

13. E. M. Moore, "The Rich Man's Mail," *Twentieth Century Magazine* 20(Aug., 1912):320–28.

14. *Moran's Dictionary of Chicago*, p. 247.

15. *South Side Sayings*, Mar. 11, 1899.

16. Harrison, "Bicycles and Billiards."

17. Edmund Gillon, *Victorian Cemetery Art* (New York: Dover Publications, 1972), pp. v–xiii; *Handbook for Cambridge and Mt. Auburn* (Boston: Russell & Richardson, 1875), pp. 25–87; *King's Dictionary of Boston*, pp. 101–3; *C.T.*, Nov. 4, 1883; *B.G.*, Sept. 21, 1902.

18. Louis Cook, ed., *History of Norfolk County, Massachusetts, 1622–1918* (New York: S. J. Clarke Publishing Co., 1918), pp. 97, 206–7; D. Hamilton Hurd, comp., *History of Middlesex County, Massachusetts* (Philadelphia: J. W. Lewis, 1890)1:210, 324–25, 632. There are dozens of references to outlying inns in Vivien Palmer Scrapbooks, C.H.S.

19. St. Ida Roman Catholic Church and St. Mathias Roman Catholic Church, in Ibid., Uptown, Doc. 25, and Ravenswood, Doc. 30, respectively.

20. *C.F.P.* 30(June–Sept., 1907) for controversy over Mt. Greenwood section of Chicago; Vivien Palmer Scrapbooks, Uptown, Docs. 7 and 10; William Pattison, "The Cemeteries of Chicago: A Phase of Land Utilization," *Annals of the Association of American Geographers* 45(Sept., 1955):245–57.

21. Massachusetts Bureau of Labor Statistics, *A.R., 1880*, pp. 263–65.

22. *C.T.*, Mar. 3, 10, 1878, Feb. 10, 1883.

23. *W.B.* 4(Apr. 15, 1879):297; McClure, *Stories and Sketches*, pp. 166–67.

24. Windsor Park Protective Association, *A.R., 1898*, n.p.

25. Frances Willard, *A Classic Town: The Story of Evanston* (Chicago: Women's Temperance Publishing Association, 1891), pp. 166–67; Everett Chamberlin, *Chicago and Its Suburbs* (Chicago: T. A. Hungerford, 1874), pp. 378–82; "The Four Mile Limit," in Newton Bateman and Paul Selby, *Historical Encyclopedia of Illinois and History of Evanston*, 2 vols. (Chicago: Munsell Publishing Co., 1906), 2:317–21.

26. *John O'Leary* v. *County of Cook*, 28 Ill. 534(1862).

27. Citizens' League (Evanston) Minute Book, Evanston Historical Society; Four Mile League, *Semi-Annual Report, June 30, 1900; C.T.*, Apr. 4, 1893; *C. Times*, Apr. 27, 1894; *M.C.* 8–9 (Oct. 1892–Apr., 1893); Ibid., 11–12(July, 1895–Dec., 1896).

28. Arthur LeGacy, "Improvers and Preservers: A History of Oak Park, Illinois," (Ph.D. diss., University of Chicago, 1967), pp. 48–67,

94, 105, 128–29, 136, 194–202; W. Hubert Morken, "The Annexation of Morgan Park to Chicago: One Village's Response to Urban Growth" (M.A. thesis, University of Chicago, 1968), pp. 4, 23, 41, 47, 63, 73, 77; *Illinois Issue* 1(May 4, 1906):1; Chamberlin, *Chicago and Its Suburbs*, pp. 395–96; *C.T.*, June 16, 1883; On Highwood, a wet town near Fort Sheridan, see Marvin Wittelle, *28 Miles North: The Story of Highwood* (Highwood, Ill.: Highwood History Foundation, 1953), pp. 22, 35, 40, 42–43, 57–58, 62–75; Cherrington, *Standard Encyclopedia*, 1:206–07.

29. "A Study in Local Option: The Development of Local Option Legislation Prior to the Year 1900," United States Brewers' Association, *Yearbook, 1910*, pp. 13–23; "Local Option in Massachusetts," Ibid., pp. 96–131; Charles Roberts, *The Working of Local Option in the Cities: The Policy of No-License in the State of Massachusetts, U.S.A.* (London: United Kingdom Alliance, 1907), especially p. 9; W. Rathbone and E. L. Fanshawe, *Liquor Legislation in the United States and Canada* (London: Cassell, 1893), pp. 51–60; Amy Acton, *Local Option in Massachusetts* (New York: Russell Sage Foundation, 1910), *passim*.

30. "A Study in Local Option," pp. 97–99; Roberts, *Working of Local Option*, pp. 10–11; William F. Hoehn, *No License in Quincy* (Quincy, Mass.: n.p., 1899), *passim*; Cherrington, *Standard Encyclopedia*, 3:971–72; see *M.C.* and *B.T.* immediately after each December's election for results and commentary; Carroll Hill Woody, "Survey of Local Option Elections," vol. 5, pp. 63–89, in U.S., National Commission on Law Observance and Enforcement, *Report*, Senate Doc. 307, 71st Congress, 3rd Session, 1931 [Wickersham Commission].

31. Rogers, "College Town," p. 10; J. Dustin Tucker, "A Study of Housing Conditions in Evanston," Seminary in Economics, Finance and Administration, Contributions, XXVI, 1912, Northwestern University; Edmund Whitman, "The Frozen Truth," in *Ten No-License Years in Cambridge* (Cambridge: Cambridge, Massachusetts No-License Committee, 1898), pp. 134–35.

32. Frank Foxcroft, "The Unsuccessful Years," Ibid., pp. 89–92; Whitman, "The Frozen Truth," pp. 126–33, 137; Edmund Whitman, "The Political Methods of the No-License Campaign," in *Ten No-License Years in Cambridge*, pp. 113–26; Edmund Whitman, "Successful Prohibition," *Lend-a-Hand* 8(Feb., 1892):129–33.

33. James Merino, "The Great City and Its Suburbs: Attempts to Integrate Metropolitan Boston" (Ph.D. diss., University of Texas at Austin, 1968), pp. 37–46. There was also much comment about Boston dealers who lived in the suburbs: *Mayor's Message Communicating the Message from the Board of Police Submitting a List of Persons Holding Licenses for the Sale of Intoxicating Liquors Who Are Not Residents of Boston*, Boston, City Doc. 85, 1894.

34. "Neighborhood Improvement Associations," a pamphlet collection, Department of Special Collections, University of Chicago

Library; C. Bancroft Gillespie, *History of South Boston* (South Boston: Inquirer Publishing Co., 1900), pp. 81–85.

35. Numerous complaints from neighborhoods, in *Proceedings of the Boston City Council*, 1885–91, which are indexed; *United Improvement Association Bulletin* 1(Oct., 1910), pp. 8, 10; that publication details Boston activities, as does *The Improvement Club News* in Chicago; Amalie Hofer, *Neighborhood Improvement In and About Chicago* (Chicago: Chicago Woman's Club, 1909), pp. 31–32; *Conference of Improving Societies of Cook County, Art Institute, October 5, 1901; C.T.*, Oct. 5, 6, 1901.

36. Warner, *Streetcar Suburbs*.

37. *B.T.*, Dec. 1, 1881, July 1, 7, 1882, May 3, 1883; *L.O.* 1(Sept. 12, 1885):394–95; *B.G.*, Feb. 7, Mar. 3, 7, 12–14, Apr. 10, 18–24, 29, May 12, 1901, May 1–6, June 9, Oct. 15–Nov. 6, 1902; *H.B. 401 for District Option in Boston: An Argument against the Bill by William B. Sullivan* (Boston: Fort Hill Press, 1908), and *H.B. 642 for District Option: Argument against the Bill by William B. Sullivan* (Boston: Fort Hill Press, 1909).

38. Pierce, *History of Chicago*, 3:50–51, 331–33; *Chicagoer Arbeiter-Zeitung*, Aug. 2, 1888; *W.B.* 13(Aug. 15, 1888):1792, 13(Oct. 15, 1888):2276; Chamberlin, *Chicago and Its Suburbs*, pp. 352–54; William G. Beale, comp., *The Revised Code of Chicago, 1897* (Chicago: W. B. Conkey, 1897), pp. 458–59, 460–63; Lucretia Harper, "Hyde Park," typescript, 1939, C.H.S.

39. *H.C.S.*, pp. 131–32; Cherrington, *Standard Encyclopedia*, 3:970; *W.B.* 13(Dec. 15, 1888):100; *The Emancipator* 1(Nov., 1900):3; *People ex. rel. Michael J. Morrison v. DeWitt Cregier, Mayor*, 138 Ill. 401(1891).

40. *South Side Sayings*, Jan. 25, 1894; *Rhea's New Citizen's Directory, 1908*, n.p.; *C.T.*, May 17, 1914; *C.F.P.* 42(Jan. 2, 1915):5.

41. Rossiter Johnson, *A History of the World's Columbian Exposition*, 4 vols. (New York: D. Appleton, 1897), 1:360–62; Washington Park, Doc. 10, p. 2, and Woodlawn, Doc, 1, pp. 5, 8, in Vivien Palmer Scrapbooks, C.H.S.; *M.C.* 8–9(Jan., 1892–Oct., 1893).

42. *People v. Heidelberg Gardens*, 233 Ill. 290(1908); Abstract of Record, *Theurer v. People ex. rel. Deneen*, 211 Ill. 296(1904), pp. 1–17, 33, 39, 44, 49, in Illinois State Archives; *C.R.-H.*, June 27, 1902, Oct. 11, 29, 1904; Melendy, "The Saloon," p. 447; the history of White City may be gleaned from White City Papers, C.H.S.; *The Midway Gardens* (Chicago: Midway Gardens Co., [1914]); on blind pigs, see Box II, Hyde Park Protective Association Papers, C.H.S.; H.P.P.A., A.R., 1895–1904, contain many references to blind pigs and other problems.

43. W. H. Stead, Illinois Attorney General, to William F. Mulvihill, Garfield Park Improvement Association, Nov. 3, 1911, in H.P.P.A. Papers, C.H.S.; *Illinois Issue* 4(June 25, 1909):3, 6(Oct. 13,

1911):7–8; *Die Abendpost*, Aug. 22, 1891; *C.T.*, Apr. 8, 18, 1892; McElwain, "The Saloon Problem in Chicago," pp. 10–12, 75–76; quote from *C.R.-H.*, Dec. 5, 1904.

44. "Hearing of Committe on Judiciary-House on Local Option Bill, April 5, 1905," typescript, William Anderson-Anti-Saloon League of Illinois Papers, U.C., especially pp. 6–10, 20, 48–52, 62, 64; *C.F.P.* 30(June 15, 1907):1.

45. *A Greater Chicago! A Greater Evanston!* (n.p., [1909]), Evanston Historical Society; [Citizens' Association of Evanston], *Annexation to Chicago?* (n.p., [1894]); Citizens' Association of Evanston, *Report of the Committee on Printing and Publications*, April, 1894; [Frank Grover], *A Call to Duty* (n.p., [1909]); *The Women of Evanston Are Unanimously in Favor of Maintaining Our Present Safeguards against Saloon Influences through Home Rule* (n.p., [1909]); on Juneway Jungle, see *An Evanston Problem* (n.p., [1913]), and *Evanston Index*, Feb. 9, 1915.

46. George H. McCaffrey, "The Disintegration and Reintegration of Metropolitan Boston," (Ph.D. diss., Harvard University, 1937), pp. 280–87; *B.T.*, Mar. 11–25, 1892.

47. Duis, "Saloon and the Public City," p. 871, note 1.

48. *C.T.*, Mar. 16, 1880, Mar. 29, 1881, Mar. 3, 1883, Jan. 12, 1884; *Wright* v. *People* 101 Ill. 126(1881); *C.I.-O.*, July 23, 1896; *Noecker* v. *People* 91 Ill. 494(1879); *M.C.* 20(Apr. 1, 1904):37, 79, 20(May 16, 1904):68.

49. *C.T.*, Jan. 1, 1896; Twyman, *History of Marshall Field*, p. 134; *M.C.* 11(Oct. 1, 1895):67; *L.T.R.* 8(Feb. 9, 1900):18.

50. *Proceedings of the Chicago City Council*, July 12, 1897, pp. 621–23; *C.T.*, July 13, 1897; *C.T.-H.*, Oct. 30, 1897; *Chicago* v. *Netcher*, 183 Ill. 104(1899), Abstract of Record, pp. 2–3, Illinois State Archives.

51. *M.C.* 17(Aug. 1, 1901):49, 21(Oct. 16, 1905):38; *A.B.R.* 15(Aug. 20, 1901):53.

52. *M.C.* 9(Jan. 16, 1893):1.

53. *Henry Kiel* v. *City of Chicago*, 176 Ill. 137(1893).

54. *M.C.* 9(Jan. 16, 1893):35, 22(June 1, 1906):32; *C.F.P.* 28(Feb. 4, 1905):4, 29(May 7, 1906):4, 32(Apr. 20, 1907):5; *Illinois Issue* 1(Feb. 9, 1906):2; Evanston, *Report of the Chief of Police 1896–1905*, lists numbers of violations; *W.B.* 3(Oct. 15, 1878):676.

55. *W.B.* 3(Oct. 15, 1878):676.

56. Unidentified clipping, Apr. 30, 1888, Pabst Scrapbooks, V, p. 29, Milwaukee County Historical Society; *L.T.R.* 6(May 30, 1899):3, 7(July 4, 1899):6; Plavchan, "Anheuser-Busch," pp. 92–94.

57. *M.C.* 7(Nov. 16, 1891):30, 10(July 1, 1894):34, 21(July 16, 1905):50; *M.D.* 2(Oct. 15, 1891):1; *T.C.* 27(Sept., 1905):1.

58. James Harvey Young, *Toadstool Millionaires* (Princeton: Princeton University Press, 1961), pp. 129–34; Woods, *City Wilderness*, pp.

84–85; *B.G.*, June 6, 1888, Sept. 8, 1889; *L.T.R.*, 6(June 6, 1889):6; *L.O.* 2(Apr. 24, 1886):1; Massachusetts, *A. and R., 1838*, Ch. 157; *1855*, Ch. 215; *1869*, Ch. 415; *1870*, Ch. 389; *1872*, Ch. 271; *1875*, Ch. 99; *1878*, Ch. 203; *1887*, Ch. 431; *1896*, Ch. 397; *1901*, Ch. 91; *1902*, Ch. 327; Citizens' Law and Order League of Massachusetts, *A.R., 1886*, pp. 13–14; Ibid., *1890*, p. 10; *Commonwealth v. Pierce*, 147 Mass. 161(1888).

59. Whitman, "The Citizens' Law Enforcement Association," in *Ten No-License Years*, pp. 101–2.

60. Citizens' Law Enforcement Association of Cambridge, *Bulletin* 1(May–Aug., 1887), n.p., 2(Jan.–Mar., 1888):2–5, 3(Apr.–June, 1889):4.

61. Arthur Lyman, *The Liquor Law and Its Administration in Suburban Cities*, Massachusetts Civic League, Leaflet No. 9, 1907; *B.G.*, Nov. 10, 1888, Apr. 17, May 1, 8, 1901, Sept. 17, 1902.

62. *L.T.R.* 9(Nov. 16, 1900):1.

63. E.g., *B.T.*, May 11, 1882, May 1, 1884; on expressmen, *B.G.*, Apr. 21, 1889.

64. Cambridge Law Enforcement Association, *Bulletin* 1(June, 1887):2; *B.G.*, June 16, 1888.

65. Massachusetts, *A. and R., 1897*, Ch. 271; *M.C.* 15(Aug. 1, 1899):38; Boston, Board of Police, *A.R., 1900*, p. 15; Ibid., *1902*, p. 27.

66. *Commonwealth v.Shea*, 185 Mass. 89(1904); *M.C.* 20(Dec. 20, 1904):40.

67. Massachusetts, *A. and R., 1906*, Ch. 421.

68. *B.G.*, May 9, 1888; Whitman, "The Frozen Truth," p. 136; Whitman, "The First Victory," pp. 93–94, and "Letters of Charles Eliot Norton," both in *Ten No-License Years*, p. 193; *Reports on the Subject of a License Law* [1867], p. 419.

69. Ibid., p. 428.

70. H. C. B., *The White-Haired Bartender* (n.p., 1887), pp. 2–3; Joseph Warren to Charles W. Eliot, president of Harvard University, Nov. 2, 1908, Eliot Papers, Box 226, Harvard University Archives.

71. Citizens' Law Enforcement Association of Cambridge, *Bulletin* 1(June, 1887):1, 1(July–Aug., 1887):3, 2(Feb., 1888):2, 3(June 1889):2; Citizen's Law and Order League of the United States, *Proceedings of the 1888 Convention*, p. 130; *M.C.* 4(May 15, 1888):10; Citizens' Law and Order League of Massachusetts, *A.R., 1890*, p. 6.

72. Boston Police Commissioner, *A.R., 1907*, pp. 7–9; Ibid., *1910*, pp. 33–34.

73. *B.G.*, July 1, 1891, May 21–23, June 3–22, 1903.

74. Alderman Thomas Garfield in *Reports on the Subject of a License Law* [1867], p. 220; see Ibid., pp. 234–35, 427–28.

75. *M.C.* 21(Mar. 16, 1903):58A.

76. Samuel P. Hays, "The Changing Political Structure of the City

in Industrial America," *Journal of Urban History* 1(Nov., 1974):6–38, stresses the role of governmental reforms aimed at parochialism as a means by which the wealthy could regain their lost political influence.

CHAPTER 8

1. Herbert Asbury, *Gem of the Prairie* (New York: Alfred A. Knopf, 1940), and Wendt and Kogan, *Lords of the Levee*, are good general works on Chicago; there is nothing comparable for Boston; Ellen Gullot, "Social Factors in Crime" (Ph.D. diss., University of Pennsylvania, 1943), pp. 138–54; quote from John M. Barker, *The Saloon Problem and Social Reform* (Boston: Everett Press, 1905), pp. 60–61.

2. L. O. Curon, *Chicago: Satan's Sanctum* (Chicago: C. D. Phillips, 1899), pp. 104–5; *C.T.*, Dec. 27, 1880, Jan. 24, 1881, Sept. 29, 1882; *C.D.N.*, Feb. 2, 1884; quote from *T.C.* 7(Oct., 1884):1.

3. Polsky, *Hustlers, Beats and Others*, chapter 1; Kingsdale, "The Poor Man's Club," pp. 472–89, applies Polsky to Calkins, *Substitutes*.

4. *The Sporting and Club House Directory* (Chicago: Ross and St. Clair, 1889), p. 40; *Chicago Broad-Axe*, Aug. 10, 1907; *C.T.*, June 11, 1911; May Churchill Sharpe, *Chicago May: Her Story* (New York: Macaulay, 1928); John Landesco, "The Criminal Underworld of Chicago in the '80s and '90s," *Journal of Criminal Law and Criminology*, pt. 1, (Sept., 1934):341–57, pt. 2(Mar. 1935):928–40; Joseph Weil, *"Yellow Kid" Weil* (Chicago: Ziff-Davis Publishing Co., 1948).

5. Landesco, "Criminal Underworld," deals with pickpockets; *B.G.*, July 21, Sept. 21, 1901, Aug. 25, 1902; *C.T.*, Dec. 3, 1883, Apr. 29, 1901.

6. *C.T.*, Feb. 8, 1874, July 27, Dec. 19, 1880, Oct. 5, Nov. 5, 1881, Nov. 2, 1903; this was happening much later also. Crime Committee Report, Aug. 24, 1914, Box 88, Folder 5, Charles Merriam Papers, University of Chicago Library; Weil, *"Yellow Kid"*, pp. 15–17; Harold Vynne, *Chicago by Day and Night: Or the Pleasure-Seeker's Guide to the Paris of America* (Chicago: n.p., 1892), p. 58; *Tricks and Traps of Chicago* (New York: Dinamore, 1859), p. 22; *Chicago After Dark* (Chicago: A. C. Anderson, 1868), p. 5; *B.G.*, July 20, 1887, Apr. 21, 1901.

7. Pierce, *History of Chicago*, 3:343–44; *C.D.D.*, Jan. 29, July 20, 1849, July 15, 26, 1852; *Chicago Daily Democratic Press*, Mar. 20, May 15, 1855.

8. *H.C.S.*, pp. 100–114; Ahern, *Great Revolution*, pp. 17–119; *Frank Schwuchow v. City of Chicago*, 68 Ill. 444(1873), Transcript of Record, Illinois State Archives; *C.T.*, Apr. 25, May 1, Aug. 7, 1873, Mar. 17, 1874, Mar. 31, Dec. 13, 1879, Feb. 17, 22, Mar. 15, 1880, Jan. 22, Feb. 19, Mar. 31, 1881, Jan. 23, 1882; *C.D.N.*, July 14, 1884.

9. *C.T.*, Nov. 24, Dec. 9, 16, 1879, Feb. 12, Dec. 7, 1882, Feb.

27, 28, Mar. 6, Dec. 22, 1883, Jan. 2–15, 1884; *M.C.* 8(Dec. 16, 1892):37, 9(July 1, 1893):45.

10. Robert E. Riegel, "Changing American Attitudes toward Prostitution, 1800–1920," *Journal of the History of Ideas* 29(July–Sept., 1968):437–52; Herbert Asbury, *Sucker's Progress* (New York: Dodd, Meade, 1938), pp. 285–95.

11. Sunset Club of Chicago, *Yearbook, 1892–93*, pp. 211–33; *C.T.*, Jan. 18, Feb. 25, Mar. 23–26, 1874; New England Watch and Ward Society, *A.R., 1894–95*, p. 21, *A.R., 1895–96*, pp. 22–32.

12. Lane, *Policing the City*, p. 99; Woods, *Americans in Process*, pp. 192–93; *North End Mission Magazine* 1(Apr., 1872):16; Boston Police, *A.R., 1851*, p. 20, *A.R., 1852*, pp. 15–16; *Boston's By-Ways to Hell: A Visit to the Dens of North Street* (Boston: J. M. Usher, 1867), pp. 3–5, 15; New England Female Reform Society, *A.R., 1851*, p. 195.

13. Savage, *Police Records and Recollections*, pp. 109, 257–59; Edward Savage, *Boston Events* (Boston: Edward Savage, 1884), p. 106; Boston Police, *A.R., 1852*, p. 15, *A.R., 1870*, pp. 57–59.

14. Lane, *Policing the City*, pp. 168–70; Joseph Ward, "Boston's South End in the 1880's and 1890's," typescript, Rare Book Room, Boston Public Library, p. 6; *B.T.*, Jan. 8, 1884, Aug. 20, Sept. 12, 1885; *B.G.*, Sept. 1, 1885, June 11, 1888, Dec. 15, 1890.

15. Helen B. Haseltine, "A History of the Chicago Home for Girls Founded in 1863 as the Chicago Erring Woman's Refuge," (M.A. thesis, University of Chicago, 1934), pp. 1–54; Pierce, *History of Chicago*, 1:255–56; Walter Reckless, "The Natural History of Vice Areas in Chicago," (Ph.D. diss., University of Chicago, 1925), pp. 1–119, contains historical material omitted from his *Vice in Chicago;* Don Fehrenbacher, *Chicago Giant: A Biography of Long John Wentworth* (Madison: American History Research Center, 1957), pp. 143–44; *C.T.*, Apr. 20, 1857.

16. *Tricks and Traps*, p. 26; *Chicago After Dark*, p. 64; Asbury, *Gem*, pp. 62–65; *C. Times*, Jan. 6–12, Feb. 8, 1864; Frederick Cooke, *Bygone Days in Chicago* (Chicago: A. C. McClurg, 1910), pp. 130–31, 171.

17. Chicago, *Fire Marshall's Report, 1874–75*, pp. 137–38; Ibid., *1875–76*, p. 118; *C.T.*, Apr. 21, 1873; John J. Flinn, *The History of the Chicago Police* (Chicago: Police Book Fund, 1887), p. 136.

18. *C.T.*, Feb. 3, 1882.

19. Citizens' League of Chicago, *A.R., 1881*, p. 13; *The Curse of Chicago; C.T.*, Jan. 15, 1882, Mar. 10, 29, 1883.

20. Massachusetts, *A. and R., 1858*, Ch. 152.

21. *C.T.*, Jan. 18, 1874; *C. Times*, Jan. 4, Feb. 8, 1874; *Chicago's Dark Places*, pp. 57–60, 74–75, 120–24; *Chicago by Day and Night*, p. 45; *C.H.*, Nov. 25–27, 1892; *C.D.N.*, Mar. 19, 1884; Asbury, *Gem*, pp. 132–41.

22. *Chicago's Dark Places*, p. 67.

23. Savage, *Police Records and Recollections*, pp. 155–59; Boston Police Department, *A.R.*, *1865*, p. 17, *1871*, pp. 28–29.

24. John P. Quinn, *Fools of Fortune* (Chicago: Anti-Gambling Association, 1892), pp. 404–5.

25. *C.T.*, Jan. 6, Mar. 5, 16, 1880, Mar. 31, 1881, Feb. 12, Nov. 28, 1882; Asbury, *Gem*, pp. 146–47.

26. *C. Times*, Jan. 25, Sept. 19, 1894; *C.T.*, Dec. 31, 1881, July 18–20, Nov. 24, 1882, Oct. 28, 1883; *Chicago by Day and Night*, pp. 74, 165; *H.C.S.*, pp. 156–57.

27. *B.T.*, Jan. 11, 23, 1884.

28. Ibid., Aug. 10, 12, Sept. 9, 1885, Feb. 16, 1892; *B.G.*, May 12, 1889, *C.T.*, Nov. 1, 1885.

29. Ibid., July 20, 21, Dec. 19, 1880, Nov. 27, 1881, July 1, 21, 1882, May 7, July 7, 1887.

30. Ibid., Oct. 14, 1885, July 30, 1902; Robert O. Harland, *The Vice Bondage of a Great City* (Chicago: Young People's Civic League, 1912), p. 36; "The Crime Committee, [c. 1915]," typescript, in Box 55, Folder 2, and data in Box 88, Folders 3 and 5, Charles Merriam Papers, University of Chicago.

31. Alexander R. Piper, *Report of an Investigation of the Discipline and Administration of the Police Department of the City of Chicago* (Chicago: City Club of Chicago, 1904), pp. 5–11; Chicago Police Operators Benevolent Association, *Directory*, *1914*, p. 455; untitled note on Democratic Ball, Box 88, Folder 5, Merriam Papers, University of Chicago; Mark H. Haller, "Police Reform in Chicago," *American Behavioral Scientist*, 13(May–Aug., 1970):649–66; *C.J.*, June 7, 1894; *Special Rules and Regulations for the Government of Boston Police* (Boston: Alfred Mudge & Sons, City Printers, 1867), pp. 12, 23; *B.T.*, May 19, 24, 1882; New England Society for the Suppression of Vice, *A.R.*, *1883–84*, p. 11.

32. *B.G.*, Apr. 29, 1902.

33. "Testimony in the Investigation of William Osborne," typescript, Massachusetts State Library, pp. 5–7, 22–29, 85–457.

34. Quote, *L.T.R.* 4(Jan. 25, 1898):1; McElwain, "The Saloon Problem in Chicago," pp. 15, 17; *C.T.*, Apr. 11, Sept. 11, Dec. 17, 1880, Mar. 19, 1881, July 23, 1883, Nov. 6, 1894; *C.I.-O.*, Nov. 11, 1903.

35. "Justice Shops in Chicago," *Graphic* [Chicago] 1(Mar. 31, 1894):1, 242–43; *C.T.*, Oct. 15, 1881; *M.C.* 17(Feb. 16, 1901):32; *B.G.*, July 6, 1890.

36. *C.T.*, Sept. 23, 1880, Jan. 11, 22, 1882; *L.O.* 1(Oct. 11, 1884):10.

37. Ibid. 1(Mar. 28, 1885–July 18, 1885), 2(Feb. 27, 1886):172–73, 176, 2(Mar. 13, 1886):188; Citizens' Law and Order League of Massachusetts, *A.R.*, *1886*, p. 12, *A.R.*, *1888*, p. 7, *A.R.*, *1889*, pp. 10–11, *A.R.*, *1890*, pp. 11–12; *N.E.T.* 2(June 6, 1885):3.

38. *Reports on the Subject of a License Law*, pp. 129–34, 150–53, 163–65, 193–96, 221, 232, 449, 452–3; *C.T.*, Nov. 8, 1883, Mar. 19, 1886.

39. "Both Sides of the Jury Question," *Century Magazine* 26(June, 1883):299–304; "Is the Jury System a Failure?" Ibid. 25(Nov., 1882):124–33; Robert C. Pittman, "Juries and Jurymen," *North American Review* 333(July, 1884):1–11.

40. Quote, *C.T.*, May 27, 1888; Ibid., Jan. 12, 1888, Feb. 14, 21, 1883; Weil, *"Yellow Kid,"* p. 13.

41. National Retail Liquor Dealers' Association, *Proceedings of the Annual Convention, 1900*, p. 32; *C.F.P.* 43(June 5, 1915):4; *C.T.*, Nov. 9, 1915.

42. New England Watch and Ward Society, *A.R., 1902–3*, gives an excellent history on its twenty-fifth anniversary.

43. Ibid.

44. Flower, *Civilization's Inferno*. Flower was also the publisher of *The Arena*, a rich source on city problems. Banks, *White Slaves;* Arthur Mann, *Yankee Reformers in the Urban Age* (Cambridge: Belknap Press, 1954), pp. 163–71, on Flower.

45. *B.G.*, Feb. 13, 1891, Feb. 6, 1892, Oct. 10, 11, 1893, June 24, July 8, 10, 29, Aug. 3–5, 8, 10, 15, 21, 28, 1894.

46. Vivia Divers, *The Black Hole* (Chicago: n.p., 1892).

47. *C. Times*, Mar. 27, 1892; *C.T.*, Oct. 29, 30, Nov. 11, 13, 1893; Stead, *If Christ Came to Chicago.*

48. Civic Federation of Chicago, *A.R., 1895*, pp. 7–25.

49. Ibid., pp. 84–95; Harry Rubens, *The Gambling Problem: An Address Delivered at the Request and on the Special Invitation of the Civic Federation* (n.p., 1894); *C. Times*, Sept. 20–22, 1894; *C.T.*, Sept. 19–29, 1894.

50. New England Watch and Ward Society, *A.R., 1895*, pp. 10–11; Massachusetts, *A. and R., 1894*, Ch. 410; Ibid., *1895*, Ch. 419.

51. New England Watch and Ward Society, *A.R., 1888*, p. 12; *B.G.*, Mar. 31, 1887.

52. New England Watch and Ward Society, *A.R., 1885*, pp. 10–11; *C.T.*, Jan. 6, 1894, June 6, 17, 26, 28, Aug. 30, Sept. 11, 1896; *Chicago Record*, Oct. 5, Dec. 1, 3, 1900; *C.R.-H.*, Apr. 17, Aug. 23, 1903.

53. *W.B.* 4(Jan. 15, 1879):46; *Weekly Chicago Democrat*, July 4, 1857; Curon, *Chicago: Satan's Sanctum*, p. 82; Mark Sullivan, "The Pool-Room Evil," *The Outlook* 77(May 28, 1904):212–16; Josiah Flynt, "The Pool-Room Spider and the Gambling Fly," *Cosmopolitan Magazine* 42(Mar., 1907): 513–21.

54. *Chicago Herald and Examiner*, Dec. 28, 1937; Richard T. Griffin, "Big Jim O'Leary: 'Gambler Box Iv Th' Yards'," *Chicago History* 5(Winter, 1976–77):213–21; Josiah Flynt, "The Men behind the Pool Rooms," *Cosmopolitan Magazine* 42(Apr., 1907):636–45; Josiah Flynt, "Telegraph and Telephone Companies as Allies," *Cosmopolitan*

Magazine 43(May, 1907):51–53; *C.R.-H.*, Sept. 15, 1904; "Affidavit of C. O. Resin, June 28, 1910," and printed letter, "To The Chicago Federation of Labor, June 4, 1910," in John Fitzpatrick Papers, Folder 4, C.H.S.

55. *B.G.*, Jan. 28, Feb. 1, 2, 4, 1892; New England Watch and Ward Society, *A.R.*, *1889–90*, pp. 9–11.

56. Ibid., *1898–99*, p. 26; Ibid., *1903–4*, p. 9; Woods, *Americans in Process*, pp. 153, 204, 220; Chicago Citizens' Association, *Bulletin 11, 1903*, n.p.; *Bulletin 13, 1904*, n.p.; *Bulletin 14, 1905*, n.p.; Chicago Citizens' Association, *A.R.*, *1904*, pp. 3–6; Ibid., *1905*, pp. 6–7.

57. Franklin Matthews, "Wide-Open Chicago," *Harper's Weekly* 42(Jan. 22, 1898):88–91; *Proceedings of the Boston City Council Board of Aldermen*, August 7, 1905, p. 437.

58. New England Watch and Ward Society, *A.R.*, *1902–3*, p. 27; Ibid., *1903–4*, p. 9.

59. Advertisements, Conrad Jackson Desk Co., in possession of author.

60. *M.C.* 14(Feb. 1, 1898):40B, 14(Nov. 1, 1898):57, 15(Apr. 1, 1899):52A; *The Emancipator* 3(Oct., 1902):8.

61. New England Watch and Ward Society, *A.R.*, *1892–93*, pp. 3–5.

62. *B.G.*, Jan. 10, 11, June 19, 20, July 23, 1894.

63. Ibid., Jan. 13–Feb. 27, 1900, Feb. 6, 1901; Woods, *City Wilderness*, pp. 159–70; Woods, *Americans in Process*, pp. 198–99, 213–17; quote, New England Watch and Ward Society, *A.R.*, *1894–95*, p. 22.

64. Ibid., *1899–1900*, pp. 16–17.

65. Quote, *B.G.*, March 7, 1901; *Closing Argument of Michael J. Murray, Esq. before Legislative Committee on the Liquor Law, 1901*.

66. Ibid.

67. *M.C.* 17(June 1, 1901):37, 18(Mar. 1, 1902):75; *B.G.*, Apr. 9, 1902.

68. Ibid., Jan. 13–Feb. 27, 1901.

69. Ibid., Feb. 14, 19, June 29, 1901, Mar. 8, 1903.

70. Ibid., Mar. 15, 23, Apr. 11, 1903.

71. Ibid., Apr. 13, 22, May 5, 6, 11, 25, June 6, 13, 28, 1903; May 25, 1904.

72. *M.C.* 15(Dec. 16, 1899):55, 16(Feb. 1, 1900):71; *L.T.R.* 8(Jan. 26, 1900):7; *Chicago Record*, Jan. 15, 1901; *C.R.-H.*, Nov. 22, 1903, Aug. 11, 1904, May 21, 26–29, Aug. 16, 29, 1905.

73. Ibid., Oct. 1, 1902; *C.F.P.* 25(Nov. 22, 1902):4; *M.C.* 29(Feb. 16, 1904):53.

74. Ibid. 17(Nov. 1, 1901):37; *C.F.P.* 27(Oct. 21, 1903; *C.R.-H.*, Nov. 16, 1900, Nov. 29, Dec. 10, 13, 14, 1901, Oct. 27, 1902, May 18, 1904.

75. Davis, *Spearheads for Reform*, pp. 174–80; Richard Becker,

"Edward Dunne: Reform Mayor of Chicago, 1905–1907" (Ph.D. diss., University of Chicago, 1971).

76. *B.G.*, July 1, Dec. 23, 1903, Mar. 30, May 18, July 1–31, 1904.

77. Ibid., July 23, Aug. 28, Sept. 4, 1901, Aug. 7, Oct. 18, 19, 1903, June 10, 1904.

78. *M.C.* 22(Apr. 16, 1906):82.

79. Massachusetts, *A. and R.*, *1906*, Ch. 395; *M.C.* 22(Jan. 16, 1906):74B, 22(Apr. 16, 1906):74D; Boston Licensing Board, *A.R.*, *1907*, p. 7.

80. Ibid.

81. Unidentified clippings, Stephen O'Meara Papers, Boston Public Library; *B.J.*, Jan. 30, 1917; *Christian Science Monitor*, Jan. 17, 1910.

82. Boston, Licensing Board, *A.R.*, *1906*, pp. 16–18.

83. *M.C.* 20(Feb. 16, 1904):53.

84. Ibid.; *C.F.P.* 29(Mar. 17, 1906):4; *Abendpost*, Oct. 4, 1905, Mar. 17, Apr. 6, 1906, *Chicago Broad-Axe*, Feb. 4, 1905.

85. *C.J.*, Oct. 12–Nov. 2, 1903; Ambler Scrapbook Collection, City Administration, Vol. 5, C.H.S., has thousands of clippings; *C.I.-O.*, Sept. 24, 1903; *C.T.*, Nov. 14, 1903; *C.D.N.*, Nov. 16, 1903.

86. "Special Investigating Committee," *Proceedings of the Chicago City Council*, Mar. 7, 1904, pp. 2501–19; Piper, *Report on Police, Chicago; The Voter* 1(Apr., 1904):14–16.

87. *C.R.-H.*, Jan. 19, Feb. 3–28, Mar, 5, 1906; *C.T.*, May 6, 1906.

88. Ibid., Feb. 27, 28, Mar. 19, May 6, 1906; *C.F.P.* 29(Mar. 24, 1906):1; *M.C.* 22(June 1, 1906):80.

89. Timberlake, *Prohibition and the Progressive Movement*, pp. 125–48; "History of the Illinois Anti-Saloon League," typescript in William Anderson, Anti-Saloon League of Illinois Papers, University of Chicago.

90. *Abendpost*, Mar. 19, 1906.

91. *C.I.-O.*, Dec. 8, 17, 1903; *C.T.*, Dec. 10, 17, 1903; *C.R.-H.*, Jan. 3, Feb. 1, 21, 1904.

92. Perry Duis, *Chicago: Creating New Traditions* (Chicago: Chicago Historical Society, 1976), pp. 69–71.

93. Louise DeKoven Bowen, *Our Most Popular Recreation Controlled by the Liquor Interests* (Chicago: Juvenile Protective Association, 1912); "The Public Dance Hall and Its Relation to Vice," typescript, 1912, Folder 104, Juvenile Protective Association Papers, U.I.C.C.; Balcomb, *Our Municipal Government*, Part II, pp. 26–28.

94. New England Watch and Ward Society, *A.R.*, *1907–8*, p. 31, quote; Ibid., *1909–10*, pp. 9, 23, 29–32; Ibid., *1910–11*, pp. 10–12.

95. *New England Magazine* 41(Jan., 1910):531–39.

96. New England Watch and Ward Society, *A.R.*, *1910–11*, pp. 7–9; Woods and Kennedy, *Young Working Girls;* Charles W. Eliot, "The Double Standard of Chastity," *The Light* 14(May, 1911):30–34.

97. New England Watch and Ward Society, *A.R.*, *1910–11*, pp.

9–10; Boston Licensing Board, *A.R.*, *1913*, p. 13.

98. Roe reprinted in E. A. Bell, *War on the White Slave Traffic* (Chicago: Charles C. Thompson, 1909), pp. 155–62; New England Watch and Ward Society, *A.R.*, *1910–11*, pp. 7–9; *Vigilance* 23(May, 1910):30.

99. Seth Cook Rees, *Miracles in the Slums* (Chicago: Seth Cook Rees, 1905); E. A. Bell, *Fighting the Traffic in Young Girls* (Chicago: G. S. Ball, 1910); F. M. Lehman, *White Slave Hell, or With Christ at Midnight in the Slums of Chicago* (Chicago: Christian Witness Co., 1910); O. B. D. [Olive Bell Daniels], *From the Epic of Chicago: Ernest A. Bell, 1865–1928* (n.p., [1928]); *The Philanthropist* 23(Apr., 1909):19–23.

100. Chicago Vice Commission, *The Social Evil in Chicago*, *1911*, pp. 176–83; Asbury, *Gem*, pp. 266–69; *M.C.* 24(Aug. 16, 1908):80–D; *The Illinois Issue*, vols. 5–7, contains numerous anti-Wayman articles.

101. Boston Police Commissioner, *A.R.*, *1907*, pp. 5–7.

102. Boston Police Commissioner, *A Record of the Enforcement of Laws against Sexual Immorality since December 1, 1907* (Boston: City Printing Dept., 1912); Boston Licensing Board, *A.R.*, *1907*, p. 3; Ibid., *1909*, p. 4; Ibid., *1911*, pp. 7–8; *M.C.* 26(July 1, 1910):708–16.

103. Carl Hovey, "The Police Question: The 'Cop' Answers in Cleveland, the Radical in Toledo, the Gentleman in Boston," *Metropolitan Magazine* 31(Mar., 1910):708–16.

104. Boston Licensing Board, *A.R.*, *1911*, pp. 6–7.

105. Boston Police Commissioner, *A Record of the Enforcement*, *passim*.

106. Graham Taylor, "The Police and Vice in Chicago," *The Survey* 23(Nov. 6, 1909):165.

107. *The American Issue* 7(June 28, 1912):11.

108. *West Side Amusement News*, described in Calkins, *Substitutes*, p. 52; *Report of the Juvenile Court Committee, 1907–08* (corrected to read *1906–07*) in Folder 16, Juvenile Protective Association Papers, U.I.C.C.; Carl Hovey, "The Police Question: Chicago Struggling To Solve It, Philadelphia Blinded and Bound," *Metropolitan Magazine* 33(Apr., 1910):40–41; *C.R.-H.*, Feb. 10, Aug. 12, Oct. 8–14, Nov. 20, Dec. 21, 1910.

109. *C.T.*, Sept. 4, 1898.

110. *Chicago Broad-Axe*, Sept. 4, 11, 1909; *C.R.-H.*, Apr. 13, Oct. 27, 1902, Nov. 22, 1903, Mar. 14, 1904, May 1, 1910; *C.F.P.* 30(Nov. 9, 1907):1, 32(Mar. 27, 1909):1; *Illinois Issue* 4(Jan. 15, 1909):5, 6(Oct. 13, 1911):3.

111. Asbury, *Gem*, pp. 281–84; Chicago Law and Order League, *Summarized Report, 1909–10*, p. 4; Wendt and Kogan, *Lords of the Levee*, pp. 153–58, 268–81, 288–89; *C.T.*, Oct. 19, 1909.

112. Chicago Vice Commission, *The Social Evil in Chicago*, pp. 329-30; *C.T.*, Apr. 28-30, 1910.

113. Eric Anderson, "Prostitution and Social Justice: Chicago, 1910-1915," *The American Journal of Sociology* 44(June, 1974):203-28, is more narrowly concerned with the commission than the title suggests; Chicago Vice Commission, *The Social Evil in Chicago*, pp. 1-9; *The Survey* 23(Feb.12, 1910):695-96, 23(Mar. 26, 1910):961-62; see secret police investigation in Committee on Public Order and Policing, Civic Committee, V, pp. 65-71, City Club of Chicago Papers, C.H.S.

114. Anderson, "Prostitution and Social Justice," p. 214.

115. *Report of the Massachusetts Commission for the Investigation of the White Slave Traffic, So-Called*, Massachusetts House Doc. 2281, 1914, pp. 9-14, 19; J. Frank Chase, "The Massachusetts Commission for the Investigation of the White Slave Traffic, So-Called," *The Light* 17(Sept.-Oct., 1914):40-42; Chicago Vice Commission, *The Social Evil in Chicago*, pp. 91-95, 152-53.

116. *Report . . . White Slave, So-Called*, pp. 14-19; Chicago Vice Commission, *The Social Evil in Chicago*, pp. 72, 330; many popularized accounts based on the Chicago report quickly appeared, including C. C. Quale, *Thrilling Stories of White Slavery* (Chicago: Hamming Publishing Co., 1912), and Leona Prall Groetzinger, *The City's Perils*. 4th ed. (n.p., n.d.).

117. Chicago Vice Commission, *Social Evil in Chicago*, pp. 25-30.

118. Walter Lippman, *A Preface to Politics* (New York: Mitchell Kennerly, 1914), pp. 122-31; Chicago Civil Service Commission, *Final Report of Police Investigation* (n.p., 1912), p. 16.

119. Quote, *C.T.*, Jan. 13, 1913; clippings, Clifford Barnes Papers, C.H.S.; *C.I.-O.*, Oct. 30, 1912; *C.T.*, Oct. 23, Nov. 12, 1912; *The Continent* 43(Oct. 10, 1912):1408.

120. Paul Boyer, *Urban Masses and Moral Order in America, 1820-1910* (Cambridge: Harvard University Press, 1978), pp. 162-219. Mark Thomas Connelly, *The Response to Prostitution in the Progressive Era* (Chapel Hill: University of North Carolina Press, 1980), is an excellent general account, and pp. 91-113 deal with the Chicago vice scene. Don S. Kirschner, "The Perils of Pleasure: Commercial Recreation, Social Disorder and Moral Reform in the Progressive Era," *American Studies* 20(Fall, 1980):27-42, is also excellent.

CHAPTER 9

1. Henry Barrett Chamberlin, "The Public Bar vs. Private Sideboard," *Chamberlin's* 13(Nov., 1915):39.

2. Ibid.

3. Clifford W. Barnes, "The Story of the Committee of Fifteen of

Chicago," *Social Hygiene* 4(Apr., 1918):145–56; see clippings and autobiographical sketch, Clifford Barnes Papers, C.H.S.

4. *Proceedings of the Chicago City Council*, May 5, 1912, pp. 265–68; *Testimony on Segregation and Commercialized Vice, Presented before the City Council's Committee of Nine* (Chicago: American Vigilance Association, 1912); Barratt O'Hara, "The Work of the Illinois Senate Vice Committee," *The Light* 19(May–June, 1916):3–11; *Report of the Senate Vice Committee, 1916* (Springfield: State of Illinois, 1916), pp. 28–41; *Report of the City Council Committee on Crime* (Chicago: [City of Chicago], 1915), p. 8; many reports of the Crime Committee are in Charles Merriam Papers, University of Chicago.

5. *The American Issue* 9(Dec. 11, 1914):4; *Proceedings of the Chicago City Council*, Nov. 15, 1915, pp. 2103–08.

6. New England Watch and Ward Society, *A.R., 1907–8*, p. 14, *1913–14*, p. 15.

7. *C.T.*, Aug. 31, Sept. 12, 1913; *Chicago's American*, Sept. 5, 1958.

8. *City Council Committee on Crime*, pp. 167–70; *Illinois Senate Vice Committee*, p. 45.

9. New England Watch and Ward Society, *A.R., 1915–16*, p. 17, *1916–17*, p. 5.

10. Boston Licensing Board, *A.R., 1915*, pp. 8–9; *Report by the Committee on License, Chicago City Council on the Public Licensing, Regulation and Control of the Liquor Traffic in Boston and New York City* (Chicago: Chicago City Council, 1918), pp. 29–31.

11. "Address of Mr. Frank J. Chase, Secretary of the New England Watch and Ward Society," in Ibid., pp. 52–56.

12. Massachusetts, *A. and R., 1915*, Ch. 180.

13. *Proceedings of the Chicago City Council*, Nov. 25, 1912, p. 2858; Ibid., Dec. 9, 1912, p. 2358; *Hoyt v. McLaughlin*, 250 Ill. 442(1912); *The Appomatox of Open Tolerated Vice* (Chicago: Chicago Law and Order League, 1913).

14. Henry Barrett Chamberlin, *"50–50" Fighting Chicago's Crime Trusts* (n.p., 1916); *City Council Committee on Crime*, p. 10; *C.F.P.* 37(Sept. 27, 1913):5, 41(Nov. 8, 1913):4, 41(Dec. 13, 1913):1, 42(Feb. 14, 1914):5; *M.C.* 29(Nov. 16, 1913):47.

15. *L.T.R.* 9(Nov. 16, 1900):6; *Current Thought* 2(Aug. 16, 1913):10; *National Herald* 8(Apr. 11, 1914):13.

16. *The Cooperation of the Retail Liquor Trade in Saloon Regulation* (Boston: Massachusetts Liquor League, 1914); *Northwestern Liquor and Tobacco Journal* 5(Oct., 1913):404; *Brewers' Journal* 39(Feb. 1, 1913):166; *W.B.* 46(Feb., 1916):54.

17. *C.F.P.* 43(July 24, 1915):4.

18. Chicago Commission on the Liquor Problem, *Preliminary Report* (Chicago: n.p., 1916), pp. 1–5.

19. *B.H.*, Mar. 20, Apr. 8, 9, 1914; *B. Ad.*, Mar. 2, 15, 1914; *B. Am.*, Mar. 29, 1914; *B.J.*, Oct. 9, 1914; *M.C.* 30(Feb. 1, 1914):47; *B.T.*, Mar. 2, 1915, clippings in scrapbook collection, James Michael Curley Papers, Holy Cross College; see Herbert M. Zolot, "The Issue of Good Government and James Michael Curley: Curley and the Boston Scene from 1897–1918," (Ph.D. diss., State University of New York at Stony Brook, 1975).

20. *B.J.*, June 24, Oct. 9, 1914; *B.P.*, Nov. 5, 1915; *Boston Record*, Jan. 26, 27, 1917; *B. Ad.*, Mar. 15, 1915.

21. Becker, "Edward Dunne," p. 3; *C.F.P.*, 26(June 25, 1904):1, 33(Apr. 30, 1910):4, 34(May 6, 1911):5, 34(Oct. 28, 1911):4; *M.C.* 27(Jan. 16, 1911):48, 27(Feb. 16, 1911):35.

22. Paul Michael Green, "The Chicago Democratic Party, 1840–1920: From Factionalism to Political Organization," (Ph.D. diss., University of Chicago, 1975), pp. 122–71.

23. Ibid., pp. 221–25; Carter H. Harrison, *Stormy Years: The Autobiography of Carter H. Harrison, Five Times Mayor of Chicago* (Indianapolis: Bobbs-Merrill, 1935), pp. 307–14, 345–39.

24. Alex Gottfried, *Boss Cermak of Chicago: A Study of Political Leadership* (Seattle: University of Washington Press, 1962), pp. 3–24.

25. *C.F.P.* 30–31(Nov. 30, 1907–July 25, 1908); *M.C.* 24(Jan. 1, 1908–Nov. 16, 1908).

26. *Brewers' Journal*, 35(Feb. 1, 1911):160, 35(Mar. 1, 1911):207.

27. Susan B. Anthony and Lucretia Harper, eds. *The History of Woman's Suffrage*, 6 vols. (Indianapolis: Hollinbeck Press, 1902), 4:701–54.

28. *Current Thought*, 2(June 21, 1913):16; *Day-Book* 2(July 2, 1913):n.p.; *The American Issue*, 8(Aug. 8, 1913):6, 8(Sept. 12, 1913):2.

29. *Objections to License Suffrage from a No-License Point of View: Address of Frank Foxcroft before a Massachusetts Legislative Committee* (n.p., 1898), and his letter in *The Congregationalist*, Sept. 11, 1913; Massachusetts Anti-Suffrage Pamphlet Collection, stacks, University of Chicago Library.

30. Green, "The Chicago Democratic Party," pp. 221–25.

31. Eleanor H. Woods, *Robert A. Woods: Champion of Democracy* (Boston: Houghton Mifflin, 1929), pp. 286–96; Louis Epple, *Liquor Laws of Massachusetts*, pp. 1, 9.

32. *B.W.S.G.* 75(Nov. 10, 1910):42; *National Herald* 6(July 25, 1912):15; *M.C.* 29(Sept. 16, 1913):88.

33. Ibid.

34. Robert A. Woods, "Social Workers' Temperance Bill," *The Survey* 23(Mar. 12, 1910):924–26; Robert A. Woods, "Undermining Drunkenness," *Harvard Theological Review* 8(Oct., 1914):497–506; *B.T.*, June 24, 26, 27, 1916.

35. Ibid.

36. *B.J.*, Nov. 3, Dec. 31, 1914; *B. Ad.*, Nov. 30, 1914; *B.G.*, Dec. 31, 1914, Jan. 1, 1915, all from scrapbooks, David I. Walsh Papers, Holy Cross College.

37. *B. Ad.*, May 12, 1915; *B.J.*, Oct. 14, 1915; *B.G.*, May 13, 1915; Howie, *Three Hundred Years of the Liquor Problem*, pp. 244–45.

38. *B.J.*, Jan. 5, Mar. 30, 31, Nov. 4, 7, 9, 12, 1915; *National Herald* 9(Apr. 24, 1915):7; *W.B.* 46(Jan., 1916):34.

39. Woods, *Robert Woods*, pp. 294–95.

40. "Address of Frank Chase," in *Chicago City Council, Report on . . . Boston and New York City*, p. 55.

41. Ibid., p. 54.

42. Lloyd Wendt and Herman Kogan, *Big Bill of Chicago* (Indianapolis: Bobbs-Merrill, 1953), on Thompson's background; Green, "The Chicago Democratic Party," pp. 242–54; *C.T.*, Feb. 17, 20, 21, 23, 24, Apr. 5, 7, 9, 1915.

43. *C.F.P.* 43(Apr. 24, 1915):1. *C.F.P.* has many articles June–Aug., 1915, on the Sunday issue. *C.T.*, Oct. 5–15, 1915; *Brewers' Journal* 40(Nov. 1, 1915):3; Municipal Voters' League, *A.R.*, *1916*, p. 14; *Svenska Kurien*, Oct. 7, 1915.

44. *C.F.P.* 43(Oct. 9, 1915):1, 4; *M.C.* 31(Oct. 16, 1915):83.

45. *C.F.P.* 43(Dec. 18, 1915):4, 44(Feb. 5, 1916):8, 44(Feb. 28, 1916):5, 44(Sept. 30, 1916):4, 45(June 23, 1917):4; "Directors' Meeting," notebook, p. 19, Box 1, Hyde Park Protective Association Papers, C.H.S.

46. *B.W.S.G.* 86(Sept. 10, 1916):284, 87(Nov. 25, 1916):56, 87(Dec. 10, 1916):93; *B.G.*, Dec. 17, 20, 1916.

47. *M.C.* 21(Mar. 16, 1903):58A, based on Boston Licensing Board, *A.R.*, *1906–20*, and *Lakeside Directory of Chicago*, 1910 and 1914.

48. *Bar. vs. Bottle: A Unique Divorce Case* (Boston: Massachusetts Anti-Saloon League, 1911).

49. *The Boston Common* 1(Apr. 30, 1910):7, 1(May 7, 1910):13; *M.C.* 26(May 16, 1910):47; "The Effect of the Bar and Bottle Bill," and "The Effect of the Double License in Boston," manuscripts in Robert Woods Papers, Harvard University.

50. *House Bill No. 627: Argument against the Bill by William B. Sullivan* (Boston: Fort Hill Press, 1910).

51. Massachusetts, *A. and R.*, *1910*, Ch. 476; *M.C.* 26(May 16, 1910):47, 26(July 16, 1910):37; attempts to repeal it described in Ibid. 27(May 1, 1911):75, *B.G.*, May 1, 21, 1911, and *Boston Common* 1(Mar. 25, 1911):2; on impact, Boston Licensing Board, *A.R.*, *1910*, p. 3, *1911*, p. 3, *1912*, p. 16.

52. *B.J.*, Apr. 14, June 1, 4, 13, 14, 1916.

53. Chamberlin, "Public Bar vs. Private Sideboard," pp. 40–41; "Profitable Local Newspaper Advertrising," *Brewers' Journal* 3(Sept. 1, 1914):498.

54. *C.F.P.* 34(Sept. 9, 1911):1, 34(Oct. 28, 1911):1, 36(Nov. 23, 1912:1, 36(Nov. 30, 1912):8, 36(Dec. 21, 1912):1, 36(Mar. 15, 1913):1.

55. *Current Thought* 2(Aug. 16, 1913):10; *National Herald* 8(Apr. 11, 1914):13; *M.C.* 30(Apr. 16, 1914):38.

56. *B.W.S.G.* 74(Sept. 10, 1910):456.

57. Ibid. 77(Mar. 28, 1912):490; *L.T.R.* 8(June 8, 1900):14; *C.F.P.* 45(July 17, 1917):4.

58. New England Watch and Ward Society, *A.R., 1905–6*, p. 22; Twentieth Century Club of Boston, *The Amusement Situation in Boston* (Boston: n.p., 1915), pp. 4–7; *C.F.P.* 32(Feb. 20, 1909):5; Fred Gordon, "The Movies in Chicago: Early Growth and the Rise of Censorship," unpublished seminar paper, University of Chicago, 1968; *The Worker* 1(Apr.–May, 1916):3, a temperance paper, draws parallels between saloons and movies.

59. *B.J.*, Feb. 25–27, May 22, June 23, 1914, Mar. 23, Aug. 3, 1917; *B. Am.*, Apr. 10, 1914, Mar. 19, 1916; *Boston Herald*, Aug. 3, Dec. 6, 11, 1917.

60. *Illinois Senate Vice Committee*, pp. 479–80; Committee of Fifteen, *A.R., 1918*, p. 7; *Abendpost*, Feb. 12, 1916; *C.T.*, Aug. 11, 1914; Robert McIntosh, "Ten Cents a Dance," typescript, 1933, Box 45, Folder 4, Louis Wirth Papers, University of Chicago Library.

61. Keitel, *Government by the Brewers?*, pp. 66–68; "Report of the Morals Commission," *Proceedings of the Chicago City Council*, July 6, 1915, pp. 951–53; Juvenile Protective Association, *A.R., 1915–16*, pp. 41–47; Louise DeKoven Bowen, *The Straight Girl on a Crooked Path* (Chicago: Juvenile Protective Association, 1916); *Dziennik Zwiazkowy*, Sept. 28, 1917.

62. *Proceedings of the Chicago City Council*, June 30, 1913, p. 1117; Ibid., July 14, 1913, p. 1349; *City of Chicago v. Drake Hotel Company*, 274 Ill. 408(1916).

63. *B. Ad.*, Feb. 6, 1914, Feb. 18, 1916; *B.P.*, Nov. 6, 10, 26, 1915; *B. Am.*, Feb. 6, 1916; Boston Licensing Board, *A.R., 1915*, p. 9.

64. *T.C.* 25(July, 1903):1; *B. and B.* 2(Mar., 1907):7, 2(Apr., 1907):13; *C.F.P.* 44(Aug. 26, 1916):1.

65. Ibid. 42(Jan. 23, 1915):4.

66. *M.C.* 12(Feb. 1, 1896):40, 21(Jan. 1, 1905):34; *B.W.S.G.* 67(Nov. 10, 1906):52; Massachusetts, *A. and R., 1914*, ch. 484; Epple, *Liquor Laws of Massachusetts*, pp. 96–98.

67. Chicago Department of Health, *Report, 1911–18*, p. 979; *American Issue* 7(Oct. 4, 1912):6, 8(Apr. 11, 1913):4; *C.F.P.* 25(Nov. 22, 1902):1, 25(Dec. 6, 1902):1, 33(June 25, 1910):6, 34(Jan. 4, 1911):5, 41(Dec. 20, 1913):4.

68. Ibid. 45(May 19, 1917):4, 45(June 30, 1917):4; *B.W.S.G.* 76(May 10, 1911):16, 87(Dec. 15, 1917):583.

69. Ibid. 74(May 25, 1910):114, 75(Apr. 10, 1911):744.

70. *B.W.S.G.* Boston column in each issue, especially vols. 74–86, give copious information about trade conditions as affected by weather, the European war, and local laws.

71. *C.F.P.* 42(Nov. 21, 1914):4, 44(May 6, 1916):2, 44(July 1, 1916):8, 44(Oct. 4, 1916):1; *Brewers' Journal* 36(Sept. 1, 1912):522, 38(May 1, 1914):314, 38(June 1, 1914):368, 39(Mar. 1, 1915):217, 39(June 1, 1915):369, 39(July 1, 1915):406. The most complete bankruptcy record is that of the Ernst Tosetti Brewing Company, Docket n. 23081, District Court of the United States, Northern District of Illinois, in the Chicago Regional Center, National Archives. On suicides, *Brewers' Journal* 36(Apr. 1, 1912):282, 36(July 1, 1912):426, 42(June 1, 1918):279.

72. *C.F.P.* 43(Feb. 13, 1915):3, 43(Sept. 4, 1915):1, 44(Jan. 8, 1916):4; *B.W.S.G.* 87(Nov. 15, 1917):559.

73. *C.F.P.* 31(July 25, 1908):5; *Illinois Issue* 4(Aug. 13, 1909): 6–7.

74. *Abendpost*, May 11, 1907; *Illinois Staats-Zeitung*, Jan. 12, 1914; see letterhead, Box 7, Raymond Robins Papers, S.H.S.W.; *Brewers' Journal* 38(Oct. 1, 1914):567; *C.F.P.* 43(Dec. 18, 1915):5.

75. *C.F.P.* 44(June 3, 1916):1, 45(Apr. 28, 1917):5, 45(June 23, 1917):4; *Brewers' Journal* 42(May 1, 1918):257, 42(Sept. 1, 1918):381, 43(Nov. 1, 1918):43.

76. Ibid. 41(July 1, 1917):370, 41(Aug. 1, 1917):414, 42(Sept. 1, 1918):381.

77. Ibid. 42(Feb. 1, 1918):135, 138; *Christian Science Monitor*, Dec. 29, 1917, Jan. 1, 3, 28, 29, 1917.

78. *C.F.P.* 45(Mar. 24, 1917):5.

79. New England Watch and Ward Society, *A.R.*, *1918–19*, p. 7; Executive Committee Minutes, October 1, 1918, Citizens' Association Papers, C.H.S.

80. Research Notebooks, vols. 10–12, numerous places, Committee of Fifteen Papers, University of Chicago; Folder 3, Graham Taylor Papers, C.H.S.; "Conference and Observation at Grant Park, Committee on Protective Work for Girls," typescript, Elizabeth Dummer Papers, Folder 380, Schlesinger Library, Radcliffe College.

81. The best summary is Timberlake, *Prohibition and the Progressive Movement*, pp. 148–84; Anti-Saloon League, *Yearbook, 1918*, pp. 42–73; see numerous stories in *C.F.P.*, vol. 45, especially (June 30, 1917):4.

82. Chicago's Mayor Thompson also held a meaningless "Prohibition Referendum" in 1919, in which 80 percent of Chicago's voters preferred a wet future.

83. *C.T.*, May 16–30, 1918; *B.G.*, May 14–30, June 1, 1919.

84. Ibid., May 31, June 2, 3, 1919; *C.T.*, June 3, 1919.

Index

Note on the Author

Perry R. Duis, a native of Illinois, received his Ph.D. from the University of Chicago and now teaches history at the University of Illinois-Chicago. He also writes a monthly column on Chicago history for *Chicago* magazine. He is the author of *Chicago: Creating New Traditions* and *The People of Chicago* (forthcoming).